Regulating the Web

Regulating the Web

Network Neutrality and the Fate of the Open Internet

Edited by Zack Stiegler

LEXINGTON BOOKS
Lanham • Boulder • New York • Toronto • Plymouth, UK

Published by Lexington Books
A wholly owned subsidiary of The Rowman & Littlefield Publishing Group, Inc.
4501 Forbes Boulevard, Suite 200, Lanham, Maryland 20706
www.rowman.com

10 Thornbury Road, Plymouth PL6 7PP, United Kingdom

British Library Cataloguing in Publication Information Available

Library of Congress Cataloging-in-Publication Data

Library of Congress Cataloging-in-Publication Data Available
ISBN 978-0-7391-7868-3 (cloth : alk. paper) — ISBN 978-0-7391-7869-0 (electronic)

♾™ The paper used in this publication meets the minimum requirements of American National Standard for Information Sciences—Permanence of Paper for Printed Library Materials, ANSI/NISO Z39.48-1992.

Printed in the United States of America

Contents

Acknowledgments

An edited volume is by its very nature a collaborative effort. Even beyond the authors however, this book came to fruition through the assistance of many people for whom I and the authors wish to extend our gratitude.

This volume originated as a panel at the 2011 meeting of the National Communication Association in New Orleans. I wish to thank NCA's Partnership for the Progress on the Digital Divide for their sponsorship of that initial panel. I also extend thanks to the members of that presentation panel and attendees who offered valuable feedback: Benjamin Cline, Brian Dolber, Daniel Faltesek, Joy Hayes, Dan Sprumont, David Hingtsman, and John Nathan Anderson. The rich dialogue initiated between these scholars directly lead to the creation of *Regulating the Web*.

Without the enthusiastic guidance and support of Lenore Lautigar, Lindsey Frederick, Alison Northridge, and Johnnie Simpson at Lexington Publishing, this book would not exist. Their assistance, guidance, patience, and professionalism made the publication process both efficient and pleasurable. Special thanks is also due to Samantha Nogueira Joyce for her assistance in navigating the publication process.

I am grateful to be surrounded by supportive colleagues in the Department of Communications Media at Indiana University of Pennsylvania. I am especially grateful for the support that Luis Almeida, Nurhaya Muchtar, Mark Piwinsky, David Bruce Porter, and B. Gail Wilson showed for this project. I especially wish to thank Mary Beth Leidman, whose shared interest in media law and policy helped to shape the concept and structure of this book.

As a Graduate Assistant, Robyn Defelice was an exemplar of logic and reason when oftentimes I lacked such virtues. Robyn was instrumental in the creation of *Regulating the Web* from the very beginning, and without her, its completion would have been impossible.

In addition, Kate Lukaszewicz and James Pobst provided invaluable feedback to portions of *Regulating the Web*, and the book is stronger for it.

Lastly, I would like to thank those closest to me: my parents, my sister Kristi, and my partner Kate. Their unyielding love and support anchors me, even as they sustain the collateral damage of my work life.

Regulating the Web: An Introduction

Zack Stiegler

As communication technology evolves, it does so with an increasing swiftness that is by now taken for granted. Consider that 400 years passed between Gutenberg's printing press (c. 1440) and Morse's telegraph in 1837. There was then a lapse of a mere 60 years between the introduction of the telegraph and the onset of earnest experimentation in radio communication in the late nineteenth century. Although television broadcasting was still in its experimental stages, the first TV sets appeared on the commercial market simultaneously with the rise of radio's golden age in the 1930s. The genesis of the Internet began just a few decades later in 1969, when the collaborative ARPANET project connected military and research institutions. Nearly 20 years later, Tim Berners-Lee introduced the World Wide Web, ushering in a global revolution in communication technology.

Yet as the temporal gaps between new media developments shrink, there remains a significant lag between technological development and the implementation of regulatory policy to manage those technologies. Although educational institutions, electronics firms, and hobbyists had been broadcasting for nearly 30 years, it wasn't until 1927 that the cacophonic result of laissez-faire regulation required Congressional intervention into radio broadcasting. Congress passed comprehensive communication legislation in 1934, but it would be another 32 years before the Communications Act received a major overhaul, despite intervening technological developments.

Continuing this pattern, the Internet went relatively untouched by regulatory hands from its popularization in the 1990s until 2010. In those intervening years, judicial, legislative, and regulatory attention on the Internet focused on addressing children's access to salacious content, digital defamation, managing intellectual property, and curbing spam messages.[1] Although significant in their own right, these initiatives were narrowly tailored to specific issues raised by contemporaneous online culture. Policy discourse addressing the regulation of the Internet on a broader, structural level did not emerge until the mid-2000s. It was not until 2010 that the Federal Communications Commission (FCC) took any substantial regulatory stance on Internet communication, nearly 20 years after Berners-Lee's World Wide Web made its debut.

1

Net Neutrality: An Overview

The history of the FCC's net neutrality policy is well documented in the chapters that populate this volume. As a matter of preface, however, a brief discussion is necessary to establish a foundational understanding of the FCC's policy and the multi-faceted debates that surround it.

Network (or "net") neutrality is the principle that those who manage networks should provide access to all applications, content, platforms, and websites on a non-discriminatory basis.[2] That is, as consumers navigate the World Wide Web, they should be able to access all legal content at the same rate of speed; Internet Service Providers (ISPs) should not have authority to prioritize any one application or website with greater speed or higher quality access than any other. A subscriber to Verizon FIOS, for example, should be able to access the Fox News webpage at the same rate of speed and quality that they can access their coworker's political blog. Likewise, a Comcast subscriber should be able to access video content on YouTube at the same speed and quality that they access video content on Hulu (in which Comcast now has a stake, following its 2011 merger with NBC-Universal). In short, net neutrality is the fundamental design principle of the Internet that allows users to access information without discrimination or interference levied by the network operator or ISP, as has been the case up to this point. As Tina Sikka notes in this volume however, design principles are imposed by external actors such as ISPs, network managers, and federal regulators—there is nothing inherently neutral about the technological nature or structure of the Internet.

By the middle of the 2000s, ISPs pursued imposing alternate design principles onto the structure of Internet communication. Corporations such as AT&T and Comcast considered altering their network management practices in ways that would maximize their profitability, but would also change the very structure of the Internet, as well as users' navigation of the World Wide Web. Until that point, ISPs simply provided the bandwidth and the connections between web users and online content. In 2003, AT&T CEO Ed Whitacre boldly articulated a new approach:

> Now what they would like to do is use my pipes free, but I ain't going to let them do that because we have spent this capital and we have to have a return on it. So there's going to have to be some mechanism for these people who use these pipes to pay for the portion they're using. Why should they be allowed to use my pipes? The Internet can't be free in that sense, because we and the cable companies have made an investment and for a Google or Yahoo! or Vonage or anybody to expect to use these pipes [for] free is nuts![3]

As ISPs considered new approaches to network management, citizen activists and media interest groups rallied to preserve net neutrality. A series of legislative attempts to enshrine net neutrality as the status quo in Internet regulation failed to gain traction in the 109th and 110th Congress, perhaps unsurprising when one considers the lobbying power of U.S. telecommunications corporations.[4] In recent years, media and technology firms consistently rank among industries with the highest lobbying expenditures.[5]

The FCC first took up the matter of net neutrality under Chairman Kevin Martin. Although it did not directly lead to formal policy adoption, the Commission's 2005 Internet Policy Statement initiated policy discourse about net neutrality.[6] However, a 2010 decision by the United States Court of Appeals for the District of Columbia put into question the FCC's jurisdiction over Internet and broadband services. Vacating the FCC's 2008 censure of Comcast for undisclosed throttling (altering the speeds at which users access content online), the Court's ruling held that the FCC did not have even ancillary authority over Internet service under the Communications Act. Noting that the Court's decision "invalidated the prior Commission's approach to preserving an open Internet," the Commission held firmly that "the Court in no way disagreed with the importance of preserving a free and open Internet, nor did it close the door to other methods for achieving this important end."[7]

The FCC thus continued pursuit of codifying net neutrality via regulatory policy, despite continued pressures from the telecommunications industry. Yet as is often the case, the FCC began to work closely with the very industry that it set out to regulate.[8] Throughout the summer of 2010, the Commission collaborated with ISPs and content developers in closed door meetings. These discussions led to concessions to the telecommunications industry at the expense of consumers' interests, as evidenced in the parity between the Google-Verizon proposal and the FCC's eventual Order.

The FCC adopted its Report and Order in the Matter of Preserving the Open Internet in December 2010. Yet the Commission's adoption of an open Internet policy did little to settle the controversy over Internet regulation. Instead, the FCC's policy stoked already heated debates on the matter. Anti-regulatory conservatives pointed to the *Comcast* decision to argue that the FCC had no legitimate authority over the Internet. To this end, Verizon quickly filed suit against the FCC, challenging the agency's authority to create and enforce Internet regulation.

Meanwhile, advocates of net neutrality criticized the FCC's policy for not going far enough. Media reformers dubbed the policy "net neutrality lite," and went on to denounce the FCC's lax provisions for the blocking and discrimination of mobile Internet traffic.[9] In his statement concurring with the FCC's Order, public interest stalwart and FCC Commissioner Michael Copps acknowledged the policy's shortcomings, and his somewhat reluctant support of the Order:

> So, in my book, today's action could—and should—have gone further. Going as far as I would have liked was not, however, in the cards. The simpler and easier course for me at that point would have been dissent—and I considered that very, very seriously. But it became ever more clear to me that without

some action today, the wheels of network neutrality would grind to a screeching halt for at least the next two years.[10]

Across the social and political spectrum, then, few were satisfied with the Commission's net neutrality policies as adopted. Although net neutrality may no longer be in the media spotlight as it was in 2010, the challenges to the FCC's policy from diverse political affiliations indicate that the 2010 Order is by no means the final word on Internet regulation in the United States. As Robert McChesney argues, the early twenty-first century is a critical juncture for media policymaking, where the law and policy that we adopt now will set the course for the next several decades; net neutrality has in fact become "a defining issue for this critical juncture."[11] Assessing this critical juncture, *Regulating the Web* inserts itself into net neutrality discourse to provide an in-depth, multi-faceted examination of net neutrality from a diversity of academic perspectives. This volume addresses and dissects net neutrality directly, but also provides a snapshot of the policy, procedure, and impact of media regulation in the digital age.

Overview and Structure

Regulating the Web is divided into four main sections. The first of these provides analysis of the foundational principles and approaches to regulating Internet communication. Opening this section, Michael Felczak takes a historical perspective in his examination of data management initiatives by telephone carriers beginning in the 1970s. Framed through changing definitions as well as evolving design infrastructure protocols and technologies, Felczak shows how this rich history has positioned Internet operators to control the future development and workings of the Internet. In chapter 2, Danny Kimball takes a broader historical view of net neutrality as a discursive construction to underscore the symbiotic relationship that such discourse has with the policy and practice of Internet regulation in the United States.

At issue throughout net neutrality debates is the principle of transparency, a central point of contention in the *Comcast* case. Patrick Schmidt, Jeremy Carp, and Isabella Kulkarni argue that there is a duality in the principle of transparency: although desirable for consumers, it is easily exploited as rhetorical tokenism by the industry and its regulators. The authors chart the appeal and failures of past transparency policies, countering with new approaches aimed at ensuring ISPs' accountability to their customers.

Another key principle throughout the history of utility and media regulation in the United States is common carriage, stipulating that qualifying providers must treat all traffic with the same quality of service. Echoing the regulation of broadcasting, telegraphy, and telephony, common carriage figured prominently in debates about net neutrality. In the lead-up to the FCC's Order, a number of net neutrality advocates supported reclassification of broadband under Title II regulation, a means to treat broadband as a common carrier. Although the FCC abandoned this initiative, Mark Grabowski and Pallavi Guniganti engage a rich historical and comparative study of the common carriage principle to argue that it is a particularly valuable approach to Internet regulation.

Regulating the Web's second section presents institutional analyses central to net neutrality in the United States. Daniel Faltesek examines the FCC's rule-making to parse out two competing visions of the market within the regulatory discourse. Both offer critical insights into the future of the investment, regulation, and the Internet in general, yet both also illustrate the rather tenuous position of market discourses in policymaking. Faltesek investigates how discursive formations shape our understanding of the relationship between the market and policy, while also illustrating the ways in we can productively grapple with these formations to forge alternative conceptions of the market.

From an alternate angle, Benjamin Cline interrogates the ideological framework of the FCC's Order to establish the policy as a rhetorical artifact within a larger ideological process. Cline argues that from a rhetorical standpoint, the Order amounts to an axiological shift in our collective thinking about the Internet and its regulation, one that will shape future discourse of Internet regulation.

To date, net neutrality discourse has been fairly contentious, even controversial. As legislators and the FCC considered Internet regulation, consumers, mass media, politicians, and telecommunications firms engaged in an impassioned and wide-ranging debate on the issue. *Regulating the Web*'s third section assesses two particular areas of these larger debates. In the year preceding the FCC's adoption of its Open Internet Order, net neutrality received significant mainstream media attention, unusual for matters of media policy. Zack Stiegler and Dan Sprumont employ framing analysis to assess mass media's presentation of net neutrality to the public, and how such coverage attempted to shape public perception of the issue.

In the course of the last decade, increasing numbers of citizens have become active in advocating media reform. Brian Dolber outlines three segments within the media reform movement (activist groups Free Press and the Save the Internet Coalition; the Congressional Black Caucus and the Civil Rights community; and the Communications Workers of America) to argue that reformers inadvertently helped to reinforce the dominance of industry players in shaping net neutrality policy. Noting these failings, Dolber argues for a countering of the ideological frameworks that inherently support the status quo, instead opting for a broader conception of the political economy of media.

Regulating the Web concludes with three chapters addressing the social and cultural implications of net neutrality in the United States. Approaching net neutrality through a critical theory of technology, Tina Sikka delineates the sociology, technology, and policy levels of net neutrality to determine how such an approach can help to preserve an open Internet. Ultimately, Sikka argues that this preservation can lead to increased public participation in media policymaking, as well as a democratization of Internet design.

Public participation is also the focus of Michael Daubs' contribution to this volume. As noted earlier, one of the most glaring flaws of the FCC Order is its decidedly lax approach to regulating the mobile Internet. Daubs argues that this loophole poses a significant danger to social and political movements, which increasingly make use of mobile platforms to communicate, mobilize, and organize. In this context then, the non-neutral Internet's impact on free speech is not mere hyperbole, but can in fact hinder citizens' ability to publicly organize and demonstrate for social and political causes.

Finally, John Nathan Anderson looks to net neutrality as a case study of media reform in the United States. While media reform activists have been moderately successful preventing law and policy that threaten the open Internet, Anderson argues that significant work remains before we can truly claim that citizens shape media policy in any significant way. Anderson considers ways forward that may allow citizens to more actively and meaningfully engage in media policy debates, to the extent that resultant policy is shaped by public rather than commercial or political interests.

At its most basic level, the Internet deals in information exchange. As Tim Wu observes, "the flow of information defines the basic tenor of our times, the ambience in which things happen, and, ultimately, the character of society."[12] Culturally, how we structure and regulate the Internet will decide the parameters of access to and flow of information in the United States. Ultimately, *Regulating the Web* aims to add to the discourse of Internet regulation so that we may move forward toward an open Internet, one that values public access to this information-rich resource that is seemingly inextricable from our educational, occupational, and personal lives in the twenty-first century.

Notes

1. See for example the *Communications Decency Act* (initially incorporated as Title V of S. 652, the *Telecommunications Act of 1996*); *Child Online Protection Act* H.R. 3783 (1998), 105th Cong., 2d. sess.; the *CAN-SPAM Act of 2003*, Public Law 108–187; *Digital Millennium Copyright Act of 1998*, Public Law 105–304; *United States v. Thomas* 74 F.3d 701 6th Cir. 1996; *Zeran v. American Online, Inc.*, 129 F.3d 327 (4th Cir. 1997); *Blumenthal v. Drudge* 992 F. Supp 44 (D.D.C. 1998); *A&M Records v. Napster, Inc.* 239 F.3d 1004 (2001); *MGM Studios, Inc. v. Grokster, Ltd.* 545 U.S. 913 (2005).

2. Tim Wu, "Network Neutrality FAQ," *timwu.org*, http://timwu.org/network_neutrality.html (accessed August 8, 2012).

3. Ken Fisher, "SBC: Ain't No Way VoIP Uses Mah Pipes!" *Ars Technica*, October 31, 2005. http://arstechnica.com/old/content/2005/10/5498.ars (accessed August 8, 2011).

4. *Internet Freedom and Nondiscrimination Act of 2006* H.R. 5417, 109th Cong., 2d. sess.; *Communications Opportunity, Promotion and Enhancement Act of 2006*, H.R. 5252, 109th Cong., 2d. sess.; *Network Neutrality Act of 2006*, H.R. 5273, 109th Cong., 2d. sess.; *Communications, Consumer's Choice and Broadband Deployment Act of 2006*, S 2686, 109th Cong., 2d. sess.; *Internet Freedom and Nondiscrimination Act of 2006*,

H.R. 5417, 109th Cong., 2d. sess.; *Internet Freedom Preservation Act of 2008*, H.R. 5353, 110th Cong., 2d. sess.

5. In 2011, for example, the country's three largest ISPs (AT&T, Comcast, and Verizon) collectively spent $55,315,000 in lobbying expenditures. See the Center for Responsive Politics' Lobbying Database at http://www.opensecrets.org/lobby/index.php.

6. Federal Communications Commission, *Policy Statement in the Matter of Inquiry Concerning High Speed Access to the Internet Over Cable and Other Facilities*, 2005 http://www.publicknowledge.org/pdf/FCC-05-151A1.pdf (accessed January 20, 2011).

7. Federal Communications Commission, "FCC Statement on *Comcast v. FCC Decision*," April 6, 2010, hraunfoss.fcc.gov/edocs_public/attachmatch/DOC-297355A1.pdf (accessed August 18, 2012).

8. On industry's "capture" of regulatory agencies see David Hilliard and Michael Keith, *The Quieted Voice: The Rise and Demise of Localism in Radio* (Carbondale: Southern Illinois University Press, 2005), and Robert Britt Horwitz, *The Irony of Regulatory Reform: The Deregulation of American Telecommunications* (New York: Oxford University Press, 1989).

9. Matthew Lasar. "It's here: FCC adopts net neutrality (lite)," *Ars Technica*, December 21, 2010, http://arstechnica.com/tech-policy/news/2010/12/its-here-fcc-adopts-net-neutrality-lite.ars (accessed August 8 2011); Adam Holofcener, "Net Neutrality Besieged by *Comcast Corp. v. FCC*: The Past, Present and Future Plight of an Open Internet," *Journal of Business and Technology Law* 7, no. 2 (2012): 403–424.

10. Michael J. Copps. "Concurring Statement of Michael J. Copps re: Preserving the Open Internet, GN Docket No. 09-191, *Broadband Industry Practices*, WC Docket No. 07-52," December 21, 2010. http://hraunfoss.fcc.gov/edocs_public/attachmatch/FCC-10-201A3.pdf (accessed August 18, 2012).

11. Robert McChesney, *Communication Revolution: Critical Junctures and the Future of Media* (New York: The New Press, 2007), 181.

12. Tim Wu, *The Master Switch: The Rise and Fall of Information Empires* (New York: Alfred A. Knopf, 2010), 12.

Part I: Background and Principles

Chapter 1

Visions of Modernity: Communication, Technology, and Network Neutrality in Historical Perspective

Michael Felczak

In the summer of 2005 the U.S. Federal Communications Commission (FCC) reclassified broadband Internet access via the telephone network from a regulated communication service to an unregulated information service.[1] This move followed an earlier decision in 2002 whereby the FCC reclassified broadband Internet access via cable as an unregulated information service.[2] Although U.S. federal courts initially blocked the 2002 reclassification, the U.S. Supreme Court ruled in a case in 2005 that broadband Internet access constituted a type of information service and that the FCC did have the authority to classify broadband in this way.[3] The Supreme Court did not rule on the merits of whether the FCC should classify broadband Internet as an information service, but it nonetheless upheld the authority of the FCC to classify it as such.

Within a few months of the 2005 Supreme Court decision, the FCC classified telephone broadband Internet as an unregulated information service, responding to the ongoing and well-funded lobbying efforts of U.S. network operators. The classification and the consequent move from state to market regulation marked a significant reversal in U.S. telecommunication policy dating back to at least 1934, when the Communications Act granted the FCC with the authority to regulate telephone companies as common carriers. To encourage competition, the FCC has required since the early 1980s that major U.S. telephone companies provide non-discriminatory interconnection and access to their networks. In so doing, the FCC prohibited telephone companies from using their monopoly market positions to prioritize their immediate revenue streams at the expense of serving the public good and public communication. The FCC's move in 2005 from state to market regulation not only eradicated these established communication rights and incentives for competition, but also effectively authorized network operators to control and develop the Internet's infrastructure according to their visions and interests.

The purpose of this chapter is to add an often-missing historical dimension to network neutrality debates. The political economy of the Internet has deep historical roots that date back to the earliest experiments with data networking. Not only have telephone carriers always attempted to control the telephone infrastructure and telephone communications, but they have since the earliest days of data networking attempted to define the nature of network communication in such a way that leverages to the widest extent possible their privileged position as providers of the infrastructure that makes this communication possible.

In contradistinction to historical analyses that focus exclusively on the institutional and political landscape of telecommunication and how this landscape has changed over the years, a critical constructivist methodology[4] is employed in this chapter to trace the efforts of telecommunication providers to achieve representation in the very technologies that constituted early data networking initiatives and that define what the Internet is and is not today. This examination illustrates that, given the opportunity, network operators have historically attempted to define and structure networking in ways that maximize their control of both the network and the forms of communication made possible on this network. The historical record suggests that when network operators are granted too much independence, the primacy of revenue generation guides technical considerations and decisions in ways that privilege profit margins at the expense of public, non-commercial, and diverse forms of communication and expression. Given this historical record and pattern of technology development, there is good reason to be skeptical of recent claims of corporate responsibility and the sufficiency of industry self-regulation. On the contrary, the historical record suggests the continued need for network neutrality legislation that protects the full diversity of communication and expression on the Internet.

Drawing primarily on the histories of data networking protocols and technologies, the analysis will begin with a consideration of national videotex initiatives in Europe and North America in the 1970s, where national telephone carriers were central to the implementation of state-supported data networking and modernization projects. Within these initiatives, telephone carriers were given much freedom to define the exact nature of data networking and its technologies. In particular, telephone carriers designed their core networking protocols and associated technologies in such a way as to concentrate and extend their power over the telephone infrastructure, limit the number and capacity of private network operators, and, to a large extent, define the nature of communication for users.

With the exception of the French system, most national videotex initiatives failed to achieve mass adoption and were quickly forgotten with the advent and eventual popularity of the Internet. Nonetheless, the technical politics of national videotex initiatives are instructive when compared to those of the early Internet, which is the focus of the second part of the chapter. Unlike national videotex initiatives, telephone carriers were notably absent from the Internet design process and consequently, the Internet's core technologies do not reflect the carriers' concerns or priorities. In the Internet model of networking, telephone carriers are but one provider of one type of network medium in a system that supports private network operators and user-defined communication and applications.

The chapter concludes with an examination of the design process of next-generation Internet technologies and suggests that telephone carriers in particular and network operators more generally are well represented by these new technologies. Although telephone carriers were largely absent from both the early Internet design process as well as more recent design undertakings, they nonetheless have managed to achieve technical representation in next-generation Internet technologies by way of a congruence of interests and needs with other groups and organizations, namely the U.S. Navy, U.S. corporations, and the U.S. cable industry. These organizations managed to successfully convince the Internet's technical community to extend and amplify design features that allow network operators to prioritize data flows and that enable network users to reserve network resources.

In addition to these design features, next-generation Internet technology is designed in such a way that network operators and equipment manufacturers may supplement and extend it through the addition of new functionality and features. Although the Internet has yet to fully transition to these next-generation technologies, it is evident that without adequate legislation to limit the power of network operators, the next-generation Internet is well suited to the expansion of the operators' control over the Internet's infrastructure and, consequently, over the nature of communication that will be encouraged and hindered.

Data Networking According to the Telephone Carriers

National telephone carriers became increasingly interested in data networking in the early 1970s as a result of increased computer deployment and use.[5] To the carriers, dropping computer prices and increased computer use represented new and as yet untapped telecommunication markets that could be incorporated into their existing monopolies. However, in order to be able to control these new markets, carriers sought to gain independence from manufacturers and their proprietary networking products and protocols.

This independence was important for two reasons. First, by avoiding the use of proprietary protocols and networking components, carriers would not be dependent on a single manufacturer.[6] A nonproprietary protocol developed by the carriers would make it possible for multiple manufacturers to implement it, and in turn would enable carriers to choose between multiple suppliers and network products. More importantly, by defining networking protocols themselves, carriers would be able to define public data networking according to their vision, values, and priorities.[7] By providing products that conform to carrier-defined protocols, manufacturers would simply be supporting this vision as opposed to defining their own. By defining, controlling, and promoting widespread use of their own protocols, carriers could pressure manufacturers to adjust and conform to the carriers' priorities and needs.

To this end, the carriers were largely successful. In 1975, an ad hoc group within the Consultative Committee on International Telegraphy and Telephony (CCITT), led by representatives from national carriers in Canada, France, and Britain, began to outline and define the X.25 data networking protocol.[8] By 1976, X.25 had received approval from the CCITT, which recommended it as the standard for data networking to be adopted by its members. Computer manufacturers began to introduce networking products with support for the new protocol shortly after the CCITT's recommendation. The first public, national networks based on X.25 became operational shortly thereafter in Canada (1977), France (1978), Japan (1979), and Britain (1980).[9]

To understand some of the unique characteristics of the X.25 networking protocol, it is important to first understand the essential features of packet-switched networking. Packet-switched networking differs from traditional circuit-switched networking used in telephone networks where a connection is established between two communicating parties and maintained for the duration of the conversation. In this scenario, the telephone network establishes a physical circuit between the two communicating parties and maintains this circuit until the end of the conversation. This method of connection is resource intensive, since the network resources that are allocated to one connection cannot be used for other connections.

In contrast to circuit-switched networking, packet-switched networking does not maintain a physical network connection between the two communicating parties. Instead, the message that is to be transmitted is divided into multiple packets, each of which is transported across the network independently of other packets. The sender is responsible for the breaking up of messages into packets and the receiver is responsible for assembling the packets to reconstruct the original message. In this networking model, the network provides a simple data transport service for packets based on their source and destination addresses.

There are two additional aspects of packet switching that are important for the discussion that follows. First, although packet-switched networks provide a simple data transport service, it is sometimes desirable to also be able to have some control over the flow and ordering of the packets in the system. For example, if packets arrive at their destination out of order, the recipient may wish to reassemble them in the correct order. Second, if an error occurs somewhere along a packet's path and the packet arrives at its destination with corrupted data, the receiver may wish to be able to detect this so that another copy of the packet may be requested from the sender. Error and flow control of this sort are thus two additional features that may be provided within a packet switching network in addition to the actual transport of packets.

Technical Representation

To understand the carriers' approach to and implementation of packet switching, it is important to consider their vision of data networking and the sociotechnical network that X.25 was designed to interweave with, preserve, and extend. Perhaps not surprisingly, the national carriers understood data networking as an extension of their telephony business and operations.[10] The existing telephone infrastructure provided a basis for data networking that simply needed to be supplemented by data networking components. Since the carriers owned the network infrastructure, it was assumed that they should also maintain the technology necessary to regulate the flow of data and provide congestion and error control to users.[11] Since the carriers owned the infrastructure, they believed that they were in the best position to provide this network functionality.

In addition to this belief, the carriers also assumed that users would engage a simple interface to access the network, the computer equivalent to the telephone.[12] According to the carriers, this simple terminal interface was in the best interest of the user, who would have easy operation and access as well as minimal responsibility for the operation of the network. The terminal, like the telephone, should not be expected to handle complex network functionality such as flow and error control. Instead, it would establish a connection with the network, which would then look after and handle the more complex functionality needed to actually make use the network.[13]

The carriers also assumed that the majority of users would be individuals who would directly access the network via their terminals and not via intermediary networks. The carriers' vision of data networking did not include much room for private networks and commercial network operators who could compete with the carriers for users.[14] Minimizing the number and need for private networks was also central to the internetworking of national networks. In the carriers' model of networking, users would connect to their respective national networks, which, in turn, would be connected to each other.[15]

Not only were there very few network addresses available for private networks, but once connected, private network operators could not control the default flow and error handling therein.[16] Network communication that did not require error control nonetheless received it from the network, consequently incurring the associated performance costs. In addition, the carriers designed X.25 in such a way that it was inflexible with respect to the internal networking protocols used within private networks.[17] If a private network wished to internetwork with a carrier's network, it needed to use X.25 within its own internal network, regardless of whether other networking protocols were more suitable for their particular needs.

Defining packet switching in their own interests was a key step for carriers and the utilization of the existing telephone infrastructure for data communication. By defining the manner of this utilization and controlling the points of entry for both users and private network operators, the carriers placed themselves in a favorable position to enter, define, and monopolize emerging telecommunication markets.

Network Development and Sociotechnical Dynamics

In addition to having their interests represented within the actual X.25 standard, the carriers were also well positioned within the sociotechnical networks of national videotex initiatives in Europe, as videotex made use of X.25 and packet switching to deliver information services to the home. In Germany, Britain, and France, for example, carriers aligned themselves with state initiatives in such a way that they played a central role within national videotex systems.[18] These sociotechnical arrangements were well aligned with the carriers' desire to create new telecommunication services and to stimulate the use of telephone networks beyond existing telephone services.[19]

In all three national initiatives, the carriers controlled the infrastructure at both "ends" of the system.[20] At one end, users needed to use their videotex terminals to connect to the system via the telephone network. At the other end, commercial providers of information services needed to connect their remote databases to the carriers' network. In Germany and Britain, the carriers also owned and controlled centralized databases that commercial information providers could use to provide their content in addition to or in lieu of managing their own remote databases.[21]

In Germany and Britain, the new revenue streams corresponding to the carriers' strategic positioning included monthly standing charges (collected from users who connected to the system), time-based charges (collected from users for using the telephone network to connect to the videotex system), and storage charges (collected from commercial information providers who housed their information pages on centralized databases).[22]

In France, the initial plan was to require each information provider to implement and manage their own billing and subscription system. However, over time carriers implemented a broader, time-based billing system to both lessen the technical burden on information providers and to enable users to move seamlessly from one information service provider to another.[23] In this time-based system, the carrier charged the user according to a fixed, per-minute rate. The resulting revenue was then divided between the carrier and the commercial information service provider.

Although the carriers were able to successfully position themselves at strategic points within national videotex systems and were able to define the protocols used by these systems, the rewards of this positioning and technical representation could only be realized if the videotex system itself was successful and taken up by both users and information providers. Unfortunately for the carriers, with the exception of the *Teletel* in France, the majority of national videotex initiatives failed to achieve mass appeal and adoption. Over the years, some videotex operators began to adopt elements of the French system, but in the end it was too little, too late. Even the popular *Teletel* was soon dwarfed by the exponential growth of the Internet, in large part facilitated by the introduction of the World Wide Web in 1993 by Tim Berners-Lee.

Data Networking
According to the ARPANET Community

Although carriers were largely successful in gaining a measure of independence from computer manufacturers through their definition of protocols that represented their interests, they were ultimately unsuccessful in achieving widespread adoption of X.25 and their vision of data networking. Likewise, the carriers' efforts to control and commodify key points within the network, including connection, transmission, and content, were ultimately unrewarded with the decline of videotex systems. With the exception of the *Teletel* in France, national efforts to establish and promote data networking failed to achieve the sort of mass appeal anticipated by designers. Consequently, the carriers' strategic positioning within the sociotechnical networks of national videotex initiatives was short-lived and the technical representation that carriers were able to achieve by way of the X.25 standard over time has become irrelevant. Despite this lack of mass adoption, the history of videotex initiatives highlights for us the particularity of the carriers' commercial vision for networking and the ways in which carriers attempted to commodify communication by way of technologies and institutional arrangements designed to realize this vision.

Early national videotex initiatives not only trace for us their respective sociotechnical arrangements and relations, but also provide insight into the data networking alternatives available at the time, particularly the data networking model advocated by the then young Internet community. From the time of X.25's approval in 1976 until the late 1980s, the carriers became entangled in an intense debate with the networking community of the U.S. Advanced Research Projects Agency (ARPA) regarding the merits of X.25 vis-à-vis ARPA's packet switching protocols—the Transmission Control Protocol (TCP) and the Internet Protocol (IP).[24]

Although it is tempting to view such debates as sealing the fate of the respective protocols, the debates are better understood as a source of detailed insights into the sociotechnical networks and power dynamics of data networking at the time and the extent to which carriers attempted to defend and put forward their vision and model of data networking. These debates, along with a detailed understanding of ARPA's experiences with data networking, enable us to account for the parallel efforts of the ARPA community to promote the widespread adoption of their technologies and their model of networking as an alternative to that of the carriers. Although they have undergone some revision since their initial specification, the ARPA community networking protocols (TCP/IP) continue to provide the core functionality at the heart of the Internet today, and unlike carrier-defined protocols, support network growth and interconnection, accommodate a diversity of underlying media and devices, and do not dictate forms of use, communication, or application.

Technical Representation

Perhaps the most significant difference between the sociotechnical arrangements of national videotex initiatives and that of the ARPANET may be the position occupied by ARPA system builders relative to that occupied by those of the carriers. Unlike the carriers, who were well positioned within national videotex initiatives, controlled the videotex network infrastructure, and were relatively free to define the network and its protocols according to their needs and priorities, ARPA designers were bound both by the general needs of the military as well as the specific needs of academic research sites and their directors, who were skeptical of the project's success and reluctant to give up control of their computing resources. As a result, ARPA's designers needed to accommodate a heterogeneous networking environment that included a wide diversity of computers, networks, and underlying media.

More specifically, although the computers at research sites were purchased using ARPA funds and, consequently, research directors at these sites had little say in whether they would participate in the network, it was nonetheless crucial for ARPANET's designers to elicit as much support and cooperation as possible from these sites to increase the likelihood of the network's success.[25] To reduce complexity and ease the effort required from participating research sites, ARPA's first network required that research sites write only the software necessary for their host computers to be able to communicate with network interface computers. These network interface computers, in turn, looked after the more complex tasks and operations associated with exchanging data via the network.[26] In this way, ARPANET's system builders were able to accommodate diverse host computers at participating research sites while simultaneously reducing each site's efforts and delegating the more complex implementation tasks to a private contractor.

Following the success of the first, small-scale ARPA network, additional academic research sites were connected and ARPA began to experiment with packet radio (PRNET) and satellite (SATNET) networks.[27] By the mid-1970s, ARPA was operating all three experimental networks, and began to consider the possibility of their interconnection. The key challenge was a technical one. Although each network used packet switching, the three networks were incompatible, since in each network packet switching was implemented in such a way as to account for the affordances and shortcomings of the underlying medium: leased telephone lines in the case of the ARPANET, packet radio in the case of PRNET, and satellite links in the case of SATNET.[28]

Together, the Transmission Control Protocol and the Internet Protocol constitute the core of the Internet, and their development was grounded in the practical concerns of interconnecting heterogeneous networks utilizing diverse media. Although ARPA's system designers played an important role in the design of TCP/IP, ARPA was not the only group that was experimenting with networking at the time. The International Network Working Group (INWG) was formed at the 1972 International Conference on Computer Communication to share networking strategies and knowledge. The group included members from ARPA, the French research network *Cyclades*, the British National Physical Laboratory (NPL), and Xerox PARC.[29] The insights and experiences brought forth by these members significantly altered ARPA's original protocol design.[30]

To begin with, both ARPA and members of the INWG were concerned with scalability—the ability of the internetwork to accommodate growth and future networks without sacrificing reliability and performance. ARPA's needs were common to the INWG more broadly: whether connecting future ARPA networks together or future international research networks, the resulting protocols should scale well and be able to accommodate growth. In this regard, the National Physical Laboratory's past networking experiments and research were instructive. NPL researchers argued that translation between different protocols, while tolerable in small internetworks, would not scale well in larger internetworks. Instead, a common internetworking protocol should be adopted by all networks that wish to interconnect.[31]

In similar fashion, French researchers from the *Cyclades* network argued that in order for the internetwork to scale well over time and to ensure compatibility with all existing and future networks, the resulting protocol would need to be as simple as possible. Based on their own research network and experiences, the French INWG members argued that the internetwork should only be responsible for handling the transmission of individual packets. More complex functions such as flow and error control should be handled by the host computers. In this way, complexity would be handled on the periphery of the internetwork by the communicating hosts, and the internetworking protocol would simply be responsible for delivering packets.[32]

Third, both ARPA and Xerox PARC researchers had experience with networks that used media other than conventional telephone lines. ARPA's PRNET utilized radio, which was even less reliable than the telephone network. Packets could be lost or corrupted as a result of errors or interference resulting from radio transmission. In the case of Xerox PARC's Ethernet networking, computers were connected directly to each other via network cables with no intermediate network nodes managing the exchange of data. If the internetwork protocol was to support these types of networks and media, it would need to include all of its logic and intelligence at the "ends," in the host computers to alleviate the aforementioned technological shortcomings of existing networks.[33]

In sum, the concerns and priorities of INWG members were translated into a protocol design that foregrounded scalability and network diversity. The Internet Protocol was designed to provide a simple data transport service, required communicating hosts to implement more complex networking logic, and supported to the widest extent possible a diversity of computers, networks, and underlying media. In addition, by separating data transport functions from more complex networking functions, INWG members were not only addressing the technical difficulties associated with network interconnection on a large scale, but were also endorsing a form of social organization with respect to the development and implementation of the network and its use.

As Janet Abbate suggests, the "layering" of protocols such that each protocol is functionally separate from other protocols is well suited to the coordination of diverse groups.[34] By dividing complex networking tasks into modular building blocks with well-defined and specified interfaces, different groups may focus on the implementation of different aspects of the system without needing to be concerned with the progress of other groups or with the details of other aspects of the system. A modular, layered protocol design reduces the social complexity of implementation and supports the coordination and interconnection of many complex parts.

In addition, a layered network design that includes a data transport layer that provides the foundation for an application layer is well suited to encouraging network use.[35] Rather than designing the network protocol in such a way that predefines network services and applications, a layered design separates the delivery of data packets from the actual network applications that make use of this data delivery. To a large extent, this leaves open the question of how the network should be used and what applications users may deem most suitable.

The sort of application creativity that ARPA managers had hoped for and encouraged could only be realized in practice if it was possible for software developers to make use of a well defined and functioning network layer that would deliver data reliably between communicating hosts. It is worthwhile to note that layering as a design principle was not unique to the ARPANET or even to other INWG members.[36] However, the growth and popularity of the Internet did establish layering as a proven design approach to networking and similarly established the TCP/IP protocol "stack" as a de facto referent for other network designs.

In sum, the sociotechnical network that TCP/IP was designed to accommodate, transform, and extend was quite different from the sociotechnical networks of national videotex initiatives of the time. The technical representation achieved by ARPA and INWG members resulted in a protocol suite that, unlike that of X.25 and its related protocols, prioritized computer, network, and media diversity, future growth, and application flexibility. These priorities were quite different from the priorities of national carriers, who sought to control a network infrastructure that was assumed to be relatively homogeneous. The carriers' protocols and associated technologies severely limited interconnection, restricted growth and private networks, and at least initially, were generally inflexible with respect to network applications and uses.

The absence of the carriers from the INWG enabled INWG members to define the sociotechnical network of TCP/IP in such a way that carriers were constituted solely in terms of their ability to provide one form of underlying media for the internetwork. This is a significant decrease in power relative to national videotex initiatives, where carriers occupied a central place both in the provision of network service as well as in its operation, management, and design. Unlike the protocol suites and technologies based on X.25, which were designed to extend carrier control over both the operation of the internetwork and its uses, the TCP/IP protocol suite was designed to accommodate to the widest extent possible the needs of network operators and users.

It is tempting to view these design features as solely responsible for the eventual popularity of TCP/IP and the Internet. While it is certainly the case that the design of the TCP/IP protocol suite made the Internet model of internetworking an attractive option to network operators considering interconnection, it is nonetheless crucial to take account of the considerable effort, understood both in terms of political and economic support, exerted by ARPA and other organizations to promote the adoption of TCP/IP.

Network Development and Sociotechnical Dynamics

At the First International Conference on Computer Communications in 1972, ARPA managers scheduled a demonstration of ARPANET to convince computer users and connected research sites of the utility of data networking. ARPA's need to do so illustrates the lack of widespread interest in packet-switched networking at the time. The demonstration was ultimately successful in bringing positive attention to the ARPANET and signified a turning point for the network, marked by a significant increase in network traffic as well as increased interest within academic and professional circles.[37] Given this early success, ARPA sought to transfer control of the ARPANET in 1972 with the hope that data networking would be developed into a nationwide public service. However, neither government agencies nor commercial carriers were interested in managing the network. Most notably, AT&T, the largest carrier in the United States, declined the opportunity to manage and develop the ARPANET into a public data network.[38]

With little interest outside of ARPA and the Department of Defense, day-to-day operation and management of the ARPANET was transferred to the Defense Communications Agency (DCA) in 1975. Although the ARPANET had been available to the armed forces prior to this transfer of control, it was only after the DCA began managing the network that the ARPANET was used by the military in any significant way.[39] With this increased usage, the DCA began to increasingly depend on the ARPANET and when DCA managers began to consider the interconnection of various military networks the Department of Defense (DoD) turned toward TCP/IP as its solution.[40] Even though ARPA had funded the implementation of TCP/IP for popular computers and operating systems prior to the DoD's endorsement, most ARPA research sites continued to use the older ARPANET protocols, which were well implemented and understood. TCP/IP, in contrast, was still experimental, difficult to implement, and subject to modifications and improvements with early trials and testing efforts.[41]

Thus, the DoD's endorsement of TCP/IP and additional ARPA funding to support TCP/IP implementation were integral to increased adoption and usage of the Internet protocols.[42] In the case of the DoD's endorsement, all ARPANET sites were mandated to implement TCP/IP on their hosts by January 1, 1983. While the transition was expensive and difficult, it contributed to the practical feasibility of TCP/IP and made it possible to connect the ARPANET to other TCP/IP networks.

Likewise, by making available a $20 million fund to finance computer manufacturers' implementation of TCP/IP in their computers and networking products, ARPA helped ensure that TCP/IP was readily and widely available to managers and operators considering data networking. According to Janet Abbate, this funding and the resulting availability of TCP/IP "gave a tremendous momentum to the spread of the ARPA protocols, helping to ensure that they would become a de facto standard for networking."[43]

(Re)Designing the Internet:
A Congruence of Interests

With increased adoption of TCP/IP and the eventual abandonment of X.25, the privileged position occupied by carriers within national modernization projects--and secured by carrier–defined networking models and technologies—gave way to a much weaker position within TCP/IP networks that emerged from the specific contingencies and considerations that guided ARPA network designers. Within TCP/IP networks, carriers became but one provider of one medium that could provide a foundation for the transport of data packets across a diverse internetwork. Equally importantly, TCP/IP networks did not include any of the commercialization provisions that were integral to national videotex projects and which included billing mechanisms for network connection and use as well as accessing content. Given the lack of these mechanisms, it should not be surprising that AT&T declined the offer to manage and develop the ARPANET into a public data network.

Despite this bleak outlook for carriers and early failure to control and commercialize emerging telecommunication services, subsequent developments and changes to the Internet's core technologies have provided network operators with new means to control and prioritize traffic flows in ways that could support new models for the commercialization of Internet communication and the privileging of commercial expression on the Internet. Interestingly, these modifications to the Internet's core protocols took place despite the absence of carriers in the development process. However, as providers of the Internet's infrastructure, all network operators are in a position to exploit and further develop these affordances according to their needs. To understand this turn of events, we need to return to the history of Internet development and the growing popularity of TCP/IP networks and their interconnection.

The adoption of TCP/IP was eventually so successful that by the late 1980s and early 1990s networking experts within the Internet community began to express concerns regarding the exhaustion of the available IP network addresses.[44] Host computers require network addresses in order to be able to identify each other on the network and, in turn, to exchange data. In the early 1990s, it was estimated that if the Internet continued to grow at a constant pace, all network addresses would soon be exhausted.

In response to these concerns, the Internet Engineering Task Force (IETF), now responsible for looking after and defining the Internet's standards and protocols, began to explore solutions that would enable the Internet to grow into the foreseeable future. At first, the IETF was not sure whether in addition to expanding the Internet address space there was sufficient time to add new functionality to the IP Version 4 (IPv4). However, predictions indicated that sufficient time was available and based on these forecasts the IETF decided to both expand the Internet's address space and to add new features to the existing IP.[45] Since Internet users and network operators would already need to upgrade their networking software to support a new version of the protocol, it was eventually agreed upon within the IETF that this inconvenience and transition should also be used to improve other aspects of the protocol.

The ethos of diversity with respect to the inclusion of diverse computers, networks, and applications that informed both ARPA's and the INWG's vision of data networking continued to flourish within the IETF. In 1993, the IETF called on the Internet community to provide input into the protocol definition process, and to formally express its needs and requirements based on experiences with the existing IP and anticipated future network uses.[46]

The resulting protocol, IP Version 6 (IPv6), is in many ways similar to its predecessor, IPv4. Based on input from the Internet community, there was general agreement that the new protocol should continue to provide a simple data transport service and that it should be possible for network users to specify when and whether flow and error control is used.[47] Likewise, most groups already using expected that the new protocol would continue to support a diversity of networks and underlying media so that network operators could tailor data networking to their unique environments.[48]

Despite these similarities, new features were also introduced into IPv6 such that the resulting protocol may be said to amplify and extend certain features of its predecessor. In particular, IPv6 includes explicit support for network resource reservation and the prioritization of traffic flows.[49] That is, in addition to being able to specify whether flow and error control should be utilized, users of IPv6 would also able to reserve network bandwidth for particular applications and to prioritize certain traffic flows over others. Prior to the introduction of IPv6, such capabilities were mainly experimental and only partially supported within the IPv4 design.

To understand the rationale for resource reservation and traffic prioritization, we need to examine briefly the networking requirements of some of the groups that responded to the IETF's call for input and that were accommodated by the IPv6 design process.[50] The U.S. Navy and U.S.-based corporations including the U.S. cable television industry requested that the IETF include explicit support in IPv6 for resource reservation and traffic prioritization. Although all three parties are U.S.-based, their requirements do not appear to be bound by national borders in any significant way. It seems reasonable to expect military and corporate representatives outside of the United States making similar requests of the IETF.

By 1993, the year that the IETF began to solicit input from the Internet community, the U.S. Navy was already a heavy user of the IP both to connect computers within its internal networks as well as to interconnect these networks. Such connectivity allowed the Navy to manage a complex and distributed information infrastructure that included networked workstations, communications equipment, weapons systems, and mobile ships, aircraft, and troop deployments.[51] Within this computing environment, the U.S. Navy used networking to transmit a variety of data, including voice, audio, video, image, text, and sensor information. In the case of multimedia applications, the ability to reserve network resources in advance would ensure that packets arrive on time and that audio and video streams are free of timing-based lags and distortions.[52]

The U.S. Navy also requested that IPv6 include the ability to prioritize traffic flows to ensure that high priority information always arrives as quickly as possible to its destination.[53] To this end, the U.S. Navy asked that the IETF include the necessary support within IPv6 that would enable network operators to prioritize certain users or even individual data packets within a network. In this way, high priority tactical messages would not be delayed as a result of low priority messages and network traffic.

Although the networking environments of corporations are quite different when compared to that of the military, similar concerns regarding the scarcity of networking resources motivated U.S. companies to request that the IETF include support for resource reservation and traffic prioritization. Companies that made extensive use of the IP expected to be able to receive a set level of network service for a set cost; they also expected to be able to lower their total costs of networking as much as possible.[54] With these interests in mind, representatives for U.S. corporations requested that the IETF include provisions for resource reservation and traffic prioritization, which could be used by companies for multimedia applications and time-sensitive information, whereas non-multimedia applications and lower priority information could be transmitted across the network at the lowest cost possible, using any remaining bandwidth not utilized by multimedia and high-priority applications.[55]

The U.S. cable industry also supported the need for these features by arguing that resource reservation was necessary for the expansion of the industry's markets.[56] According to industry representatives, compressed digital video signified the future for the industry and was expected to deliver a variety of commercial services to viewers' Internet-ready TVs. These "information services" included interactive video, video-on-demand, multiparty games, computer supported collaborative work, home shopping, customized advertising, and various multimedia applications. Within the projected sociotechnical network of the cable industry, Internet users were understood as consumers of various predefined services that could be accessed for a predefined cost. In order to guarantee an acceptable level of video quality for these services, the industry sought the inclusion of resource reservation mechanisms within IPv6. To ensure the low delay times required by multimedia applications, network bandwidth would need to be reserved in advance and made available to consumers on a pay-per-access basis.

In addition to U.S. companies and the U.S. Navy, other groups that responded to the IETF's call for input were to a large extent accommodated in the design of IPv6 and, in turn, were able to achieve technical representation in the new protocol. Moreover, the IETF's call for input and design process continued a tradition that began with ARPA's Network Working Group and that was taken up by the INWG: allowing the future users of the future network to define the network's features in such a way that their needs and requirements were satisfied. Stated in another way, the IETF employed a strategy of enrollment through inclusion. By including the needs and interests of as many potential users as possible, the IETF was able to increase the likelihood that these users would want to use the protocol when it became available.

Although over 20 groups made formal submissions in response to the IETF's call for input, telephone carriers were not among these groups. Despite this absence, carriers were nonetheless able to achieve technical representation in IPv6 by means of congruent interests with groups that requested support for resource reservation and traffic prioritization. The U.S. Navy requested these features to support its strategic operations and the U.S. cable industry was interested in the delivery of commercial multimedia applications to the home. Yet telephone and cable Internet providers could use resource reservation and traffic prioritization to introduce tiered service to the Internet in such a way that premium network service and data transport can be offered to content producers based on the economics of the market. In this scenario, content producers that cannot afford premium service are relegated to lower levels of service resulting in a hierarchy of content producers and grades of content.

Network Neutrality

Some critics of network neutrality argue that legislation is not necessary, since in practice network providers cannot actually implement a multi-tiered system. That is, although there has been some success with implementation of resource reservation and traffic prioritization mechanisms, technical experts claim that these implementations do not scale well beyond small deployments and could not be used widely on the Internet. As a consequence, these experts argue, legislation is unnecessary, since despite the best efforts of broadband providers to introduce tiered Internet service, the technical obstacles are simply insurmountable.

Although it is possible to accept the fact that current resource reservation and traffic prioritization implementations may not scale well to the size and requirements of the Internet, to judge the necessity of network neutrality legislation solely on the basis of this fact is short-sighted for at least three reasons. First, current technical difficulties should not be used as a basis for decision-making regarding legislation. Not only do network providers have the necessary resources and means to continue to challenge these technical difficulties, but developments in digital processing power, storage, and transmission are likely to diminish the scope and scale of present-day obstacles to the implementation of resource reservation and traffic prioritization.

Second, it is worthwhile to note that IPv6 is designed to support future extensions and features, which in principle may be used to overcome or skirt existing technical difficulties. Unlike its predecessor, IPv4, IPv6 was designed with extensibility as a design goal.[57] Consequently, existing resource reservation and traffic prioritization methods may be modified or supplemented with new functionality in the future, making possible wide-scale implementation and deployment of these methods or similar methods on the Internet.

Lastly, it may be argued that there is little need for concern given the wide prevalence of IPv4 on the Internet and the slow adoption of IPv6. Is it possible that a subsequent version of the IP will be developed before IPv6 achieves widespread implementation and usage? Despite the efforts of the IETF to try and maximize the likelihood of IPv6 adoption, the protocol is still not widely used today. Although it is tempting to view this shortcoming as a failure on the part of the IETF, the slow adoption of IPv6 has less to do with the IETF and more to do with the success of IPv4. Despite IPv6's slow adoption, several key indicators suggest that IPv6 is here to stay and that it will increasingly define the core operation of the Internet, even if this operation will be shared with the existing IPv4 infrastructure. Three factors seem especially relevant to the pace and extent of IPv6 adoption and deployment: the continued scarcity of IPv4 network addresses, the growth of Internet-enabled electronics, including mobile devices and phones, which place increasing pressure on this scarcity, and the now wide availability of IPv6 implementations in networking software and products that enable network operators and users to begin to transition their systems to next-generation technologies.

Although key indicators such as manufacturer support and address depletion suggest that IPv6 is likely here to stay, perhaps the most important reason for considering the value of network neutrality legislation has more to do with the democratic process and less to do with the likelihood of IPv6 adoption. Legislation in a democratic society needs to be grounded in public deliberation and judgment regarding its merits and capacity to serve the public good. Network providers that oppose network neutrality legislation define this public good in economic terms: new, non-neutral service models are good for the economy and will help fund future investments in Internet infrastructure. In contrast, network neutrality supporters define the public good in terms that are not limited solely to the single dimension of economics: network operators should not have the right to privilege the expression of certain content producers based on market considerations; society is better served when Internet users are able to choose between diverse forms of expression and content producers, regardless of these producers' market position and economic arrangements with Internet service providers.

Conclusion

What would a multi-tiered Internet look like? Who would gain and lose the most as a result of such arrangements? It is difficult to answer questions such as these with any certainty given ongoing policy debates and the ways in which tiered service may be regulated in the future, if at all. However, if we assume that industry self-regulation is not supplemented by state regulation with nondiscrimination provisions, then we can easily delineate the losers of the future Internet.

Given the inability of the market to prevent discrimination among content producers and the willingness of network operators to offer certain content producers premium services, all content producers who do not or cannot afford to enter into agreements with network operators will over time be relegated to the Internet's margins. We can anticipate at least three major losers that today rely heavily—and in some cases almost exclusively—on the Internet to exist and operate: alternative media content producers, civil society groups and organizations, and free and open source software users.

First, alternative media content producers such as news websites that operate exclusively on the Web would be severely hindered by a tiered Internet. Although some of the more popular alternative news sites and blogs have some form of revenue that could in principle be used to cover the costs of premium network service, most sites are run by volunteers and individuals for whom additional costs would be prohibitive. These content producers would be relegated to the "slow lanes" of the Internet to the extent that the transmission of their content would be degraded or compromised. In the case of multimedia or streaming content, including audio and video, the resulting degradation of network service may render these modes of communication no longer feasible. The end result would be that the diversity of expression on the Internet would be diminished.

In a similar way, the ability of many civil society groups to share information, coordinate activities, and publicize concerns would be greatly undermined by a tiered Internet. As with non-mainstream content producers, the majority of civil society groups operate on a not-for-profit basis and struggle with the costs and constraints entailed by their operations. Over the past decade, civil society groups have leveraged the affordances of the Internet to not only lower their communication costs, but also to transform their communicative practices. The Internet has enabled civil society groups to share information and coordinate their efforts, form short- and long-term alliances, as well as share their concerns with citizens and publics. A tiered Internet would undermine these capacities and limit the ability of civil society groups to participate in local, national, and international political processes.

Lastly, a tiered Internet has the potential to compromise the vibrancy and success of free and open source software and the communities that rely almost exclusively on the Internet to develop and share software. Although the sharing of computer source code dates back to the earliest days of computer programming, recent decades have witnessed an explosive growth in the number of free and open source projects and communities that make use of the Internet to distribute source code and coordinate development efforts. As an alternative to proprietary software, whereby users do not have access to source code, free and open source software is politically significant since it enables user communities to develop software that best meets their needs. Equally importantly, once free and open source software is developed it may be shared with others, who are then free to use or modify it to suit their needs. As with many content producers and civil society groups, the majority of free and open source projects operate on shoestring budgets and rely on the generosity of volunteers. A tiered Internet with slow, erratic, and unpredictable data transmissions would be prohibitive for most free and open source software communities. Furthermore, a tiered Internet would undermine the ability of all computer users to select and use software according to their needs and requirements. Software innovation and diversity would thus be diminished by a tiered Internet.

Each of the previous examples highlights the shortcomings that result from discriminatory network practices. Exclusive agreements between network operators and content producers clearly exert costs on society as a whole: the range and diversity of expression and activity on the Internet is diminished. Governments and citizens who value not only the right to freedom of expression, but also its meaningful realization will need to carefully consider these costs in light of other alternatives.

Notes

1. "FCC Classifies DSL as Information Service," *Tech Law Journal*, last modified August 5, 2005, http://www.techlawjournal.com/topstories/2005/20050805a.asp.

2. "FCC Classifies Cable Modem Service as 'Information Service': Initiates Proceeding to Promote Broadband Deployment and Examine Regulatory Implications of Classification," *Federal Communications Commission*, last modified March 14, 2002, http://www.fcc.gov/Bureaus/Cable/News_Releases/2002/nrcb0201.html.

3. *National Cable and Telecommunications Association et al. v. Brand X Internet Services et al.*, U.S. 04–277 (2005), http://www.supremecourtus.gov/opinions/04pdf/04–277.pdf.

4. Andrew Feenberg, *Questioning Technology* (London: Routledge, 1999).

5. Janet Abbate, *Inventing the Internet*, 2nd ed. (Cambridge, Mass.: MIT Press, 2000), 152.

6. Ibid., 152–153.

7. Ibid., 152.

8. Lawrence G. Roberts, "The Evolution of Packet Switching," 1978, last modified January 28, 2001, *Dr. Lawrence G. Roberts: Homepage*, http://www.packet.cc/files/ev–packet–sw.html; Peter H. Salus, *Casting the Net: From ARPANET to Internet and Beyond*, (Reading, Mass.: Addison-Wesley, 1995), 110–112; Abbate, *Inventing the Internet*, 154.

9. Roberts, "The Evolution of Packet Switching"; Abbate, *Inventing the Internet*, 154.

10. Renate Mayntz and Volker Schneider, "The Dynamics of System Development in a Comparative Perspective: Interactive Videotex in Germany, France, and Britain," in *The Development of Large Technical Systems*, ed. Renate Mayntz and Thomas P. Hughes

(Frankfurt: Campus Verlag, 1988), 282; Salus, *Casting the Net*, 112; Abbate, *Inventing the Internet*, 152.

11. Abbate, *Inventing the Internet*, 156–157.

12. Mayntz and Schneider, "The Dynamics of System Development in a Comparative Perspective," 272–274; Abbate, *Inventing the Internet*, 152.

13. Abbate, *Inventing the Internet*, 157–158.

14. Ibid., 164–166.

15. Ibid., 162–163.

16. Ibid., 160.

17. Ibid., 162.

18. Mayntz and Schneider, "The Dynamics of System Development in a Comparative Perspective," 282.

19. Ibid., 282–283.

20. Ibid., 274.

21. Ibid., 287.

22. Ibid., 276, 287.

23. Ibid., 287.

24. Salus, *Casting the Net*, 111–112; Abbate, *Inventing the Internet*, 155.

25. Abbate, *Inventing the Internet*, 50.

26. Ibid., 53.

27. Ibid., 118–122.

28. Salus, *Casting the Net*, 102; Andrew Tanenbaum, *Computer Networks*, 4th ed. (Upper Saddle River, NJ.: Prentice Hall, 2002), 54; Abbate, *Inventing the Internet*, 121–122.

29. Abbate, *Inventing the Internet*, 123.

30. Salus, *Casting the Net*, 99–102; Abbate, *Inventing the Internet*, 124–130.

31. Abbate, *Inventing the Internet*, 125–126.

32. Ibid., 125.

33. Ibid., 126.

34. Ibid., 51, 54.

35. Salus, *Casting the Net*, 101–102; Abbate, *Inventing the Internet*, 67.

36. Abbate, *Inventing the Internet*, 51, 67.

37. Ibid., 80.

38. Roberts, "The Evolution of Packet Switching"; Abbate, *Inventing the Internet*, 135.

39. Abbate, *Inventing the Internet*, 136.

40. Ibid., 139.

41. Ibid., 133.

42. Salus, *Casting the Net*, 130–131; Tanenbaum, *Computer Networks*, 54; Abbate, *Inventing the Internet*, 142–143.

43. Abbate, *Inventing the Internet*, 143.

44. Michael Felczak, "(Re)Designing the Internet: A Critical Constructivist Analysis of the Next Generation Internet Protocol" (MA diss., Simon Fraser University, 2005), 44.

45. Ibid., 106.

46. Ibid., 44, 94.

47. Ibid., 92.

48. Ibid., 93.

49. Ibid., 83–89.

50. Ibid., 89–94.

51. Ibid., 61–62.

52. Ibid., 62–63.
53. Ibid., 62–63.
54. Ibid., 64–65.
55. Ibid., 64–65.
56. Ibid., 71–73.
57. Ibid., 84.

Chapter 2

What We Talk about
When We Talk about Net Neutrality:
A Historical Genealogy
of the Discourse of "Net Neutrality"

Danny Kimball

The Federal Communications Commission's (FCC) Open Internet Order of 2010 that went into effect in November 2011 is generally understood to be the first binding network neutrality policy in the United States. These "Open Internet protections" require three things of broadband network operators consistent with network neutrality: transparency in their traffic management; no blocking of any legal content, service, application, or device on the network; and "reasonable" justification for any discrimination in transmissions.[1] However, in its different treatment of wireless networks and "specialized services" separate from the wired "public Internet," the FCC's policy diverges from the principle of network neutrality in significant ways. The Open Internet Order has been understood as going too far toward enacting network neutrality by network operators who oppose such regulation, but as not going far enough by net neutrality advocates.

Network neutrality is ultimately a principle of Internet governance that exists independent of any particular policy drafted or enacted in its name. To understand what this principle is and how it has, or has not, informed policymaking, we must look historically at how "net neutrality" has been identified, translated, and deployed over time. In the decade-long debate about net neutrality, the principle has been defined several ways by a number of groups. As the term has been translated by various stakeholders to particular situations, it has absorbed the values and interests of those who employ it through a process of discursive construction. Although it has taken on different meanings in different contexts—and despite being called by some a hollow term with no real meaning at all[2]—a relatively stable common sense interpretation of "net neutrality" as a principle has been articulated to the term. At the heart of network neutrality is the notion that access to network resources should be granted on a universal and nondiscriminatory basis.[3]

In this chapter I trace a history of "net neutrality" through its different meanings across various technical, economic, and political contexts. I focus on the various ways that "net neutrality" has been defined as a principle by following its historical "genealogy"—a term I use in line with Michel Foucault's understanding of history unfolding as the mutation of discourses.[4] Rather than a simple linear history, this study follows the discursive construction of "net neutrality" in its evolution from technical principle to its association with broader economic and civic notions. I argue that these shifts in the discourse of "net neutrality," with the converging and diverging of the alliance that both produced and was a product of this discourse, enabled and constrained significant developments in U.S. broadband policy and practice.

The "network neutrality" discourse began in the technologist community in the early 2000s to describe efficient network design encouraging technological innovation. It was further taken up by online application, service, and content providers such as Google and used in the economic context of fair marketplace competition that maximizes consumer choice and eliminates discriminatory advantages from vertical integration. As debates about broadband policy became more prominent by the mid-2000s, "net neutrality" became an advocacy issue for public interest groups such as Free Press, and it began to take on more political meanings related to freedom of expression, civic engagement, and democratic participation. As the interests of these groups coalesced within the discourse of "net neutrality"—terminology that, despite its frequent usage as synonymous with "network neutrality," is important to distinguish as a more rhetorically targeted and specific discursive formation—they formed a discursive alliance that led a push for policy informed by the principle of network neutrality in the mid- to late 2000s. Yet, they were opposed by telecommunications and cable corporations such as Verizon and Comcast and supporters of deregulation that used "net neutrality" to conjure images of overreaching and unnecessary government intervention that would stifle investment in broadband networks.

By the late 2000s however, as the interests of technologists, online services, and interest groups began to overlap less, the coalition that came together around net neutrality began to splinter. The "net neutrality" that gained traction in the policy sphere by 2010 was a very loosely translated version of the principle—the result of several levels of compromise between Google (representing online services) and Verizon (representing network operators), with little input from legal and technological experts or public interest groups. It is telling that policymakers tended to refer to principles of "Internet freedom" and the policy that was enacted by the FCC was "Open Internet protections"—a discursive shift away from "net neutrality" that is more than mere semantics. Indeed, we can see through the historical genealogy of "net neutrality" that while the principle itself solidified discursively, the embodiment of the principle in policy became significantly diluted.

Discourse, Principles, and "the Politics of Policy"

In undergoing a discursive analysis of policymaking, this chapter brings a cultural studies approach to policy. We too often take policymaking at face value, buying into the positivist assumptions that it is a pure, factually defined, rational process. However, as especially evident when viewed through this cultural lens, we can see that policymaking is actually messy political business, depending as much on cultural legitimization and rhetorical strategy as on technical or legal "facts."

The discursive power within the "definition of the situation" is the power to structurally enable certain practices and delimit others; a cultural studies approach prompts us to ask who holds that power of defining. Looking at policymaking from this perspective allows us to see why and how discourse matters for important political decisions—rhetoric is never "just rhetoric." Then we cannot only see more clearly the conflicts and contradictions inherent in the policymaking process, but also perhaps take the first steps toward making that process work better to encourage more fair and equitable structures of communication, information, and expression.

As held by Foucauldian discourse theory, the language, actions, and practices that become associated with a particular matter work to form the matter itself—the way that we talk about issues can end up shaping the way we think and act on those issues.[5] Words matter, that is, because the terms we use to describe something delimit the sense we make of it and its potentials. For Foucault, "discourse" is our way of identifying, classifying, thinking about, talking about, and acting toward topics and situations.[6] These discursive practices add up to constitute certain "discursive formations" at various conjunctures; as a function of discourse, these formations appear as natural properties of that which is being described, but they are in actuality socially, culturally, and historically contingent.

Despite its always transitory nature, discursive construction does come together in particular times at particular sites to suggest a stability and coherence. Stuart Hall explains this as the process of "articulation": the linking of elements of a discourse to elements of other discourses.[7] Hall uses articulation to describe how power concentrates within certain discursive formations to serve specific interests in a discourse. Within discursive construction, the process of articulation is how terms become linked to discourses to take up particular meanings and how diverse groups are able to come together in a kind of discursive alliance. It is through articulation that the phrase "net neutrality" became linked to such discourses as technical efficiency, marketplace competition, and freedom of expression and how technologists, online service companies, and public interest groups came together for a time in support of "net neutrality" policy.

Especially at the level of structuring institutions like the government, discursive construction holds great consequences for our conceptions of possible action, and that discursive power is not equitably distributed in society. The social position of the policy sphere means that the discourse there holds a unique authority and influence in shaping important social structures, including technological systems. Of concern here is that discourse that plays out at the level of the FCC has an especially powerful role in constituting the institutional and technical structures of communications in the United States, including the Internet.

Thomas Streeter's groundbreaking work on media policymaking points to the power of discourse at the FCC as a "legal inscription on technology": in classifying, defining, enabling, and constraining the uses, practices, and possibilities of communications media in the United States, FCC discourse shapes technologies it often fails to describe.[8] Streeter's critical studies of FCC broadcasting and cable policy provide especially great insight into the structuring power of regulatory decisions, as well as recognizing the values and principles that underlie and inform policy decisions and the conflicts and contradictions inherent to "the politics of policy."[9] Streeter's work serves as a model for this study in looking at how changes in the ways of talking about a technology in and around the policymaking arena can lead to structural changes in communications media—changes that have historically encouraged consumer access but stifled public participation.

I employ the methods of Foucauldian discourse analysis here to understand the discursive construction of "net neutrality" and trace the intellectual genealogy of the principle. I follow terms like "network neutrality," "net neutrality," "Internet freedom," and "open Internet" through policy proceedings including reports, orders, hearings, filings, and comments at the FCC; academic literature such as articles and papers in technical and legal journals, books, and conferences; and reports, statements, and commentary in the press, on blogs, and from involved corporations and interest groups. By tracing a breadth of discursive practices across various sites where the terms in question are used, we can map the discursive genealogy of "net neutrality" and, situating it within its larger social-historical context and relations of power, come to understand its role in broadband policymaking.

The Discursive Construction of "Net Neutrality"

Tim Wu coined the term "network neutrality" in his 2003 article "Network Neutrality, Broadband Discrimination."[10] It is worth noting here that Wu's choice of words in this article is significant for the construction of the discourse that grew up around the term. "Neutrality" as a signifier brings with it important connotations of impartiality, equality, fairness, and justice that have proven to be powerful conceptual vehicles for this discourse.[11] Rather than introducing a new concept though, Wu more than anything was putting a name to a long-standing principle that had informed the design and governance of the Internet since its development and operation by the technologist community of computer scientists, network engineers, and academics.

The principle that Wu describes as "network neutrality" in this article is closely related to the "end-to-end argument" that informed the early structure and operation of the Internet and common carriage regulations that governed the first generation of Internet access providers.[12] The universal and nondiscriminatory access to network content, services, applications, and devices that Wu refers to as "network neutrality" was a built-in consequence of the end-to-end structure of the early Internet and was once enforced by the common carriage regulations that applied to any transmissions over telephone lines, including dial-up Internet traffic. However, changes to the technical and institutional structures of the Internet at the turn of the millennium brought with them more incentive and ability for network operators to discriminate among Internet uses and fewer regulatory preventions against such practices.[13]

"The end-to-end argument," first advanced by network engineers Jerome Saltzer, David Reed, and David Clark, emphasizes control by end-users of a network over those who manage the core by building network infrastructures that provide only general services that can be used by any application, service, or device.[14] Legal scholars including Mark Lemley and Lawrence Lessig began arguing in the early 2000s that by originally structuring the Internet end-to-end, an "evolutionary model" of innovation was put into place.[15] By not discriminating in favor of any particular use, such a model created a relatively level playing field that enabled the sort of competition among applications, devices, and services that encouraged a wave of rapid and socially beneficial technological innovation. The development and implementation of technologies like deep packet inspection, firewalls, and content filters, however, allowed for more control at the core of the network through the 2000s.

This control over network transmissions began to be exercised more aggressively and intrusively in the early-2000s, as many of the incentives to operate networks on an open and nondiscriminatory basis were removed during the transition from dial-up to broadband Internet access. First, as the Internet access market grew broader and more commercial, the primary Internet access providers became not nonprofit parties like universities and research institutes as in the early days of the Internet but rather, profit-maximizing corporations. Further, as Internet access came to be primarily provided over direct subscriber lines and coaxial cable rather than telephone lines, the Bush FCC reclassified Internet access as an "information service" rather than a "telecommunications service," as previously defined by the Telecommunications Act of 1996. This reclassification removed many of regulations on network operators—including, importantly, common carriage rules that were similar in intention and effect to network neutrality. "Open access" regulations for network operators were also rescinded in this move, eliminating requirements for physical network infrastructure operations to be "functionally separate" to allow other firms to share lines with network operators and provide competing Internet access services. The Supreme Court's 2005 ruling in *National Cable and Telecommunications Association v. Brand X Internet Services* upheld the FCC's decision and was the final determination that common carriage and open access regulations would no longer apply to the Internet.

With no regulatory protections against exploiting dominant incumbent market positions, the telecommunications and cable companies that already owned and operated DSL and cable networks effectively became the sole providers of high speed wireline Internet access, creating a duopoly in virtually every local market in the United States by the mid-2000s.[16] Further, telecommunications firms who had historically been common carriers were joined in the broadband access market by cable companies used to the "electronic publisher" regulatory framework that enables them more control of the flow of content over the networks they operate. With profit-maximizing motives and the technological capacities for discrimination in place, the removal of incentives for openness from either regulatory protections or a competitive market meant that network operators began taking tighter control of Internet transmissions. Indeed, by the early-to mid-2000s there was a rise in discriminatory network management practices by Internet access providers, such as AT&T, Comcast, and Cox blocking subscribers' access to devices and services like virtual private networks and home Wi-Fi networks.[17]

Network neutrality began as a technical principle for efficient network design. Wu's notion of "network neutrality" was a response to the situation of increasing technological discrimination on broadband networks in the early-2000s. Wu proposed network neutrality as a principle to inform broadband nondiscrimination policy, which he explicitly opposed to calls for a return to "open access" regulation of Internet infrastructures that were quite loud during this period. Advocates of reinstating open access rules for the Internet argue that by again separating infrastructure management from service provision, competition in access services would be introduced back into the market, bringing with it incentives to provide neutral and nondiscriminatory Internet access and more widely distributing the management of Internet transmissions. However, Wu argued that if the ultimate goal is to encourage better Internet access service, including openness and nondiscrimination in online content and services, then straightforward network neutrality rules inscribed in policy are a more effective solution than relying on indirect structural remedies such as open access. In many ways, Wu's network neutrality proposal was to put back in place openness and the "evolutionary model of innovation" through policy rather than technology.

Wu's notion of network neutrality as the most efficient means to encourage technological innovation was drawn from the Internet technologist community, and his terminology was taken up there soon after. We can see how this discourse serves the interests of these computer scientists, network engineers, and scholars of high technology: the assumption is that, because the Internet was originally built to adhere to norms of openness and that those now in control of the network's infrastructures are not adhering to those norms, policy should be enacted to make those standards mandatory. That is, because commercial Internet access providers are not acting in accordance with the values that these scientists and engineers embedded in the design of the technologies (neutrality and nondiscrimination), technologists would like to reinscribe those values through regulation of those technologies.

Within the technologist community, by the mid-2000s the question of how best to govern Internet transmissions increasingly came to be answered in the terminology of "network neutrality." This can be seen in statements from prominent computer scientists and network engineers such as Vint Cerf, one of the inventors of the Internet Protocol; Tim Berners-Lee, the inventor of the World Wide Web; and David Reed, one of the founders of the end-to-end argument, as well as in the work of technology law scholars such as Barbara van Schewick, Brett Frischmann, and Susan Crawford.[18]

Network neutrality discourse soon grew out of the technologist community and took on a different discursive formation: the more concise "net neutrality." More than simply an abbreviated version of the same exact notion, "net neutrality" carries some small but important distinctions. For one, it is a bit pithier phrase that is slightly more publicly appealing and memorable, which has been important to its articulation to the allied discursive group that developed around it. Also notable is the move in terminology from general to specific: "net neutrality" makes the issue a concern for the Internet in particular, not a broadly-applicable design principle for any network architecture. This frames the issue in such a way as to hail any and all Internet users to the discourse.

Internet application and service providers like Google, Amazon, Yahoo, eBay, and Microsoft had also been discussing the need for broadband access regulations since the FCC's reclassification in 2002, and they soon began to call for "net neutrality."[19] As these content providers adopted it, the discourse expanded beyond efficiency, innovation, and technological development to become more closely articulated to economic matters of free markets and consumer choice. From the perspective of the discursive site of Silicon Valley, net neutrality became about ensuring a fair marketplace where no online applications or services have a discriminatory advantage from network operators, leaving Internet users to decide what content succeeds.[20] With this, a neutral network is in the interests of online service providers as a way to assure their control of the content made available online, therefore maintaining their ability to profit from its circulation without letting network operators get a cut. Open network design inverts the power relations of production and distribution typical to traditional media systems, where distributors' control of content delivery infrastructures give them leverage over content producers who must rely on these closed networks to reach consumers. Much of the conflict in the net neutrality debates, then, has been a struggle between the largest content providers like Google and Amazon and the largest access providers such as Verizon and Comcast over the latter's ability to assert more control over and profit extraction from the products of the former. Internet access providers' battles with Internet application providers have been especially heated over voice over Internet Protocol (VoIP) and streaming video services, which threaten their incumbent dominance over telephone and cable services.[21]

By 2005, several conspicuous instances of material and clearly threatened discriminatory network management practices began to spark some public attention. Incidents such as telecom company Madison River blocking access to the VoIP service Vonage, Canadian Internet access provider Telus blocking access to their workers' labor union website during a lockout, AT&T CEO Ed Whitacre's quickly notorious "ain't going to let them use my pipes for free" interview, and Verizon executives complaining of Google's "free lunch" were picked up by the press and major blogs, giving more visibility to net neutrality issues.[22]

The discourse of net neutrality began to rise to public prominence in 2005 and 2006, not only at the hands of technologists and content providers, but largely led by public interest groups. At the forefront of this movement was the Save the Internet campaign, launched in 2006 by the media reform organization Free Press to push for net neutrality policy. At that point, the coalition included many citizen and media advocacy groups in the United States—from the American Civil Liberties Union, the Consumers Union, and the American Library Association to Public Knowledge, the Media Access Project, and Reporters Without Borders,—as well as a wide range of interest groups from Left to Right,—from MoveOn.org, the Service Employees International Union, and the Feminist Majority to the Gun Owners of America, the Christian Coalition of America, and the Parents Television Council.[23] These interest groups expanded the discourse of "net neutrality" to address people not just as Internet users or consumers, but as citizens: here, net neutrality became articulated to issues like freedom of expression, civic engagement, and political participation.[24] This is where we began to see the images of gatekeepers, tollbooths, and tiers used as rhetorical devices to represent the troubles apparent in discriminatory network management practices. Public interest campaigns such as Save the Internet were able to successfully sell the issue in these powerful social and political terms to enlist larger public support for network neutrality principles and a push for such policy.

Discursive Shifts for "Net Neutrality"

By 2006, then, an allied discursive bloc of technologists, online content providers, and public interest groups had come together around the discourse of "net neutrality," by then understood as a matter of technological, economic, and civic importance. The discourse fully blossomed in the public sphere at that point: "net neutrality" became a widely heard term and the issue was covered regularly in the press, on cable news, and on social media including blogs and YouTube videos. Around that time, proceedings at the FCC and the Federal Trade Commission dealing directly with network neutrality issues were joined by several "net neutrality" bills introduced into Congress. By this point, supporters were paying close attention to these events in the policy sphere, culminating perhaps most prominently in the quick infamy of Senator Ted Stevens' declaration that "the Internet is a series of tubes" during a Congressional committee debate.[25]

The term "net neutrality" did not hold up well under the stress of being a popular buzzword and rallying point for many different interests. For one, its technical origins haunted it in the public sphere, as it comes across in many ways as too wonky and oblique to call forward the major social and political concerns that have become attached to it. Other terminology was attempted, such as referring to net neutrality as "the First Amendment of the Internet" and saying it is essential to ensuring a "democratic Internet."[26] Some prominent net neutrality supporters even explicitly called for a "rebranding," most notably Arianna Huffington, who called the term "net neutrality" "marketing death" and looked for something that she hoped would better "capture the public imagination."[27]

The phrase "Internet freedom" became key to the discourse of net neutrality as it developed in the public sphere, manifesting most importantly in the FCC's first official forays into network neutrality policy: the Internet Freedom guidelines and the Internet Policy Statement of 2005. In 2004, then Chairman of the FCC Michael Powell introduced what he called the four "Internet Freedoms": that Internet users have the "freedom" to access content, run applications, attach devices, and obtain service plan information.[28] In 2005, Powell's successor Kevin Martin, adapted these "Internet Freedoms" into the Internet Policy Statement, with a notable translation of the user from citizen to consumer, and an important caveat: here "consumers" are "entitled" to the content, applications, and devices of their choice, along with competition in the marketplace, all subject to "reasonable network management practices."[29]

Importantly however, the FCC's Internet Policy Statement is simply a set of guidelines and is not enforceable regulatory policy. It was issued in the midst of advocacy groups' concerns over mergers in the telecom industry and the lack of regulatory oversight resulting from the FCC's reclassification of Internet access. Issuing this statement was the agency's way to appease net neutrality supporters and divert attention from its actual deregulation of the Internet access market. Nonetheless, it was the FCC's first official recognition of network neutrality principles, making it a touchstone for net neutrality discourse—one that notably refers to these principles of "Internet freedom" and features the repetition of its stated purpose to preserve and promote the "open Internet."[30]

Following the Internet Policy Statement and building on the broadly defined technical, economic, and political discourse of net neutrality, "open Internet" began to become very significant as a discursive formation. "Open" signifies concepts that hold great power for public support for the issue of net neutrality: gaining access, being communicative and receptive, connotations of being "open to the public" and "open for business," and conjuring images of unblocked, unobstructed, unrestricted passageways and unlimited, unenclosed expanses.[31]

While it has not wholly replaced "net neutrality" in public discourse, the phrase "open Internet" has played an important part in the discursive construction of the issue in institutional and regulatory contexts especially—for example, it provided the name for the Open Internet Coalition, the advocacy group representing Internet content providers.[32]

The "open Internet" has been an especially prominent discursive formation in the policy sphere, beginning with the FCC's 2009 Notice of Proposed Rulemaking (NPRM) for Open Internet Protections. This document, issued by the FCC in its first year under the Obama administration, opened the Commission's proceedings for drafting binding net neutrality regulations. This was expected given that the Obama FCC made net neutrality a signature issue. As a presidential candidate in 2008, Barack Obama tapped into the popular appeal of net neutrality through a campaign promise to enact it as policy. The proposal for rulemaking initiated proceedings that explicitly built on the Internet Freedom recommendations for the broadband industry under the Bush FCC, and therefore adopted much of that language.[33]

The NPRM clearly demonstrated that, at the policymaking level, the net neutrality issue was officially rebranded as one of "protecting the open Internet." The word "open" appears 255 times in the NPRM's 107 pages, while the word "neutrality" shows up only 47 times and every single instance is either a quotation or a footnote referring to the word's usage elsewhere.[34] This clearly conscious effort to shift the discourse was an understandable rhetorical strategy for the FCC in its goal of passing net neutrality regulations: any stakeholders that engaged in the policymaking arena on the issue were forced to take up the discourse through these particular terms. At the level at which the policy decisions were made, the issue became defined foremost by characteristics such as openness and freedom, which seem so unassailable as to make support more agreeable.

The risk of steeping an issue so fully in terminology generally revered across so many contexts is that it can prove especially susceptible to being recontextualized. Notions like "open" and "free" are quite open and free themselves to be applied however a particular interest wishes. This proved true for "open Internet:" the efforts of net neutrality advocates and the FCC to articulate "openness" and "freedom" to regulatory policy were countered strongly by telecom and cable companies, along with their neoliberal and Right-libertarian sympathizers, who have worked to articulate the issue to "open" markets that are "free" from government regulation.[35] With the discursive formation of "open Internet," then, the discourse of net neutrality grew wide enough to be used as an instrument of potential policy change—though perhaps too blunt an instrument.

Tensions in the discursive alliance that came together around net neutrality began to grow as understandings of the issue changed and the contexts around it shifted. The sound bite demands of enlisting public support for net neutrality as a mainstream political issue saw the rhetoric of public interest groups grow more reductive. As tends to be the case for social movements, the discourse that drives them becomes simplified so as to absorb as many different interests as possible and incite action on the issue.

The shift to talking less about "net neutrality" and more about "Internet freedom" and the "open Internet" was in some ways a part of this process. At the same time, the discourse from academics and technologists increasingly moved to more nuanced discussions of the issue, as the work of scholars such as Christian Sandvig, Milton Mueller, Ed Felten, Jon Peha, Sascha Meinrath, and Victor Pickard demonstrates.[36] Indeed, many supporters of net neutrality in the academic technologist community began to frame it as a matter of principle which brings with it complications and complexities when embodied in regulatory policy—that there is no such thing as pure network neutrality and that it perhaps works better as abstract governance principle than as strictly binding policy that could bring with it unintended consequences.

The coalition that formed in support of net neutrality began to splinter as the FCC moved forward with the Open Internet proceedings and several more ultimately unsuccessful legislative attempts were introduced in Congress. In the midst of the hyper-partisan Republican reception to any goals of the Obama administration, net neutrality came to be seen by conservatives no longer as a bipartisan free speech issue but more as a signature Democratic issue to be obstructed.

Indeed, Tea Party discourse was able to reframe nondiscrimination regulations as a "Marxist takeover of the Internet" by the Obama administration.[37] As the issue became more politically divisive in the United States surrounding the 2010 Congressional elections, the Save the Internet coalition lost some members, most prominently the Gun Owners of America.[38] This discursive framing as dangerous government intervention clearly serves the interests of the network operators that were able to employ and exploit the renewal of Right-Libertarian fervor by the Tea Party movement to serve their deregulatory neoliberal interests.

In many ways, the cornerstone of the discursive alliance built around net neutrality was the advocacy of powerful online service corporations such as Amazon, Skype, and Facebook, and led by Google. However, as Google's interests in particular began to diverge from those of the technical or public interest advocates of net neutrality, Google's definition of the principle came to differ significantly from technologists and interest groups. By the late 2000s, in fact, Google's translation of net neutrality had more in common with Verizon—one of the biggest Internet access providers, but also by that point Google's close business partner in the Android mobile device project. Verizon had claimed along the way that it had no problem with network neutrality in principle but is just opposed to heavy-handed net neutrality policy, preferring voluntary self-regulation. The definition of "network neutrality" that Verizon said it supported, however, is particularly circumscribed—applying to the "open Internet," of course, but in this usage implying the existence of another closed Internet.[39]

Google and Verizon were leaders in the FCC's closed-door negotiations in 2010 between corporations with the biggest financial stakes on either side of the net neutrality issue. After breaking off from these talks, Google and Verizon negotiated a voluntary agreement between themselves that they intended to serve as a framework for net neutrality governance. At the core of the Verizon-Google compromise is "openness" for the "public Internet," but not "differentiated services" that could become *de facto* "private Internets," open only to network operators and the content providers with whom they have exclusive deals.[40] In this accord, Google met Verizon much further than halfway, committing itself—and by extension, the rest of the discursive alliance in support of net neutrality that it once led—to a greatly weakened position in the net neutrality debate. The Verizon-Google agreement on "open Internet protections" quickly became the accepted solution in the policy sphere, as this highly compromised definition of the network neutrality principle was enshrined in the regulations adopted in the FCC's Open Internet Order of 2010.

Conclusion

That Internet access policy based in the principle of "net neutrality" was adopted by the FCC speaks to the powerful discursive alliance of technologists, online service providers, and public interest groups that came together in the 2000s; that the policy ultimately enacted by the end of the decade was, in fact, deeply compromised "open Internet protections" speaks to the contingent and contested nature of discursive construction and the fragile existence of articulation of interests in such a discursive alliance.

The discursive construction of "net neutrality" linked the term to technical, economic, and civic discourses that brought in wide support. As with all discursive formations, though, the meaning of "net neutrality," is defined in struggle: it increasingly became linked to discourses of excessive government intervention and unintended consequences. By the end of the 2000s "net neutrality" was perhaps too loaded of a term, packed with contested meanings, positive and negative connotations, and a great deal of confusion. By that point, the discursive alliance of technologists, online service companies, and advocacy groups disarticulated, as the shared interests that were once absorbed into the discourse of "net neutrality" slid apart. What followed was an articulation of the discourse of net neutrality in the policy sphere to "protecting the open Internet," the rearticulated discursive construction that resulted in a compromised set of FCC regulations that is as close as the United States has come to network neutrality policy.

The standing of the FCC's Open Internet policy itself is tenuous, as the rules are, at the time of this writing, the subject of a major court battle. A judicial challenge from Verizon asserts not only that the rules go beyond the FCC's legal authority to regulate broadband access services, but also that the policy is an unconstitutional violation of the corporation's First Amendment rights to "edit" their Internet access services and their Fifth Amendment property rights over their network infrastructures.

It is important to note that net neutrality rules were only able to gain traction in the policy sphere once they became known more by "Internet freedom" and "open Internet." This vague terminology was itself a usefully open vessel for the deeply compromised version of net neutrality that was able to get barely enough grudging support from stakeholders on both sides to be passed as the FCC's "open Internet protections." While this rhetorical shift to such unassailable discourses as "freedom" and "openness" may have been necessary to achieve binding "net neutrality" policy, it also played a crucial role in watering it down to the point of enforcing very little of the actual principle of network neutrality. The difference between "net neutrality" and "open Internet protections" is not merely one of semantics, but is right at the core of a serious deviation in values. This discursive shift, from support for "net neutrality" by a broad discursive alliance to the enactment of "open Internet protections" that serve certain interests more than others, came with real material consequences for Internet users today and in the future.

Notes

1. United States, Federal Communications Commission, *Report and Order In the Matter of Preserving the Open Internet*, FCC 10-201, GN Docket No. 09-191 (Washington, DC: GPO, December 21, 2010): http://hraunfoss.fcc.gov/edocs_public/attachmatch/FCC-10-201A1_Rcd.pdf.

2. See, for example: Barbara van Schewick and David Farber, "Point/Counterpoint: Network Neutrality Nuances," *Communications of the ACM* 52, no. 31 (2009): 34.

3. Milton Mueller provides, in my estimation, the most clear and succinct definition of network neutrality, along these lines. See Milton Mueller, et al., "Net Neutrality as Global Principle for Internet Governance," Internet Governance Project (Syracuse, NY: Syracuse University, 2007): http://www.internetgovernance.org/pdf/NetNeutralityGlobal Principle.pdf.

4. Michel Foucault, "Governmentality," in *The Foucault Effect: Studies in Governmentality*, ed. Graham Burchell, Colin Gordon, and Peter Miller (Chicago: University of Chicago Press, 1991), 87–104.

5. Foucault, "The Order of Discourse," in *Untying the Text*, ed. Robert Young, translated by Ian McLeod (New York: Routledge, 1981): 48–78; Foucault, *The Archaeology of Knowledge and the Discourse on Language*, translated by Rupert Swyer (New York: Vintage, 1982); Foucault, *The History of Sexuality, Volume II: The Use of Pleasure*, translated by Robert Hurley (New York: Vintage, 1990).

6. Foucault, *Discourse on Language*; Foucault, *History of Sexuality, Vol. II*.

7. Stuart Hall and Lawrence Grossberg, "On Postmodernism and Articulation: An Interview with Stuart Hall," *Journal of Communication Inquiry* 10, no. 2 (1986): 45–60.

8. Thomas Streeter, *Selling the Air: A Critique of the Policy of Commercial Broadcasting in the United States* (Chicago: University of Chicago Press, 1996), 1.

9. Streeter, *Selling the Air*; Streeter, "The Cable Fable Revisited: Policy, Discourse, and the Making of Cable Television," *Critical Studies in Media Communication* 4, no. 2 (1987): 174–200; Streeter, "Blue Skies and Strange Bedfellows: The Discourse of Cable Television," in *The Revolution Wasn't Televised: Sixties Television and Social Conflict*, edited by Lynn Spigel and Michael Curtin (New York: Routledge, 1997), 221–242.

10. Tim Wu, "Network Neutrality, Broadband Discrimination," *Journal on Telecommunications and High Technology Law* 2 (2003): 141–179.

11. See "neutrality, *n.*," *The Oxford English Dictionary*, 3rd edition, 2003, Oxford University Press: http://www.oed.com/view/Entry/126461.

12. Jerome H. Saltzer, David P. Reed, and David D. Clark, "End-to-End Arguments in System Design," *ACM Transactions in Computer Systems* 2, no. 4 (1984): 277–288; Christian Sandvig, "Network Neutrality Is the New Common Carriage," *Info: The Journal of Policy, Regulation, and Strategy for Telecommunications, Media, and Information* 9, no. 2/3 (2007): 136–147.

13. See van Schewick, *Internet Architecture and Innovation* (Cambridge, Mass.: MIT Press, 2010).

14. Saltzer, Reed, and Clark, "End-to-End Arguments."

15. Mark A. Lemley and Lawrence Lessig, "The End of End-to-End: Preserving the Architecture of the Internet in the Broadband Era," *UCLA Law Review* 48 (2000): 925. See also Wu, "Network Neutrality:" 145–47; Lessig, *The Future of Ideas: The Fate of the Commons in a Connected World* (New York: Random House, 2004).

16. Charles B. Goldfarb, *Access to Broadband Networks*, Congressional Research Service (Washington, D.C.: Library of Congress, August 31, 2006): http://opencrs.com/document/RL33496/2006-08-31/download/1005/.

17. Wu, "Network Neutrality."

18. See, for example, Alan Davidson, "Vint Cerf Speaks Out on Net Neutrality," *Google Official Blog*, November 8, 2005: http://googleblog.blogspot.com/2005/11/vint-cerf-speaks-out-on-net-neutrality.html; Vinton G. Cerf, "Prepared Statement of Vincent G. Cerf," February 7, 2006: http://commerce.senate.gov/pdf/cerf-020706.pdf; Tim Berners-Lee, "Net Neutrality: This Is serious," Decentralized Information Group, MIT Computer Science and Artificial Intelligence Laboratory, June 21, 2006: http://dig.csail.mit.edu/breadcrumbs/node/144; Berners-Lee, "The Neutrality of the Net," Decentralized Information Group, MIT Computer Science and Artificial Intelligence Laboratory, May 2, 2006: http://dig.csail.mit.edu/breadcrumbs/node/132; Vinton G. Cerf, Stephen D. Crocker, David P. Reed, Lauren Weinstein, and Daniel Lynch, "Open Letter to FCC Chairman Julius Genachowski," *Open Internet Coalition*: http://www.openinternetcoalition.org/files/FCC_NN_Letter_Cerf.pdf; van Schewick, "Towards an Economic Framework for Network Neutrality," *Journal on Telecommunications and High Technology Law* 5 (2007): 329–391; Brett Frischmann, "An Economic Theory of Commons and Infrastructure Management," *Minnesota Law Review* 89 (2005): 917–1030; Susan Crawford, "The Internet and the Project of Communications Law," *UCLA Law Review* 55 (2007): 359.

19. See, for example, "Net Neutrality," *Google Policy Blog*: http://googlepublicpolicy.blogspot.com/search/label/Net%20Neutrality; Eric Bangeman, "Amazon Exec: Net Neutrality Necessary Because of 'Little Choice' for Consumers," *Ars Technica*, May 12, 2006: http://arstechnica.com/uncategorized/2006/05/6817-2/; Mario Armstrong and Farai Chideya, "Net Neutrality Battle Goes to Washington," NPR, June 26, 2006: http://www.npr.org/templates/story/story.php?storyId=5511150; "Net Neutrality," *eBay Main Street*: http://www.ebaymainstreet.com/issues/net-neutrality; Declan McCullagh, "eBay tries e-mail in Net neutrality fight," *CNET News*, June 1, 2006: http://news.cnet.com/eBay-tries-e-mail-in-Net-neutrality-fight/2100-1028_3-607 9291.html; McCullagh, "Microsoft's new push in Washington," *CNET News*, June 30, 2003: http://news.cnet.com/2010-1071_3-1021938.html; Tom Keating, "Amazon, Google, Yahoo, eBay Fight for Net Neutrality with Letter to Congress," *TMCnet*, July 13,

2006:   http://blog.tmcnet.com/blog/tom-keating/news/amazon-google-yahoo-ebay-fight-net-neutrality-with-letter-to-congress.asp.

20. See, for example Eric Schmidt, "A Note to Google Users on Net Neutrality," *Google Policy Blog*, 2006: http://www.google.com/help/netneutrality_letter.html.

21. See, David Clark, "Network Neutrality: Words of Power and 800-Pound Gorillas," *International Journal of Communication* 1 (2007): 701–708.

22. Jonathan Krim, "FCC Probes Blocking of Internet Phone Calls," *The Washington Post*, February 16, 2005: http://www.washingtonpost.com/wp-dyn/articles/A31082-2005Feb16.html; Cory Doctorow, "Phone Company Blocks Access to Telecoms Union's Website," *BoingBoing*, July 24, 2005: http://boingboing.net/2005/07/24/phone-company-blocks.html; Ken Fisher, "SBC: ain't no way VoIP uses mah pipes!," *Ars Technica*, October 31, 2005: http://arstechnica.com/old/content/2005/10/5498.ars; Arshad Muhammed, "Verizon Executive Calls for End to Google's 'Free Lunch,'" *The Washington Post,* February 6, 2006: http://www.washingtonpost.com/wp-dyn/content/article/2006/02/06/AR2006020601624.html.

23. On the Internet Archive we can see the list of members shortly after its founding and at the height of its bipartisan support: *The Internet Archive Wayback Machine*, "Join Us," *Save the Internet*, October 12, 2007: http://web.archive.org/web/20071012025915/http://www.savetheinternet.com/=coalition. For the current list of supporters, see, "Join Us," Save the Internet: http://www.savetheinternet.com/members.

24. See, for example, "Statement of Principles," *Save the Internet*: http://www.savetheinternet.com/statement-principles; "Join the Fight for Internet Freedom," *Free Press*: http://www.freepress.net/savetheinternet; "Future of the Internet," Free Press: http://www.freepress.net/media_issues/internet.

25. For an example of how these comments were taken up in the online public sphere, see "DJ Ted Stevens Techno Remix: 'A Series of Tubes,'" *YouTube*: http://www.youtube.com/watch?v=EtOoQFa5ug8.

26. See, for example, Evan Derkacz, "Markey Introduces Net Neutrality Act: The fight for the First Amendment of the Internet Is On," *AlterNet*, May 2, 2006: http://www.alternet.org/story/35728//; Adam Cohen, "Why the Democratic Ethic of the Web May Be About to End," *The New York Times*, May 28, 2006: http://www.nytimes.com/2006/05/28/opinion/28sun3.html; "Keeping a Democratic Web," *The New York Times*, May 2, 2006: http://www.nytimes.com/2006/05/02/opinion/02tue3.html.

27. Arianna Huffington, "'Net Neutrality:' Why Are the Bad Guys So Much Better at Naming Things?," *The Huffington Post*, May 3, 2006: http://www.huffingtonpost.com/Arianna-huffington/net-neutrality-why-are-th_b_20311.html.

28. Michael Powell, "Preserving Internet Freedom: Guiding Principles for the Industry," speech delivered at the Silicon Flatirons Symposium on The Digital Broadband Migration: Toward a Regulatory Regime for the Internet Age (University of Colorado Law School, Boulder, February 8, 2004): http://hraunfoss.fcc.gov/edocs_public/attachmatch/DOC-243556A1.pdf.

29. United States, Federal Communications Commission, *Policy Statement, In the Matter of Inquiry Concerning High Speed Access to the Internet Over Cable and Other Facilities*, FCC 05-151, GN Docket No. 00-185 (Washington, D.C.: GPO, August 5, 2005): http://hraunfoss.fcc.gov/edocs_public/attachmatch/FCC-05-151A1.pdf.

30. Ibid.

31. See: "open, *a.*," *The Oxford English Dictionary*, 3rd edition, 2004, Oxford University Press: http://www.oed.com/view/Entry/131698; "open, *v.*," *The Oxford English*

Dictionary, 3rd edition, 2004, Oxford University Press: http://www.oed.com/view/Entry/131700.

32. See: "Why an Open Internet," Open Internet Coalition: http://openinternetcoalition.org/index.cfm?objectid=8C7857B0-5C6A-11DF-9E27000C296BA163.

33. United States, Federal Communications Commission, *Notice of Proposed Rulemaking In the Matter of Protecting the Open Internet*, FCC 09-93, GN Docket No. 09-191 (Washington, D.C.: GPO, October 22, 2009): http://hraunfoss.fcc.gov/edocs_public/attachmatch/FCC-09-93A1.pdf.

34. Ibid.

35. See, for example, Andrew Moylan, "Spare Us the Broadband Plan," *The Washington Times*, March 31, 2010, http://www.washingtontimes.com/news/2010/mar/31/spare-us-the-broadband-plan/; Neil Stevens, "Danger at the FCC: An Omnibus Warning," *RedState*, March 27, 2010: http://www.redstate.com/neil_stevens/2010/03/27/danger-at-the-fcc-an-omnibus-warning/.

36. Sandvig, "New Common Carriage"; Mueller, *Principle for Internet Governance*; Edward W. Felten, "Nuts and Bolts of Network Neutrality," *Center for Information Technology Policy* (Princeton, N.J.: Princeton University, 2006): www.cs.princeton.edu/courses/archive/fall09/cos109/neutrality.pdf; Jon Peha, "The Benefits and Risks of Mandating Network Neutrality, and the Quest for a Balanced Policy," *International Journal of Communication* 1 (2007): 644–668; Sascha Meinrath and Victor Pickard, "The New Net Neutrality: Criteria for Internet Freedom," *International Journal of Communication Law and Policy* 12 (2008): 225–243.

37. See, for example, "Beck through the Looking Glass: Smears Net Neutrality as a Marxist Plot to Take Over the Internet," *Media Matters for America*, October 21, 2009, http://mediamatters.org/research/200910210026.

38. Sara Jerome, "Net-neutrality group challenged by ties to MoveOn.Org; ACORN," *The Hill*, August 23, 2010: http://thehill.com/blogs/hillicon-valley/technology/115367-as-elections-near-net-neutrality-backers-challenged-by-moveonorg-and-acorn-ties.

39. See, for example, John Czwartacki, "Preserving the Open Internet," *Verizon PolicyBlog*, September 22, 2009: http://policyblog.verizon.com/BlogPost/668/PreservingtheOpenInternet.aspx; Lowell McAdam, "Finding Common Ground on an Open Internet," *Verizon PolicyBlog*, October 21, 2009, http://policyblog.verizon.com/BlogPost/675/FindingCommonGroundonanOpenInternet.aspx; Alan Davidson and Thomas J. Tauke, "Google and Verizon Joint Submission on the Open Internet," In the Matter of Preserving the Open Internet, FCC GN Docket 09-191 (January 14, 2010): http://fjallfoss.fcc.gov/ecfs/document/view?id=7020378826.

40. "Verizon-Google Legislative Framework Proposal," Google Public Policy Blog, August 9, 2010: http://www.google.com/googleblogs/pdfs/verizon_google_legislative_framework_proposal_081010.pdf.

Chapter 3

Transparency, Consumers, and the Pursuit of an Open Internet: A Critical Appraisal

Jeremy Carp, Isabella Kulkarni, and Patrick Schmidt

"In the United States, transparency is becoming an ideal worthy of Mom and apple pie."[1] The debate over "net neutrality" regulations in the United States, one of the most significant regulatory battles on the rapidly changing technological landscape, has not occurred in a vacuum. The clash between access providers, on the one hand, and consumers and public interest advocates on the other, over the scope of content limits and consumers' awareness of those limits, has been framed by the conceptual vocabulary and apparatus made available to the interested parties. Importantly, one of the key principles enshrined in the FCC's Open Internet regulations adopted in September 2011 was the language of transparency: that broadband providers "must disclose the network management practices, performance characteristics, and terms and conditions of their broadband services."[2] In providing for this, the parties to the struggle were drawing on what is a comfortable foundation of both the ideological landscape of American regulation and the wider contemporary Zeitgeist.

Transparency serves as both an imperative and an aspiration. As apparent in the United States and elsewhere, it has immediate appeal and a developing record as an instrument of public policy. The roots of transparency are not new either, even within the early discussions of network management and competition. Yet, the motivations for its emergence in regulatory schemes and its effects in practice can remain obscure. The FCC's net neutrality regulations provide a valuable opportunity to observe the rapid rise of the "transparency" agenda for regulation. In this chapter, we trace the development of that frame, an account that highlights the significance of civil society advocacy and a critical window for policy reform in making the rule take shape. In trying to understand the emergence of the transparency frame within debates on network neutrality, we argue that transparency has significant appeal because of the way in which it evades the most difficult political questions about the extent of government regulation on network providers, and suggest that it takes root because of both general and specific factors. However, as we further note, it is difficult for the transparency frame to live up to its appeal; indeed, our second ambition here is to highlight the many vulnerabilities of transparency in the effort to ensure an open Internet.

In order to consider the compromises and limits of the transparency frame, this chapter first examines the individuals and organizations that played a role in an evolving agenda of disclosure for Internet access providers, focusing on both the Comcast enforcement action of 2008 and the 2010 Open Internet Regulations. The second part turns to the uncertain prospects of the latest regulations, using frameworks and evidence from across regulatory sectors to suggest some possibilities for the path ahead. Ultimately, we provide a critical account, one that is more skeptical about the role of transparency in policy design than the wider discourse often allows. However, we argue that the FCC's multi-faceted approach to regulation appears designed to answer some of these objections, at least in part.

The Rise of Transparency in Net Neutrality Regulation

The expectation that public policies will promote transparency has deepened over the last forty years, as trust in political institutions has dropped precipitously in the post–Watergate era. Accountable public administration and the regulation of private entities have come to share the same interest in ensuring a broad measure of openness, allowing those outside either type of organization to understand the purposes and processes by which action is taken.[3] Although transparency has not always been a central principle or even a readily identifiable element of the regulation of communication networks and media, reflections of the idea have consistently and naturally manifested themselves in the rhetoric of public interest groups, government bodies, and even businesses. In time, those ideas took on a sharper form.

Toward Consumer Disclosure

By the early 2000s, both practitioners and academic observers were concerned about the basic principles of competition and the need for fair practices in the marketplace for Internet services.[4] These paralleled much older concerns about discrimination on common carriers, whether the network in question was a telegraph or a railroad. Perhaps echoing this conceptual ancestry, the earliest discussions of network neutrality made no direct mention of transparency, instead deploying the ideas of informed consumption or industry disclosure as crude placeholders. In these initial discussions, ideals tied to transparency were used sparingly and narrowly, lacking a strong and clear rationale beyond informed consumer choice.[5] This subordinate manifestation of transparency contrasts sharply to later formulations and the eventual elevation of transparency to the status of a central principal for network neutrality. Although a consensus quickly emerged around the benefits of informing consumers about basic broadband industry practices through increased transparency, early engagement with the concept did not mark it as a coherent, guiding principle.

The first group to publicly advocate for the importance of informed consumers was, in fact, the broadband industry itself. Shortly after law professor Tim Wu advanced the term "network neutrality" in early 2003 (building on nineteenth century concepts), an industry advocacy group known as the High Tech Broadband Coalition (HTBC) published a brief document titled "Broadband Principles for Consumer Connectivity," outlining the broadband industry's preliminary position and recommendations vis-à-vis the degradation of internet connections.[6] In this document, the HTBC proposed to the Federal Communications Commission (FCC) four broadband connectivity principles designed to ensure that consumer interests remained protected, while simultaneously warning against the harms of overregulation.

First among these principles was the idea that "consumers should receive meaningful information regarding their broadband service plans."[7] The ability to access such information, the HTBC tacitly suggested, would make obsolete the need for harmful regulations on the still nascent broadband industry. However, far from being an overarching and ringing endorsement of transparency, this principle represented a limited, vague, and non-binding commitment to truth in advertising. Nevertheless, the industry's preliminary approach to network neutrality would function to position basic information disclosure as an intuitive dimension of the emerging network neutrality debate.

Less than a year later, then FCC Chairman Michael Powell offered his own perspective on transparency and network neutrality practices. During a February 2004 speech titled "Preserving Internet Freedom: Guiding Principles for the Industry," Chairman Powell outlined an unofficial preliminary guide to the Commission's evolving broadband management philosophy.[8] Echoing the broadband industry's statement, Powell articulated a central goal of consumer empowerment through the freedom to obtain meaningful information regarding broadband service plans. "Simply put," stated Powell, "such information is necessary to ensure that the market is working, as it allows broadband consumers to make rational choices among different pricing and service plans."[9] The policy goal articulated here does not reflect a normative good but a utilitarian need. The logic underpinning this principle closely echoed that used by the broadband industry, suggesting that although the FCC recognized some form of transparency as a necessary step, its scope could be limited to basic service information and be enforced by the market rather than by mandatory regulations. In this way, Chairman Powell positioned transparency as a supporting rather than central principle, conducive to limited regulation and aimed primarily at strengthening consumer protection.

Although less pronounced than in later rounds of the network neutrality debate, the classic tension between government mandates and voluntary regulation was apparent. This tension sets the deeper ambitions and expectations for how the interested parties believed transparency would function in a scheme of network neutrality. In the earliest documents discussed above, the FCC and broadband industry were in almost full agreement over transparency's appropriate role: non-mandated and limited. Indeed, the absence of the "transparency" label suggests that the fullest conception of openness wasn't yet at play. However, within these same comments, both groups hinted at how they might approach transparency differently in the future. For instance, Chairman Powell noted that, "although most in the industry recognize that providing basic information is in their own self-interest, [the FCC] must nevertheless keep a sharp eye on market practices that will continue to evolve rapidly."[10] Similarly, the HTBC was careful to qualify its suggested management principles, indicating in passing that they need only be codified under extreme circumstances.

This emerging tension between mandated and non-mandated transparency manifested itself prominently in the FCC's 2005 Internet Policy Statement.[11] In this document, the Commission outlined its official, proposed approach to maintaining an open and interconnected Internet, offering four general policy principles. Whatever the advancement represented by the statement, in terms of transparency the FCC didn't expand upon the idea of informed consumer choice as discussed by Chairman Powell in 2004. Omitted was any reference to the need for basic service information or specifications from broadband service providers.

While one of the principles did make an exceedingly subtle allusion to the context for disclosure when it stated that "consumers are entitled to competition among network providers, application and service providers, and content providers,"[12] it removed any direct mention of basic service information as a component of a viable scheme for industry competition. This virtual erasure of transparency from the document was a direct nod to the broadband industry's interest in a voluntary ethos of disclosure rather than an imposed system of rules. In the following years, however, this deference to industry interests regarding transparency would disappear as the debate surrounding network neutrality gained momentum. Instead, transparency would come to inhabit a prominent and uncompromising position within the discourses of network neutrality. It is to this shift that we now turn.

The Disclosure Agenda

In the wake of the FCC's 2005 Policy Statement, and among extensive discussion of the course of broadband regulation, the issue of transparency began to attract increasing attention from public interest advocates and academics.[13] Still lacking a solid foothold in the lengthy debate over net neutrality, a campaign to promote open Internet practices through increased government regulation gave new momentum to transparency in this industry sector. In 2006, the public interest group Free Press teamed up with the Consumers Union and the Consumer

Federation of America to publish a harsh rebuttal of the FCC's Policy Statement and its lack of attention to disclosure.[14]

Although the coalition's comments dealt largely with the implementation of the Commission's policy principles, the absence of transparency guidelines elicited sharp criticism as well. "[These policy principles] sound good," the document stated, "but say nothing about *how* and *whether* a network owner must disclose to its subscribers that discriminatory terms of service have been established on the network."[15] The coalition was not alone in noting the need for greater consumer protection, though the evidence of discriminatory practices at this time was still uneven.[16] The criticisms marked the beginning of an extended exchange with the broadband industry over transparency's optimal role in preventing content discrimination. As mentioned in the previous section, this tension would deeply impact all parties' (i.e., industry, public interest, government) understandings and expectations of transparency. Although the broadband industry was initially successful in advancing its own laissez-faire approach to the provision of consumer information, this dynamic gradually changed as (1) Free Press and other public interest groups focused their efforts on the importance of mandated transparency, and (2) it became increasingly clear that the broadband industry could not or would not sufficiently regulate its own disclosure practices.

In the meantime, it did not take long for the FCC to internalize the public pushback against its policy principles and direct its gaze back toward questions of transparency. In its 2007 Notice of Inquiry on Broadband Industry Practices, the Commission sought feedback on a wide range of issues related to network management practices, including disclosure.[17] "With regard to all practices commenters describe [in regards to content discrimination]," wrote the Commission, "we ask whether providers disclose their practices to their customers, to other providers, to application developers, and others."[18] This is a rhetorically small change, advancing a simple question about industry disclosure practices, but it represents a renewal of the agenda and a broadening of the scope of inquiry, one that divorces disclosure from consumer protection alone to a wider need for industry transparency. Moreover, the document itself was premised on the very essence of transparency, with the Commission gathering detailed information about broadband industry practices in order to assess an appropriate course of action regarding network management rules. In this way, the Notice of Inquiry elevated openness to a new position of prominence.

As the discussion on network neutrality intensified, so too did the salience of transparency. In the short period between April 2007—when the FCC published its Notice of Inquiry—and August 2008, public interest groups and broadband providers ratcheted up their transparency-driven rhetoric and worked to more fully outline their positions regarding the concept. By the later date, marking the publication of the FCC's opinion in an investigation of Comcast (discussed below), it was clear that transparency was no longer ancillary, but in some respects had become the leading edge of regulatory efforts.

In February 2008, AT&T and Verizon submitted comments to the FCC that devoted entire sections to the appropriate role of disclosure in promoting responsible broadband practices.[19] To this point, the word "disclosure" appears to have been used only sparingly outside of academic circles, and discussions of the term had been limited to three lines of text or less. However, with its latest comments, AT&T argued forcefully that the government should avoid mandated disclosure rules, especially as regards network management practices: "The Commission should encourage broadband networks to make voluntary disclosure of *customer-usage limitations* as *consumers* will experience them. The Commission should not expect, let alone require, broadband networks to disclose actual *network-management practices*."[20] AT&T reasoned that the technical methods used by service providers were highly proprietary and might leave networks open to gross breaches of security and performance. Mandated disclosure, moreover, would be superfluous, since "private initiative is more than sufficient to protect consumer interests in the well-functioning Internet marketplace."[21] From this perspective, openness had its limits, and the needs of the marketplace produced its own supply of information. Verizon, in its comments, made a similar nod toward the ideal way of protecting consumers. The expansion of the discussions given over to disclosure didn't move the battle lines on the issue, but it did mark the increasing emphasis given to transparency. For AT&T, Verizon, and other industry advocates, reports of voluntary disclosure were becoming the counter-burn to stop the forest fire: one tool in opposition to regulatory mandates.

Naturally, Free Press and other public interest advocates advanced a much different position.[22] The group called for disclosure but had begun to think more carefully about what consumers needed in order to make such regulation useful. "The FCC," they wrote, "should issue a rule that requires full disclosure to consumers of what services and applications are being affected when and in what ways."[23] Laissez–faire was not good enough. "Even in a competitive market, disclosure must be *meaningful* and *understandable* . . . Customers should be provided with enough undisguised information to have the ability to know when to expect that network management practices are taking place."[24] Beyond consumers, industry needed to explain "network management activities with sufficient detail for a programmer reasonably skilled in the field to write applications meeting and taking advantage of these management activities."[25] And it couldn't be voluntary: the penalties for violating disclosure rules had to be large enough to deter possible attempts to hide information.

More importantly, however, Free Press made clear in separate comments that mandated transparency alone, although highly desirable, was not itself sufficient to maintain a free and open Internet.[26] "Disclosure is necessary," the group wrote, "but disclosure is not enough."[27] New evidence was emerging from the field, casting into doubt whether the market, at least at its present levels of concentration, could support market outcomes desired by consumers. Disclosure would not prevent discrimination if "all network providers had the same incentive to discriminate against applications."[28]

In the midst of this debate, the FCC recognized the importance of the transparency issue. In its 2008 public hearings at Harvard, Stanford, and Carnegie-Mellon, members of the Commission made their first direct references to the term transparency and noted that the Commission had "teed up before us questions about the role of transparency and disclosure between providers and consumers, an area that warrants further exploration."[29] For instance, Commissioner Adelstein, drawing directly from language previously used by Free Press, stated that he strongly believed broadband providers should provide "clear and accurate information—in plain English—about their policies and how they affect consumers' use."[30] Seeking a balance between the poles of the debate, Commissioner Tate emphasized that the Commission needed to "ensure that consumers are informed and protected," while avoiding "intrusive governmental action."[31] The Commission's other conservative member, Robert McDowell, further channeled the broadband industry's skepticism in his comments, writing that "disclosure might be beneficial to the public interest, but isn't the private sector the best forum to initially try to resolve these conflicts?"[32]

Providing the backdrop to these administrative proceedings, and a factor helping participants to recognize "transparency" as an issue, was the FCC's enforcement action against Comcast. In August 2008, the FCC issued an Opinion and Ruling in an investigation of the industry giant.[33] The run-up to that ruling had done more than anything else to elevate transparency to a guiding principle. The case emerged when in 2007, Robb Topolski discovered active measures by Comcast to block BitTorrent-based file trading. Comcast had denied the claim but later admitted its practices and settled a class action lawsuit. After pursuing their own investigation, the FCC, in addition to concluding that Comcast had participated in unreasonable network management practices, strongly emphasized that the company's failure to disclose its discriminatory practices had seriously exacerbated the situation. "Although we have not adopted today general disclosure requirements," they wrote, "the anti-competitive harm perpetuated by discriminatory network management practices is clearly compounded by failing to disclose such practices to consumers."[34] In its discussion, the Commission reasoned that legible and comprehensive disclosure was paramount for four reasons.

First, disclosure was necessary to prevent customers from improperly blaming applications rather than Internet connections for service limitations. This was especially important if an application could be used to provide services that competed with the broadband operator's own service. Second, disclosure was necessary to ensure proper consumer choice and a "vibrant and competitive free market."[35] Third, disclosure was necessary for the FCC itself to accurately understand industry practices and to ensure compliance with regulations. Finally, and most importantly, the Commission made clear that "reasonable" network management practices were defined by a provider's willingness to be transparent about them. "A hallmark of whether something is reasonable," they wrote, "is whether an operator is willing to disclose fully and exactly what they are doing."[36] In short, by advancing new mechanisms for regulating the market, transparency was now becoming central to the FCC's understanding of fair network management practices.

Transparency as a Rule

The D.C. Circuit Court of Appeals ultimately overturned the FCC's Comcast order, declaring that the FCC lacked sufficient statutory authority,[37] but the incident seems to have solidified the regulator's conviction about the problems in the broadband marketplace. The Comcast Order aggressively propelled the FCC closer to the vision of transparency articulated by public interest advocates, but the Commission stopped short of taking direct and binding action. However, as Free Press and its allies continued to demand mandated disclosure regulations and overall increased transparency,[38] the FCC further lost faith in the industry's capacity to regulate itself, inching closer to reifying transparency as a prominent rule and principle of network management. In a September 2009 speech at the Brookings Institute, Chairman Julius Genachowski proposed a "sixth principle" of network management centered on transparency. It was clear, he argued, that "we cannot afford to rely on happenstance for consumers, businesses, and policymakers to learn about changes to the basic functioning of the Internet."[39] In particular, Genachowski reasoned that greater transparency would give consumers the confidence of "knowing that they're getting the service they've paid for," "enable innovators to make their offerings work effectively over the Internet," allow policymakers to ensure that broadband providers are "preserving the Internet as a level playing field," and help "facilitate discussion among all the participants of the Internet ecosystem," thereby reducing the need for government involvement in network management disagreements.[40] Although the Chairman made clear that certain proprietary and security information could be withheld, there was nevertheless a definitive widening of the gap between the Commission's approach to network management and that of the broadband industry.

The FCC's Notice of Proposed Rulemaking in December of 2009 brought its conceptualization of transparency into line with wider societal framings, using the classic Louis Brandeis formulation to argue that "sunlight is the best disinfectant and that transparency can discourage inefficient and socially harmful market behavior."[41] To serve this end, the FCC drafted a transparency rule, broadly outlining the obligations of broadband Internet providers: "Subject to reasonable network management, a provider of broadband Internet access service must disclose such information concerning network management and other practices as is reasonably required for users and content, application, and service providers to enjoy the protections specified in this part."[42]

This somewhat vague principle amounted to a coming out party for transparency, providing it with a tentative yet central place in the FCC's governing philosophy. Consumers would benefit by acquiring the ability to overcome information asymmetries, thus allowing users to make informed purchasing and usage decisions. But the Commission also believed service providers and poli-cymakers would benefit. By reducing uncertainty, mandated disclosure would "benefit content, application, and service providers and investors" by providing incentives to invest in research and development.[43]

Service providers like Verizon,[44] Comcast,[45] and AT&T[46] uniformly at-tacked the FCC's evolving position on transparency. In addition to forcefully reiterating their argument that transparency should be promoted within a volun-tary and self-regulating framework, broadband providers further challenged the Commission's proposed rules on three levels. First, they argued that any disclo-sure guidelines needed to place an exclusive emphasis on informing and educat-ing broadband consumers. Disclosing additional technical details and network management practices to the public, content providers, and application provid-ers, they reasoned, would be both needless and harmful. Indeed, such compelled disclosure would serve "only one conceivable purpose: to facilitate network manipulation by third parties."[47] Second, service providers attempted to paint the proposed rule as arbitrary, reasoning that it would be unfair to create a new legal burden for service providers without doing so for application and content providers alike. "If there is an issue in the Internet eco-system about transparen-cy and disclosures," Comcast explained in its January 2010 comments, "it makes no sense to impose a new duty on broadband providers alone."[48] Finally, broadband providers argued that, should the FCC choose to enact new network regulations, the scope of its proposed transparency rule would need to be nar-rowed significantly.

Conceding some ground, Comcast offered its own revised transparency rule: "Subject to reasonable network management, broadband ISPs and Internet application and service providers must disclose such information about its ser-vice as is reasonably required for consumers to enjoy the protections specified in this part."[49] Although superficially similar to that of the FCC, Comcast's pro-posed rule greatly narrowed the requirement and made consumers (not potential competitors) the sole audience of service information.

Rulemaking involves posturing and position-taking within a legal frame.[50] While proposing approaches to the FCC, parties to a rulemaking are also build-ing a record on which they could mount a challenge in court, where they would be questioning the logic or adequacy of the government's conclusions. Free Press and other public interest groups submitted their own comments in January and April 2010, demanding that the FCC go even further in its commitment to mandated transparency.[51] They asked for a transparency policy that was com-prehensive, requiring both "high-level information concerning network man-agement practices, geared towards a general audience," and "detailed infor-mation on purposes, methods, and triggers of network management, sufficient to enable third party providers and savvy users to make effective choice and opti-mal use of the service."[52] Doing battle with the industry, Free Press attacked vague formulations and pushed for a rule that would support effective enforce-ment.[53]

After approving new rules in December 2010, the FCC delayed publication of the regulations until September 2011. When it did so, the Commission's movement away from self-regulated transparency was complete. The FCC's rationale for the rule had blossomed and matured, containing a defense of mandated transparency for its ability to "promote competition throughout the Internet ecosystem," to reduce providers' "incentive and ability" to use discriminatory practices, to "increase consumer confidence," to facilitate "innovation, investment, and competition," and ultimately, to "increase the likelihood of providers' compliance with other "open Internet principles" and encourage collective, expedient solutions to any "problematic conduct."[54] As such, a revised version of the transparency principle previously suggested in the Notice of Proposed Rule Making was codified as a rule, and reads as follows:

> A person engaged in the provision of broadband Internet access service shall publicly disclose accurate information regarding the network management practices, performance, and commercial terms of its broadband Internet access services sufficient for consumers to make informed choices regarding use of such services and for content, application, service, and device providers to develop, market, and maintain Internet offerings.[55]

Although superficially similar to the original proposed rule, the adopted version incorporated public interest critiques and added more specific language throughout. In addition to noting that providers must "publicly" and "accurately" disclose not just their network management practices but also performance and commercial terms, the rule specified that disclosures must be sufficient for a broad array of parties to productively use this information. The Commission stopped short of mandating a specific disclosure format and left some flexibility in terms of what information needed to be disclosed and how to disclose it. Transparency wasn't enough. If the industry had hoped that transparency regulations could be used as a rationale for fending off other regulations, it wasn't to be. In a direct nod to Free Press, the Commission wrote that "although transparency is essential for preserving Internet openness, we disagree with commenters that suggest it is alone sufficient to prevent open Internet violations[;] the record alone does not convince us that a transparency requirement by itself will adequately constrain problematic conduct."[56]

Though for our purposes here the rule represented a significant step in the progression toward a transparency framework, in a wider light the FCC's rule was a compromise that many consumer groups viewed as insufficient. Andrew Jay Schwartzman, senior vice president and policy director for the Media Access Project, tersely summarized the mood by saying that, "there is a reason that so many giant phone and cable companies are happy, and we are not."[57] In the immediate reaction, some tried to see the rule as "a vital first step,"[58] or "a floor, not a ceiling,"[59] but others were much harsher in their criticism, predicting that the rules would be "subject to manipulation" by industry firms unless the FCC enforced them vigorously.[60] Free Press, for its part, filed a challenge to the

FCC's rules, joining U.S. mobile phone company Verizon in doing so. With litigation continuing, net neutrality regulation remains a work in progress.

Making Transparency Effective

Transparency was not the sole approach employed by the FCC in its most recent efforts to ensure network neutrality, but so much had changed since the FCC's 2005 statement of principles that one observer could now claim that transparency is "the most important component of a net neutrality definition."[61] Given the other legs the FCC planted in its regulatory stool, transparency might become the most relied upon feature. Courts have long struggled to define "reasonable" in any context, and the FCC's regulations do no better in explaining what "reasonable discrimination" providers may impose upon the regulation of lawful network traffic.[62] If, in practice, some discrimination is inevitable in network management, transparency then at least becomes the very important backstop by which those discriminations could be known to consumers. The primacy of disclosure in this case matches the emergence of transparency as the perhaps the most significant trend to emerge in the regulation of government and by government. Yet, transparency is similarly prone to vagueness, and skepticism is needed to question how effective it will be as a scheme of regulation. In this section, we first locate the manifestation of transparency regulation within the wider net neutrality movement; we then situate net neutrality's place in the wider understanding of transparency to suggest the driving forces and possible outcomes in this context for regulation.

Of Ideology and Aspiration

Why did transparency rise so swiftly as a key concept from what at first appeared a simple desire for greater consumer choice? It is all too easy to link the march of transparency to a drumbeat of inevitability. To be sure, a progressive narrative can be told, starting in the American case with the maxims of James Madison ("a popular government without popular information or the means of acquiring it, is but a prologue to a farce, or a tragedy, or perhaps both") and Louis Brandeis ("Sunlight is said to be the best disinfectant").[63] The latter's invocation extended the concept from beyond governmental openness to sunlight as a tool for the regulation of the private economy. Brandeis' opposition to corporate trust fraud later gained wider salience following the stock market crash of 1929, and his advocacy of disclosure and publicity influenced the role of disclosure by financial market participants as the core of the Securities and Exchange Acts of 1933 and 1934.[64]

A more self-sustaining politics of transparency was birthed in Cold War distrust and raised on a steady diet of scandal, from Watergate to Guantanamo.

As a tool of accountability, transparency became "the antidote to the wrong of excessive governmental secrecy," the so-called golden ticket out of a repressive regime into one of greater democracy.[65] At the governmental level, the U.S. Freedom of Information Act became a model for such laws around the world, so much so that in recent years more voices have called for the recognition of the right of access to information as a human right.[66] The normalization of the "right to know" increasingly extended beyond governmental accountability, now enshrined as part of the 2007 Open Government Act and subsequent Obama administration initiatives, to virtually all policy sectors. The effect has to been to naturalize the language of transparency, that whether you are a citizen or a consumer, if you are affected by an organization it automatically follows that you should receive access to information about its activities.

Specific currents in recent decades may provide a clearer understanding of the ideological forces at work. From one perspective, the spread of transparency values may simply be reactive, a turn against the inefficient markets of the status quo, which had allowed resources to be "inaccessible, invisible and/or concealed."[67] The push toward market values, particularly since the Reagan administration's deregulatory efforts of the 1980s, arguably has elevated the need for information. But transparency's current "quasi-religious authority as a contemporary doctrine of governance"[68] can also be linked to the rise of accountability, particularly in a globalizing world that has raised up new, complicated technologies of social organization.[69] In this light, "for institutions to be held accountable, their actions must be visible."[70] This "values dimension" might then be seen as an outgrowth of the classic constitutional aim of checking otherwise unchecked power and giving over the ultimate direction of the state to popular authority. In an age suspicious of regulatory power—to its critics, both unaccountable and inefficient—the FCC's support for transparency could disperse information and thus power, in ways that enhance democracy.[71]

A more critical view would see transparency less as "better" regulation and more as simply "weaker" regulation. For regulated firms, the appeal of transparency in net neutrality regulation may be that the noninterventionist, market-supporting aims of transparency provide businesses with the type of flexible accommodation that would not greatly threaten the status quo. For the regulator, transparency is politically possible, even if less than ideal. As it was, the FCC's regulations spurred efforts in Congress to overturn the rules; a more vigorous set of regulations would have been more difficult to defend. With critics on all sides and recent threats of both legislative and judicial oversight, the FCC has faced particular pressure to compromise.

Across sectors of the economy, disclosure regulations are something that can be passed, sometimes with bipartisan agreement, because they have intuitive appeal for advocates of regulation but do not fundamentally upset the established market dynamics. Disclosure regulations impose administrative costs, but those costs can be less tangible than direct regulations that curtail a current business practice. That isn't to say that disclosure regulations are merely symbolic, but that they can be criticized in some cases for leaving a significant gap between the aspiration or assumed impact and the reality.[72] Numerous broadband industry groups reacted to the rules by praising the spirit of compromise embodied in the FCC's net neutrality rule, acknowledging that the FCC could have gone much further with a direct regulatory approach.[73] Whether transparency is a hollow gesture in the area of net neutrality will depend on the experience with it in the years ahead.

Critical Possibilities

Despite the fact that net neutrality regulation is too new to begin an evaluative analysis in earnest, the conceptual model underlying transparency regulations—such as the FCC's Open Internet rule—can still direct our scrutiny to those points in the process where the hopes of regulators and consumer advocates might be most easily dashed.

An elegant model for transparency, helpfully elaborated by Fung, Graham and Weil, describes an "action cycle" consisting of two primary actors: the disclosers and the users.[74] The public policy aim of disclosure is not disclosure for its own sake, but as a trigger to a series of effects, direct and anticipated. Once an initial requirement to disclose information has been established, the users—here, the consumers and content providers—will begin to receive the information from disclosing organization. The information sought by the regulation should not be trivial but calculated to shape the market decisions of the consumers and relatively more sophisticated recipients of the information. A broadband provider disclosing information about its network management practices may find users prepared to change service providers, depending on what the disclosures reveal.

But it is not necessary for consumers to actually get that far for transparency to do its work; the anticipation by companies of possible negative publicity, coupled with the knowledge that certain types of activities will now be disclosed, could discourage those behaviors to begin with. Thus, disclosure regulations can promote a virtuous cycle of responsiveness by firms to consumer or market wishes, real or anticipated. In that way, the net would remain neutral because no firm wants to see what could happen if they were used as an example in the way that Comcast was.

Many steps of the action cycle invite scrutiny. First, what is the information that the regulation requires and how vital is it to the decisions being made by consumers? Here the FCC has provided for a degree of circularity, by defining the type of information to be disclosed through reference to that which is "sufficient" for good decision-making by interested parties. What is it that will be sufficient? The answer may depend on the kind of response the FCC wants from consumers—and knowledge of what will move consumers to play a role as "enforcer" in the marketplace. The range of interpretations that these allow makes for rules that can easily be swayed by the changing politics of the highly divided five-member Commission and the rapidly changing technological setting for further net neutrality orders and enforcement actions.[75] "What the FCC wants" will require a continuing action by a divided Commission. There can be incentives to default to maximum disclosure, including of information that is tangential to the kinds of decisions consumers and competitors actually need to make.[76] The formal enforcement powers available to the FCC may provide a credible threat, but their sufficiency cannot be guaranteed.

However, the FCC continues to have the advantage of being merely the formal enforcer. As seen in the Comcast case, technically proficient consumers possess some ability to identify practices that are affecting performance, and they may help to ensure that providers stay forthright with all of the technical practices that shape service use. Securing compliance with regulations remains a significant challenge in both theory and practice. Disclosure can be very difficult to regulate, because firms can be tempted into thinking—sometimes justifiably—that a secret can be kept, or that the risk of it being revealed is worth it in light of the immediate economic interests.[77] Even though transparency regulations philosophically aim to bring market incentives to bear on companies by simply providing a more informed marketplace, the mandate for disclosure requires enforcement, which opens up all the classic challenges of winning compliance with the law.[78]

The next juncture for scrutiny occurs once information has been released to the public, and there are numerous ways that the model can break down. For one, scholars and policy makers have learned in recent years that the passive release of information, especially in fields with large volumes of information, may not make waves in the marketplace. A regulator cannot take for granted that information will be "visible" to its intended audience simply because it has been released to the public.[79] As a case in point, the large volume of data available about donations to political campaigns has not enlightened voters, despite efforts of public interest organizations to pull it all together in easily digestible websites. Civil society organizations including interest groups and the media can be essential in receiving the information and processing it in a way that wider consumers can understand more readily. Over time, regulations can evolve to require that organizations package their disclosures in formats that ease the digestion of information further.[80] As net neutrality regulations evolve, greater emphasis will need to be placed on the audience for the communication: who needs what information, and how can transparency be better targeted to the different types of consumers?[81] "Plain English" initiatives, common to both the FCC and other regulatory bodies such as the Securities and Exchange Commission, take their cue from the recognition that the highly legalized form of disclosures can work against clarity of meaning and understanding. The contract language written in a small font and sent to consumers is unlikely to be read or integrated into a consumer's behavior.

It is not enough for consumers to be presented with the data. Further challenges plague how potential users employ data. First, will recipients make good decisions because of this data? Even if information is understood, consumers may not give much weight to that information. Under the 1990 Food and Nutrition Labeling Act for example, health advocates have observed that the clear and simple statistics about calories and fat grams on the side of a Ben & Jerry's container simply hasn't guided many consumers in making good dietary choices. In the more complicated technical world of broadband regulation, information may fail to become "embedded" in consumer decision-making when users fail to see the relevance of disclosed information to the decisions they're making.

Second, for consumer choice to serve as a check on corporate decision-making, individuals must have practice options if they are going to act on it in the marketplace. Driving a skeptical view about the prospects for transparency in the Open Internet regulation, it isn't clear that consumers will always have alternatives, or if they do, that those appear sensible for reasons such as cost and convenience. And, vitally, if transparency were ever the only mechanism, then market collusion or similar behavior could nullify the potential of greater information in the marketplace: if all providers offer the same type of services and conditions, consumers would have no alternatives, no matter how much they know and how much they wish to change service providers. Boycotts against individual firms, which could emerge as a result of disclosure, are also no solution. Comcast faced calls for boycotts following the revelation of their bandwidth management practices, but those attempts fizzled. In other sectors, it has been very difficult to find evidence that well-organized and salient boycotts facilitated by disclosures could have much impact on large corporations.[82] The ISP market may be particularly difficult for many consumers, due to the contract barriers or simple inconvenience with switching service providers. Industry consolidation may further shrink consumer choice. Some of the most significant challenges to net neutrality may ultimately have to be met by antitrust investigation rather than the FCC. Using transparency as a tool for regulating mobile services could prove even more problematic in light of the limits of consumer choices.

All told, there are serious concerns one can hypothesize about the future of transparency regulation as a way of jump-starting the action cycle toward net neutrality. But long-term concerns also intervene in a system that is well enforced and initially effective. Over time, well written regulations can fall victim to efforts to undermine the rules, or those whom a rule regulates begin to play a greater part in the regulatory process.[83] The "life cycle" of regulations often sees the advocates of regulation disappear after a victory, allowing opponents of the regulation to mount a successful fight-back. As an independent regulatory commission, the FCC is still linked to political winds through Presidential appointment. As administrations change, the closely balanced structure of the FCC similarly tilts. Even minor differences of emphasis within a scheme of transparency could meaningfully change what consumers know and what firms are able to do.

Even this account of the action cycle doesn't complete a survey of the possible challenges to effective regulation through transparency. Some of the most vexing challenges are the unanticipated adaptive responses to transparency regulation that have been observed in other sectors of the economy. Political adaptation—from a posture of opposition to one of support for transparency—may be particularly likely in the telecommunications sector, as suggested by many of the responses of industry groups to the FCC rules. Support for transparency can often be used as a rhetorical wedge against stronger regulations when the acceptance of transparency as a necessary element is rhetorically turned into the sufficiency of transparency. Organizational adaptation is another common outcome unanticipated by regulators and advocates of transparency regulations. All firms naturally seek to minimize the disruption of regulations, and unless well designed, transparency regulations offer particularly broad avenues for creative compliance. Information is a particularly malleable and manipulable commodity. As regulators establish categories and requirements, firms—particularly with the contributions of legal counsel—work to frame disclosures in such a way as to avoid drawing the interest or ire of consumers and regulators.[84] Techniques that allow "nondisclosing disclosure" have emerged in areas such as tax and securities regulation, and network neutrality regulations may be equally vulnerable.

At times, nondisclosing disclosures can be the product of an explicit effort by firms to remain "perfectly legal" with disclosures, while manipulating the text (such as contract terms or notices) in whatever way necessary to obscure the meaning of the disclosure. At the heart of research and commentary on transparency over the past decade lies a vital difference of meaning between transparency and disclosure. In the FCC's rule, the terms are used interchangeably: disclosure is a tool to produce transparency, transparency simply requires disclosure. That pairing is simplistic and inadequate. The disclosure of information does not ensure that the provision of broadband services is transparent. In the work ahead for the FCC, the agenda may need to include discussion of ways to monitor company disclosures and the informational marketplace available to users, including close scrutiny of ISPs' terms of service that are inordinately complex, detailed, or vague. The FCC may also need to support the work of civil society organizations who attempt to collect and disseminate such information, or it may need to take on some of that work itself, such as through a central repository of information or public information campaigns. There remain alternatives to disclosure, of course: one answer to the failures of transparency regulation is to fall back on direct regulation, such as specifically barring certain practices.[85]

The FCC's Open Internet rule allowed for "flexibility in implementation of the transparency rule" but Commissioners were clearly concerned about making disclosures "effective" and suggested that they be "timely and prominently disclosed in plain language."[86] The first years of the rule are essential in setting the meaning of these practices. Individual companies will model their disclosure activities around the practices that become the norm, because there is safety within that norm. The "look and feel" of disclosures can become routinized, an environment in which disclosures are formally made but become something that consumers ignore because they know what to expect, and decide that the information does not help them. The energy and attention surrounding new disclosure requirements fades over time, and if the design and care of the transparency system do not support it, the ability to shape the behavior of marketplace participants will be lost.

Conclusion

It is easier to explain the past than to predict the future. From a virtual absence to its status as the dominant strain in the FCC's Open Internet rulemaking, the rise of transparency in network neutrality discussion fits easily within the wider narrative of American regulation. The FCC's path to transparency in the Open Internet regulation reflects a common desire across sectors of the economy to subject organizations to a scheme of disclosures, so that the marketplace itself can provide the regulation and accountability, as an alternative to direct regulation. The ideological acceptability of transparency regulation also makes the availability of information about network management and practices an appealing point of compromise when compared to even more contentious tools of regulation. Transparency resonates well with the ideals of information technologies—the capacity for generativity in a world of open competition.[87]

As the net neutrality debate moved to a transparency frame, it employed a model that has become increasingly well understood. Whatever its "mom and apple pie" quality, as a regulatory tool, disclosure is fickle and can fall short of expectations for many different reasons. The FCC's definition and enforcement, firm adaptation, and how others actually consume the information that is generated will all be essential for transparency to sustain an open Internet. We sound a note of caution and warning for the road ahead: disclosure mechanisms cannot be instituted and then left to run on auto-pilot. They require care and initiative in order to be effective. The FCC recognized as much when it encouraged third-party experts and Internet "end users and edge providers" to play a role in monitoring the field.[88] Even more importantly, the FCC rejected the idea that transparency is "alone sufficient to prevent open Internet violations." No rhetoric or appeals to an ideal conception should be allowed to obscure the ways in which the semblance of transparency regulation could legitimate distortions in the marketplace and constrain the promise of an open Internet.

Notes

1. Sandy Lutz, "Transparency–'Deal or No Deal'?" *Frontiers of Health Services Management* 23, no. 3 (2007): 13–23.

2. Federal Communications Commission, "Preserving the Open Internet", Docket No. 09–191. Available at: http://www.fcc.gov/rulemaking/09-191.

3. Christopher Hood, "Transparency in Historical Perspective," *Transparency: The Key to Better Governance? Proceedings of the British Academy.* (135). Eds. Hood and David A. Heald (Oxford: Oxford University Press, 2006), 4–5.

4. See *Analysis to Aid Public Comment on America Online, Inc. and Time Warner Inc. Proposed Consent Agreement*, 65 Fed. Reg. 79861 (December 20, 2000); Sarah G. Lopez, "Evaluation of the AOL Time Warner Consent Decree's Ability to Prevent Antitrust Harm in the Cable Broadband ISP Market," *St. John's Journal of Legal Commentary* 17, no. 1 (Winter 2003): 127–175.

5. E.g., Christopher S. Yoo, "Would Mandating Broadband Network Neutrality Help or Hurt Competition? A Comment on the End-to-End Debate," *Journal of Telecommunications and High Technology Law* 3 (2004): 23–68.

6. High Tech Broadband Coalition, *Broadband Principles for Consumer Connectivity*, September 25, 2003. Available at: http://www.netcompetition.org/docs/others/htbc_principles.pdf. Reflecting the state of the dialogue at the time, neither "transparency" or "disclosure" merited a mention in Wu's influential, "Network Neutrality, Broadband Discrimination," *Journal of Telecommunications and High Technology Law* 2 (2003): 141–179.

7. High Tech Broadband Coalition, 1.

8. Michael Powell, "Preserving Internet Freedom: Guiding Principles for the Industry," (remarks given at the Silicon Flatirons Symposium on 'The Digital Broadband Migration: Toward a Regulatory Regime for the Internet Age', University of Colorado School of Law, Boulder, Colorado, February 8, 2004). Available at: http://hraunfoss.fcc.gov/edocs_public/attachmatch/DOC-243556A1.pdf.

9. Ibid., 6.

10. Ibid., 3.

11. Federal Communications Commission, *Policy Statement*, Docket No. 05–151, August 5, 2005. http://hraunfoss.fcc.gov/edocs_public/attachmatch/FCC–05–151A1.pdf.

12. Ibid., 3.

13. For helpful reviews, see Davina Sashkin, "Failure of Imagination: Why Inaction on Net Neutrality Regulation Will Result in a de Facto Regime Promoting Discrimination and Consumer Harm," *CommLaw Conspectus* 15, no. 1 (Fall 2006): 261–309; and Douglas A. Hass, "The Never-Was-Neutral Net and Why Informed End Users Can End the Net Neutrality Debates," *Berkeley Technology Law Journal* 22 no. 4 (Fall 2007): 1565–1635.

14. Ben Scott, Mark Cooper, and Jeannine Kenney, for Free Press et al., *Why Consumers Demand Internet Freedom*, May 2006. Available at: http://www.freepress.net/files/nn_fact_v_fiction_final.pdf (accessed August 8, 2012).

15. Ibid., 20.

16. Jerry Brito and Jerry Ellig, "A Tale of Two Commissions: Net Neutrality and Regulatory Analysis," *CommLaw Conspectus* 16, no.1 (2007): 1–51.

17. Federal Communications Commission, *Notice of Inquiry, In the Matter of Broadband Industry Practices*, Docket No. 07–52, March 22, 2007. Available at http://hraunfoss.fcc.gov/edocs_public/attachmatch/FCC–07–31A1.pdf.

18. Ibid., 5.

19. AT&T, Inc., *Comments of AT&T on Petitions of Free Press and Vuze*, FCC Docket No. 07–52. February 13, 2008. http://apps.fcc.gov/ecfs/document/view?id=6519841106 (accessed August 8, 2012); and Verizon and Verizon Wireless, *Comments of Verizon and Verizon Wireless*, FCC Docket No. 07–52, February 13, 2008. http://apps.fcc.gov/ecfs/document/view? id=6519841190 (accessed August 8, 2012).

20. AT&T *Comment of AT&T on Petitions of Free Press and Vuze*, 4. Emphasis in original.

21. Ibid., 34.

22. Free Press, *Reply Comments of Free Press et al.*, FCC Docket No. 05–72, February 28, 2008. Available at: http://apps.fcc.gov/ecfs/document/view?id=6519856406.

23. Ibid., 5.

24. Ibid., 6. Emphasis added.

25. Ibid., 5.

26. *Comments of Free Press et al.*, FCC Docket No. 05–72, February 13, 2008. Available at: http://apps.fcc.gov/ecfs/document/view?id=6519841216.

27. Ibid., 59.

28. Ibid., 64.

29. Statement of Commissioner Jonathan S. Adelstein at En Banc hearing on Broadband Management Practices, Harvard Law School, Cambridge, Massachusetts, February 25, 2008, 3. Available at: http://hraunfoss.fcc.gov/edocs_public/attachmatch/DOC–280441A1.pdf.

30. Statement of Commissioner Jonathan S. Adelstein at En Banc Hearing on Broadband Network Management Practices, Stanford Law School, Palo Alto, CA (April 17, 2008), 3. Available at: http://www.law.stanford.edu/publications/projects/lrps/pdf/wilsons–rp21.pdf.

31. Statement of Commissioner Deborah Taylor Tate at En Banc hearing on Broadband Management Practices, Stanford Law School, Palo Alto, CA, April 17, 2008, 2. Available at: http://hraunfoss.fcc.gov/edocs_public/attachmatch/DOC–281629A1.pdf.

32. Opening Statement of Commissioner Robert M. McDowell (at Second Public En Banc hearing on Broadband Management Practices, Stanford Law School, Palo Alto, California, April 17, 2008), 8. Available at: http://hraunfoss.fcc.gov/edocs_public/attachmatch/DOC–281646A1.pdf.

33. Federal Communications Commission, Memorandum Opinion and Order, Docket No. 07–52, August 1, 2008. Available at http://hraunfoss.fcc.gov/edocs_public/attachmatch/FCC–08–183A1.pdf.

34. Ibid., 31.

35. Ibid., 32.

36. Ibid., 34.

37. *Comcast Corp. v. FCC*, 600 F.3d 642 (D.C. Cir. 2010).

38. See Free Press, *Notice of Ex Parte Filing*. Docket No. 07–52, October 24, 2008. Available at: http://apps.fcc.gov/ecfs/document/view?id=6520179100; and *Comments of Free Press*, FCC Docket No. 09–51, June 8, 2009. Available at: http://www.freepress.net/files/FP_National_broadband_plan.pdf.

39. Prepared Remarks of Chairman Julius Genachowski, "Preserving a Free and Open Internet: A Platform for Innovation, Opportunity, and Prosperity" (at The Brookings Institution, Washington, D.C., September 21, 2009), 6. http://hraunfoss.fcc.gov/edocs_public/attachmatch/DOC–293568A1.pdf (accessed August 8, 2012).

40. Ibid., 6.

41. Federal Communications Commission, *Notice of Proposed Rulemaking*, Docket No. 07–52, October 22, 2009, 45. Available at: http://hraunfoss.fcc.gov/edocs_public/attachmatch/FCC–09–93A1.pdf.

42. Ibid., 45.

43. Ibid., 45, 47.

44. *Comments of Verizon and Verizon Wireless*, FCC Docket No. 07–52, January 14, 2010. Available at: http://apps.fcc.gov/ecfs/document/view?id=7020378541.

45. *Comments of Comcast Corporation*, FCC Docket No. 07–52, January 14, 2010. Available at: http://apps.fcc.gov/ecfs/document/view?id=7020376090.

46. *Comments of AT&T Inc.*, FCC Docket No. 07–52, January 14, 2010: http://apps.fcc.gov/ecfs/document/view?id=7020377279 (accessed August 8, 2012),

47. *Comments of AT&T, Inc.* (2010) 193.

48. *Comments of Comcast* (2010), 47.

49. Ibid. 50.

50. Patrick Schmidt, *Lawyers and Regulation: The Politics of the Administrative Process* (New York: Cambridge University Press, 2005); Cornelius M. Kerwin and Scott R. Furlong, *Rulemaking: How Government Agencies Write Law and Make Policy*, 4th ed. (Washington, D.C.: CQ Press, 2011).

51. Free Press, *Comments of Free Press*, FCC Docket No. 07–52, January 14, 2010. Available at: http://apps.fcc.gov/ecfs/document/view?id=7020378792; Free Press, *Reply Comments of Free Press et al.*, Docket No. 07–52, April 26, 2010. Available at: http://apps.fcc.gov/ecfs/document/view?id=7020437471.

52. Ibid., 112–113.

53. Ibid., 120.

54. FCC, "Final Rule: Preserving the Open Internet," *Federal Register* 76, no. 185 (September 23, 2011): 59192–59235; 59202–3. http://www.gpo.gov/fdsys/pkg/FR–2011–09–23/pdf/2011–24259.pdf (accessed August 13, 2012).

55. Ibid., 59203.

56. Ibid., 59204.

57. Chloe Albanesius, "Net Neutrality: The Heavy Hitters React," *PC Magazine*, December 21, 2010.

58. Leslie Harris, President, Center for Democracy and Technology, quoted in Albanesius (2010).

59. Rep. Henry A. Waxman (D–CA), quoted in Albanesius (2010).

60. Gigi B. Sohn, President and co-founder, Public Knowledge, quoted in Albanesius (2010).

61. Alexander Reicher, "Redefining Net Neutrality after *Comcast v. FCC*," *Berkeley Technology Law Journal* 26, no. 1 (2011): 736.

62. Ibid., 740.

63. See also Hood, "Transparency in Historical Perspective," 5–10.

64. Marc Allen Eisner, *Regulatory Politics in Transition*, 2nd edition (Baltimore, M.D.: Johns Hopkins University Press, 2000), 107.

65. Mark Fenster, "Seeing the State: Transparency as Metaphor," *Administrative Law Review* 62, no. 3 (2010): 619.

66. Patrick Birkinshaw, "Transparency as a Human Right," in Hood and Heald (2006); Archon Fung, Mary Graham, and David Weil, *Full Disclosure: The Perils and Promise of Transparency* (New York: Cambridge University Press, 2007), 24.

67. Elizabeth Fisher, "Transparency and Administrative Law: A Critical Evaluation," *Current Legal Problems* 63 no.1 (2010): 275.

68. Christopher Hood, "Beyond Exchanging First Principles? Some Closing Comments," in *Transparency: The Key to Better Governance?*, ed. Christopher Hood and David Heald (Oxford: Oxford University Press), 19.

69. Hood, "Beyond Exchanging First Principles," 216.

70. Fenster, 619. See also Cass R. Sunstein, "Open Government Is Analytic Government and Vice-Versa," Speech on the Occasion of the 30th Anniversary of the Regulatory Flexibility Act (September 21, 2010), http://www.whitehouse.gov/sites/default/files/omb/inforeg/speeches/Sunstein_Speech_2010–0921.pdf (accessed August 8, 2012).

71. Sunstein, 5.

72. Fisher, 278.

73. See Albanesius.

74. Fung, Graham, and Weil, 54.

75. Elizabeth Austin Bonner, "Network Neutrality Disclosures: More and Less Information," *I/S: A Journal of Law and Policy for the Information Society* 8, no. 1 (2012): 197.

76. Omri Ben-Shahar and Carl E. Schneider, "The Failure of Mandated Disclosure," *University of Pennsylvania Law Review* 159, no. 3 (February 2011): 647–749; Bonner, 197.

77. Adrian Henriques, *Corporate Truth: The Limits to Transparency* (Sterling, VA: Earthscan, 2008), 3.

78. For a general overview, see Keith Hawkins, *Law as Last Resort: Prosecution Decision-Making in a Regulatory Agency* (Oxford: Oxford University Press, 2002) and Cary Coglianese and Robert A. Kagan, ed., *Regulation and Regulatory Processes* (Burlington, VT: Ashgate, 2007).

79. Fung, Graham, and Weil, 66–67; Henriques, 91; Carolyn Ball, "What Is Transparency?" *Public Integrity* 11 no. 4 (October 2009): 293–307 .

80. Richard Briffault, "Campaign Finance Disclosure 2.0," *Election Law Journal* 9 no. 4 (December 2010): 302.

81. See also Bonner, 207.

82. Taren Kingser and Patrick Schmidt, "Business in the Bulls-Eye? Target Corp. and the Limits of Campaign Finance Disclosure," *Election Law Journal* 11 no. 1 (March 2012): 21–35.

83. Fung, Graham, and Weil, 110–111.

84. Doreen McBarnet, "Whiter Than White Collar Crime: Tax, Fraud Insurance and the Management of Stigma," *British Journal of Sociology* 42 no. 3 (September 1991): 323–344; Patrick Schmidt, "Securities Lawyers and the Ethical Quagmires of Disclosure," in *Lawyers in Practice: Ethical Decision Making in Context*, ed. Leslie Levin and Lynn Mather (Chicago: University of Chicago Press, 2012).

85. Ben-Shahar and Schneider, 749.

86. FCC, *Final Rule*, 59203.

87. Jonathan Zittrain, *The Future of the Internet and How to Stop It* (New Haven, C.T.: Yale University Press, 2008), 178–181.

88. FCC, *Final Rule*, 59203.

Chapter 4

Applying Common Carriage to Network Neutrality in the United States

Pallavi Guniganti and Mark Grabowski

In this chapter, we argue that lessons learned from the history of common carrier regulation, and from the contemporary example of countries that regulate Internet Service Providers (ISPs) as common carriers, provide the appropriate regulatory foundation for Internet access in the United States.

Common carriage is a legal concept that dates back to Roman law and medieval England, where a village's sole dock, inn or surgeon was required to serve all customers at a reasonable price. It was adopted in the United States and evolved with new technologies to include other businesses that were considered public services, such as steamships, railroads and telephone carriers. Internet access was initially subject to common carrier regulations, but lawmakers removed most regulations between 1996 and 2008, hoping less government involvement would spur more competition and better Internet service. When ISPs failed to deliver on their promises and began censoring traffic, lawmakers called for new regulations. At the moment, the Federal Communications Commission (FCC) is pursuing quasi-common carrier regulations for ISPs, but whether the agency has the authority to regulate Internet access and whether their regulations are strict enough remains unclear. There are both technical and economic considerations to weigh.

Opponents of applying common carrier regulations to Internet access argue that it is unlike telephone service because Internet access service comes with a variety of additional services beyond just the transportation of the communications services—services like caching and Domain Name System. Some say any government involvement would stifle innovation and investment, claiming that this was the result for past common-carrier regulated industries like railroads and the telephone.

But proponents argue that Internet service is fundamentally like a common carrier service because it involves a communications network. Indeed, personal Internet access for many people—especially those who are younger, less educated or from minority groups[1]—is primarily through smartphones and thus through cellular service, which the FCC already regulates under common carrier rules. Proponents contend that common carrier regulations could help resolve disputed issues such as duty to serve, nondiscrimination and interconnection, just as they did in the past for other industries involved in communications and commerce. They also believe it could help spur innovation and competition among ISPs.

In many other countries, Internet speed and connectivity have improved dramatically since ISPs have been regulated as common carriers. The United States, meanwhile, now ranks behind several of those.[2] The Internet has not become the competitive communications medium that lawmakers envisioned, despite more than a decade of non-involvement and hundreds of billions of dollars in taxpayer handouts. In many U.S. markets, only one ISP provides service.

The common carrier concept arose specifically from a situation in which there was only one entity offering an important public service; thus there was a necessity to oblige that sole service provider to do so in a fair manner. Given that, this chapter argues that the same policy is needed for ISPs. That is not to say that the rules of docks, railroads, or telephone carriers should be imported wholesale to govern Internet access. Rather, the history of common carrier regulation and its modern success in other countries demonstrates the fundamental importance of imposing on ISPs a duty to serve the public, along with interconnectivity and nondiscrimination requirements.

History of Common Carriage

The regulation of common callings has two main roots: one in a liability for damages, and the other in an obligation to serve the public. The former appears to have arisen earlier, during ancient times, but the latter is the basis for achieving some aspects of net neutrality through common carriage. Throughout its 1,500-year history, common carriage policies have been applied in various nations to inns, docks, trains, telephones, the Internet, and more.

Inns, Ferries, and Farriers

The law of common carriage can be traced back to the edicts of the Roman emperor Justinian in the sixth century: "When sailors, innkeepers, and the proprietors of stables have received property for safe keeping, I will grant an action against them if they do not restore it."[3] This edict was passed to protect victims from proprietors conspiring with thieves to claim that the property had been taken and could not be returned to the owner. "No one should think that this Edict imposes any hardship upon them, for they have the choice of refusing to receive anyone."[4]

Unlike its Roman antecedent, English law distinguished between common, or public, callings and private ones on the basis of whether the general public would reasonably think that they could avail themselves of the service. A tailor who worked only for a few households, who had no place of her own business and did not advertise for customers, was a private tailor; a tailor who had a shop open to the community was a common tailor. Under English law, the term "common carrier" commingled two distinct legal concepts, liability and duty to serve.[5] Thus, a common tailor was obligated to serve all who came into her shop. "Common carriers" were a subset of "common callings," serving the general public specifically by carrying people's physical possessions.

Post-Independence, American law largely retained the two aspects of the "common carrier" idea; in an 1848 decision, the Supreme Court states that a carrier "is in the exercise of a sort of public office . . . bound to receive and carry all the goods offered for transportation, subject to all the responsibilities incident to his employment, and is liable to an action in case of refusal."[6]

Telegraphs and Railroads

Since the introduction of telegraph in the United States in the early nineteenth century, common carriage has been a staple in regulating the nation's telecommunications. Shortly after Samuel Morse began successfully demonstrating and licensing his electrical telegraph across America, state legislation regarding the telegraph sprang up requiring nondiscriminatory, first come, first serve service to all customers. Two years later, New York made divulging the contents of a private communication entrusted to the telegraph company, or refusing to transmit it, a misdemeanor.[7]

Congressional enactments regarding the construction of telegraph lines to the Pacific in the early 1860s similarly provided that "messages received from any individual, company, or corporation, or from any telegraph line connecting with this line at either of its termini, shall be impartially transmitted in the order of their reception," and that the line "shall be open to the use of all citizens" upon payment that "shall not exceed three dollars for a single dispatch of ten words."[8]

States' designation of telegraph and telephone companies as common carriers of messages, comparable to the traditional common carriers of goods, soon received support from the Supreme Court, which noted, common carriers "are corporations chartered for the promotion of the public convenience."[9] In 1881, the Court opined, "A telegraph company occupies the same relation to commerce as a carrier of messages, that a railroad company does as a carrier of goods . . . [T]hey are both indispensable to those engaged to any considerable extent in commercial pursuits."[10]

The Court in *Wabash v. Illinois* limited states' ability to regulate interstate business, thereby catalyzing the 1887 creation of the Interstate Commerce

Commission.[11] The ICC enforced the Telegraph Lines Act of 1888's requirements of nondiscrimination "in favor of or against any person, company or corporation whatever," and of "terms just and equitable" in each company's business with connecting telegraph lines. In *Western Union Telegraph Co. v. Call Publishing Co.*, the Supreme Court held that discrimination in rates charged to competitors was actionable at common law as well.[12]

While the duty-to-serve element of common carrier obligations thrived, strict liability for damages waned due to the dissimilarity between an object, which could be entrusted to only one carrier at a time, and a message, which might be "held" by an unlimited number of people. The Supreme Court stated, "Telegraph companies resemble railroad companies and other common carriers, in that they are instruments of commerce, and in that they exercise a public employment, and are therefore bound to serve all customers alike, without discrimination . . . But telegraph companies are not bailees, in any sense."[13] The lack of intrinsic value in messages, contrasted with the market value of goods carried or held by inns, ferries and railroads, meant that telegraph companies could not be held liable for damages beyond what value they and the sender had previously agreed the message had.

Person-to-Person Telecommunications

In 1876, with the invention of the electric telephone and the telephone switchboard, states added nondiscrimination rules for telephone companies to those existing for telegraphy, though with the new obligation of furnishing the equipment necessary for people to send and receive messages, i.e., telephones and necessary fixtures. Several states' laws declared telegraph companies to be common carriers, and many of these designated telephone companies to be such as well.

In the Mann Elkins Act of 1910, Congress declared that "telegraph, telephone, and cable companies . . . shall be considered and held to be common carriers . . . All charges made for the transmission of messages . . . shall be just and reasonable."[14] Combined with the Sherman Act of 1890, the Mann Elkins Act empowered federal regulators to respond to the independent telephone companies' concerns regarding AT&T's purchase of local competitors and its refusal to connect other companies to its interstate long-distance network. The Department of Justice began an antitrust inquiry and the ICC investigated "the operations, rates and practices of the various telephone companies."[15]

In December 1913, AT&T forestalled the completion of these reviews by declaring itself willing to submit to regulation. According to the Kingsbury Commitment, AT&T would (1) divest itself of Western Union; (2) allow noncompeting independent telephone companies to interconnect with the AT&T long distance network; (3) stop acquiring competing independent telephone companies; and (4) balance its acquisitions of noncompeting companies with sales of its properties to independents.[16] In return, telecommunications would remain in the hands of the private sector, and the DOJ would not break up AT&T as it had done with the railroads and Standard Oil.

But throughout the time period, the ICC focused on its original mission of regulating the railroads and gave little attention to the communications sector, over which it still had much more limited power. For example, while telephone interconnection was largely based on the Kingsbury Commitment, a series of statutes had steadily enlarged the ICC's ability to mandate railroad interconnection, even to the point of requiring railroads to extend their lines and to build new constructions to facilitate interconnection.

Telecommunications Gets Its Own Regulator

A Senate Committee complained in 1934, "Under the existing provisions of the Interstate Commerce Act, the regulations of the telephone monopoly has been practically nil."[17] The charge of monopoly was substantiated by reports showing that in 1932, Bell accounted for 94.3 percent of the operating revenues of all substantial telephone companies. Western Union accounted for over 75 percent of operating revenues in the telegraph business, and its main rival Postal Telegraph was a weak competitor that was interested in merging with it.

With the Communications Act of 1934, Congress created a new agency, the Federal Communication Commission (FCC), to take over from the ICC the regulation of telephone and telegraph companies. The Act defined a common carrier as "[a]ny person engaged in rendering communications service for hire to the public" and largely copied the common carrier provisions of the Interstate Commerce Act.[18] The Act also required interconnection upon FCC order, as a backstop against Bell's Kingsbury Commitment to interconnect with independent local telephone companies.

With jurisdiction over both common carrier and noncommon carrier communications, the FCC decided to divide its staff by subject matter and established a Common Carrier Bureau in 1949. The CCB regulated entities "which furnish interstate or foreign communications service for hire—whether by wire, radio, cable or satellite facilities."[19] A parallel bureau was created for persons engaged in broadcasting, whom the Communications Act of 1934 had forbidden to be deemed common carriers.

Cable TV

AT&T laid its first experimental coaxial cable lines between New York and Philadelphia in 1936, originally carrying only one television program at a time. The FCC initially tried to avoid having jurisdiction over cable; in a 1958 agency ruling against broadcasters, the FCC held that cable was not a common carrier.[20]

But by 1962, almost 800 cable systems serving 850,000 subscribers were in business. The FCC first established rules in 1965 for cable systems that received signals by microwave antennas. In 1966, the FCC established rules for all cable systems (whether or not served by microwave).[21]

The Supreme Court affirmed the FCC's jurisdiction over cable in 1968, ruling that its "regulatory authority over CATV is imperative" to performing its duty of preserving local broadcast service and an equitable distribution of broadcast services among the various regions of the country.[22] However, a decade later the Court ruled that since cable systems acted as *broadcasters* of content, which the 1934 Act had forbidden to be treated as common carriers, the FCC "may not regulate cable systems as common carriers . . . We think authority to compel cable operators to provide common carriage of public-originated transmissions must come specifically from Congress."[23] In 1984, Congress adopted the Cable Communications Policy Act, an unusually extensive regime of regulation for a noncommon carrier. The new law also defined jurisdictional boundaries among federal, state, and local authorities for regulating cable television systems.

Computer Services

In 1971, the FCC declared that computer services would not be regulated common carrier services under the Communications Act.[24] In a foreshadowing of later rationales, the FCC reasoned that this new computer processing industry was currently competitive and would better innovate without the burden of regulation. To protect against cross-subsidy and discrimination, common carriers had to establish separate operations to offer data processing services.

In 1993, Congress amended the Communications Act of 1934, creating a new regulatory classification designated "commercial mobile services," and classified all mobile services as either "commercial mobile service" or "private mobile service."[25] The revised Act specified common carrier treatment of commercial mobile services and non-common carrier treatment of private mobile services. The statute emphasized the interconnection element of common carrier regulation: "Upon reasonable request of any person providing commercial mobile service, the Commission shall order a common carrier to establish physical connections with such service." On the other hand, commercial mobile services "shall not be required to provide equal access to common carriers for the provision of telephone toll services."

While the Telecommunications Act of 1996 gave the FCC expansive power to refrain from applying the 1934 Act where competition had taken root, even this provision declared that regulation could be eliminated only where nondiscriminatory service would continue in its absence.[26] Statutory authority requiring all incumbent local exchange carriers to permit physical collocation—i.e., that the telephone companies offer opportunities for information service providers to physically place their equipment in telephone company offices, similar to the opportunities enjoyed by the telephone companies' own affiliates—was added to the 1934 Act by the 1996 Act.

Common Carriage in Internet Access Regulation

In the United States

Internet access in the United States was initially subjected to common carriage. In its early days, consumers connected through a call over a telephone line to an ISP. Because the local loop of telephone copper was already a common carrier, it was open to any ISP. This gave small firms equal footing with dial-up giants such as CompuServe and America Online.[27] "America's Internet flourished in the dial-up era because federal regulators . . . forced local phone companies to act as common carriers, allowing competing service providers to use their lines," according to Princeton University economist Paul Krugman.[28]

All that began to change in the late 1990s as deregulation, already applied to transport common carriers such as railroads, airlines, and trucks came into vogue for telecommunications.[29] Cable operating companies commenced a major upgrade of their distribution networks to build higher capacity hybrid networks of fiber optic and coaxial cable. These "broadband" networks could provide multichannel video, two-way voice, high-speed Internet access, and high definition and advanced digital video services all on a single wire into the home. The upgrade to broadband networks enabled cable companies to introduce high–speed Internet access to customers in the mid-1990s, and competitive local telephone and digital cable services later in the decade. Cable and telephone companies assured Congress that they would enter each other's markets and compete against one other if the government would relax regulations. Lawmakers agreed to deregulation believing that the resulting competition would remove the need for public oversight.[30]

The Clinton administration and Congress took the first steps toward deregulation in 1996 when they overhauled telecommunications law for the first time in more than 60 years.[31] Under the Telecommunications Act of 1996, different forms of media were subject to varying levels of regulation. Title I of the Act applied to information services, which were not subject to any statutory rules and over which the FCC had limited regulatory authority. Title II, however, was applied to telecommunications services and allowed for far more stringent regulation. A telecommunications carrier was defined as a company offering "telecommunications services" and "shall be treated as a common carrier."[32] Telecommunications service "means the transmission, between or among points specified by the user, of information of the user's choosing, without change in the form or content of the information as sent and received."[33] In contrast, an "information service" was defined as a provider offering the "capability for generating, acquiring, storing, transforming, processing, retrieving, utilizing, or making available information via telecommunications, and includes electronic publishing, but does not include any use of any such capability for the management, control, or operation of a telecommunications system or the management of a telecommunications service."[34]

Since the law did not explicitly state which categorization Internet access fell under, the decision was left up to the FCC.[35] The Commission ruled that "Internet service does not meet the statutory definition of a 'telecommunications service.'"[36] This distinction was premised on the fact that at the time, 98 percent of all households with Internet connections used traditional telephone service to "dial-up" their ISP. The FCC thus treated Internet access as "information service" because these ISPs owned no telecommunications facilities. When telecommunications companies began to offer their own DSL (digital subscriber line) services, the transmission component of their Internet access service remained under Title II regulation.[37] Originally, DSL was short for "digital subscriber loop," because the service began by utilizing unused bandwidth of the telephone loop.[38]

The distinction between Title I and Title II classification was significant because classifying Internet access as a Title I "information service" meant that the FCC did not have specific and direct authority to regulate ISPs, and instead relied on its "ancillary authority."[39] Such power authorizes the FCC to "perform any and all acts, make such rules and regulations, and issue such orders, not inconsistent with this chapter, as may be necessary in the execution of its functions,"[40] provided the agency demonstrates that its action is "reasonably ancillary to the . . . effective performance of its statutorily mandated responsibilities."[41] Courts soon after reaffirmed the FCC's classification of Internet access as an information service with regards to dial-up ISPs. In 1999, the Eastern District of Virginia court held that AOL was not a common carrier, reasoning that they must defer to the FCC's interpretation of information service.[42] In 2000, the Ninth Circuit Court of Appeals upheld a district court decision "that AOL is not a common carrier."[43] The court justified its decision by citing the 1996 Telecommunications Act and the FCC's interpretation of it.[44]

In 2002, following a trilogy of differing court conclusions on whether cable television companies providing Internet access were subject to common carrier regulations,[45] the FCC ruled that "when consumers purchase cable-modem service, they are buying only an 'information' service, not a traditional two-way communications service like telephone service. The decision exempted cable-modem providers from opening their lines to competing ISPs and from other rules."[46] Thus, it created a roadblock for start-up ISPs who wanted to get in on the growing demand for Internet service by using cable and phone wires to offer a competing service. They sued, and following inconsistent decisions by federal courts, the Supreme Court weighed in. In *National Cable and Telecommunications Association v. Brand X*, the high court held in favor of the FCC that cable Internet providers are an "information service," and not a "telecommunications service."[47] The Court made clear that it would also uphold a classification of other Internet services as information services. In his majority opinion, Justice Clarence Thomas said the *"Chevron* [doctrine] requires a federal court to accept the agency's construction of the statute, even if the agency's reading differs from what the court believes is the best statutory interpretation."[48]

Two months later, the FCC classified DSL services as information services. Once again, the FCC was challenged, but prevailed in court.[49] As new forms of Internet access began to emerge, including wireless and mobile services, the FCC refrained from regulating, saying it did not want to stifle development. In March 2007, the FCC ruled that wireless Internet access service was an information service.[50] The FCC's decision thus placed wireless Internet access service on the same largely deregulated footing as cable and wireline Internet services. Although mobile operators were required to obey common carrier regulations for voice signals, thus forcing wireless providers to allow other companies to use their infrastructure for voice signals, there were minimal regulations on Internet services offered by smartphones.[51]

In 2008, FCC administrators finally conceded deregulation may have gone too far and that there was a need for some Internet protections. "The Bush FCC hoped that deregulation would prompt greater competition in Internet access services," said University of Michigan Law School Professor Susan Crawford, a former special assistant to President Obama for science, technology, and innovation policy. "But a wave of mergers instead reduced it. Prices stayed high and speeds slow. And eventually the carriers started saying that they wanted to be gatekeepers—creating fast lanes for some Web sites and applications and slow lanes for others."[52] The agency handed Comcast a cease-and-desist order after discovering that the company was secretly hindering customers' access to the Web service BitTorrent because it competes with Comcast's video-on-demand services.[53] "If we aren't going to stop a company that is looking inside its subscribers' communications—blocking communication when it uses a particular application regardless of whether there is congestion on the network, hiding what it is doing by making consumers think the problem is their own, and lying about it to the public—what would we stop?" asked then–FCC Chairman Kevin Martin,[54] who approved the Order over White House opposition.[55]

Ultimately, however, the order was overturned by the D.C. Circuit Court of Appeals, which dealt a major blow to the FCC's attempts to regulate Internet access. The decision noted the FCC's "still-binding 2002 Cable Modem Order," in which "the Commission ruled that cable Internet service is neither a 'telecommunications service' covered by Title II of the Communications Act nor a 'cable service' covered by Title VI."[56] The D.C. Circuit concluded that "[b]ecause the Commission has failed to tie its assertion of ancillary authority over Comcast's Internet service to any 'statutorily mandated responsibility,'" the FCC lacked such authority to regulate cable Internet services.[57]

Since the ruling, the Obama administration has aggressively worked "to craft rules governing the entire industry,"[58] even though it remains unclear whether the FCC has the authority to regulate Internet access at all. FCC Chairman Julius Genachowski said the D.C. Circuit Court's ruling in favor of Comcast left the Commission two options: "To not regulate broadband or to classify broadband as a common carrier, subject to potentially much harsher regulation enacted during the heyday of the old Bell System."[59] Saying that neither option was ideal, the FCC in May 2010 proposed regulating Internet access in a "Third Way" that would offer a hybrid of Titles I and II. It would provide "a legal anchor that gives the Commission only the modest authority it needs to foster a world-leading broadband infrastructure for all Americans while definitively avoiding the negative consequences of a full reclassification and broad application of Title II," Genachowski wrote in a memorandum.[60]

While the new rules have common carrier components, they are not entirely common carrier. As part of its "Third Way" compromise, the FCC opted to apply only a handful of the Title II provisions, while renouncing and not enforcing the remainder.[61] For example, the new rules do not require giant ISPs to share their physical infrastructure with smaller, startup ISPs for a reasonable price. Throughout the history of railroad, telegraph and telephone regulation, an obligation to connect at a "just and reasonable price" was a policy staple. Until such open access is required for the Internet, the underlying problems in U.S. Internet service may not get fixed, some experts argue.[62] Currently, the United States faces a duopoly problem: 96 percent of households have access to two or fewer broadband service providers, according to the FCC,[63] and the situation will only grow worse as demand for higher speeds grows. FCC Commissioner Mignon Clyburn predicted that in the next year only 15 percent of households will have a choice of even two providers offering competitive world-class broadband service.[64]

Overseas

Other nations' experiences illustrate the benefits for Internet users of imposing common carrier regulations on ISPs and the dangers of taking the laissez faire approach that characterized the Bush administration and continues to be sought by telecom giants. Over the past decade almost all developed countries have extended some kind of common carrier arrangement to broadband access, according to a 2010 study by the Berkman Center for Internet and Society at Harvard University.[65]

Great Britain and France, for example, required their former monopoly telecom companies to make their infrastructure available to rival ISPs, which rent it at regulated rates and compete on price and speed. The study found evidence that these common carrier policies drove prices down and speeds up for Internet users. In France, the average Internet speed is more than three times as fast as it is in the United States, while the price for each megabyte per second is less than half.[66] Meanwhile, Britons get Internet service comparable to what is available in the United States for less than $6 a month.[67] As Rick Karr of tech blog Engadget observed last year:

> The market in the UK used to be much like ... the U.S.: British homes had two options for broadband service: the incumbent telephone company or a cable provider. Prices were high, service was slow, and ... Britain was falling behind its European neighbors in international rankings of broadband service. The solution, the British government decided, was more competition: If consumers had more options when it came to broadband service, regulators reasoned, prices would fall and speeds would increase . . . You can see evidence of the UK's competitive market on the streets of London: Broadband providers splash ads across bush shelters and train stations, touting prices that seem outrageously low by U.S. standards. Post offices sell broadband service; so does Tesco, one of the UK's largest supermarket chains.[68]

In Japan, the nation's largest phone service and Internet provider is required to resell access to its facilities to competitors at wholesale. Japan now has thousands of ISPs reselling Internet access, all competing against each other.[69] Consequently, "Japan is often cited as a global leader in broadband technology, speed, and price."[70] The average speed of a broadband connection in Japan is over 90 megabits per second, compared to only nine in the United States. Broadband access by households is around a third higher in Japan. The average price of broadband service is two to three times as high in the United States as in Japan, with a 50 megabit per second line costing less than $25 per month in Japan. Most Americans pay $38 to $44 per month just for Internet access.[71] Comcast and Cablevision want up to $140 a month for 50 megabits a second, and Verizon charges $165.[72]

Germany, by contrast, illustrates the drawbacks of weak regulation. Until recently, Deutsche Telekom (DT) had a monopoly over Internet access, controlling 97 percent of the market by refusing to open its facilities to competitors. As a result, the ISP giant was able to saddle Internet users with an overpriced service that included features many consumers did not want. Eventually, European Union officials pressured German lawmakers to put stricter regulations in place. DT now controls only 47 percent of the market, better Internet technologies are being implemented and prices are going down. The Harvard study concluded, "Regulation is seen as having promoted competition in the telecommunications market and fostering investment and growth."[73]

Why Common Carriage Is Necessary

The lessons learned from other nations show that countries with common carrier regulations enjoy better Internet service because the barrier to entry for new providers is much lower. If the ISP does not keep up with technological breakthroughs to offer faster speeds or if it starts charging excessive fees, users can switch providers. Unless the FCC takes steps to address the duopoly in the U.S.

market, America could continue to lag behind other nations. "A significant reason that other countries had managed to both expand access and lower rates over the last decade was a commitment to open-access policies, requiring companies that build networks to sell access to rivals that then invest in, and compete on, the network," argues Harvard Law School professor Yochai Benkler, who conducted the Berkman Center study.[74] ISPs that currently control the U.S. market argue that they deserve the spoils because they have invested enormous amounts of money into digging trenches and laying cables for their telecommunications network. But as Benkler points out, "other countries are exploring creative ways for competitors to share the costs and risks of fiber investments, sometimes coupled with public investment, so that incumbent companies can accommodate competitors without unnecessarily hamstringing themselves."[75] America's telecom giants should be well aware of this. After all, AT&T and Verizon have both benefited from Britain's common carrier regulations, which have given them access to incumbent telecom companies' infrastructure and enables them to take away their market share.[76]

Some opponents of net neutrality claim that common carriage has never worked in any industry.[77] However, their arguments generally assume that common carrier regulation intrinsically requires detailed price regulation.[78] On the contrary, even after the deregulation of transportation sectors with regard to price-setting, commercial airlines remain common carriers under federal law, subject to different regulations than private carriers.[79] The regulation of AT&T's rates arose from a symbiotic relationship in which the company insisted that telephone service was a "natural monopoly," and that it ought to be able to merge freely with competitors, but in return would submit to heavy government oversight.[80] As the collapse of AT&T's proposed merger with T-Mobile under antitrust scrutiny reaffirmed, that old trade-off is dead.[81] There is a case for rate setting in the context of an actual monopoly over high-speed Internet access in a particular geographic market. But such total monopolies are likely to be quite rare given proliferating methods to access the Internet and the competitive benefits of common carrier rules. Alternatively, the government might subsidize Internet access in areas where it is currently unprofitable, as happens with air service.[82]

Another problem common carrier regulation could fix is censorship. To be sure, giving the government greater control of the Internet could create a slippery slope into the valley of government censorship.[83] However, the government is limited in its ability to censor because of the First Amendment. Private companies are not. While concerns about government censorship are speculative, ISPs have already demonstrated their penchant to censor. Comcast is not the only culprit. In 2007, Verizon blocked Naral Pro-Choice America from sending text messages over its mobile network because they were "controversial" and "unsavory."[84] The same year, AT&T banned its Internet users from making critical remarks online about the company.[85] Both companies later reversed their policies following public backlash. Federal regulation as a common carrier also may limit the degree to which local governments can pressure private companies to censor or disrupt service to disfavored individuals.[86]

Some scholars, such as University of Pennsylvania Law School professor Christopher Yoo, believe FCC oversight is unnecessary because the free market can solve the censorship problem. "You might find text-messaging companies competing on their openness policies," Yoo said.[87] But, at the moment, many consumers could not change ISPs even if they wanted to. More than one-quarter of consumers do not have the choice between cable and DSL, and even in markets with both services available, customers usually face a duopoly, with one choice for each type of service. As a result, Internet users could face Chinese-like censorship and not be able to access content that their ISP bans for whatever reason, according to Columbia Law School professor Tim Wu.[88] This could also hinder innovation among tech startups. "You can't have innovation if all the big companies get the fast lane," said Gigi Sohn, president of Public Knowledge, which advocates for consumer rights on digital issues. "Look at Google, eBay, Yahoo—none of those companies would have survived if 15 years ago we had a fast lane and a slow lane on the Internet."[89]

Regulation derived from the common carriage tradition also provides positive benefits to ISPs. Prior to the passage of the Digital Millennium Copyright Act in 1998, which amended existing copyright law to limit ISP liability, the defendant ISPs described themselves as common carriers of messages or information like the telephone industry, and therefore not liable for the content of transmissions.[90] Courts countered that the ISPs could not enjoy the immunity because they did not meet the nondiscrimination requirement of 17 U.S.C. 111: "any carrier who has no direct or indirect control over the content or selection of the primary transmission or over the particular recipients of the secondary transmission." In Canada, the Copyright Board and Federal Court of Appeal premised ISPs' immunity from liability for copyright violations on their being exempt from the Copyright Act as common carriers. The Copyright Act exempts common carriers on the rationale that that they are passive intermediaries merely providing the means of communication.[91]

Finally, applying common carriage represents a return to tradition rather than a drastic change. The Internet, after all, began as a common carrier service. The very same telephone and cable companies that used to be regulated as telecommunications providers now "comprise nineteen of the largest providers of [Internet] access in the United States, serving approximately 93 percent of all [Internet] users."[92] History shows that "prior to the FCC's policy shift [deregulating the Internet], the broadband market was competitive."[93] Eliminating common carrier regulations actually hindered competition, raised prices and stifled innovation. But giant ISPs such as AT&T warn that such reclassification would "cram today's broadband Internet access providers into an ill-fitting twentieth century regulatory silo" and would "present risks and harms that dwarf any putative benefits."[94]

ISPs contend that classifying them as "telecommunication services" is inappropriate now because they offer an integrated bundle of services—not just Internet access but also e-mail, Web hosting, news groups, and other services. But, in practice, consumers increasingly use their ISPs only to connect to the Internet. Once there, a typical Internet user might send e-mail using Gmail, search for information via Bing, chat with friends through Skype, and watch a TV show on Hulu.[95] ISPs provide information services only because they want to increase their profits by forcing their bundle of services on consumers, not because consumers demand them.

Implementing Common Carriage in the United States

The road to common carriage implementation is fraught with roadblocks and uncertainty. Current FCC Chairman Julius Genachowski says he does not favor a strict common carriage scheme, and the Comcast decision has left experts speculating whether the agency even has the power to implement such regulations. U.S. Senator Michael Johanns told FCC officials at a hearing, "You've been handed your hat in your hand in the Comcast case . . . [and] you can't go to Title II, it'd be like remaking the world."[96] But some notable legal scholars disagree. University of Michigan's Susan Crawford contends the truly radical move was classifying ISPs as "informative services" in the first place, rather than "common carriers."[97] Tim Wu of Columbia Law says reverting to common carriage would require a simple "error correction."[98] He explains, "by statute, the agency retains enormous powers over every form of communications by wire; it simply has to turn them back on." For now, the only certainty is that the mega ISPs would fight any attempts to impose common carriage all the way to the Supreme Court.

Telecom giants are even opposed to the FCC's new "Open Internet" rules, which are much less restrictive than common carriage. Verizon and MetroPCS have filed lawsuits against the FCC in D.C. Circuit Court, the same court which ruled against the FCC in 2010, holding the agency did not have the authority to regulate Comcast or, for that matter, the Internet.[99] The latest challenge to the FCC's authority is expected to be heard in 2013.[100] The telecom companies contend the FCC is overstepping its bounds in trying to regulate their network management.[101] The FCC believes it now has the authority to do so because its new "Open Internet" regulations rely on the agency's authority under the Communications Act rather than its ancillary authority.[102] Legal scholars say the best way to definitively resolve the issue is for Congress to give the FCC explicit authority to regulate Internet service. Otherwise, "absent an act of Congress, the FCC will have to choose to abstain from mingling in affairs for which it does not have expressed authority or continue to face service providers in court," the legal journal *News Media and The Law* stated.[103]

However, Congress appears unlikely to come to the FCC's rescue. Since 2006, when Congress considered five different bills to reform the Telecommunications Act of 1996, U.S. lawmakers have been unable to pass any piece of legislation regarding ISP regulation, and chances for a Congressional intervention appear to be dwindling further. The House of Representatives voted in April 2012 to reject the FCC's new "Open Internet" rules, undermining the agency's already precarious authority over the Internet.[104] "Conservative Republicans philosophically oppose giving the agency more power, on the grounds that Internet providers should be able to decide what services they offer and at what price," according to the *New York Times*.[105] While President Obama is expected to veto the bill, if approved by the Senate, Congress' reluctance to enforce even modest regulations on ISPs suggests the chances of Congress imposing common carrier regulations are slim. Benkler, a professor and co-director of the Berkman Center for Internet and Society at Harvard Law School, says that the FCC has been bowing to the monopolies' pressure but must incorporate open access— i.e., allowing new entrants to use big ISPs' infrastructure at reasonable rates—to break up existing duopolies and achieve the kind of success seen in the EU and Japan. "If we stay the present course, the Commission's new policy will build a better wireless network around a more entrenched monopoly system, lodging an insurmountable obstacle in the path toward bringing America's broadband network up to speed with the rest of the world," he warns.[106]

With common carriage seemingly a pipe dream, some local governments are taking matters into their own hands. As of February 2012, more than 150 municipalities across the nation have built or are planning to build broadband networks, according to *USA Today*.[107] But such projects can be costly, and telecom lobbyists have doggedly fought similar attempts through lobbying and litigation. "Pick a battlefield," says Craig Settles, a California-based broadband analyst and consultant. Telecom companies "will figure out a way to kill as many of these projects as they can." Already, 19 states either explicitly ban communities from creating their own Internet service or make it exceedingly difficult. ISPs argue that it is unfair for their regulator to also be a competitor. Governments may charge exorbitant franchise fees to keep out private companies. In addition, critics argue, government-run services are often not as efficient as the private sector.

Despite all the evidence in support of the suitability of common carriage, policymakers appear unwilling to make it a reality. However, if the FCC survives the latest challenge to its authority, it could pursue incrementally stricter regulations and eventually adopt full-blown common carriage.

Conclusion

Both proponents and opponents of network neutrality often equate it with common carriage.[108] But common carriage principles would not perfectly fulfill all visions of network neutrality. For example, in 2005 then CEO of AT&T, Ed Whitacre, replied to the question "How concerned are you about Internet upstarts like Google, MSN, Vonage, and others?" by saying, "How do you think they're going to get to customers? Through a broadband pipe. Cable companies have them. We have them. Now what they would like to do is use my pipes free, but I ain't going to let them do that because we have spent this capital and we have to have a return on it."[109] In other words, Whitacre proposed that content and service providers (CSPs) should pay not only for the CSP's own connection to the Internet, but also an additional fee to the consumer ISPs where the CSP's traffic terminated.

So long as such fees are assessed on a nondiscriminatory basis that does not work to exclude rivals, and especially if there is no "pay for priority" that would violate the old "first come, first served" tradition of telegraph transmission, they are consistent with common carriage. An analogous fee would be the common practice of a local telephone company's charging AT&T a fee for carrying a consumer's in-state long distance and local toll calls over its lines—a cost that AT&T passes on to consumers.[110] But Whitacre's statement aroused significant outrage and such fees have been criticized as contrary to network neutrality, particularly because noncommercial content producers such as are unlikely to have the money to pay fees to each user's ISP, making such content inaccessible to most of its current audience.[111] Nonetheless, those who seek a zero–pricing rule for the Internet may have to look somewhere other than common carriage for its source.[112]

In the transition from the transportation to the telecommunications industry, the term "common carriage" dropped the baggage of strict liability for loss or damage, as the telegraph and telephone could carry no literal baggage. The remaining principles of interconnection, nondiscrimination and a duty to serve still meet the needs of consumers and telecommunications companies. Both American history and the overseas examples show that these most basic aspects of common carriage would ensure continuity of the legal treatment of telecommunications without overburdening a developing industry with new, technical regulations. Just going back to the dial-up days of regulating the Internet as a common carrier reconnects Internet service's past to the present moment of smartphone access to the Internet. Using historically dominant, traditional methods of regulation provides basic consumer protection balanced with innovation and market freedom.

Notes

1. Stephanie Chen and Chris Brown, "Saving the Open Internet: The Importance of Network Neutrality," *Greenlining Institute*, March 2012, http://stage.greenlining.org/resources/pdfs/GLIonNetNeutrality.pdf (accessed August 13, 2012).

2. See, e.g., Verne G. Kopytoff, "America: Land of the Slow," *New York Times Bits Blog*, September 20, 2011 (4:09 p.m.), http://bits.blogs.nytimes.com/2011/09/20/America-land-of-the-slow/ (accessed August 13, 2012). See also "Akamai Releases Fourth Quarter 2011 'State of the Internet' Report," Akamai Press Release, April 30,

2012, http://www.akamai.com/html/about/press/releases/2012/press_043012.html (accessed August 13, 2012).

3. *Pandects*, ninth title of the fourth book, in Samuel P. Scott, trans., *The Civil Law* (Cincinnati: Central Trust Co., 1932).

4. Ibid., 134.

5. William Blackstone, *Commentaries on the Laws of England* (Oxford: Clarendon Press, 1765–1769), 164–165.

6. *New Jersey Steam Navigation Co. v. Merchants' Bank*, 47 U.S. 344, at 382 (1848).

7. An Act to Provide for the Incorporation and Regulation of Telegraph Company, *Laws of the State of New York*, 1850, Chap. 340, p. 739.

8. *The Pacific Telegraph Act of 1860*, Chapter 137, U.S. Statutes, 36th Cong. 1st Sess.

9. *Express Company v. Caldwell*, 88 U.S. 264 (1874).

10. *Telegraph Company v. Texas*, 105 U.S. 460 (1881).

11. 118 U.S. 557 (1886).

12. 181 U.S. 92 (1901).

13. 154 U.S. 1 (1894).

14. *Mann-Elkins Act of 1910*, 61st Cong., 2nd sess., ch. 309, 36 Stat. 539.

15. Associated Press, "Investigation Dropped by Wickersham; Telephone Combine Question Referred to Commerce Commission; Deep Probe Is Planned," *Pittsburgh Gazette Times*, January 21, 1913, 1.

16. "Letter to the Attorney General from the American Telephone and Telegraph Company: Outlining a Course of Action Which It Has Determined Upon," published by the U.S. Government Printing Office, 1914.

17. Senate Report No. 781, 73d Cong., 2d Sess., 2 (1934).

18. *Communication Act of 1934*, 73rd Cong., 2d sess., ch. 652, 48 Stat. 1064

19. *Code of Federal Regulations,* Functions of the Bureau, title, sec 0.91.

20. *Frontier Broadcasting Co. v. Collier*, 24 F. C. C. 251 (1958).

21. Federal Communications Commission, "Evolution of Cable Television," *FCC Encyclopedia*, at http://www.fcc.gov/encyclopedia/evolution-cable-television#sec46 (accessed August 13, 2012).

22. 392 U.S. 157 (1968).

23. *FCC v. Midwest Video Corp.*, 440 U.S. 689 (1979).

24. Reg. and Policy Problems Presented by the Interdependence of Computer and Communications Services, Final Decision, 28 FCC2d 267, 21 Rad. Reg.2d (P & F) 1561 (1971).

25. *Omnibus Budget Reconciliation Act of 1993*, 103rd Cong, 1st. sess. Pub. L. No. 103–66, § 6002(b), 107 Stat. 312, 392.

26. *Telecommunications Act of 1996*, *U.S. Code* 47 (1996) sec. 401, § 10(a),

27. Marcia Clemmitt, "Controlling the Internet," *CQ Researcher* 16 (May 12, 2006): 409–432.

28. Paul Krugman. "The French Connections," *New York Times*, July 23, 2007, A19.

29. Joseph D. Kearney and Thomas W. Merrill, "The Great Transformation of Regulated Industries Law," *Columbia Law Review* 98, no. 6 (October 1998): 1323.

30. "The Telecommunications Act: Consumers Still Waiting for Better Phone and Cable Services on the Sixth Anniversary of National Law," Consumers Union, press release, February 6, 2002, http://www.consumersunion.org/telecom/sixthdc202.htm (accessed August 13, 2012).

31. Ibid.

32. *Telecommunications Act of 1996, U.S. Code* 47 (1996) sec. 153.

33. Ibid.

34. Ibid.

35. *America Online, Inc. v. GreatDeals.net*, 49 F. Supp. 2d 851 (E.D. Va. 1999). Citing *Chevron*, "Congress has not provided clarification on whether an information service provider is a common carrier. Where a statute is silent or ambiguous with respect to a specific issue, the Court must defer to the agency's interpretation of the statute unless it is an impermissible construction or manifestly contrary to the statute."

36. *In re Federal-State Joint Bd. on Universal Serv.*, 12 F.C.C.R. 87, 123–24 (1996).

37. *Report 112–51*, 112th Cong., 1st Sess. (April 1, 2011), p. 18, http://www.gpo.gov/fdsys/pkg/CRPT-112hrpt51/pdf/CRPT-112hrpt51.pdf (accessed August 13, 2012).

38. Edward A. Lee and David G. Messerschmitt, *Digital Communication* (Norwell, Mass: Kluwer Academic Publishers, 1994), 119.

39. Kathleen Ann Ruane, "The FCC's Authority to Regulate Net Neutrality after *Comcast v. FCC*," Congressional Research Service, December 2, 2010, p. 7, http://www.hsdl.org/?view&did=12737.

40. 47 U.S.C. §154(i).

41. *American Library Association v. Federal Communication. Commission*, 406 F.3d 689, 692 (D.C. Cir. 2005).

42. *America Online, Inc. v. GreatDeals.net*, 49 F. Supp. 2d 851 (E.D. Va. 1999).

43. *Howard v. America Online*, 208 F.3d 741, 752 (9th Cir. 2000).

44. 47 U.S.C. S 223(e)(6) (Supp. III 1997).

45. Jim Chen, "The Authority to Regulate Broadband Internet Access Over Cable," *Berkeley Technology Law Journal* 16 (2001): 667; *AT&T v. City of Portland*, 43 F. Supp. 2d 1146 (D. Or. 1999), rev'd, 216 F.3d 871 (9th Cir. 2000); *MediaOne Group, Inc. v. County of Henrico*, 97 F. Supp. 2d 712, 715 (E.D. Va. 2000); *Gulf Power v. FCC*, 208 F.3d 1263 (11th Cir. 2000), cert. granted, 121 S. Ct. 879 (2001).

46. Clemmitt, "Controlling the Internet."

47. *National Cable and Telecommunications Assn. v. Brand X Internet Services*, 545 U.S. 967 (2005).

48. *National Cable and Telecommunications Assn. v. Brand X Internet Services*, 545 U.S. 967, 980 (2005).

49. *Time Warner Telecom Inc., et. al, v. FCC*, 507 F.3d 205, 221 (3d Cir. 2007).

50. Federal Communications Commission, *Declaratory Ruling In the Matter of Appropriate Regulatory Treatment for Broadband Access to the Internet Over Wireless Networks*, March 23, 2007, http://hraunfoss.fcc.gov/edocs_public/attachmatch/FCC-07-30A1.pdf (accessed August 13, 2012).

51. Marc Oestreich, "Research and Commentary: FCC's Data-Roaming Mandate," Heartland Institute, April 3, 2011, http://heartland.org/policy-documents/research-commentary-fccs-data-roaming-mandate (accessed August 13, 2012).

52. Susan Crawford, "An Internet for Everybody," *New York Times*, April 11, 2010, WK12, http://www.nytimes.com/2010/04/11/opinion/11crawford.html (accessed August 13, 2012).

53. Declan McCullagh, "FCC Formally Rules Comcast's Throttling of BitTorrent Was Illegal," *CNET*, August 1, 2008, http://news.cnet.com/8301-13578_3-10004508-38.html. (accessed August 13, 2012).

54. Bob Fernandez, "FCC Chair Blasts Comcast," *Philadelphia Inquirer*, August 2, 2008, http://articles.philly.com/2008-08-02/business/25258241_1_michael-copps-high-speed-internet-service-jonathan–adelstein (accessed August 13, 2012).

55. McCullagh. "FCC Formally Rules."

56. *Comcast Corp. v. FCC*, 600 F.3d 642, 645 (D.C. Cir. 2010).

57. *Comcast Corp. v. FCC*, 600 F.3d 642, 661 (D.C. Cir. 2010).

58. Edward Wyatt, "U.S. Court Curbs F.C.C. Authority on Web Traffic," *New York Times*, April 6, 2010, A1, http://www.nytimes.com/2010/04/07/technology/07net.html (accessed August 13, 2012).

59. David Coursey, "Comcast May Now Regret Suing the FCC Over Net Neutrality," *PCWorld*, May 6, 2010, http://www.pcworld.com/businesscenter/article/195794/comcast_may_now_regret_suing_the_fcc_over_net_neutrality.html (accessed August 13, 2012).

60. Julius Genachowski, "The Third Way: A Narrowly Tailored Broadband Framework," *FCC*, May 2010, at http://www.broadband.gov/the-third-way-narrowly-tailored-broadband-framework-chairman-julius-genachowski.html.

61. Mark Hachman, "FCC Proposes 'Third Way' to Regulate Broadband," *PC Magazine*, May 6, 2010, http://www.pcmag.com/article2/0,2817,2363484,00.asp (accessed August 13, 2012).

62. See infra section "Why Common Carriage Is Necessary."

63. Federal Communications Commission, "Connecting America: The National Broadband Plan," March 16, 2010, 37, http://download.broadband.gov/plan/national-broadband-plan.pdf (accessed August 13, 2012).

64. Statement of Commissioner Mignon L. Clyburn, *A National Broadband Plan for Our Future*, GN Docket No. 09-51 (March 16, 2010).

65. Berkman Center for Internet and Society at Harvard University, "Next Generation Connectivity: A Review of Broadband Internet Transitions and Policy from around the World," February 16, 2010, http://cyber.law.harvard.edu/pubrelease/broadband (accessed August 13, 2012).

66. David K. Correa, "Assessing Broadband in America: OECD and ITIF Broadband Rankings," *The Information Technology and Innovation Foundation*, April 2007, http://www.itif.org/files/BroadbandRankings.pdf (accessed August 13, 2012).

67. Rick Karr, "Why Is European Broadband Faster and Cheaper? Blame the Government," *Engadget*, June 28, 2011, http://www.engadget.com/2011/06/28/why-is-european-broadband-faster-and-cheaper-blame-the-governme (accessed August 13, 2012).

68. Ibid.

69. Scott Dunn, "Net neutrality Is a Ruse," KSL TV, February 29, 2012, http://www.ksl.com/?nid=1014&sid=19286087 (accessed August 8, 2012).

70. Berkman Center, "Next Generation Connectivity."

71. Hannibal Travis, "The FCC's New Theory of the First Amendment," *Santa Clara Law Review*, 51, no. 2 (2010): 101–197.

72. "Down the Tubes: Internet Television Moves From the Computer to the Living Room," *The Economist*, http://www.economist.com/node/13562114 (accessed August 13, 2012).

73. Berkman Center, "Next Generation Connectivity."

74. Yochai Benkler, "Ending the Internet's Trench Warfare," *New York Times*, March 20, 2010, http://www.nytimes.com/2010/03/21/opinion/21Benkler.html (accessed August 8, 2012).

75. Ibid.

76. Karr, "Why Is European Broadband."

77. Bruce M. Owen, "Antecedents to Net Neutrality," *Cato Regulation* (Fall 2007): 14–17.

78. Opponents of net neutrality often treat it as synonymous with government price–setting. See, e.g, *id.* at 14 ("Net neutrality policies could only be implemented through detailed price regulation"); Geoffrey Manne, "Net Neutrality and Trinko," *Truth on the Market*, April 4, 2011, at http://truthonthemarket.com/2011/04/04/net-neutrality-and-trinko/ (accessed August 8, 2012).

79. 49 USC § 40102.

80. See supra Section II, regarding the Kingsbury Commitment.

81. David Goldman, "AT&T Kills $39 Billion Bid for T–Mobile," *CNNMoney*, December 19, 2011, http://money.cnn.com/2011/12/19/technology/att_tmobile_dead/index.htm (accessed August 13, 2012).

82. Before deregulation, airlines cross-subsidized routes by charging supracompetitive prices; AT&T similarly ran telephone lines to rural areas because as a monopolist promising universal service it was obligated to serve even unprofitable markets. Since deregulation, the federal government has had to subsidize unprofitable airline routes in order to maintain commercial service at certain airports. See U.S. Department of Transportation, "Essential Air Service Program," http://ostpxweb.dot.gov/aviation/X-50%20Role_files/essentialairservice.htm.

83. Stephen Miller, "FCC's Third Way: The FCC's Broadband Regulation Proposal and Its Impact on Journalism," *The News Media and The Law* (Fall 2010): 36, http://www.rcfp.org/browse-media-law-resources/news-media-law/news-media-and-law-fall-2010/fccs-third–way (accessed August 8, 2012).

84. Adam Liptak, "Verizon Blocks Messages of Abortion Rights Group," *New York Times*, September 27, 2007, http://www.nytimes.com/2007/09/27/us/27verizon.html (accessed August 8, 2012).

85. Daithí Mac Síthigh, "Regulating the Medium: Reactions to Network Neutrality in the European Union and Canada," *Journal of Internet Law* (February 2011): 5.

86. Harold Feld, "Forget The First Amendment, BART Messed with the Phone System. Violated CA and Federal Law," *Wetmachine*, Aug. 22, 2011, http://tales-of-the-sausage-factory.wetmachine.com/forget-the-first-amendment-bart-messed-with-the-phone-system-violated-ca–and-federal-law/ (accessed August 8, 2012).

87. Liptak, "Verizon Blocks Messages."

88. Ibid.

89. Wyatt, "U.S. Court Curbs F.C.C."

90. See, e.g., *Religious Technology Center v. Netcom On-Line Communication Services, Inc.*, 907 F. Supp. 1361 (N.D. Cal. 1995).

91. *SOCAN v. Canadian Association of Internet Providers et al.*, (2002) FCA 166.

92. Kendra Leghart, "The FCC's New Network Semi-Neutrality Order Maintains Inconsistency in the Broadband World," *North Carolina Journal of Law and Technology* 12 (2011): 207.

93. Justin P. Hedge, "Decline of Title II Common–Carrier Regulations in the Wake of Brand X: Long-Run Success for Consumers, Competition and the Broadband Internet Market." *CommLaw Conspectus* 14 (2006): 429.

94. Statement of AT&T Associate General Counsel Jack Zinman et. al., *Framework for Broadband Internet Service*, GN Docket No. 10-127 (December 7, 2010).

95. Technology experts encourage Internet users to use services from multiple providers in order to protect their privacy, as this prevents a single company from holding a complete dossier of one's online activity. See Kate Murphy, "How to Muddy Your Tracks on the Internet," *New York Times*, May 2, 2012, http://www.nytimes.com/2012/05/03/technology/personaltech/how-to-muddy-your-tracks-on-the-internet.html (accessed August 8, 2012).

96. Nate Anderson, "Blind Refs and Baby Kissers: Senators Brawl Over Neutral Net," *Ars Technica*, April 2010, http://arstechnica.com/tech–policy/news/2010/04/senate-brawls-over-network-neutrality.ars (accessed August 8, 2012).

97. Crawford, "An Internet for Everyone."

98. Tim Wu, "Is Net Neutrality Dead?," *Slate*, April 13, 2010, http://www.slate.com/articles/news_and_politics/jurisprudence/2010/04/is_net_neutrality_dead.html (accessed August 8, 2012).

99. Amy Schatz, "Net Neutrality Case Heads to D.C. Circuit Court," *Wall Street Journal*, October 6, 2011, http://blogs.wsj.com/digits/2011/10/06/net-neutrality-case-heads-to-d-c-circuit-court; Alec Dubro, "Court Rules to Hear Net Neutrality Challenge," *Speed Matters*, March 9, 2012, http://www.speedmatters.org/blog/archive/court-rules-to-hear-net-neutrality-challenge/#.T6pBbb-9-88.

100. Harold Feld, "Meanwhile, Back at the D.C. Circuit . . . . The Open Internet Litigation Plods Along," Public Knowledge, March 27, 2012, http://www.publicknowledge.org/blog/meanwhile-back-dc-circuit-open-internet-litig (accessed August 8, 2012).

101. Cecilia Kang, "Court Dismisses Verizon Lawsuit Against FCC Net Neutrality Rules," *Washington Post*, April 4, 2011, http://www.washingtonpost.com/blogs/post-tech/post/court-dismisses-verizon-lawsuit-against-fcc-net-neutrality-rules/2011/04/04/AFfxDNdC_blog.html.

102. Hachman, "FCC Proposes 'Third Way.'"

103. Miller, "FCC's Third Way."

104. Kevin Drawbaugh, "House Rejects FCC's 'Open' Internet Rules," *Reuters*, April 8, 2011, http://www.reuters.com/article/2011/04/08/us-congress-internet-idUSTRE7376UR20110408 (accessed August 13, 2012).

105. Wyatt, "U.S. Court Curbs F.C.C."

106. Benkler, "Ending the Internet's Trench Warfare."

107. Rick Jervis, "Louisiana City Blazes High-Speed Web Trail," *USA Today*, February 5, 2012, http://www.usatoday.com/news/nation/story/2012-02-01/broadband-telecom-lafayette/52920278/1 (accessed August 8, 2012).

108. Bruce Owen, "The Net Neutrality Debate: Twenty Five Years after *United States v. AT&T* and 120 Years after the Act to Regulate Commerce," Stanford Law & Econmonics Olin Working Paper No. 336, 2007, n. 6, http://ssrn.com/abstract=963623 (accessed August 8, 2012); Christian Sandvig, "Network Neutrality Is the New Common Carriage," *Journal of Policy, Regulation and Strategy* 9, no. 2/3 (2007): 136; *Moyers on America: The Net at Risk*, PBS television broadcast, October 18, 2006, http://www.pbs.org/ moyers/moyersonamerica/print/netatrisk_transcript_print.html (accessed August 8, 2012).

109. "At SBC, It's All About 'Scale and Scope'; CEO Edward Whitacre talks about the AT&T Wireless acquisition and how he's moving to keep abreast of cable competitors," *Bloomberg Businessweek Online Extra,* Nov. 7, 2005, at http://www.businessweek.com/magazine/content/05_45/b3958092.htm (August 8, 2012).

110. AT&T, "In-State Connection Fee," http://www.consumer.att.com/instate-connectionfee/ (accessed August 13, 2012).

111. Robin S. Lee and Tim Wu, "Subsidizing Creativity through Network Design: Zero-Pricing and Net Neutrality," *Journal of Economic Perspectives* 23, no.3 (Summer 2009): 61–76.

112. C. Scott Hemphill, "Network Neutrality and the False Promise of Zero-Price Regulation," *Yale Journal on Regulation* 25, no. 2 (July 2008): 135.

Part II: Institutional Perspectives

Chapter 5

Imagining Equilibrium:
The Figure of the Dynamic Market
in the Net Neutrality Debate

Daniel Faltesek

It would not be an understatement to say that the Internet has been revolution-ary. Latent demand has been connected to nascent supply, information made accessible, and social networks expanded. The capacity of the Internet has in-creased dramatically: text has been supplemented with images, sounds, videos, and interactive programs. The Internet has become an engine of commerce in as much as it decreases transaction costs and facilitates search functions, which had previously limited the scope of business. Yet for all the power of the Internet, the end of the first decade of the new millennium has brought the Internet to a crossroads: web-based retailing has matured, Facebook has reached saturation, and Google has redefined privacy so as to increase revenues from increasingly skeptical advertisers.[1] Twenty years ago the prospect of banner advertising on an unlimited Internet stoked dreams of avarice. Today, media distribution compa-nies seek rents for access to rich, but difficult to monetize content. As a re-sponse, Internet users and media production companies have sought to maintain the status quo, the open Internet.

In December 2010, the Federal Communications Commission (FCC) adopt-ed rules for net neutrality. These rules are designed to maintain the status quo against the threat of problematic traffic management techniques that would facil-itate the rent-based business models proposed by distributors. The rules passed the Commission by a vote of three to two, along party lines. The rules them-selves offer an economic argument as to why net neutrality rules would be best for promoting the values of an open Internet. The dissents against the proposed rules make the case not that the open Internet is bad, but that some economic harm would come from the rules and that this harm would damage the open web. At stake in the debate is the future of the Internet—without the rules com-panies could bring changes that could have irreversible negative implications for the Internet and the economy, an idea not contested by the dissenters. Losing the Internet, or at least making access less egalitarian would fundamentally amplify the impact of the digital divide. No longer would access and a good idea be enough to find economic and political opportunity—now the requirement would be access, an idea, and a pool of cash to pay the tolls. The net neutrality debate is a prerequisite for understanding that the politics of the Internet, and the politics of the network are important.[2]

In this chapter, I read the FCC Order on net neutrality and the dissents for their visions of the market. Through this reading, I show how two distinct concepts of the market are operating in the Order and the dissents, and that these conceptions of the market are evidence of a more fundamental issue relating to the terms by which communication policy debates take place.

Rhetoric and Economics

The market is a name given to a complex system of relationships, contexts, and technologies. Inasmuch as a market is a name for dimensions both of the means by which exchange negotiations take place and the political dimensions through which the normative, aesthetic, and moral characteristics of exchange are debated. Markets are what we call the organizational arrangements by which the private public sphere is enacted. The study of these mechanisms and their regulation is not a mechanical task, but an act of rhetorical creation. Nobel Prize winning Economist Ronald Coase emphasized the importance of this in the conclusion of his seminal article on transaction costs:

> But it is, of course, desirable that the choice between different social arrangements for the solution of economic problems should be carried out in broader terms than this and that the total effect of these arrangements in all spheres of life should be taken into account. As Frank H. Knight has so often emphasized, problems of welfare economics must ultimately dissolve into a study of aesthetics and morals.[3]

Even with this striking argument, the turn from the analytic economic question to the normative and political is treated with some trepidation. Economics gains ethos through mathematical precision and scientific thinking. What is especially useful about the Coaseian position is the way in which his larger work lends itself to rhetorical critique. Coase exposed the ways in which the framing of economic problems produced certain kinds of solutions and in the necessity for systems level thinking.

In an idealized world of market logic, the Commissioners would engage in a relatively straightforward debate, find the optimal outcome, and write a rule that would implement that outcome. No rhetoric needed. If various stakeholders did not believe the rule would facilitate the expansion of the common economic good, capital markets would react negatively. In a stark reminder of the culturally semiotic features of rationality, some stocks went up, some went down, and interpreting any chart of stock prices as a form of aggregate political will is foolhardy at best.

Perhaps this vision of a cause and effect relationship between the regulators and industries is already too deeply statist. Adam Thierer proposes that consumer reactions alone would be enough to preclude nefarious agents from damaging the Internet:

> Corporations go out of business if they no longer serve consumers. The gov-
> ernment and its agencies do not. For the former, the combination of technologi-
> cal innovation, consumer education, industry best practices and competitive
> markets all work to blunt the abuses—real or imagined—of broadband
> providers. But only the Constitution and the Bill of Rights restrain the govern-
> ment.[4]

The magical quality of the market appears here in full force. An entire prefabricated system of relationships can be inferred not from the specificity of the market itself, but from the cultural super-story of customer service. For Thierer, there is no real matter for ethical engagement as the systems theoretical capacity of the exchange technology itself overwhelms the political.

The rhetoric of economics is a developing project, and to this point there is not a consensus approach to study economic discourses, the analysis of markets and economic relationships happens on an ad hoc basis.[5] This is not to say that there has not been a discussion of materialism in the past few years. An important step in taking this position is to acknowledge the ongoing academic discussion about the materiality of rhetoric. The focus of many inquiries into the relationship between rhetoric and economics has been into the primacy of challenging oppressive power structures on the basis of their materiality or their associated cultural formations. Dana Cloud takes the position that material change should precede scholarly critique, and Ron Greene argues that affective communication theory is central to good activism, which might redress the inequalities.[6] This is an interesting and productive debate, although it does not provide us with a theoretical approach for reading forms of economic argumentation. In this sense, the materialism debate tells us about the economics of rhetoric, rather than the rhetoric of economics.

Deidre McCloskey has provided the discipline with several important books, the earlier *Rhetoric of Economics*, and the later *Bourgeois Virtues* are of particular note. In *The Rhetoric of Economics*, McCloskey argues that the discipline of economics lost its way when it traded empirical significance and persuasion, or scientific significance and abstract modeling.[7] McCloskey's argument revolves around the idea that economics is about persuasion, and that the mathematical tools that the computer revolution has given economics have eclipsed their usefulness. In her newer works, McCloskey has sought to revive the values of classical economic thinkers like Adam Smith, through an examination of the other, often ignored values of the bourgeoisie.[8] These values included more than prudence. They included self-love and benevolence among others. What weakens this account is that her diagnosis of the creeping power of prudence is on point—prudence hollows out the other virtues, and the hope that a more literate version of capitalism might strike a blow against unadulterated greed is less than brimming.

In communication studies, the approach to the rhetoric of economics turns on the discursive features of networks, more than on the fact that economics relies on persuasion. For G. Thomas Goodnight and Sandy Green, economic transactions appear as the result of network effects.[9] Bubbles and other economic maladies are the result of communicative issues, rather than transcendental economic ideas. The version of economic criticism extended by Goodnight and Green as a form of world analysis comes from a union of McCloskey's economic criticism, new institutional theory, and the theory of argumentative worlds. In a recent article, David Hingstman and Tom Goodnight historicize the Hayek-Keynes newspaper columns to reveal that in their proper context, their positions are far more nuanced and careful than political uses of their writings.[9] What Hingstman and Goodnight do so effectively is to highlight the figures used to argue about systems, without proposing a systems theory of their own.

Before turning toward the inflection of the market I would be remiss to leave the work of Michael Calvin McGee out of this analysis. Some scholars try to understand the market as an ideograph—a concept with an Althusserian lineage, referring to a term evacuated of material meaning in favor of a positive affective position.[10] In short, an ideograph is a term that means little, is not a noun, and is overwhelmingly emotionally positive. There are very few true ideographs—freedom, liberty, equality, and justice would all be fine candidates for this theoretical position. Unfortunately, critics who use the ideograph to describe terms that are hotly contested in the public sphere, or terms that are emotionally painful have hollowed out the idea of the ideograph. The concept of the ideograph also tends to speak to a coherent public, which can be interpolated toward a single position. McGee in his turn toward postmodernism argued against the idea of a unified public that might be evenly connected to a single term or idea. The structuralist bend of the ideograph is difficult for contemporary scholars to deal with—it simply does not fit with the concept of agency that accompanied post–structuralism.

What is perhaps most problematic with the move to read the market in this case as an ideograph is that the market functions as something of a pronoun for infrastructure investment. There is nothing nebulous about this concept, and surely telecommunication development practices are not enormously stirring to much of the public. Reading the market as an ideograph would lose the variety and the contestation inherent within it. If the ideograph can now be used to describe a term actively contested in public debate, the structuralist and affective power of the term has waned to the point that it no longer performs necessary work.

While these traditional rhetorical approaches are surely useful, the case of the FCC presents a few unique challenges. Notice and comment for the production of administrative regulations tends to be highly technical. The Commissioners themselves are appointed in such a way as to create lags between presidential administrations, requiring argumentation and compromise. Most importantly, the FCC is a decorous and friendly organization. Boltanski and Thevenot's work in *On Justification* is particularly helpful in this regard. In any given argumentative world there are values, which are agreed upon, and tests assigned to determine if the justifications given for a particular action are legitimate.[11] By focusing on the creation of relevant tests for values in argumentative spheres, Boltanski and Thevenot offer a useful vocabulary for reading the rhetorical dimensions of deliberations about economic problems. For example in Civil Court, the appropriate tests involve close readings of the law and the presentation of properly handled evidence. In scientific worlds, tests involve experiments, and evidence is measured with ordinal numbers. This presents a challenge for reading the argumentative world in which net neutrality is regulated. It is a civic realm; the Commissioners are public servants in a legal institution. They are conflicted because they are compelled to consider both relevant business tests of values and public tests of values. The FCC and regulatory negotiations are wedged between worlds, but should be understood to be an institution of the public sphere, a civic world. Boltanski and Thevenot argue that when values are in conflict, there is a common move to turn toward the social sciences to find some stability, to select the appropriate test for any given argumentative world. The compromises made in the civic world are ultimately underwritten by the force of their legitimation. In this sense, the constituents of parliamentary politics judge the way in which the FCC parses matters related to the market, the state, and the public.

A Pragmatic Approach to
the Rhetoric of the Market

Beyond the idea of the market in the abstract sense, there are cultural ways of figuring the market. A Google image search for Wall Street reveals images of the temple like stock exchange building, a metallic bull, and the street sign for the market itself. In everyday life the market no longer refers to a local grocery store, but a capital market. The market is important, mysterious, and serious. It should be a surprise then that one of most important theorists of fundamental analysis saw the market as less than rational and serious.

Benjamin Graham, the so-called Dean of Wall Street, author of many important early academic works on the Stock Market, and mentor of Warren Buffett, described the seductive appeal of the market and the irrationality that characterized exchange through his allegory of Mr. Market.[12] Mr. Market would approach every day frenzied, offering prices both reasonable and unreasonable for stocks. The prices were not necessarily rational or irrational, they were just prices. The key for a fundamentally sound investor is to pass by Mr. Market, to make sound evaluations of the businesses underlying the stocks and to select their purchases on that materialist basis. This allegory is the narrative version of the basis of fundamental analysis. Fundamental analysis is useful for small investors looking for dividends, but is largely regarded as old-fashioned in the stock market today. Instead, nondiscursive algorithmic devices which treat Mr. Market as something to be centrifuged are quite popular, although largely inaccessible to all but the largest investors.

Technical analysis, and the vision of the market inherent in it, depends on taking Mr. Market at his word: the underlying assets are irrelevant, only the irrational shouts of that character matter. In this sense one can make a great deal of money simply by learning his whims.[13] Analysis in this sense leads directly to the algorithmic and flash-trading systems popularized after the NYSE allowed the direct interface of electronic systems into the market. The turn back toward idealism is comforting, but the image of the market as being a source of collective intelligence is an oxymoron. The sound thinking and basic analytic skills inherent in the fundamental analysis of the last era have been given up in exchange for the guaranteed profits to be made through the pure, fast price plays. This Mr. Market character eclipses the physical market. Finding ways either to predict his decisions or even to manipulate him become more important than finding value.

The synecdoche which sees the NYSE as the market writ large is quite widespread. Consider the daily news coverage on cable television. The current activity of stocks is taken as information about what the market thinks of a given policy proposition or current event. The validity of this connection is dubious, but the idea that we have some way to get a concrete lever, an Archimedean point to move the market world through the stock price itself is comforting. Here the formulation of the stock market as a part representing the whole of market relations can flow backward—the idea of the market as a flowing space infects the idea of the market writ large. Many markets are slow moving. Consider the 1980s commodity drama of the pork belly. Pork bellies are the parts of pigs that are cut into rashers of bacon. The reason why pork bellies are traded is that when frozen they can be kept for long periods of time with little quality lost, and since bacon is a relatively valuable foodstuff, frozen bellies can be held until they are needed. Actually moving the pork bellies requires refrigerated trucks that can haul thousands of pounds of pork to a processing facility. If we think of this in a vertically integrated sense, the entire process of producing bacon—from first oink to the last sizzle takes many months if not years to complete. The image of the rapidly moving stock market changes the idea of the market itself.

Mr. Market is a useful metaphor because it engages the term as it is actually used. The market is often treated as an anthropomorphic figure: the market wants things, it fears things, and it definitely has an opinion. The history of Mr. Market is telling—long before the modern stock market was abuzz with electronic trading and derivatives, the most popular advice for traders was to treat the market as a person with problems.

What Is Net Neutrality?

The Internet as we know it has been almost completely neutral: when you input a web address into your browser, the system of routers and cables brought you the web page at the maximum possible speed. In the 1990s, this was relatively slow, as most Internet connections were made over telephone wires that were riddled with static. The new millennium brought a new wave of Internet connection technologies, most importantly the ubiquity of broadband. The penetration of broadband has been rapid—people wanted good, fast Internet.

To put this in some context, one of the first viral videos was entitled "All Your Base Are Belong to Us."[14] The video consisted of a series of crudely manipulated images and pranks designed to make it appear as if the phrase "all your base are belong to us" had proliferated widely across the United States and the world. The soundtrack for the video was a sandstorm techno–house song made from sampled sounds from the 1987 video game *Zero Wing*. This is an important early video as due to the media attention that it received, it was unlike anything users had seen before. It was a legitimately viral video, which although only three minutes in length, took just as long to load. Compare this with a viral video today: the load time is mere seconds, and the resolution is much higher. This is the power of net neutrality – we have an expectation that when we call for a file on the Internet it will arrive with all due speed.

Net neutrality is the status quo. This means that firms that provide Internet service allow traffic to cross their networks without discrimination. Firms doing business on the web expect to deliver data to customers through the Internet on this basis. The dispute about net neutrality comes at the level of the FCC rules supporting net neutrality. For reasons related to the market; the status quo arraignment is painted as damaging companies. Just as the rules are supposed to be damaging, the end outcome of net neutrality, a free and open Internet, is almost universally supported. This duality is why the case of net neutrality can tell us something important about the idea of the market—because it is the idea of the market, not the policy outcome or the transactions, that is at the heart of the policy's opposition.

The Rule and Support

The conception of the market that is most easily seen in the FCC's majority opinion is tied to the relative profitability of activities and the capacity for companies to access those profits. The market is understood as the willingness of consumers to purchase a good or service. VoIP (Voice over Internet Protocol) provides an example for the Commission both of a market and of an edge provider. Markets are low friction and expansive in the conception of the Order—providers of services who are not a part of the core of capital are understood to have an equal right to access customers as those in the center. The equality of edge access has been a central element in the digital economy. The FCC describes the market chilling effect of charging edge providers in terms of entrepreneurial endeavor:

> Fees for access or prioritization to end-users could reduce the potential profit that an edge provider would expect to earn from developing new offerings, and thereby reduce edge providers' incentives to invest and innovate. In the rapidly innovating edge sector, moreover, many new entrants are new or small "garage entrepreneurs," not large and established firms. These emerging providers are particularly sensitive to barriers to innovation and entry, and may have difficulty obtaining financing if their offerings are subject to being blocked or disadvantaged by one or more of the major broadband providers.[15]

Markets are a way for "garage entrepreneurs" to find customers. Both the consumer on the far end and the entrepreneur are central to this vision—the broadband company is not centered as an element of the market. This vision of the market would be the classic conception of "dumb pipes," where the broadband provider is akin to a postal service. Data flows between economic actors, the pipes that allow that data to flow are not a part of the economy.

The FCC uses the future tense to integrate the risks of a non-open Internet through their market logic. In answering a response that consumers would simply switch service providers, the FCC predicts that consumers are too smart to switch; theorizing that if the consumers perceive downstream throttling, they would also imagine this happening in the server center, upstream. If the home Internet connection is being slowed, the connection between companies will surely be slowed as well. Possible small business people are not going to climb a mountain to fetch a pail of water.

The discourse used in the Order speaks to incentives and counter incentives through a discussion of a clearly physical thing—the Internet. The FCC's task is to produce the conditions that would allow for competition between firms in many places. The conclusion of the persuasive element of the Order articulates the positions both for and against net neutrality. The FCC makes the risks involved in the non-open Internet clear:

> If the next revolutionary technology or business is not developed because broadband provider practices chill entry and innovation by edge providers, the missed opportunity may be significant, and lost innovation, investment, and competition may be impossible to restore after the fact. Moreover, because of the Internet's role as a general purpose technology, erosion of Internet openness threatens to harm innovation, investment in the core and at the edge of the network, and competition in many sectors, with a disproportionate effect on small, entering, and non-commercial edge providers that drive much of the innovation on the Internet. Although harmful practices are not certain to become widespread, there are powerful reasons for immediate concern, as broadband providers have interfered with the open Internet in the past and have incentives and an increasing ability to do so in the future.[16]

In this section, the Internet is a "general purpose technology," where innovation is driven from the edges, rather than the center. The case for net neutrality in this conclusion is nothing less than the case for democracy itself. Diversity of information leads to better outcomes in health, education, and the environment. This passage could not be written in the market vernacular any more than it is: there are revolutionary technologies and investment chilling effects, as well as market competition.

The remainder of the on balance section is dedicated to answering common objections. Claims that net neutrality is the status quo and would not be expensive to implement are well explicated. Further, the FCC argues that the market for Internet services is already in flux, both because the market is already the subject of potential regulation, and because the relative stability in the market is a product of the status quo of net neutrality itself. The case for net neutrality in the Order is relatively straightforward: the damage caused by traffic discrimination on the Internet would be vast, expensive, and irreparable.

Commissioner Baker's dissent is curious in that she is also entirely committed to the open Internet in its current configuration. For Baker, the reason not to promulgate the rules comes from the damage to the market. The image of the market as presented in this dissent hinges on footnote six, where three source citations are provided to demonstrate that the proposed net neutrality rule would cause substantial economic harm.[17] The first is a popular press account about a statement from a private equity researcher claiming that net neutrality would harm investment. The second is a very difficult to find statement from Bank of America that net neutrality would be bad for investment.[18] The third and final citation is a statement from the investment analyst referenced in the first citation. The analyst provides a form of heuristic expertise, since markets are a complex system of relationships. He is in a position to tell us about how that network will react to the rules, although specifics, quotes, data, engineering, and geographic information do not appear.

Presumption works in a decidedly different way for Commissioner Clyburn. Clyburn's concurrence is interesting in that no figuration of the market appears in the text. Clyburn flips the presumption that appears in Baker's dissent by arguing that the Internet is open now and that changes to current network management practices should be justified. The impact of a closing of the Internet as we know it would have incredible implications for Clyburn, which would be immediate and severe for those affected.

There are two ways to read these accounts: the market is scared of everything, or the analysis and the dissent are an attempt at a covert defense of a non-open Internet. The analyst simply states that investment will decline. The popular press report of the analyst's statement provides daily stock quotes as evidence of the statement's veracity. What is missing from the article is the relative absurdity of this form of argument. Stock prices are not a referendum and worse, not all ISP stocks went down on the day the regulation was introduced. Does this suggest that Time Warner Cable owners voted for the FCC rules while Cablevision owners voted against it?[19]

Less optimistic than an authority driven warrant, the lagging idea that the future of the web is not open could also be at stake in both Baker's dissent and in the press reports. Baker goes out of her way to argue that the Internet is not a system of "dumb pipes," and that network management is really a "marvel," which protects from threats "foreign and domestic."[20] This terminology inserts the web operator into the channel as a friend or even a hero, normalizing the idea that the closed Internet is actually beneficial. Nowhere in these reports is there mention of the supposed new technologies that would depend on highly flexible business models, or what those models would look like. If they resemble anything in the mobile telephony industry, these models will appear as a series of attempts to leverage the network, the device, or the software to extract rents from other companies: a decidedly suboptimal outcome.

Another set of economic arguments occur in footnote 13, and focus on the reasons why net neutrality may be unnecessary. The idea that consumers are quite happy with their service is interesting, but somewhat unfulfilling since it does not speak to possible business model development and the opinions of those users if the status quo were to change. Further, the concept that service providers would behave themselves because of consumer choice is attractive, as long as upstream net neutrality is preserved. It simply does not matter how innovative a downstream service provider might be if they cannot get access to high capacity fiber optic lines.

The lack of specificity becomes the heart of an agenda and an argument for a presumption against action, as the risk of action might upset the market: "Did the Commission kill the future of the Internet today? Of course not. But, in this dynamic industry, the majority also has no rational means by which to estimate the real damage it does to the development of future business models, network management practices, and core networks."[21] Even within this quote, the weakness of the inference comes through: the Internet industry is dynamic, but somehow can be damaged by the mere suggestion of the political or the normative. The ambiguous future is leveraged in this argument as a weight against any possibility of change. Just as there is no rational means for evaluating the damage caused by net neutrality, there is no rational basis for evaluating the damage that could be caused by allowing a major carrier or carriers to disrupt the web as we know it.

Commissioner McDowell's dissent is similar to Commissioner Baker's, with an important difference. Where Baker claims that there has never been misconduct (and thus no need for regulation), McDowell contends that there has been misconduct but that existing law universally resolved these matters in favor of the end user. Instead of seeing the future of the Internet as an unlimited well of profitability, McDowell envisions a future world where litigation, rather than regulation would preserve the open web. The relative risks to the market coming from litigation versus regulation are not addressed. Anti-trust law acts as the circuit breaker. If a conglomerate were to use their monopoly advantage on system access they would be roundly defeated in court on those grounds. Much like Baker, McDowell contends that there would be substantial economic harm in mandating network neutrality. McDowell derives his warrant for the claim to economic harm from the testimony of a rural Internet service provider, which has a certain empirical weight that the use of popular press articles cannot reach. The issue with the use of the testimony is that the evidence does not speak to the technical capacity of the system, but to the operator's fear that he might not find financing because of the market reaction. The logic of citation is circular—we know what the market wants so we know what the market wants.

The Market World

The market-based reasoning for net neutrality depends on the conception of the market as a technology that connects supply and demand. Arguing in this world of the market involves making claims about profit and loss, and the structure of the network. The market-based reasoning against net neutrality involves making claims as to the perception of the market. Arguers would assert their predictions for the reactions of unnamed investors; upsetting this invisible audience is to be avoided at all costs. The struggle is between those who conceive of the market as a technology for allocating and facilitating transactions and those who conceive of the market as an affective nexus. Is the market a system to be adjusted or a feeling that must be cultivated? What is particularly fascinating about the market case against net neutrality is that those involved in this kind of argument are also those who would accede to the technical analysis of investments.

If we consider the dispute from the perspective of a figural rhetoric, the issue at stake seems to be if the market should be taken as the figure or the background. In the persuasive element of the Order, those involved in transaction are the point of emphasis, the market appears in the background. Taking the other position would place the market in the sharpest relief, with the actors being only a side note. For arguers looking to join this debate, the difference between the two conceptions of the market is critical—one could argue from the perspective that the market facilitates transactions and not engage the warranting pattern of their interlocutor. Conversely, the arguer against net neutrality would be equally frustrated as their interlocutor simply cannot accept the idea that market psychology matters more than the transaction itself, and that arguments about that psychology would be nonfalsifiable—the market has spoken.

In the context of the FCC, the evidence and values are agreed upon. What is good for business opportunity and good for access to high quality Internet services should be implemented. In this sense the values are also not in dispute. What we find in the Order and the dissents is precisely what Coase found fifty years ago—an aesthetic problem. What does a market look like? What does a good market look like? And the most problematic formulation—what does a market feel like? This is a question about the possibility of using tests from the world of the market in a civic world. In a market world, the test is the negotiation of a profitable contract. In the civic world, the test is a vote promoting the public good. What is so interesting is the way in which the dissents to the rule and popular press opposition to the regulations talk of the reaction of the market without the quantitative backing employed to check the relativism between the arguers.

Mr. Market and Net Neutrality

The discourse of the Report and Order on Net Neutrality and the dissents from that Order are part of an argumentative world which is conflicted not because of a clear empirical question about investment, but an aesthetic and moral debate. Graham's allegory of Mr. Market rings true 80 years later. The vision of the market as a person with a psyche and all the entailments there too has a strong cultural purchase. If holding oneself at a reflective distance from Mr. Market were easy, Warren Buffet would be one among many successful value investors. The idea of the market as a character is far easier to take than the market being a macroeconomic network of relationships and technologies from which they are almost categorically excluded. Mr. Market is far easier to deal with than an absurd world of market relationships. The very serious character of the market approaches with great regularity, offering prices both reasonable and ridiculous. Mr. Market would be entirely willing to build a national broadband network that would provide cheap Internet service to minority communities one minute, and be so worried that he might not be able to squeeze every penny out of the network that he would choose to go out of business the next. The idea of the market in the context of the Order is more than that which can be read through an optic of figure-ground or core-periphery: the market almost always morphs into Mr. Market. Rhetoric falls into stasis if narratives about this character are treated as scientific data.

The other side of technical analysis that privileges the market is fundamental analysis that focuses on the reality of the businesses themselves. Moving toward concrete stories would offer arguers a way to talk about the market without being caught up in the whims of Mr. Market. The alternative is to continue talking with Mr. Market—a conversation that could go nowhere for decades.[22] Graham's advice is not to shut out Mr. Market, but to continue investing in a rigorous way—you can listen to and even talk with Mr. Market, but you must always be aware of what you are really talking to. This should be the answer for arguers as well, we should not avoid the discussion of the market, but we should be clear to keep the material world at the center of our cultural articulations.[23] Viewing the market as an anthropomorphic character offers one way of resolving the aesthetic and moral problems in economics by sublimating them with a narrative. As it invites a circular form of reasoning, the anthropomorphic market can be satisfying, but narcotizing. Within the cultural context of the market as a character, there is no presentation of evidence, and no test that can be deployed to engage in civic deliberation about economic policy.

This could easily be taken as a dismal conclusion—the structure of the civic world cannot effectively deal with markets—losing the moral and aesthetic dimensions of economic judgment. The market world cannot be effectively tested if a circular narrative frames the world. The Internet is sometimes a creation of industrial agglomeration. Sometimes, the Internet is a sublime marvel. It is this rupture that shows possibility—if the anthropomorphic Mr. Market is a gravity well for all economic arguments, spaces for alternative modes of legitimation open up. The task for economic criticism in rhetoric is to challenge the sophisticated ways in which Mr. Market appears in public discourse, and to offer a meta-critique of the work of that narrative for public consumption, as arguing with a fictional character is difficult at best.

Notes

1. The SEC filings for Facebook and Amazon are quite revealing in this respect. The retail units of Amazon are not as lucrative as they had been, and Facebook will likely reach $4 billion of revenue, but not expand much further.

2. There are attempts by an industry group the "Internet Innovation Alliance" to claim that net neutrality doesn't resolve the digital divide. The rationale for the argument is that net neutrality would impede education in minority communities. The press release/blog is available here: http://internetinnovation.org/blog/entry/net-neutrality-and-the-digital-divide1/. The underlying evidence for claims of minority groups opposing net neutrality is hotly contested, with groups ties to AT&T being a major reason for opposition. Adam Polaski, "Examining Other Minority Group's Opposition to Net Neutrality, Support of AT&T Merger," *The Bilerco Project* (June 12, 2011). http://www.bilerico.com/2011/06/examining_other_minority_groups_opposition_to_net.php. This was further documented when six board members of GLADD were forced to resign over their actions on behalf of AT&T: Jennifer Martinez, "Six GLADD Board Members Resign Amid AT&T Flap," *Politico* (June 22, 2011) http://www.politico.com/news/stories/0611/57515.html.

3. Ronald Coase, "The Problem of Social Cost." *Journal of Law and Economics* 3, no. 1 (1960): 1–44.

4. Adam Thierer, "Net Neutrality and the First Amendment," *The Technology Liberation Front* (August 8, 2010). http://techliberation.com/2010/08/08/net-neutrality-the-first-amendment/.

5. The number of articles that speak to these issues is very small. There have been a few special issues that address economic issues in *Popular Communication, Journal of Communication Inquiry*, and *Communication Currents*. Although there are many interesting articles in these volumes, studies of media industries and the rhetoric of economics should be thought of as different. There are two articles in recent NCA journals that would speak to this idea: G. Thomas Goodnight and Sandy Green, "Rhetoric, Risk, and Markets: The Dot-Com Bubble," *Quarterly Journal of Speech* 96, no. 2 (2010): 115–140. And, Joshua Hanan, "Home Is Where the Capital Is: The Culture of Real Estate in an Era of Control Societies," *Communication and Critical/Cultural Studies* 7 (2010): 176–201.

6. Ronald Greene "Another Materialist Rhetoric." *Critical Studies in Media Communication* 15 (1) (1998): 21–40. And the response, Dana Cloud, Steve Macek, and

James Arnt Aune, "'The Limbo of Ethical Simulacra' a Reply to Ron Greene." *Philosophy and Rhetoric* 39 (1): (2006) 72–86.

7. Dierdre McCloskey, *The Rhetoric of Economics* (Chicago: University of Chicago Press, 1994).

8. Dierdre McCloskey, *The Bourgeois Virtues* (Chicago: University of Chicago Press, 2006).

9. David Hingstman and G. Thomas Goodnight, "From the Great Depression to the Great Recession," *POROI* 7 (1).

10. Michael Calvin. McGee, "The 'Ideograph' a Link between Rhetoric and Ideology." *Quarterly Journal of Speech* 66 (1) (1980): 1–16.

11. Luc Boltanski and Laurent Thevenot, *On Justification*, trans. Catherine Porter, (Princeton, N.J.: Princeton University Press, 2006).

12. Benjamin Graham and Jason Zweig. *The Intelligent Investor*. Revised Edition. (New York: Collins Business, 2003).

13. Technical analysis is the stock and trade of cable business news. I chose to use Mr. Market since in its original context it would have been a masculine character.

14. Chris Taylor, "All Your Base Are Belong to Us." *Time*, February 25, 2001. http://www.time.com/time/magazine/article/0,9171,100525,00.html. For the video itself see: http://www.youtube.com/watch?v=qItugh-fFgg

15. Federal Communications Commission, "Report and Order in the Matter of Preserving the Open Internet" (GN Docket No 09-191), 2010: 16.

16. Ibid., 23.

17. The regulatory uncertainty arguments have been debunked in traditional macroeconomics as well. I am particularly interested in this citation and the methodology as Mischel uses the concrete world to answer the abstract economic world. Lawrence Mischel, "Regulatory Uncertainty: A Phony Explanation for Our Jobs Problem," *Economic Policy Institute Report*, (September 27, 2011). http://www.epi.org/publication/regulatory-uncertainty-phony-explanation/.

18. The information for this citation is incomplete in the order, searching for it points back toward the order itself.

19. This joke is confirmed with a quick look up of the stock prices for December 21. This was actually a very good day for stocks.

20. FCC, 187.

21. Ibid., 180.

22. See footnote 20. This is the rhetorical take taken by Mischel, Krugman, and others who are involved in economic criticism.

23. This article could be taken as a displacement of the materiality debate in that the description of material conditions offers a way to challenge a modernist fantasy of the personified market.

Chapter 6

Axiology and the FCC: Regulation as Ideological Process

Benjamin Cline

On December 21, 2010, the Federal Communications Commission (FCC) released its new rules regarding network neutrality, adding fresh fuel to an ideological fire over Internet regulation. Early in the history of broadband, the FCC began a tradition of policing Internet Service Providers (ISPs) with regard to access.[1] The process became seriously ideologized when discussions about the role of government in the protection of the Internet were brought into public debate with the House of Representatives' passage of the Internet Freedom Preservation Act.[2] At that point, the proliferation of broadband and related technologies resulted in a concern that network neutrality, the tradition of equal access by all content and equipment to the Internet, might be endangered without legal protection and government oversight of ISPs. Argument regarding that bill seemed to divide the debate along traditional political lines with conservative members claiming that further regulation is unnecessary and that free markets would continue to produce a free Internet. On the other hand, more liberal members of the House argued for the necessity of regulation to preserve the Internet as an open medium.

The Internet Freedom Preservation Act never became law. However, its directive that the FCC establish a clear broadband policy provided an impetus for regulation, one that was exacerbated by complaints that some network providers were throttling certain content. These complaints became evident when it was sufficiently proven that Comcast had indeed limited access for peer-to-peer file sharing on their network.[3] The FCC sanctioned Comcast with the intent of "preserving the open character of the Internet," according to then Chairman of the FCC Kevin J. Martin. Martin elaborated that, "[w]e are saying that network operators can't block people from getting access to any content and any applications."[4]

The ruling did not last long, however. The D.C. Circuit Court of Appeals soon ruled that under their current mandate, the FCC did not have the authority to censure Comcast.[5] Soon after, the FCC issued a press release reaffirming their commitment to promoting and protecting an open Internet. The Commission further commented that despite ruling in favor of Comcast, "the Court in no way disagreed with the importance of preserving a free and open Internet; nor did it close the door to other methods for achieving this important end."[6]

At this time, the FCC began to pursue a means to create a legal basis for FCC policing of network neutrality. The FCC described this as "a public process to determine whether and what actions might be necessary to preserve the characteristics that have allowed the Internet to grow into an indispensable platform supporting our nation's economy and civic life, and to foster continued investment in the physical networks that enable the Internet."[7] This public process and the resultant deliberations were instrumental for the FCC in creating new protections for the Internet regarding openness and regulating the industries which provide DSL and cable Internet services.

Martin's successor as Chairman of the FCC, Julius Genachowski, called the Commission's net neutrality rules "a strong sensible non-ideological framework that protects Internet freedom."[8] Yet the ideological arguments that ensued betray that neutral stance. Certainly, attacks on the FCC's Order emanated from both major political parties albeit for very different reasons. Conservatives worried that further government regulation would harm economic growth. They attacked the plan, arguing that it puts unfair limits on broadband providers and restricts their ability to offer a range of products to their consumers. Republican FCC Commissioner Robert McDowell argued that the FCC had become "vigilantes," and that this act of "regulatory hubris" spelled the "darkest days in recent FCC history."[9]

Taking heed to McDowell's criticisms, conservatives immediately went to work creating legislation to block the FCC's rules. House Energy and Commerce Committee leaders Fred Upton (R–MI), Greg Walden (R–OR), and Lee Terry (R–NE) issued a press release stating: "We Share Chairman Genachowski's goal to ensure the Internet remains open, which is exactly why we oppose the FCC's decision to impose unprecedented government regulations on a currently thriving and open Internet. Over the last several months, the FCC has failed to provide a compelling justification for its power grab."[10] Worried about what they saw as a government crackdown on private industry, House Republicans immediately presented legislation to counter that crackdown.[11] While the bill never made it through the Democratically-controlled Senate, HR 37 nonetheless provided an ideological censure from those opposed to legal regulations.

The pro-network neutrality factions were no less upset with the FCC's policy. Online technology journal *Ars Technica* summed up such criticisms arguing that the FCCs rules catered to telecommunications firms such as AT&T, particularly in light of the policy's lack of neutrality protections for wireless services.[12] Thus, despite Genachowski's claims to the contrary, the ideologically informed opposition from divergent parties suggests that the FCC's net neutrality rules are in fact not absent an ideological framework.

It is therefore incumbent upon the scholarly community to interrogate the ideology embedded in these new rules. Certainly, those with a political advantage to their interrogation have already done so on both sides of the debate, but these obvious advantages render their interpretations suspect and their critiques biased. This chapter examines the rules themselves as a rhetorical artifact which provides a snapshot of an ideological process at a particular point in time. In order to accomplish this, I explain the development of ideology as a communication process and then examine the FCC's net neutrality rules as a rhetorical act within that process.

The FCC's Rules as Artifactual Evidence in Ideological Communication Process

This chapter argues that the FCC rules function within this process of ideology construction. This process is not just an attempt to sway the ideological focus of certain auditors who read the rules, but is instead a means of attempting to construct a social ideology. The attempt not only institutes a means of understanding what is legal, but indeed a means of understanding what is right.

In order to really understand what scholars mean by ideological construction, here it is important to understand ideology as a communication process. Interrogating the ideology of rhetorical artifacts has been a hallmark of interpretive methodologies in the study of communication. Ideology itself, however, has come to mean a number of different things depending on the theoretical apparatus utilized. Cloud and Gunn recently traced one history of ideological study in communication through roots in Marxist, skeptical, materialist, and immanentist discourse.[13] Certainly, these have been common ideological methodologies of inquiry and can provide powerful insight into the latent meaning of any rhetorical artifact. In the current case, however, I am not attempting to conceive a stagnant or set ideology imposed by some dominant master class intent on maintaining the means of production. Rather, this chapter looks at the FCC's Order using a conception of ideology as process.[14]

The best way to begin understanding how ideology can be seen as a communication process is to understand that scholars in the rhetoric of social intervention do not see ideology as a stagnant worldview. Rather, ideology is a multidimensional fluctuating organic worldview wherein we have the possibility not only of processing information, but of incorporating that information in such a way that the entire ideology remains stable and can undergo constant change in relation to the barrage of stimuli it encounters. It is a system whereby an introduction to any of its parts changes the whole, and yet within that change there is stability. It is a "comprehensive complex name that we create out of symbols."[15] The FCC's 2010 Order was more than just a means of regulating the actions of ISPs; it was an intervention into worldviews and an alteration of the way that the

Commission hoped that their audience would begin to perceive the reality of the Internet.

Brown (who did most of the early work in developing the concept of ideology as a process of communication) explained that argument can be understood using the metonym, the whole in the parts.[16] To see the whole in each part it is necessary to adopt a slightly different view of knowledge itself. Instead of viewing knowledge as simply the accumulation of various "facts," knowledge must be "considered to be making sense both (1) as meaning for and (2) as experience of the world."[17] Therefore the FCC's Order couldn't simply be a small change from de facto tradition to de jure regulation. There would be inevitable ripple effects throughout the audience's ideology. Whenever a change occurs anywhere in one's ideology, the change becomes present throughout the entire ideological system. The input of new information such as a rhetorical act in one area absolutely affects all areas of the worldview, as well as the process whereby ideologizing continues to occur.

The FCC's Order, then, is not simply a means of regulating the Internet. The Order becomes something infinitely more, and something that goes on to the very core of the auditor's being. We could easily have seen that there would be repercussions, especially in those whose ideology is at some core level hostile to government intervention. As Stoner notes, studying ideology as a communication process creates "a systematic analysis that would allow a participant in or observer of a social situation to predict rhetorical behaviors of those involved."[18] While the ideology works itself out as a process, the new information and new knowledge will affect each other in predictable ways. As the ideology and new information interact, the latter will also affect the means by which further information is processed.

When seen from this perspective, creating a rhetorical intervention by means of the net neutrality rules is a means of creating ideology on a social level. Within the context of this ideology, rhetorical acts such as this one do not simply set out to change the attitudes or behaviors of a particular individual auditor. Rather, they are meant to change the ideologies of an entire society; they are rhetorical acts of social intervention.[19]

Brown claimed that this process was central to the creation of humans' worldview due to our propensity toward symbol use. According to Brown, "ideology is grounded in the abstracting process of *all* symbol-making."[20] There are three aspects of necessary abstraction that force ideologies to come into being: "(1) by our very senses, (2) by our reification of some 'kinds' and not others, and (3) by the tacitly agreed upon *rules* for constituting 'kinds.'"[21] Brown goes on to explain each of these processes in detail. The basic concept that Brown attempts to deliver in this portion of his argument is that human abstraction leads to generalization. This generalization is necessary because the human senses cannot possibly take in all the data of the world around them. Even what they can collect is divided into arbitrary rhetorically and socially constructed categories within the mind. Those categories themselves are dictated by a previously constructed framework, which in turn selects which categories can even exist. The FCC's net neutrality rules then, posit an entirely new way of categorizing existence. They argue for a view of government and the Internet different from what was currently in existence. There may have been some inclination that putting into practice regulations that were already being enacted by tradition was merely rubber stamping an existing reality, yet the Order did something more: it reified a particular understanding of the Internet. It assumed rules for constituting one kind of Internet as a public good and denying the legitimacy of an Internet constituted by the needs of corporations. It allowed for the government to constitute the "kinds" of data that are being produced, but reduced the abilities of business people to constitute those "kinds."

This abstracting and categorizing continues, according to Brown, until it reaches "the abstracted dimension of ultimacy, the carrying to its nth degree the principle of perfection available through language symbols."[22] This final dimension of ultimacy is ideology: "that category of experience on which one is willing to bet the meaning of one's life."[23] Different forms of rhetorical intervention constantly take place that either affirm or alter the ideology. We can see that even after the rules were developed, multiple rhetorical interventions began to take place. New legislation was proposed and all sides brought their cases before the media.

When ideology is seen as a communication process, a rhetor can work in one of three areas in order to effect a change in ideology. These are the three sub-cycles of social intervention: "the needs sub-cycle, the power sub-cycle and the input switching sub-cycle."[24] The "input–switching sub-cycle" is also commonly referred to as the "attention sub-cycle,"[25] because it shifts the attention of the receiver from one data organizing framework to another.

The FCC's net neutrality Order constitutes a rhetorical intervention in the attention, or input switching sub cycle. The intent of the Order is a means of socially persuading the audience to accept some data and patently reject other data.

The FCC Order developed because of a deviance amplifying state that came into existence due to previous rhetorical interventions on the part of two main parties: the legislators who assumed the FCC had legal authority to regulate the Internet,[26] and Comcast,[27] whose actions while perhaps legal[28] were nonetheless ethically suspect, especially with regard to their lack of transparency.

The FCC's rhetorical intervention was an attempt to compensate for a deviance amplifying cycle that was caused by two simultaneous trends. The first were a series of court cases increasingly restricting the FCC's ability to regulate ISPs. Second, industry actors developed practices of discriminating users' access for the ISP's benefit.

In order to stop a self-destructive cycle, a rhetor may intervene to "shift" the view of a person or group from one source of data to another. Before this can be fully accomplished, three prerequisites must be in place: "(1) at least two patterns or interpretive 'templates' [must] always be potentially involved in our sizing up a situation; (2) each pattern itself [must] be capable of rendering the situation coherent; and (3) *movement* from one to another—with a consequent restructuring of the situation—[must] be necessary before a 'switch will have occurred."[29] With all of these factors in place, a rhetor can attempt to shift "the attention of an audience from one specific issue or belief to ideas that subsume the original issue."[30] This is precisely the function of the FCC's net neutrality Order.

According to Brown, one can change between varying modes of epistemology, axiology and ontology.[31] One does this through "conceived-anomaly-masking and -anomaly-featuring,"[32] accomplished via "shifting levels of interpretation, changing metaphors, and so on."[33] Opt and Gring explain that anomalies are recognized when "[l]ived experience fails to match the expectancies generated by our naming process." They go on to write: "Because we foreground some aspects of experience and background others to categorize symbolically, our names for experience are always *incomplete.* Our symbolic constructions always direct our attention *away* from parts of experience."[34] Therefore, there are anomalies in every worldview that arise "when someone asserts that an accepted categorization of lived experience is 'inadequate.'"[35] The end result is the development of a new system of accepting input either in how one knows (epistemology), how one values (axiology), or how one perceives her or his being (ontology).

The FCC Order recognizes that the ideology which they advocate is not the only possible ideology. The Order repeatedly refers to alternative ideological positions. In fact, it seems that the FCC Order openly recognizes its critics, and its anomaly masking and featuring appears to be done in the most direct way possible. The resultant shift is in the axiology of its readers.

For example, those who oppose regulation argue that it is an unnecessary and unwanted government intrusion. A corollary argument is that market pressures inherently require an open Internet, as those who discriminate users' access will lose customers to competitors. The FCC's Order responds to this alternative template: "Some commenters argue that an end user's ability to switch broadband providers eliminates these problems"[36] By shifting the discussion from a conversation regarding the ability of customers to switch providers to a discussion of access, the Order features an anomaly in the market driven ideology, namely that a competitive market is not readily available to everyone.

The method continues in discussions regarding transparency: "Although transparency is essential for preserving Internet openness, we disagree with commenters that suggest it is alone sufficient to prevent open Internet violations."[37] Here, the Commission provides the same basic reasoning: that transparency alone would suffice in a truly free market, but in monopolistic conditions it does not.

This is an interesting shift in axiology. The FCC does not challenge the American mantra that a free market and competition can solve the problems. Instead, they write that we do not yet have a free market. They accept the overarching axiological supposition that the free markets are beneficial, but point out that the existing monopoly is detrimental to consumers. In fact, competition and free market pressures are encouraged by the FCC Order: "Some commenters suggest that open Internet protections would prohibit broadband providers from offering their subscribers different tiers of service or from charging their sub-scribers based on bandwidth consumed. We are, of course, always concerned about anti-consumer or anticompetitive practices, and we remain so here."[38] This virtual homage to competitive practice attempts to protect the rhetors from accusations of unnecessary regulation and inhibition of capitalist markets. The overall rhetorical effect is to create a shift in the value suppositions of the audi-ence regarding the ISPs, which puts the providers on the defensive and makes them, not regulation appear to be the threats to the free market.

Another aspect of an alternative ideology opposed to regulation is concern that regulation will reduce investment in further broadband connection. The de-tractors from enforcement of network neutrality believe that people will no longer invest in connections unless they can fully utilize those connections to their own advantage. Without the advantages that privileging their own content can give them, detractors believe that Internet service providers will not create new products and services for their customers: "Some commenters contend that open Internet rules are likely to reduce investment in broadband deployment. We disagree. There is no evidence that prior open Internet obligations have dis-couraged investment."[39]

The Order attempts to change the conversation from deliberative to forensic rhetoric, from a discussion about the results of decisions on future discussions to ones about the past. In so doing, the FCC masks the anomaly that they cannot necessarily predict the overall effect that regulation will have on future invest-ment. A largely unregulated market in the past has certainly encouraged invest-ment. However this market has traditionally espoused the very concepts that will be required by regulation. Whether or not any change will take place is unclear and there is no real reason to assume that investment will not be hampered by regulation. There is also, as the FCC Order clearly states, no reason to think that it will be inhibited.

The shift from a deliberative to forensic method of seeing the world might seem a shift in epistemology rather than in axiology. Given the interconnected-ness of the various sub-cycles within the attention shift, an epistemological shift in an overall axiological artifact would be a reasonable action. However, I argue that in this case it is still an axiological shift that is taking place. Certainly, the concern about future investments is a question of value; in many ways monetary value is the overarching metaphor by which all other value is understood. How-ever, axiology is more the way in which something is valued rather than the re-sultant values that are produced. Thus, the argument for stability is valued by both sides, but the FCC Order produces a shift claiming that stability, and the stable investments that have come from it, are more readily maintained through regulation as opposed to laissez-faire nonintervention.

This is not the only time that the FCC Order makes use of the shift from deliberation to forensics. Elsewhere, the Order functions as an axiological call for stability through regulation as well: "Although some commenters assert that a disclosure rule will impose significant burdens on broadband providers, no commenter cites any particular source of increased costs, or attempts to estimate costs of compliance."[40] This shift from the future- to past-oriented rhetoric masks the overall anomaly that exists in all questions of deliberation: namely, that the future cannot with any reasonable degree of certainty be proven. The artifact's insistence on detractors' provision of proof continues to mask the fact that it is equally agnostic as to the overall effects of the regulation.

Not all alternative ideologies are opposed to regulation. Another argument calls for clearer regulation with fewer ambiguities and loopholes. For instance, one rhetorical shift that the FCC Order enacts is to move from an axiology which privileges clarity to one which privileges the ability of the regulatory agencies to respond: "We believe that at this time the best approach is to allow flexibility in implementation of the transparency rule, while providing guidance regarding effective disclosure models."[41] Here, an axiological shift replaces precision with plasticity, which the Order claims is necessary to adjust to changing situations as they arise.

Certainly not all of the FCC's disagreements are dealt with via rhetorical shifts that mask a lack of clarity. At times, a simple legal explanation suffices:

> We disagree with commenters who argue that a rule against unreasonable
> ination violates section 3(51) of the Communications Act for those broadband
> providers that are telecommunications carriers but do not provide their broad-
> band Internet access service as a telecommunications service. Section 3(51)
> provides that a "telecommunications carrier shall be treated as a common car-
> rier under this Act only to the extent that it is engaged in providing telecommu-
> nications services." This limitation is not relevant to the Commission's actions
> here.[42]

This is another type of axiological shift which creates a valuing system that narrowly defines FCC regulations. This is an interesting move on the part of the FCC. While the Order clearly expands the FCC's regulatory power by switching clarity for plasticity, they value a narrow understanding of the limits of their own power both by legislative oversight and judicial interpretation:

> In arguing that broadband service is protected by the First Amendment, AT&T
> compares its provision of broadband service to the operation of a cable televi-
> sion system, and points out that the Supreme Court has determined that cable
> programmers and cable operators engage in speech protected by the First
> Amendment. The analogy is inapt. When the Supreme Court held in *Turner I*
> that cable operators were protected by the First Amendment, the critical factor
> that made cable operators "speakers" was their production of programming and
> their exercise of "editorial discretion over which programs and stations to in-
> clude" (and thus which to exclude).[43]

Using the text of this rule to narrowly limit their own culpability in advance of any judicial action or legislative proposal, the Order limits the extent to which such oversight can apply to the FCC.

Perhaps foreseeing this potential critique, the Order further protects the FCC against accusations of espousing policies that function as little more than grabs for power beyond the scope of Constitutional authority:

> Our Section 706(a) authority is limited in three critical respects. First, our mandate under Section 706(a) must be read consistently with Sections 1 and 2 of the Act, which define the Commission's subject matter jurisdiction over "interstate and foreign commerce in communication by wire and radio." As a result, our authority under Section 706(a) does not, in our view, extend beyond our subject matter jurisdiction under the Communications Act. Second, the Commission's actions under Section 706(a) must "encourage the deployment on a reasonable and timely basis of advanced telecommunications capability to all Americans." Third, the activity undertaken to encourage such deployment must "utilize[e], in a manner consistent with the public interest, convenience, and necessity," one (or more) of various specified methods.[44]

Thus any axiological notion that the FCC is attempting to overreach its authority by the use of this rule is headed off, not by a rebuttal, but by shifting the metaphor to an FCC acting only in submission to Congressional authority. They are not overreaching their authority, but are acting as servants within the limits and under the auspices of legislative oversight. The attempt here is to shift the axiology from a hermeneutic of suspicion to one which assumes the FCC is acting within Congressional authority.

Overall, the axiological shift engaged in the Order is one which tries to establish the FCC as valuing reasonable oversight, adaptability, and traditional legislative oversight. The axiological shift works itself out both epistemologically and ontologically as well, in that when ideology is seen as a communication process, all parts of an attention shift are interconnected. Ontologically, they attempt to appear to be the metaphoric "adult in the room." They are seen as the reasonable party, stern when required to be, adaptable when necessary and submissive to reasonable authority. Epistemologically, they demand a theory of knowledge which is equally reasonable and adaptive to the particular nuances of technological change.

It is this attempt to show a value of "reasonableness" that also gives rise to perhaps the strangest part of the Order, the exclusion of the same legal requirements to providers of wireless Internet technology:

> Some commenters express concern that wireless providers could favor their own applications over the applications of unaffiliated developers, under the guise of reasonable network management. A number of commenters assert that blocking or hindering the delivery of services that compete with those offered by the mobile broadband provider, such as over-the-top VoIP, should be prohibited . . . Although some commenters support a broader no-blocking rule, we believe that a targeted prophylactic rule is appropriate at this time, and necessary to deter this type of behavior in the future.[45]

This ultimate value of "reasonableness" and an entire axiology that hinges upon that value becomes the focus of the FCC Order. That value works itself through the entire ideological system at until at last, the FCC is bound by that Order to what seems a strange exclusion. Ultimately, an ideology that hinges on the value of reasonableness cannot act to effectively regulate technology still in its infancy. The Order seems to be saying that it is unreasonable to put limits on these at this time because they do not know what these infant technologies will eventually become.

Conclusion

That we do not know what technologies will become is certainly a clear fact. Nor do we know what future rhetorical acts will affect the conversation about network neutrality. It is difficult to see how technological development will play itself out within the confines of the Order. Still, it is clear that however technology and its surrounding rhetorics develop, they will be in some way confined by this Order. Even if the FCC's Order is overthrown through Congressional or Judicial action, it will still have had a rhetorical affect on the conversation. The Order created an ideology in which reasonable oversight, adaptability, and submission to the legislature are now terms that will color any future rhetorical interventions. They are axiological constructs around which future axiologies will have to align or oppose.

While the Order did not end the conversation about network neutrality, it significantly affected that conversation. According to the theories espoused in this chapter however, we know that the ideology is not a communication construct, but a communication process. So while we can clearly see how reasonable oversight, adaptability, and submission to the legislature were used to alter the social ideology regarding network neutrality here, we can also be certain that future rhetorical interventions will continue to affect and change this ever fluid ideology.

Notes

1. Declan, McCullagh, "Telco Agrees to Stop Blocking VoIP calls," *CNET*, March 3, 2008, http://news.cnet.com/Telco-agrees-to-stop-blocking-VoIP-calls/2100-7352_3-5598633.html (accessed August 30, 2011).

2. *Internet Freedom Preservation Act of 2008*, HR 5353, 110th Cong., 2nd sess., http://www.govtrack.us/congress/billtext.xpd?bill=h110–5353 (accessed September 1, 2011).

3. Free Press and Public Knowledge, *Formal Complaint of Free Press and Public Knowledge against Comcast Corporation for Secretly Degrading Peer-to-Peer Applications*, 23 FCC Rcd 13028, November 1, 2007 http://www.publicknowledge.org/pdf/fp_pk_comcast_complaint.pdf (accessed August

13, 2012).

4. Saul Hansel, "F.C.C. Vote Sets Precedent on Unfettered Web Usage," *New York Times*, August 2, 2008, http://www.nytimes.com/2008/08/02/technology/ 02fcc.html?_r=1 (accessed August 8, 2011).

5. *Comcast Corp. v. FCC*, 600 F.3d 642, 645 (D.C. Cir. 2010).

6. Jen Howard, "FCC Statement on Comcast v. FCC Decision," *FCC.gov*, April 6, 2010. http://hraunfoss.fcc.gov/edocs_public/attachmatch/DOC-297355A1.pdf (accessed August 5, 2011).

7. Federal Communications Commission, *Report and Order in the Matter of Preserving the Open Internet Broadband Industry Practices*, December 23, 2010, http://www.fcc.gov/Daily_Releases/Daily_Business/2010/db1223/FCC-10-201A1.pdf (accessed January 20, 2011), 2.

8. Matthew Lasar, "It's Here: FCC Adopts Net Neutrality (lite)," *ArsTechnica*, December 2010, http://arstechnica.com/tech-policy/news/2010/12/its-here-fcc-adopts-net-neutrality-lite.ars (accessed August 8, 2011).

9. Nate Anderson, "Why Everyone Hates New Net Neutrality Rules—Even NN Supporters," *ArsTechnica*, February 2011, http://arstechnica.com/tech-policy/news/2010/12/why-everyone-hates-new-net-neutrality-ruleseven-nn-supporters.ars (accessed September 1, 2011).

10. "Upton, Walden, and Terry Find FCC's Economic Analysis Lacking," House Energy and Commerce Committee press release, March 8, 2011, on the House Energy and Commerce Committee website, http://energycommerce.house.gov/news/PRArticle.aspx?NewsID=8315 (accessed September 7, 2011).

11. *Dissaproving the Rule Submitted by the Federal Communications Commisssion with Respect to Regulating the Internet and Broadband Industry Practices*, H.J. Res. 37, 112th Cong, 1st sess. http://republicans.energycommerce.house.gov/Media/file/ Hearings/Telecom/030211_FCC/hjrES37.pdf (accessed June 1, 2011).

12. Anderson, "Why Everyone Hates."

13. Dana L. Cloud and Joshua Gunn, "Introduction: W(h)ither Ideology," *Western Journal of Communication* 75, no. 4 (2011): 407–420.

14. William R. Brown, "Ideology as Communication Process," *Quarterly Journal of Speech* 64, no. 2 (1978): 123–180.

15. Susan K. Opt and Mark A. Gring. *The Rhetoric of Social Intervention: An Introduction* (Los Angeles: Sage, 2009), 57.

16. William R. Brown, "The Holgraphic View of Argument," *Argumentation* 1, no. 1 (1987): 89–102.

17. Ibid., 115.

18. Mark R. Stoner, "Understanding Social Movements: Rhetoric of Social Intervention," *The Speech Communication Annual* 3 (1988): 27–43.

19. William R. Brown, "Attention and the Rhetoric of Social Intervention," *Quarterly Journal of Speech* 68, no. 1 (1982): 17–27; William R. Brown, "Power and the Rhetoric of Social Intervention," *Quarterly Journal of Speech* 53, no. 2 (1986): 180–199; Opt and Gring.

20. Brown, "Ideology," 125.

21. Ibid., 125.

22. Ibid., 126.

23. Ibid., 126.

24. Ibid., 135.

25. Brown, "Attention"; Alberto Gonzalez, "Participation" at WMEX–FM: Interventional Rhetoric of Ohio Mexican Americans," *Western Journal of Speech Communication* 53, no. 4 (1989): 398–410; Shaorong Huang, *To Rebel Is Justified: A Rhetorical Study of China's Cultural Movement, 1966–1969* (Lanham, M.D.: University Press of America, 1996; Neil Leroux, "Frederick Douglas and the Attention Shift," *Rhetoric Society Quarterly* 21, no. 2 (Spring 1991): 36–46; Opt and Gring.

26. *Internet Freedom Preservation Act.*

27. Free Press and Public Knowledge.

28. *Comcast Corp. v. FCC,* 600 F.3d 642 (United States Court of Appeals for the District of Columbia, April 6, 2010).

29. Brown, "Attention," 18.

30. Leroux, 36.

31. Brown, "Attention," 22.

32. Ibid., 22.

33. Mark R. Stoner, "Understanding Social Movements," 30.

34. Opt and Gring, 72.

35. J. Russ Corley, "A Communication Study of Arthur F. Holmes as a Worldview Advocate" (Doctoral Dissertation, The Ohio State University, 1983). Vol. 44, in *Dissertation Abstracts International,* 1983.

36. Federal Communications Commission, *Report and Order,* 17.

37. Ibid., 37.

38. Ibid., 41.

39. Ibid., 24

40. Ibid., 36.

41. Ibid., 34.

42. Ibid., 46.

43. Ibid., 78.

44. Ibid., 56.

45. Ibid., 56–57.

Part III:
Net Neutrality as
Cultural and Political Debate

Chapter 7

Framing the Net Neutrality Debate

Zack Stiegler and Dan Sprumont

Hailed by advocates as the First Amendment issue of this generation and reviled by critics as overbearing governmental regulation, net neutrality is perhaps the most hotly debated media policy issue in recent years. At root, debates over net neutrality raise the evasive matter of who controls the Internet, and to what ends. As net neutrality gained greater public awareness, two clearly defined, vocal and opposing camps emerged. A number of public interest groups rallied to advocate for codifying network neutrality in the interest of preserving unrestricted web access for American consumers. On the other side, telecommunications firms such as AT&T and Comcast worked to prevent legislation or Federal Communications Commission (FCC) policy protecting net neutrality, expressing concern of government intrusion into private enterprise.

Although the issue of net neutrality received regulatory attention as early as 2005, only recently has it received much mainstream media exposure. This was especially true in the lead up to the formal adoption of net neutrality rules by the FCC in December 2010. During this time, net neutrality evolved from a somewhat arcane policy issue to a source of widespread debate across a variety of media outlets. This chapter examines media discourse about net neutrality by applying framing analysis through the lens of rhetorical criticism. Such an analytic approach presents a clearer understanding of these particular media messages, including the motivations shaping them, their validity, and how they have shaped cultural discourse about net neutrality. As a matter of preface, we first provide a historical overview of network neutrality in the United States.

From its popularization in the 1990s, the Internet has operated as a neutral information network. This foundational principle holds that consumers have equal opportunity to access all legal Internet sites and applications at the same rate of quality and speed. An Internet based upon neutrality prevents the telecommunications industry from segregating the flow of information, instead facilitating continued freedom of access, expression, and innovation online. In contrast to owners of broadcast and print media, to date the telecommunications industry has had little say as regards the types of applications and content users choose to access and develop online, a fact that web users have taken for granted.

During the first decade of the twenty-first century however, the conversation began to change. In 2005, the FCC issued its Internet Policy Statement. Alternately known as the Open Internet Policy or Broadband Policy Statement, the document outlined core principles intended to offer continued protection of online innovation and freedom of expression.[1] Shortly thereafter, the nation's largest ISPs quietly initiated a push for greater control over the Internet. Corporations such as AT&T and Comcast sought to breach net neutrality, arguing for their rights to discriminate among the applications and websites their subscribers accessed under the auspices of network management. As with telecommunication law and policy more generally, debates over net neutrality received minimal coverage in the popular press, leaving Americans generally unaware of the issue.

Americans were similarly unaware that some ISPs were in fact tampering with their access to legal content online. In 2002, Comcast blocked e-mails sent from anti-war group AfterDowningStreet to supporters with Comcast e-mail accounts; Comcast and Cox Communications also blocked e-mails from Cindy Sheehans's anti-war organization meetwithcindy.org.[2] In 2005, DSL provider Madison River Communications blocked its subscribers' access to Vonage, a VoIP (Voice over Internet Protocol) that competed with Madison River's own digital voice service.[3] During a live webcast of a Pearl Jam performance, AT&T deleted front man Eddie Vedder's explicitly anti-Bush comments from their audio stream, despite the comments' lack of obscene or indecent content.[4] Just one month later, Verizon blocked Naral Pro-Choice from utilizing its mobile network to distribute mass text messages to subscribers who had opted-in for such announcements from Naral.[5] Collectively, these examples illustrate the willingness of ISPs to act as gatekeepers of content traversing their networks, a practice that net neutrality principles seek to prohibit.

Barack Obama's campaign for and eventual election to the U.S. presidency provided a major turning point in public discourse about net neutrality. On the campaign trail, Obama vowed to protect American consumers from corporate tampering with Internet access, data transferring speeds, and freedom of speech.[6] Obama continually voiced his support for net neutrality during the campaign, declaring, "I will take a backseat to no one in my commitment to network neutrality."[7] With this bold proclamation, Obama put the protection of a free and open Internet at the forefront of his technology agenda.

Upon taking office, Obama appointed Julius Genachowski as Chairman of the FCC. Like Obama, Genachowski explicitly stated his objective to preserve Internet openness, prioritizing net neutrality upon joining the Commission.[8] However, a 2010 ruling by a Federal Court of Appeals dealt a significant blow to the FCC's authority to regulate Internet communications.

The case came in response to a 2007 Commission Order that revolved around Internet "throttling," a practice wherein an ISP degrades access speeds among heavy bandwidth users. The FCC reprimanded Comcast, arguing that the company's throttling practices violated the Internet Policy Statement's entitlement of consumers' access to "the lawful internet content of their choice."[9] In response, Comcast filed suit, claiming that the FCC had overstepped the boundaries of its regulatory jurisdiction. Ultimately, the Court of Appeals for the D.C. Circuit ruled that in fact, the FCC did lack clear authority to regulate broadband.[10]

Although a clear victory for ISPs wishing to operate without regulatory intervention, the Court's ruling was a major setback for net neutrality advocates. After backing down on a proposal to reclassify broadband as a Title II common carrier telecommunications service, the FCC placated industry criticisms by inviting corporate influence to shape the policy, including AT&T, Google, and Verizon. Google and Verizon independently drafted a compromise proposal in August 2010 that in many ways served as the template for the FCC's rules adopted later that year.

On December 21, 2010, the FCC issued its Report and Order in the Matter of Preserving the Open Internet Broadband Industry Practices. The adopted policy reflects compromise between the agency and broadband providers, introducing a rather limited set of regulations for ISPs. Most notably, the Report and Order's provision of "No unreasonable discrimination" applies only to fixed, wireline broadband providers, leaving the rapidly growing mobile broadband sector vulnerable to discrimination.[11] The Commission also failed to codify rules preventing a tiered pricing system for consumers, which had been a primary concern among net neutrality advocates.

Shortly after adopting the rules, the FCC faced Congressional and judicial challenges. A Resolution of Disapproval that would eradicate the FCC's net neutrality rules passed the Republican-led House in 2011, but was rejected by the Senate.[12] Meanwhile, Verizon filed suit against the FCC, challenging the Commission's authority to regulate Internet communication. Although initially dismissed on a technicality, the D.C. Circuit Court of Appeals has agreed to hear the case.[13]

With these unresolved legal challenges, the future of net neutrality is uncertain. Yet it remains a hotly debated political issue. As net neutrality becomes an increasingly controversial subject, press coverage can play a greater role in shaping public opinion of the issue. In considering media coverage of net neutrality, employing framing analysis as a mode of rhetorical criticism facilitates a greater understanding of how mass media frame net neutrality.

Framing Analysis as Rhetorical Criticism

Rooted in the work of Erving Goffman, framing initially developed as a means of analyzing social interactions to understand how the organization of information and experience shapes individuals' perceptions and ways of understanding.[14] Framing further involves "taking some aspects of our reality and making them more accessible than others."[15] Frames may be understood as filters through which the world is presented, allowing certain elements to pass through those filters and preventing the transmission of others. As an organization of information then, frames significantly shape our perceptions, serving as one mechanism through which we make sense of the world.

Moving beyond the purely sociological realm, scholars of journalism and mass media adopted frame analysis as a method for examining how audiences understand news media. As Entman explains, "To frame is to *select some aspects of a perceived reality and make them more salient in a communicating text, in such a way as to promote a particular problem definition, causal interpretation, moral evaluation, and/or treatment recommendation* for the item described."[16] Framing analysis thus provides insight not only into audience perception, but also message construction and effectiveness.

The last decade has seen a growing group of scholars adapt framing analysis as an instrument of rhetorical criticism.[17] This approach provides a rich lens of analysis that builds upon social-scientific methodology to examine media framing as a strategic process engaged to shape audience perceptions of news stories.

Kuypers was at the forefront of introducing rhetorical criticism to framing analysis. In constructing a rhetorical model of framing analysis, Kuypers builds upon the concept of agenda-setting to present his concept of agenda-extension. Agenda–setting holds that mass media tell us not what to think, but what to think about. When mass media engage in agenda-extension on the other hand, they advocate a particular interpretation of the message with the conscious intent of influencing audience perception and by extension, public opinion.[18] It is here that a combination of framing analysis and rhetorical criticism is particularly beneficial, illuminating how agenda-extension operates to encourage a particular interpretation of a given media message.[19]

This is not to say that media audiences are uncritical dupes who interpret messages in the same manner that media institutions encode them.[20] However, it is true that audience attention is necessarily selective in our media-saturated environment, and as Kuypers notes, "we too often rely upon and accept information that is easily accessible."[21] While we cannot overgeneralize assumptions about audience interpretation, we can analyze how news media frame certain issues to foster particular interpretations, whether audiences take up these interpretations or not.

Kuypers' incorporation of rhetorical criticism and framing analysis is informative in a more general sense, in relation to how media define and present issues to their audiences.[22] Of concern here is that despite the high valuation of accuracy and objectivity within American news media,[23] in practice news organizations shape perceptions of their reportage via framing, whether consciously or unconsciously. By doing so, media frames "act to define problems, diagnose causes, make moral judgments and suggest remedies," while obscuring information contrary to the adopted frame.[24]

It is precisely this matter of problem definition that is at play in media coverage of network neutrality. Mass media's relative inattention to net neutrality prior to 2010 speaks to their reluctance to report on matters that challenge their commercial interests. By 2010 however, mass media could no longer ignore the issue, as the FCC's action on an open Internet policy grew imminent.

Methodology

In a discussion of media framing, Entman posits that effective framing analysis looks at news frames over a sustained period of time to discover consistent frames employed by news media.[25] In gathering data for analysis, we looked to national broadcast, cable, and print news outlets. Via Lexis Nexis, we ultilized the search terms "net neutrality" and "network neutrality" within the period of January 1, 2010 through December 31, 2010. Although net neutrality received some press attention prior to this time period, 2010 shows the greatest concentration of the topic in light of the FCC's impending action on net neutrality that year. As such, we feel that this period produces the richest data set for analysis. Because of their national prominence, we included the following fourteen media outlets in our search:

- CNN
- CNBC
- Fox News
- MSNBC
- ABC News
- CBS
- Newsweek

- National Public Radio
- *The Wall Street Journal*
- *The Washington Times*
- *The Los Angeles Times*
- *The New York Times*
- *The Washington Post*
- *USA Today*

This sampling cuts across broadcast, cable, and print media, providing a broad spectrum of data sources for analysis.

Our search yielded a total of 319 news stories published in 2010. We then organized the stories into four general categories of "positive," "negative," "neutral," and "irrelevant." "Positive" stories were those that advocated net neutrality, "negative" stories spoke against legislative or FCC action on net neutrality, while "neutral" stories presented a balanced view on the topic or were otherwise indeterminate. Stories marked "irrelevant" were those that mentioned net neutrality, but did so in a cursory manner in unrelated news stories. With these broad categories established, we set out not only to attain quantitative data on their occurrence, but also to determine how media framed net neutrality, and to what ends.

Analysis, Results, and Discussion

At the outset, we anticipated a greater frequency of negatively framed stories on net neutrality. However, this proved to be false. Overwhelmingly, stories included in our sample were neither positive nor negative, but presented the issue in a neutral manner. With 124 occurrences, these neutral stories nearly doubled positive and negative stories, which accounted for 71 and 66 stories respectively (see Figure 7.1).

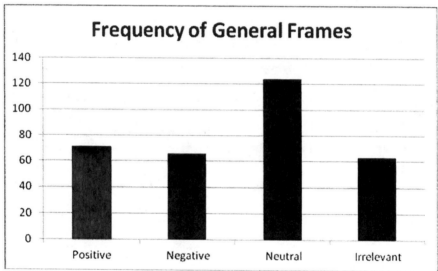

Figure 7.1: Frequency of General Frames

Positive Net Neutrality Frames

Analysis of the 71 positive stories revealed little in the way of rhetorical framing. CNN, NPR, and *The Washington Post* produced the highest concentrations of positive stories (see Figure 7.2).

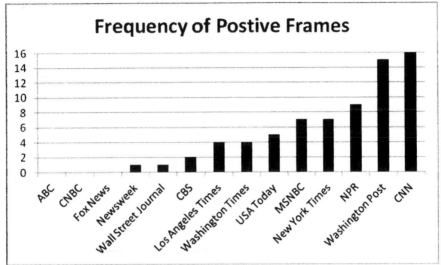

Figure 7.2: Frequency of Positive Frames

Certain trends did emerge, however. For example, a number of stories discussed the need for net neutrality's "equal treatment" of websites and services, lest policies open the door for "preferential treatment" of some content over others. Similarly, many stories discussed the possibility of erecting a "toll booth" or "fast-lane" on the Internet, allowing those with greater capital to pay to reach end users faster and more directly than competitors.

We cannot accurately label these trends as rhetorical frames however, as they are congruent with language used by the FCC.[26] Thus, the recurrence of phrases such as "equal treatment," "prioritization," "toll booth," and "fast-lane" do not constitute a rhetorical move to frame net neutrality. Instead, such stories merely employ language consistent with the relevant policy discourse.

Negative Net Neutrality Frames

More interesting and rhetorically rich however were the negatively charged stories. The majority of stories negatively portraying net neutrality hailed from three sources: *The Washington Times* (10), *The Wall Street Journal* (23), and the Fox News cable channel (20), the latter two owned by Rupert Murdoch's News Corporation conglomerate. Negative stories did not appear exclusively in these media outlets however, as Figure 7.3 indicates.

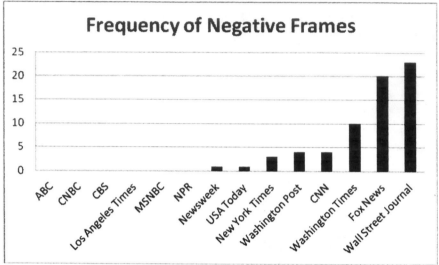

Figure 7.3: Frequency of Negative Frames

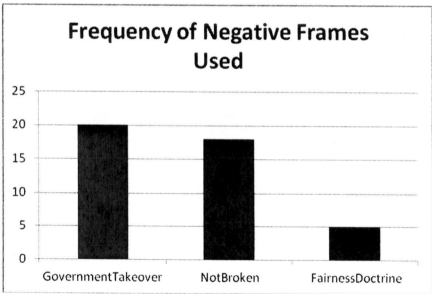

Figure 7.4: Frequency of Negative Frames Used

Across various sources, three frames emerged in stories portraying net neutrality negatively:

1. Net neutrality constitutes a government takeover of the Internet
2. Net neutrality constitutes a Fairness Doctrine for the Internet
3. The Internet is not broken, and therefore not in need of regulation

Figure 7.4 shows the frequency of these frames across all sources included in our study.

Mirroring the occurrence of negative stories more generally, the majority of stories utilizing these specific frames appeared in decidedly conservative media outlets: Fox News (15), *The Wall Street Journal* (11), and *The Washington Times* (10). The same pattern holds within each individual frame as well. Note also that some stories incorporated two or three of these frames simultaneously. We analyze each of these frames in kind.

Negative Frame 1: "Government Takeover of the Internet"

The "Government Takeover" frame presented the net neutrality issue as illustrative of a larger perceived trend, "big government." In the wake of the health care debate of 2009–2010, particularly conservative analysts and commentators decried "big government," seemingly viewing any form of federal regulation as intrusive. Indeed, some commentators levied similar criticisms at the Environmental Protection Agency and the Food and Drug Administration.

Similar rhetoric is evident in the "Government Takeover" frame in stories covering net neutrality. Stories utilizing this frame frequently cite net neutrality policies as a "power grab" by the FCC and the Obama administration.[27] *The Wall Street Journal* called net neutrality "invasive government regulation" and "a naked lunge for political power."[28] In another piece, the same publication simply stated that "so long as government keeps out the way, the Internet can stay free."[29]

One strain within the "government takeover" frame depicts net neutrality as government censorship of Internet content, when in fact one of the policy's primary aims is to ensure that users can freely access whatever legal online content that they wish. In portraying net neutrality as censorship, news stories draw on historical references to buoy their claims. For example, Glenn Beck frequently labeled net neutrality as "Marxist" on his program. However flawed Beck's definition of Marxism may be, he often invokes the German philosopher to stand in for government control and censorship:

> Net neutrality is also getting support from religious groups like the Christian Coalition. The Christian Coalition? Among the coalition 2010 agenda, prevent discrimination on the Internet by passing net neutrality. This is Marxism![30]

> But that's what this so-called net neutrality effort is really all about. Your kids have heard about it, I can guarantee. It's about eliminating traditional constitu-

tional points of view from the public arena, but that's not the way it's being billed. It is about stopping debate, but nobody will tell you that. It's about ending free speech. It is about Marxism.[31]

It's about eliminating traditional, constitutional points of view from the public arena. But that's not the way it's being built. It is about stopping debate. Nobody will tell you that. It's about ending free speech. It is about Marxism. No, our kids aren't taught that. That's not the way they're positioning it. No.[32]

In a similar vein, StopNetRegulation.org Editor in Chief Seton Motley labeled the regulations "socialism for the Internet" in an interview on Beck's program.[33] Representative Marsha Blackburn (R–TN) likewise told Sean Hannity that net neutrality was "a taking, if you will. And I look at this and say, this is a step toward nationalizing the Internet."[34]

Other stories utilizing the "government takeover" frame engaged literary rather than historical references. In a discussion of net neutrality in the spring of 2010, *The Washington Times* referred to the FCC as an "Orwellian commission" with intent to "deem exactly how stakeholders and the public should feel about their drive to regulate portions of the Internet ecosphere."[35]

CNN also conjured *1984* in an opinion piece claiming that "the real 'Big Brother' threat here is a government with the power to completely foreclose all speech under threat of fine or imprisonment—a power the private sector lacks even if you buy into the silly notion that it is out to bottle up speech or speakers."[36] Here, CNN writers Thierer and Wendy evoke images of the totalitarian Big Brother in relation to the FCC's power to censor expression online, should net neutrality pass. Although the final version of the FCC's policy differed from earlier models discussed by the agency, from the FCC's perspective, net neutrality was never about content regulation. In fact, a primary goal of the FCC in the net neutrality rulemaking was to ensure that consumers could continue to express themselves and access all legal content without their ISP serving as a gatekeeper. One could counter however that the Internet currently thrives as an unprecedented forum for expression and information without any federal regulation. This is the core of the second negative frame in our sample.

Negative Frame 2: The Internet Isn't Broken
With 18 occurrences, the second most frequent negative frame in our sample is that "The Internet Isn't Broken." In a guest editorial for *The Wall Street Journal*, Republican FCC Commissioner Robert McDowell stated simply, "nothing is broke that needs fixing," a sentiment echoed in a number of other stories utilizing this rhetorical frame.[37]

A common remark within the "Internet isn't broken" frame is that net neutrality is a solution in search of a nonexistent problem. Appearing on *Hannity*, Marsha Blackburn (R–TN) called the push for net neutrality "a hysterical reaction to a hypothetical problem"; John Fund of *The Wall Street Journal* called net neutrality a "nonproblem," while Glenn Beck referred to the need for net neutrality as a "bogus nonexistent crisis."[38] *The Wall Street Journal* pointedly asked, "Doesn't the Obama Administration have enough to do other than mess with a part of the U.S. economy that is working well?"[39] Beck also cited the lack of existing problems on his Fox News cable program:

> Who's complaining about the neutrality on the Internet? I mean, is there some major outcry that I just haven't heard about yet? Americans have never had more access to more outlets to express themselves than they do now. Anyone in America with a computer and an Internet connection can sit in their basement in their underpants, eating biscuits, while they bang on their keyboards all night and day while mom is upstairs sleeping . . . They can literally say whatever they want any time they want. So, what is the problem? It seems to me there isn't one if free speech really is your goal.[40]

Here, Beck very clearly expresses the heart of this rhetorical frame: the Internet is operating effectively as a democratic means of expression of and access to information, and the function of federal regulation ought to be reactive to rather than preventative of corporate abuses of power.

In addition to claiming that "the Internet is not broken," a few stories in our sample claim that current law and policy is sufficient to prevent ISPs from tampering with subscribers' access.[41] More frequent however are arguments that market forces are an adequate means of regulating corporate behavior. Such stories hold that a lack of any offenses by ISPs to date indicates that there is no need for federal regulation; to remain profitable, ISPs know that they cannot interfere with users' service, lest they lose customers and jeopardize the company's existence.

For example, in an interview for *The Wall Street Journal*, Time-Warner Cable CEO Nat Worden proclaimed that "nothing has happened that would cause a need for intrusive regulation."[42] Another *Wall Street Journal* piece claims that "Net neutrality proponents say government regulation is necessary to prevent these companies from suppressing political views or favoring one service over another. Yet there's no evidence that such behavior has occurred. And it's unlikely to occur so long as consumers have a variety of Internet service options."[43]

Phil Kerpen of *The Washington Times* shared the sentiment that market forces would fetter out any impropriety on the part of ISPs:

> The scare story has always been that if government doesn't step in immediately, the phone and cable companies will block access to websites, interfere with traffic and otherwise ruin the Internet. It hasn't happened, and it won't happen, because of competition. It works. A company that messed with its customers would lose them to a competitor. And competition is only increasing as next-generation wireless becomes an increasingly viable option for home broadband Internet.[44]

In the same publication, Andrew Moylan concurred that "Companies that impose draconian tolls or block services will lose customers. Existing laws already offer a number of protections against anti-competitive behavior, but it's not clear under what law Mr. Genachowski thinks he can stick his nose into the businesses that comprise the Internet."[45]

Similarly, a pair of CNN reporters questioned Senator Al Franken's (D–MN) concerns over ISPs acting as gatekeepers of information online:

> And really, why would any company want "to control the flow of information in America," as Franken suggests? First, it's bad for business. There's just no good business case for censorship. Internet service providers make more money by delivering more bits, not fewer. Second, censorship is hard. Internet service providers simply don't have the technology or manpower necessary to effectively filter online content by viewpoint. Third, trying to control information would quickly create public relations nightmares for carriers. There'd be hell for them to pay with the press, industry watchdogs and especially their subscribers. The white-hot spotlight of public attention is the best disinfectant. Finally, any attempt to censor would backfire and actually draw attention to the speech or speaker in question.[46]

An August 2010 piece from CNN goes further, arguing that the in the current unregulated Internet environment, consumers ultimately wield the most power:

> The truth is that if Verizon and AT&T wanted to cannibalize their broadband business with premium broadband services, they'd already be doing it. But they aren't, because there hasn't been a market for it. The reality is that consumers are in control of what type of services are offered. If the public Internet can adequately deliver a service for free, then there's no need to pay for it.[47]

These stories' claims ring hollow however as they ignore the substantial list of instances of service degradation or outright censorship on the part of ISPs including Madison River's blocking of Vonage, Comcast and Cox's blocking of emails from Cindy Shehan's anti-war group, AT&T's censorship of Eddie Vedder's anti-Bush remarks, and Verizon's blocking of text messages from Naral Pro-Choice. To claim that no record exists of content discrimination by ISPs is patently false, which raises questions of journalistic integrity. Certainly, columnists and commentators should be free to express their personal analyses and opinions. Such expression becomes problematic however when doing so incorporates blatantly false information—particularly when such commentary and disinformation is presented to media audiences as "news." Reliance upon disinformation is also common within the third and final negative frame in our study, which maintains that net neutrality is a Fairness Doctrine for the Internet.

Negative Frame 3: The Fairness Doctrine

Although this frame occurred with the least frequency, it is noteworthy due to the misinformation that it propagates regarding net neutrality and FCC policy. The FCC enacted the Fairness Doctrine in 1949 as a mechanism to ensure broadcasters acted in the public interest through their news and public affairs programming. The Doctrine simultaneously required broadcasters to cover controversial issues of public importance, and to present multiple viewpoints when covering those issues. The FCC eliminated the Fairness Doctrine in 1987, one of many deregulatory steps taken by the Reagan-era Commission.

Twenty-three years after it was taken off the books, a handful of media outlets claimed that net neutrality policies were merely an online version of the Fairness Doctrine, requiring websites to present multiple viewpoints in their content. In our sample, the most frequent harbinger of the online Fairness Doctrine frame was Glenn Beck. In late November, Beck announced that "the FCC is announcing plans next week for regulations that would ban the ISPs, like Comcast, from blocking or favoring content online. This is basically a Fairness Doctrine for the Internet. America, you lose the Internet, you lose the war, I think."[48]

Appearing on *The O'Reilly Factor* around the same time, Beck expanded his explanation of the net neutrality policy and it's connection to the Fairness Doctrine.

> O'REILLY: OK. They [the left] want net neutrality. What does that mean?
> BECK: Net neutrality, what it means is they say that you can't—it's basically the Fairness Doctrine on the Internet.
> O'REILLY: So, they want to regulate Internet content those on the left.
> BECK: Correct.
> O'REILLY: So, why would they want to do that it's a left wing cesspool?
> BECK: How great was it for the left when you shut down opposing voices on talk radio?
> O'REILLY: But they didn't. Talk radio is dominated by the right wing.
> BECK: No, as soon as the Fairness Doctrine went away. Before that, if the Fairness Doctrine was on talk radio, you couldn't do what we've—
> O'REILLY: Well, you have—you could do it but then they have to put somebody on opposite.
> BECK: There is no way that you could do all of the paperwork, et cetera, et cetera now. There's no way you could have that balanced [content].[49]

Beck's colleague at Fox News Bret Baier also discussed net neutrality in relation to the Fairness Doctrine. While Baier didn't explicitly label net neutrality as the "Fairness Doctrine of the Internet," he did make a clear tie between the two policies as products of the Obama administration.

> When the head of a party that is trying to impose the fairness doctrine that would shut off debate and kill talk radio is talking retaining the spirit, the democratic spirit of the Internet, I would reach—I would have a little skepticism in

that. And I'd say perhaps when someone shows up at your door and says "I'm from the government and here to help," I'd worry about that.[50]

Before entering an extraneous discussion of the Fairness Doctrine and broadcasting, Wesley Pruden of *The Washington Times* commented that "anyone paying attention can see how [net neutrality] would be a first step toward revival of the so-called Fairness Doctrine, sought by Barack Obama and the Democrats since he first arrived in Washington."[51]

It is again worth noting that the FCC's net neutrality policies never proposed to give the agency authority over the regulation of content online. The guiding principle of net neutrality is to preserve the freedom and openness online that consumers currently enjoy, not to dictate what constitutes permissible content and expression online. The many instances of ISPs blocking or otherwise interfering with legal content illustrate the desire of dominant Internet corporations to regulate users' access to certain kinds of content and services. We have been unable to find similar instances of the FCC interfering with consumers' access to online content.

Equally as important is the fact that the Obama administration has not made any concerted effort to revive the Fairness Doctrine, in broadcasting or online. In the leadup to the 2008 presidential election, conservative media was aflutter with talk of the Fairness Doctrine's pending return, despite the multiple statements by outgoing President George W. Bush, Barack Obama and his FCC appointees to the contrary.[52] In fact, Obama-appointed Chairman Genachowski successfully led a vote in 2011 to formally revoke the defunct Fairness Doctrine from the *Federal Register.*[53] Why then, would some media outlets discuss net neutrality as a "Fairness Doctrine for the Internet," particularly as part of a larger agenda to reinstate the Doctrine in broadcasting?

Explained as a threat to our nation's founding principles of free speech and expression, the Fairness Doctrine provides an easily identifiable issue for pundits and audiences to rally behind. Who wouldn't be motivated by threats to the freedoms enshrined in the First Amendment? With the Fairness Doctrine scare of 2007–2009 still fresh in audience's minds, resurrecting that red herring to discuss net neutrality frames the latter as an assault on our First Amendment rights to speech and expression. The shock value of this frame is enhanced by a common perception of the Internet as inherently democratic; an electronic public sphere where everyone has the ability to participate. Framing net neutrality as a threat to that openness and exchange makes it an easy target for conservative media, though these are actually the principles that net neutrality seeks to protect.

Conclusion

The three negative frames above raise concern over attempts to shape audience perceptions of net neutrality, arguably the single most important policy issue currently facing U.S. media. Collectively, frames purporting that the U.S. government is plotting to takeover of the Internet, that the Internet isn't broken and needs no regulation, and that net neutrality constitutes an online Fairness Doctrine do a disservice to the quality of discourse about net neutrality. As Kuypers points out, "facts remain neutral until framed; thus how the press frames an issue or event will affect public understanding of that issue or event."[54] Although absolute objectivity is impossible to attain, the three negative frames discussed above go beyond simply providing an argument opposing net neutrality. To some degree, these frames actually narrow the scope of debate surrounding net neutrality, providing little in the way of information.

In light of these findings, our suggestions are threefold. First, there needs to be more extensive coverage of media policy issues. Coverage of net neutrality in 2010 is indicative of an ongoing trend in which news outlets minimize coverage of media policy debates. Our study illustrates that net neutrality received coverage across a wide spectrum of mainstream media news outlets. Yet in the larger scheme of media coverage over an entire calendar year, a total of 261 stories culled from our sample is not a particularly impressive amount, especially considering the stakes of the debate and the prominence of the Internet in American culture. If the Internet is truly the most democratic communication medium to date and is to remain so, the public must not only be privy to debates surrounding its governance, but should have a greater presence in those policymaking debates as well. Otherwise, the free flow of discourse and information is in jeopardy as its control is out of the hands of the public.

In addition to increased coverage of media policy issues, such coverage should also be more balanced in presenting these debates. We are encouraged by the fact that within our sample, the majority of stories (124) provided a neutral perspective. Rather than mere opinion, these neutral stories display key points from multiple sides of the argument, substantiated by facts and statistics. The value of the neutral stories in our sample is that they tend to provide audiences with the most information about net neutrality, presenting various aspects of the debate for audience members to evaluate. This is in stark contrast to the three dominant frames that emerged within the negatively charged stories in our sample, which often functioned to narrow the scope of debate to the detriment of circulating discourse about net neutrality. This is the fundamental problem with agenda-extension of policy issues and news stories in general.

In their frame analysis of media discourse about gun control policies, Callaghan and Schnell note that through agenda-extension,

> Journalists can actively limit the public's right to access and evaluate different policy platforms and thus diminish the quality of political dialogue. Such actions have the potential to inhibit pluralism by blocking out the preferred

themes of interest groups and politicians. When complex policy issues are reduced to a single issue frame, regardless of the complexity of the issue, the
public is shortchanged, policy solutions are ignored, and a window of opportunity is closed.[55]

We do not mean to suggest that the negative frames in our study are problematic
simply because they oppose net neutrality. Stories limiting net neutrality to a
single positive frame can be equally damaging to the quality of discourse. Our
sample did not produce any clear frames in the stories that treated net neutrality
positively, however.

Yet negative stories employing frames of government takeover, an unbro-
ken Internet and a digital Fairness Doctrine do limit the information provided to
audiences and oversimplify the issue while often providing false information.
This is indicative of a much larger problem facing American journalism: it's
declining quality.[56] A greater sense of balance in media coverage can help to
combat this problem while enhancing public discourse. This is particularly important for coverage of media policy debates, which generally occur behind
closed doors with minimal input from the public, if any. The difficulty lies in the
fact that many media outlets have stakes in these debates, and thus are unlikely
to publish stories that conflict with their corporate interests. This is quite common with the continuing consolidation of media ownership among an ever-
shrinking number of corporate firms. This suggests the need not only for more
independent media sources, but for an end to the merger-mania that continues to
plague our media systems and hinder the quality and flow of discourse in American society.

Finally, there must be greater accountability of media outlets in relation to
the validity of information that they report. Two of the negatively charged
frames in our sample ("The Internet isn't Broken" and "Net neutrality is a Fairness Doctrine for the Internet") often rely upon false information to support their
frame. The effect is that news media present falsity as fact, and misinform their
audiences about the fundamentals of net neutrality.

Audiences may very well take it upon themselves to exercise critical faculty
and check various new sources against each other. However, the impact of stories perpetuating false information is heightened due to the limited amount of
coverage given to media policy debates. There are mechanisms in place that can
help to hold news media more accountable for knowingly disseminating false
information. The two dominant professional organizations for journalism have
both established codes of ethics for print and electronic journalism that speak
against deliberate distortion and publication false information, advocate diversity of viewpoints, and endorse accountability to the public.[57]

The codes of ethics developed by SPJ and RTNDA are voluntary attempts
at formalizing industrial self-regulation. However, as the SPJ code emphasizes,
"journalists should encourage the public to voice grievances against the news
media."[58]

This is perhaps the most effective way to facilitate news media accountability. With a vocal public who willingly air their grievances, news media are more likely to adhere to ethical standards of journalism, including distortion and knowing publication of false information, for it is audiences whose attention indirectly funds commercial news media.

More frequent and balanced coverage of media policy issues by an accountable news industry enhances public discourse on media policy. Collectively, these practices provide more information to the public, which significantly increases not only their understanding, but their ability to evaluate media policy debates. In turn, enhanced discourse improves the ability of the public to participate in policy debates through voting, petitioning Representatives and Senators as well as filing comments in FCC rulemakings. Thus, enhancing discourse becomes a way to increase participation in media policy debates by those most directly affected by media policy: the public.

Notes

1. Federal Communications Commission, *Policy Statement* (2005), http://www.publicknowledge.org/pdf/FCC–05–151A1.pdf (accessed January 20, 2011).

2. Dawn Nunziato, *Virtual Freedom: Net Neutrality and Free Speech in the Internet Age* (Stanford: Stanford University Press, 2009), 5–6.

3. Federal Communications Commission, *Consent Decree in the Matter of Madison River Communications, LLC and affiliated companies,* (2005), http:// hraunfoss.fcc.gov/edocs_public/attachmatch/DA-05-543A2.pdf (accessed January 20, 2011).

4. Carol M. Hayes, "Content Discrimination on the Internet: Calls for Regulation of Net Neutrality," *University of Illinois Journal of Law, Technology and Policy* 2009, no. 2 (Fall 2009): 500.

5. Ibid.

6. John D. Sutter, "FCC Chairman Proposes 'Net Neutrality' Regulations," *CNN Tech*, December 1, 2010, http://articles.cnn.com/2010–12–01/tech/ fcc.net.neutrality_1_google-and-verizon-mobile-internet-net-neutrality?_s=PM:TECH (accessed March 5, 2011).

7. Bianca Bosker, "Watch Obama's Net Neutrality Promises, Promises, Promises," *Huffington Post*, August 13, 2010, http://www.huffingtonpost.com/2010/08/13/net-neutrality-obama-see_n_681695.html (accessed March 10, 2011). Obama made a series of public pledges to protect net neutrality including the following addresses: November 14, 2007 in Mountain View, CA; a February 1, 2010 YouTube Interview; April 21, 2008 in Blue Bell, P.A.

8. Julius Genachowski, "Preserving a Free and Open Internet: A Platform for Innovation, Opportunity and Prosperity," address to The Brookings Institution (September 21, 2009), http://hraunfoss.fcc.gov/edocs_public/attachmatch/DOC-293568A1.pdf (accessed March 5, 2011).

9. FCC, *Policy Statement.*

10. *Comcast v. Federal Communications Commission*, 600 F. 3d 642 U.S. Court of Appeals (2010), sec. 644, 661.

11. Federal Communications Commission, *Report and Order in the Matter of Preserving the Open Internet Broadband Industry Practices* (2010) http://www.fcc.gov/Daily_Releases/Daily_Business/2010/db1223/FCC-10-201A1.pdf (accessed January 20, 2011).

12. *Joint Resolution Disapproving the Rule Submitted by the Federal Communications Commission with Respect to Regulating the Internet and Broadband Industry Practices.* H.J. Res. 37 112th Cong., 1st sess.; *Disapproving the Rule Submitted by the Federal Communications Commission with Respect to Regulating the Internet and Broadband Industry Practices.* S.J. Res. 6. 112th Cong., 1st sess.

13. United States Court of Appeals, Order No. 11-1014, February 11, 2011; Maisie Ramsay, "Verizon, MetroPCS Net Neutrality Suit to Proceed," *Wireless Week*, March 2, 2012, http://www.wirelessweek.com/News/2012/03/Policy-and-Industry-Verizon-Metro PCS-Net-Neutrality-Suit-to-Proceed-Legal/ (accessed March 10, 2011).

14. Erving Goffman, *Frame Analysis: An Essay on the Organization of Experience* (Boston: Northeastern University Press, 1986).

15. Jim A. Kuypers, *Rhetorical Criticism: Perspectives in Action* (Lanham: Rowman & Littlefield, 2009), 181.

16. Robert Entman, "Framing: Toward Clarification of a Fractured Paradigm," *Journal of Communication* 43, no. 4 (1993): 52 (emphasis in original).

17. See, for example, Jason A. Edwards, *Navigating the Post–Cold War World: President Clinton's Foreign Policy Rhetoric* (Lanham: Lexington Books, 2008); Kathy Elrick, "Themes from Clinton's 1992 Speeches: Frames, Puritan Influence, and Rhetoric" (paper presented at the annual meeting of the Midwest Political Science Association, Chicago, IL, April 2007); Jim A. Kuypers, *Press Bias and Politics: How the Media Frame Controversial Issues* (Westport: Praeger, 2002); Brian L. Ott and Eric Aoki, "The Politics of Negotiating Public Tragedy: Media Framing of the Matthtew Shepard Murder," *Rhetoric & Public Affairs* 5, no. 3 (2002): 483–505; Joseph.M. Valenzano III, "Framing the War on Terror in Canadian Newspapers: Cascading Activation, Canadian Leaders and Newspapers, *Southern Communication Journal* 74, no. 2 (2009): 174–190.

18. Jim A. Kuypers, *Doing News Framing Analysis: Empirical and Theoretical Perspectives* (New York: Routledge, 2010), 299; see also Kuypers, *Rhetorical Criticism*, 182–184.

19. Kuypers, *Doing News Framing Analysis*, 300.

20. Stuart Hall, "Encoding/Decoding," in *Media and Cultural Studies: Key Works*, ed. Gigi Meenkashi Durham and Douglas M. Kellner (Malden: Blackwell Publishing, 2006), 163–173.

21. Kuypers, *Rhetorical Criticism*, 181.

22. Kuypers, *Press Bias.*

23. See for example Society of Professional Journalists, "Code of Ethics," n.d., http://www.spj.org/ethicscode.asp (accessed April 2, 2011).

24. Kuypers, *Rhetorical Criticism*, 182, 186.

25. Cited in Kuypers, *Rhetorical Criticism*, 185.

26. FCC, *Report and Order*, 37–47, 137.

27. Holman Jenkins, "End of the Net Neut Fetish?" *Wall Street Journal*, April 7, 2010, http://online.wsj.com/article/SB10001424052702303411604575168053474388236 .html (accessed March 20, 2011); Phil Kerpen, "Silencing Voices of Internet Dissent: FCC's 'Net Neutrality' Puts New Congress to the Test," *Washington Times*, December 15, 2010, http://www.washingtontimes.com/news/2010/dec/14/silencing-voices-of-internet-dissent/ (accessed March 25, 2011); "Net Neutrality End Run," *Wall Street Journal*, December 4, 2010, http://online.wsj.com/article/SB10001424052748704369300

4575632522873994634-lMyQjAxMTAxMDIwMzEyND MyWj.html (accessed March 20, 2011); Wesley Pruden, "Pruden on Politics: Nothing Neutral about This Unholy Scheme," *Washington Times*, December 21, 2010 (accessed March 25, 2011); "www.internet.gov" *Wall Street Journal,* December 30, 2010, http://online.wsj.com/article/SB10001424052970203525404576049951815563410.html (accessed March 20, 2011).

28. "Government Gobbles the Web," *Wall Street Journal*, December 22, 2010, http://online.wsj.com/article/SB10001424052748703581204576033772053001588.html (accessed March 20, 2011); Steve Largent, "Providers Need Flexibility," *Wall Street Journal*, August 18, 2010 (accessed March 20, 2011).

29. L. Gordon Crovitz, "Do Monopolies Rule the Internet?" *Wall Street Journal,* November 28, 2010, http://online.wsj.com/article/SB10001424052748704693104575638401052783466.html (accessed March 20, 2011).

30. *Glenn Beck*, Cable television, Fox News Channel, May 18, 2010.

31. *Glenn Beck*, Cable television, Fox News Channel, September 9, 2010.

32. *Glenn Beck*, Cable television, Fox News Channel, April 5, 2010.

33. *Glenn Beck,* Cable television, Fox News Channel, December 16, 2010. Note that Beck often uses Marxism and socialism interchangeably.

34. *Hannity*, Cable television, Fox News Channel, December 21, 2010.

35. Kelly William Cobb, "Defining and Confining the Internet: Regulation by Another Name Is Still Regulation," *Washington Times*, May 26, 2010, http://www.washingtontimes.com/news/2010/may/25/defining-and-confining-the-internet/ (accessed March 25, 2011).

36. Adam Thierer and Mike Wendy, "Big Government the Real Threat to the Internet," *CNN.com* August 6, 2010, http://articles.cnn.com/2010-08-06/opinion/thierer.net.neutrality_1_net-neutrality-first-amendment-al-franken?_s=PM:OPINION (accessed March 5, 2011).

37. Robert M. McDowell, "The FCC's Threat to Internet Freedom," *Wall Street Journal,* May 24, 2010, http://online.wsj.com/article/SB10001424052748703395204576023452250748540.html (accessed March 20, 2011).

38. John Fund, "The Net Neutrality Coup," *Wall Street Journal*, December 21, 2010, http://online.wsj.com/article/SB10001424052748703581204576033772053001588.html (accessed March 20, 2011); *Hannity*, December 21, 2010.

39. "A 'National Broadband Plan,'" *Wall Street Journal,* Jan. 20, 2010, http://online.wsj.com/article/SB10001424052748703652104574652501608376552.html (accessed March 20, 2011).

40. *Glenn Beck*, April 5, 2010.

41. McDowell, "The FCC's Threat"; "www.internet.gov."

42. Nat Worden, "Time Warner Cable CEO Wary of Net Rules Limiting Options," *Wall Street Journal,* August 16, 2010, http://online.wsj.com/article/SB10001424052748704023404575430252734689506.html (accessed March 20, 2011).

43. "The Google-Verizon Deal," *Wall Street Journal,* August 14, 2011, http://online.wsj.com/article/SB10001424052748704164904575421472481509784.html (accessed March 20, 2011).

44. Kerpen, "Silencing Voices."

45. Andrew Moylan, "Spare Us the Broadband Plan; Everything Is Working Just Fine without Obama's Meddling," *Washington Times*, April 1, 2010, http://www.washingtontimes.com/news/2010/mar/31/spare-us-the-broadband-plan/ (accessed March 25, 2011).

46. Thierer and Wendy, "Big Government."

47. Marguerite Reardon, "Debunking the Internet Apocalypse," *CNN.com*, August 17, 2010 (accessed March 5, 2011).

48. *Glenn Beck*, Cable television, Fox News Channel, November 22, 2010.

49. *The O'Reilly Factor*, Cable television, Fox News Channel November. 22, 2010.

50. *Fox Special Report with Bret Baier*, Cable television, December 21, 2010.

51. Pruden, "Pruden on Politics."

52. John Eggerton, "Obama Does Not Support Return of the Fairness Doctrine," *Broadcasting and Cable*, June 25, 2008, http://www.broadcastingcable.com /article/ 114322-Obama_Does_Not_Support_Return_of_Fairness_Doctrine.php (accessed March 18, 2011); John Eggerton, "President Says He Would Veto Fairness Doctrine Imposition," *Broadcasting and Cable*, March 11, 2008, http://www.broadcasting cable.com/article/112821-President_Says_He_Would_Veto_ Fairness_Doctrine_Imposition.php (accessed March 18, 2011); John Eggerton, "Genachowski, Again, Voices Opposition to Fairness Doctrine," *Broadcasting and Cable,* September 17, 2009, http://www.broadcastingcable.com/article/354411– Genachowski_ Again_Voices_Opposition_to_Fairness_Doctrine.php (accessed March 18, 2009); John Eggerton, "Obama Restates Opposition to Return of Fairness Doctrine," *Broadcasting & Cable,* February 18, 2009, http://www.broadcastingcable.com/article/174455- Obama_Restates_Opposition_to_Return_of_Fairness_Doctrine.php?rssid=20065 (accessed March 18, 2009); "FCC Nominees Oppose Fairness Doctrine Reincarnation," *Radio World,* July 16, 2009, http://www.rwonline.com/article/fcc-nominees-oppose-fairness-doctrine-reincarnation/1480 (accessed February 18, 2011).

53. Federal Communications Commission, "Broadcast Applications and Proceedings; Fairness Doctrine and Digital Broadcast Television Redistribution Control; Fairness Doctrine, Personal Attacks, Political Editorials and Complaints Regarding Cable Programming Service Rates," *Federal Register* 76, (2011): 55817–55819.

54. Kuypers, *Press Bias,* 7.

55. Karen Callaghan and Frauke Schnell, "Assessing the Democratic Debate: How the News Media Frame Elite Policy Discourse," *Political Communication* 18, no. 2 (2001): 203.

56. Robert McChesney, *The Problem of the Media: U.S. Communication Politics in the 21st* Century (New York: Monthly Review Press, 2004); Robert McChesney and John Nichols, *The Death and Life of American Journalism: The Media Revolution That Will Begin the World Again* (Philadelphia: Nation Books, 2010).

57. Radio Television Digital News Association, "Code of Ethics and Professional Conduct," 2000, http://www.rtdna.org/pages/media_items/code-of-ethics-and-professional-conduct48.php (accessed April 2, 2011); Society of Professional Journalists, "Code of Ethics."

58. Society of Professional Journalists, "Code of Ethics."

Chapter 8

Informationism as Ideology: Technological Myths in the Network Neutrality Debate

Brian Dolber

On August 11, 2010, the *San Francisco Chronicle*'s editorial page declared that network neutrality had been lost. The mega-search engine corporation Google, who had long argued in favor of maintaining nondiscrimination principles online, agreed to concessions with the ISP and telecommunications behemoth Verizon, seemingly putting an end to the policy debate. "Google has turned its back on its promise to insist on Internet neutrality," the *Chronicle* stated. "Its just-announced proposal with Verizon would prohibit carriers from discriminating against competitors but allow them to charge websites more for better service. It excludes wireless mobile networks, which means that websites on mobile phones wouldn't even have safeguards against nondiscrimination. Because the two companies are so huge—and because the FCC has been unable to issue its own policy on net neutrality—their proposal will shape the debate."[1]

Until this point, the two firms were seen as being at odds with each other, as their strategies for capital accumulation were at cross-purposes. But as the *Chronicle* predicted, the agreement between Google and Verizon became the cornerstone for FCC policy. In December 2010, the regulatory body voted three to two to ban discrimination by network providers of any specific online service, but did not bar ISPs from charging more money for faster service. In addition, the rules differed between "wired" and "wireless" providers. Wireless companies could block apps and services if they do not compete directly with their own products.[2]

The Google-Verizon agreement and the FCC's adopted policy should be understood as expressions of class solidarity among the corporate elites of the information economy. While a popular movement for network neutrality had taken hold and successfully shaped some aspects of federal policy between 2005 and 2010, the pervasive ideology of informationism worked to limit its success.

In this chapter, I develop an ideology critique of arguments made during the network neutrality policy debates by representatives of the SavetheInternet coalition, the Communication Workers of America (CWA), and the African American civil rights community. Michelle Rodino-Colocino argues that "Understanding how ideology works can help critical media and communication scholars craft more effective critiques and aim actions at the wellspring of . . . ideology—material reality—so that we do not, as Marx and Engels cautioned in The German Ideology, fight "phrases with phrases."[3]

Thus, ideology critique is particularly crucial in the realm of policy discourses, because it enables activists to reframe their arguments and achieve particular goals, and allows for a conceptualization of reform-oriented projects that put the interests of the working class, and other intersecting oppressed groups, at their core. By locating the myths of informationism in arguments that were made both for and against network neutrality legislation, I demonstrate that reformers inadvertently helped to solidify corporate power in policy decisions, rather than creating a unified front in favor of democratically organized communications networks articulated along class lines. Informationism divided potential allies in the fight to preserve network neutrality, linked civil society organizations to corporate players, and helped to ensure that the Internet's future will be structured through privatized decision-making processes serving the needs of corporations rather than citizens.

Informationism as Ideology

Informationism, according to Robert Neubauer, is a corollary to neoliberalism. Rather than critically examining the role that ICTs have played in the ascent of deregulated, global capitalism, informationists envision "a global citizenship in which an emerging transnational citizenry is empowered by technology to usher in meaningful social change on a scope previously unimaginable." This notion has enabled "the resurgence of capitalism and the subsequent rejuvenation of global class power since the 1970s."[4]

Such utopian visions tend to accept declines in democratic participation and growing economic inequality that have characterized social life during the last several decades as part of a transition to a better, online future. Neubauer argues, "That these changes are described as technologically induced not only obscures the political intervention of neoliberalism and its hegemonic aspirations, but also helps form the basis of prescriptions for socio-technological changes without which global neoliberal regimes of flexible accumulation would simply not be possible."[5] As Douglas Kellner points out, informationism "exaggerate[s] the role of knowledge and information . . . occludes the connections between industrial manufacturing and emergent hi-tech industries," and downplays "the role of capitalist relations of production, corporate ownership and control, and hegemonic configurations of corporate and state power."[6]

Informationism works to rationalize the very real contradictions embedded in the capitalist system, obfuscating political-economic relationships. This variety of distortion is central to Marx's conceptualization of ideology. As Rodino-Colocino demonstrates, a close reading of Marx and Engels shows that ideology need not be articulated by members of the ruling class alone—but also "may emanate from any individual or cultural organ attached to any class or class fraction."[7] As such, individuals and groups from across civil society often perpetuate informationism through communications policy discourses. Dispelling the myths of informationism, therefore, will be essential to restructure the communications system along democratic lines in the epoch of what Dan Schiller terms "digital capitalism."[8]

During the debates over network neutrality, the SavetheInternet coalition, CWA, and representatives of the African American community, perpetuated three interrelated myths upon which informationism is predicated. These myths are: (1) there is no fundamental conflict between labor and capital; (2) access to advanced communication technologies will enable political participation and full citizenship; and (3) corporate elites within the new media sector are defenders of democracy under neoliberalism. Ultimately, these myths did the ideological work of dividing segments of civil society and enabling the endurance of corporate power in communications policymaking.

The first myth is that there is no fundamental conflict between labor and capital. While this idea is at the core of neoliberalism, its roots were ingrained in U.S. capitalism during the postwar period. Lizabeth Cohen argues that the United States transformed into a "consumer's republic" in the late 1940s and 1950s, as citizenship and consumerism became mutually constituted identities. Liz Fones-Wolf demonstrates how corporate trade associations, such as the National Association of Manufacturers (NAM), sold this ideology to the American public with the assistance of the Advertising Council. In addition, the Taft-Hartley Act of 1947 placed new legal restrictions on unions, and labor leaders sought to distance themselves from radicalism in light of Cold War anxieties. Thus, trade unions turned toward "business unionism," representing themselves as strengthening the private enterprise system rather than challenging it.[9]

Under neoliberalism, this myth has mutated into an extreme form that enables widespread reverence for information technology. According to informationism, the Internet would not only help keep capitalism afloat—it would also make it more humane and equitable. The myth of "the new economy" that circulated during the late 1990s held that technological advancement would boost production and put an end to the business cycle, as economic inequality reached staggering degrees in the United States.[10] While slow growth through the first decade of the twenty-first century and the financial collapse of 2008 have put an end to the hyperbolic, optimistic claims of the Clinton era, politicians continue to offer technological solutions to economic sluggishness. President Obama has emphasized the need for technological investment, education in the STEM (science, technology, engineering, and math) fields, and technological superiority as a competitive edge in the global economy.[11]

All of this ignores the fact that inequality has grown dramatically alongside the development of the Internet and digital technologies. As Robert Reich asserts,

> Although productivity continued to grow and the economy continued to expand, wages began flattening in the 1970s because new technologies—container ships, satellite communications, eventually computers and the Internet—started to undermine any American job that could be automated or done more cheaply abroad. The same technologies bestowed ever larger rewards on people who could use them to innovate and solve problems. Some were product entrepreneurs; a growing number were financial entrepreneurs. The pay of graduates of prestigious colleges and M.B.A. programs—the "talent" who reached the pinnacles of power in executive suites and on Wall Street—soared.[12]

While the Internet has been quite useful in the pursuit of capital accumulation, this has not led to widespread economic benefits throughout society.[13] During the Keynesian era, between 1947 and 1979, wages and compensation actually did rise alongside productivity. However, between 1980 and 2009, compensation increased by only 8 percent while productivity increased by 80 percent. As the poorest fifth of U.S. society actually lost ground during this period, the top fifth increased their wealth by 55 percent, and the top 1 percent has increased its share of the national income from 10 to 23.5 percent.[14]

Thus, informationism acts as an ideology by assuming unity of interests across class lines in capitalist economies, despite the stark, empirical evidence to the contrary. Since informationism confirms the neoliberal myth that all members of society may share the benefits of capitalism, it also suggests that technological access can curb neoliberalism's democracy deficit. This leads to the second myth of informationism, that access to advanced communication technologies is essential for political participation and full citizenship. This is evident in some discussions about the digital divide among academics, activists, policymakers and corporations where the discourse often elides the role of technologies in the broader political economy and assumes their inherent democratizing power.

For example, the Pew Internet and American Life Project has charted the adoption of the Internet in American homes across a variety of demographics since 2000. In their latest report, survey data suggested that, "The internet access gap closest to disappearing is that between whites and minorities. Differences in access persist, especially in terms of adults who have high-speed broadband at home, but they have become significantly less prominent over the years—and have disappeared entirely when other demographic factors (including language proficiency) are controlled for." However, "having a low household income (less than $20,000 per year) [is one of] the strongest negative predictors for Internet use."[15]

It is unclear, however, what "access" means for democratic participation. The sole concern with access seems predicated on accepting the cultural production thesis, which argues that new media technologies open up the possibilities of user-generated content, disrupting the top-down flow of information characterized by the broadcast era.[16] These views have been largely affirmed by the commercial press, such as in *Time Magazine*'s decision to name "You" 2006's Person of the Year.[17] Despite the increasingly important economic links between new and old media, the dominant view of "Web 2.0" contends that universal access to broadband technology could mean the development of a radically democratic public sphere, where marginalized groups retain greater control over their own representations. Some, such as MIT professor and self-described "critical utopian" Henry Jenkins, argue that too much focus on the limitations to technological access abstracts from the forms of democratic cultural participation which are already taking place.[18]

The cultural production thesis tends to downplay the ways in which new media users are workers within the neoliberal economy, providing personal information and creating value for large corporations such as Google, Facebook, and Amazon.[19] But because informationism ignores the competing interests between labor and capital, uses of new media are typically lauded as democratic self–expression. This gives rise to a third myth—the corporate elites of the new media sector are the defenders of democracy within the neoliberal environment. Because new media are the tools through which citizens may participate in the public sphere, the multinational corporations that provide access to new media platforms are viewed as being on the side of citizens, the defenders of democracy. Owners are, thus, on the side of users.

This belief is so strong that even those who might be critical of corporate capitalism's excesses frequently ignore the ways in which the system's problematic tendencies are reproduced in the technology sector. This was perhaps made most clear in the media discourses surrounding the death of Apple CEO Steve Jobs. At the very moment when the Occupy Wall Street movement was garnering news coverage and making its critique of inequality part of the national and global conversation, Jobs was roundly hailed as a technological genius who improved the lives of millions through innovative Apple products. The liberal *Huffington Post* blog posted a slideshow of sixty-two front pages of newspapers from around the world mourning the billionaire's passing. "Thought Differently," declared the *San Francisco Examiner*. The *Tampa Tribune* called Jobs a "revolutionary." "He changed the world," proclaimed the *Chicago Tribune*. "Apple Visionary Brought the World to Our Fingertips," stated the *Houston*

Chronicle.[20] As President Barack Obama stated in his 2012 State of the Union Address, "We should support everyone who's willing to work, and every risk-taker and entrepreneur who aspires to become the next Steve Jobs. After all, innovation is what America has always been about."[21]

Jobs and Apple were considered exceptional within the higher echelons of corporate capitalism because their products were widely understood as providing a public service, making our world a better place. The extreme praise obfuscated the fact that Jobs had cut Apple's philanthropy programs, as well as the harsh working conditions at the China's Foxconn factory where Apple products are manufactured.[22] Thus, informationism does the ideological work of perpetuating what Marx described as commodity fetishism, concealing the ways in which ICTs as consumer products are always already linked to the inherently exploitative processes of capitalism.[23]

These three myths were all present in the discourse around network neutrality, produced both by its opponents and its advocates. Rather than uniting around a broad conception of a democratically controlled communications infrastructure, media reformers, labor unions and some components of the African American political community became divided from each other, as they articulated their concerns alongside the visions of competing components of the corporate class. This enabled an eventual consolidation of corporate power through the Google-Verizon pact, shaping the future of Internet policymaking.

Free Press and the SavetheInternet.com Coalition

The major force behind the pro-network neutrality movement from within civil society was the media reform organization Free Press. Founded in 2002 by media scholar Robert McChesney and progressive journalist John Nichols, Free Press emerged as a political force in the wake of the fight to protect media ownership regulations in 2003. The group became the central organizing body behind the SavetheInternet.com coalition, composed of 800 groups from across the political spectrum—national and local progressive media reform organizations such as the Alliance for Community Media and the Consumers Union of America; conservative organizations such as the Gun Owners of America and the Christian Coalition; and labor unions such as the Service Employees International Union (SEIU) and the Writer's Guild of America. "Much of the business community—including big Internet companies like Google and E–Bay, but also countless electronics retailers and small businesses—supported Net Neutrality, too," writes McChesney. "But the story was often miscast in the press as a corporate clash of the titans—Google versus AT&T, or Yahoo! versus Verizon—when the real story was the unprecedented involvement in a media policy issue from the grassroots."[24]

Indeed, the massive outpouring of concern regarding network neutrality from the public demonstrated the impressive commitment and skill of Free Press' staff. Critics of the media reform movement, however, have charged that the organization's focus on policy has marginalized many media activists and their concerns. Advocating a "media justice" approach to activism, Dan Berger writes that the media reform movement is quite limited in its critique and potential "without a broader focus on the underlying ideologies and structures which uphold the current arrangement of society, and which are far more determining in the function and orientation of modern communication systems . . . [W]ithout a deeper challenge to the routines and commonsense notions that both uphold the media system and tether it to systems of injustice, progressive media policy may still uphold conservative politics."[25]

This may be due, in part, to the limits of acceptable political discourse within the beltway. As Thomas Streeter observes in his history of broadcasting policy, Washington is an "'interpretive community,' a community of individuals that interact with one another in such a way as to generate a shared, relatively stable set of interpretations." While policy may be hotly debated, it tends to occur "within a broad framework of underlying assumptions." Violating those assumptions does not necessarily make one "a heretic, but uninteresting, incomprehensible, or at best quaint."[26]

Thus, policy reform activists must be in conversation with the values and norms of the dominant institutions in order to be taken seriously. While Free Press has enjoyed "stunning and unanticipated success in Washington," McChesney argues that the organization might do better to pursue "a more ambitious agenda that pushes the bounds of policy options beyond beltway parameters and emphasizes grassroots mobilization." Characterizing himself as a "sympathetic critic," the co-founder says "what Free Press is doing is [not] sufficient to encompass the full range of media reform activism, or media activism writ large, that is necessary."[27]

Thus, despite the fact that its founders are quite critical of capitalism and the media system's role within it, Free Press' focus on policy work led it to make arguments in favor of network neutrality within an informationist discourse. As an ideology, informationism provides an acceptable framework to make claims for reform in Washington, rendering more radical critiques of the political economy and its relationship to technology invisible. The tendency toward informationism was clear from the organization's entree into the policy fight, and left it open to criticism that it was merely shilling for new media companies, such as Google.[28]

The myths of informationism were present throughout Free Press' arguments in favor of network neutrality. First, Free Press linked network neutrality to a version of competitive capitalism where consumers benefit from a vibrant marketplace, echoing the notion that there is no inherent conflict between capital and labor. Immediately following the Supreme Court's landmark 6–3 Brand X ruling in 2005, undermining the nondiscrimination principle online, Free Press' policy director Ben Scott said that the decision was "an insult to the American ideals of competitive markets, equal opportunity, and the free flow of information." Decrying telecom companies as "gatekeepers taxing innovation and throttling the free market," Scott said, "There will be no competitive broadband carriers. There will be no independent ISPs. The thriving new market for Voice Over Internet Protocol (VoIP) may be badly destabilized."[29] Alongside the Consumers Union and the Consumer Federation of America, Free Press released another statement calling for a policy "that meets the needs of consumers, entrepreneurs, ISPs and applications developers."[30]

Free Press also singled out the Internet as a force for economic progress, despite previously mentioned evidence to the contrary. "Net neutrality is the reason why the Internet has driven economic innovation, democratic participation, and free speech online—and the public demands Congress not dismantle it," claimed Free Press campaign director Tim Karr in a press release.[31] Here, Free Press linked "digital capitalism" to a thriving democracy, ignoring the contradictions between these to which political economists within communications studies are well attuned. Thus, we see the second myth of informationism emerge within Free Press' discourse—that access to new technologies is an essential component of democracy, despite its often contradictory relationship with "economic innovation," or capital accumulation.

Because online tools are assumed to have strongly democratic attributes regardless of their relationship to capital, the content provider corporations that emerged within the new media environment were given a privileged place within Free Press' arguments. "The next great idea, the next Google or eBay or Napster or whatever, won't have the capital to get themselves in the fast lanes right away. The reason the big e-companies were so successful were that they started on the same level playing field as everyone else," Scott said.[32] The notion that public policy should enable "the next Google" assumes that it would deliver some widespread social benefit. Thus, Free Press reinforced the third myth of informationism, that new media corporations bring democratic possibilities to the masses, giving credence to the notion that these companies are somehow exceptional within corporate capitalism.

Corporations like Google have worked hard to make themselves seem indispensable. As Siva Vaidhyanathan argues, "Our dependence on Google is the result of an elaborate political fraud."[33] Asserting corporate responsibility under its mantra, "Don't be evil," Google represents itself as being "weightless and virtual," unlike like the large corporations of the industrial age. Google argues that they are vulnerable to competition, still a mere startup. This ignores the enormous capital they have invested in "physical sites such as research labs, server farms, data networks, and sales offices." While their positions such as their initial stance on network neutrality may "correspond roughly with the public interest," it is essential that media activists realize that this is more of a convenient coincidence than a corporate commitment to a particular set of progressive politics. Quite frequently, Google's positions "such as fighting against stronger privacy laws in the United States" undermine the public interest.

Thus, the desire for "the next Google" among reformers is in no small part due to the company's enormous efforts to cultivate a progressive image through successful branding and public relations. While many within the SavetheInternet coalition undoubtedly understood this, the informationist rhetoric likely resonated with its "netroots" membership base. By definition, this demographic understands the Internet as a political tool. But as Matthew Hindman demonstrates, only a small percentage of the population utilizes the Internet for such purposes. There are no political sites among the top fifty most frequently visited nonadult web pages. In April 2007, the most frequently visited, the *Huffington Post* ranked 796th. Hindman's conception of "Googlearchy" demonstrates how Google directs searchers to the most frequently linked websites, constricting the online public sphere. Furthermore, the most widely read bloggers—the very root of the "netroots"—tend to be white, highly educated, upper-middle class men, reflecting the same segment of society as the elite media.[34]

Thus, SavetheInternet's informationism was predicated on a familiarity with and a connection to online services to which many people do not have access or do not use. Believing that content providers are working in the service of democracy requires some level of interaction with, and affinity for, those providers. While arguments that were inherently critical of capital's relationship to technology might have resonated across the digital divide, informationist discourses allowed potential allies to view ISPs—not content companies—as the true emissaries of democracy in neoliberal societies. Representatives of those who would build the network infrastructure, and those who have very limited access to the online world, were thus able to argue that the public at large would be better served by policies that favor the telcos rather than websites and applications.

The Communications Workers of America

The Communications Workers of America (CWA) represents 700,000 members, including 300,000 workers in cable and telephone services. Describing itself as "the union for the information age," the CWA emerged out of AT&T's "company unions" that were made illegal by the Wagner Act in 1935. While the union has presented a challenge to the telecom industry in terms of its employment practices, it has often found itself between a rock and a hard place in advocating for telecommunications policies. On the one hand, they must protect and, if possible, expand the number of jobs at the employing companies of CWA members.

On the other hand, this means maintaining a corporate-controlled communications system. This has the tendency to promote an anti-labor culture and the increasingly efficient accumulation of capital at the expense of working people.[35]

Founded during the Fordist era, the CWA has long perpetuated the first myth of informationism: there is no inherent conflict between the interests of labor and capital. As a result they have protected the short-term interests of unionized workers at the expense of a more democratically controlled communications system. In 1942, for example, the NFTW fought against the War Department, alongside employers at Western Electric, in order to prevent the government from setting up their own communications repair shops in direct competition with the private, unionized company.[36]

The CWA brought this approach to unionism, steeped in compromise, into the neoliberal era following the federal breakup of AT&T in 1984. Having been against the divestiture, the union did at first oppose efforts by the Regional Bell Operating Companies (RBOCs)—also known as the "Baby Bells"—to scrap strict federal regulations. By the 1990s however, CWA had come to support allowing the RBOCs to go into "information services," and argued that the 1996 Telecommunications Act would help create jobs in the growing information sector.[37]

CWA President Larry Cohen continued the tradition of reflecting AT&T's telecommunications policy goals when he wrote to the House Judiciary Committee to oppose the Internet Freedom and Nondiscrimination Act in 2006. In his letter, he argued that the bill would delay "deployment of high-speed networks, with particularly negative impact on underserved communities." Because the bill would require broadband providers to offer network services for free to all content providers, Cohen echoed the phone and cable companies' claims.

> Broadband network providers would not be able to recover the billions of dollars they invest in the construction of high-speed networks. As a result, investment in the physical infrastructure necessary to provide high-speed Internet will slow down, the U.S. will fall even further behind the rest of the world, and our rural and low-income populations will wait even longer to enter the digital age.[38]

Instead, Cohen recommended passage of H.R. 5252, the Communications Opportunity Promotion and Enhancement (COPE) Act. Despite the SavetheInternet coalition's strong opposition to the bill, the CWA argued that its passage would encourage network build-out. The FCC would retain the power to institute nondiscrimination rules, but they would not be written into law. Rather, the FCC would oversee a service complaint process.[39]

Here, Cohen reinscribed the three myths of informationism. First, as a union leader, Cohen demonstrated a belief that there is no fundamental opposition between capital and labor, showing faith in the profit motive as a sufficient arbiter of communications resources. Taking this as a given, Debbie Goldman of the CWA told *In These Times*, "We're America, where there's capitalism, and companies invest where there's a return on their capital." "How are the companies going to pay for this? Their business model, and our position, is that, in order to pay for the public good of the high speed network, these companies should be able to have a private video network."[40] As a labor union, the CWA argued that it was in their members' and the public's interest to allow cable and telephone companies to shape the nature of the network. Indeed, broadband providers would help keep the U.S. competitive in the global economy, lest the country "fall even further behind the rest of the world."[41]

This leads to the second myth of informationism—access *uber alles*. Without questioning "access to *what*?", the CWA assumes Internet access to be an end in and of itself. In order to participate in neoliberal society "rural and low-income populations" must be served by the telecom giants. Presumably, access will enable these communities to empower themselves culturally and economically. However, this presumption rests on a denial of class conflict, particularly in advocating for a policy that leaves open the potential for corporate discrimination.

As such, the CWA started its "Speed Matters" campaign. The campaign website declares, "We must act now on universal Internet access and the digital divide," because "high speed Internet access is essential for economic growth, job creation and global competitiveness." Placing primary emphasis on broadband speed, and encouraging site visitors to think primarily about download and upload rates as the central concern with broadband policy, the site features a "speed test" where you can find out how your own broadband access stacks up in relation to your state, the United States, and a selection of other nations (Germany, the Netherlands, Sweden, Japan, and South Korea).[42]

This primary focus on network technology at the expense of democratic control of media stands somewhat in contrast to CWA's recent history in advocating for a more democratic media system. CWA is not a monolithic organization; there are competing interests within it. Since the 1990s, convergence in media industries has prompted convergence of media labor, and CWA now represents workers on the content-production side of the equation, as well as those who maintain the networks. The Newspaper Guild (TNG), which has represented journalists since the 1930s, became affiliated with CWA in 1997. TNG has worked alongside Free Press, playing a central role in media reform efforts, particularly around issues of media ownership consolidation.[43] However, CWA has also supported policies that have allowed for the re-consolidation of AT&T. In this respect, the CWA's approach to the network neutrality question has forced it to reconcile tensions between the short-term interests of members in network operation versus content provision.

Speed Matters' "Four Principles for High Speed Internet Policy" demonstrate how CWA has navigated these concerns, leaning towards the side of its historic support for AT&T and reproducing the ideology of informationism. Seemingly contrary to the CWA's anti-neutrality position, the third principle is an "open Internet." But Speed Matters suggests that this can be accomplished through network self-regulation and technological development. They say,

> We must protect free speech on the Internet so that people are able to go to the websites they want and download or upload what they want when they want on the Internet. There should be no degradation of service or censoring any lawful content on the Internet. At the same time, reasonable network management is necessary to preserve an effective and open Internet. Most important, building high-capacity networks will ensure that all Americans have fast, open access to all content on the Internet.[44]

Thus, as suggested by the third myth of informationism, telecom giants are the defenders of democracy under neoliberalism, especially for those across the digital divide. Rather than critiquing their employers for not building out high speed networks where they are not most profitable, CWA accepted the need for profit as a legitimate reason for perpetuating the digital divide. In this case, government regulations and those calling for them were keeping the digitally disenfranchised down.

The Speed Matters campaign worked to divide the labor movement as a whole from media reformers supporting network neutrality. While SEIU, the main force behind the Change to Win labor coalition, supported SavetheInternet, endorsers of Speed Matters include the AFL-CIO, the American Federation of Teachers (AFT), the Coalition of Black Trade Unionists, the International Brotherhood of Electrical Workers (IBEW), and other labor groups. Some of the Speed Matters proponents were also members of SavetheInternet, such as the American Library Association.[45] While seemingly at cross-purposes, Speed Matters carefully called for "reasonable network management," but did not specifically object to legislation that would enforce that principle.[46] However, schisms between media reformers and labor demonstrate the need for a coherent critique of technology's role in the economy within media policy debates.

The Congressional Black Caucus and the Civil Rights Community

While CWA's position reflected the interests of the major telecommunications industry employers, there is little evidence that this happened as the result of direct manipulation by AT&T or other industry behemoths. Members of the Congressional Black Caucus (CBC) who often represent poor, racialized communities, were seemingly influenced by corporate benefactors to oppose network neutrality. Like CWA officials, they made informationist arguments, discussing broadband access in and of itself as the key concern.

Many black members of Congress argued alongside telecom companies that removing neutrality protections through the COPE Act in 2006 would enable broadband providers to advance racial equality by expanding online access. Rep. Bobby Rush (D–IL), the former Black Panther who represents part of Chicago's largely African American South Side, supported the "great bill" on civil rights grounds. He proclaimed that opponents were "trying to confuse" people from realizing that that it would "drive the cost of cable down for my community in my district and districts like mine across the country. More than that, this bill . . . will allow for diversity and ownership diversity in programming. This bill will allow minorities to get into the cable industry and into the telecommunication industry."[47]

Thus, Rush and other CBC members understood technological access—without regard for Internet content—as the way to curb racial inequality. This was so urgent that efforts to ensure neutrality protections were a hindrance to justice and represented the privilege of middle-class white reformers. This narrative displaced the potential for a critique of corporate influence over communications that unjustly shapes access as well as content within communities of color. By separating "access" and "neutrality" from each other, anti-neutrality CBC members could support equal rights for the consumption of media over broadband while implicitly rejecting rights to participatory communication.

Corporate supporters of the COPE Act invested large sums in a massive public relations and lobbying campaign. In 2006, AT&T was the most active telecom lobbyer in Washington, devoting $22,405,497 to their cause on Capitol Hill.[48] Verizon, the second most active lobby, spent $13,202,500, while the National Cable and Telecommunications Association (NCTA), which represents both the phone and cable companies spent an additional $14,020,000 on promoting legislative efforts.[49] In addition, the 2006 election cycle saw the communication and electronics firms give $77,301,680 in federal campaign contributions. Within the sector, AT&T and Verizon were the most politically active corporations, spending $4,317,072 and $2,116,785 on contributions, respectively.[50]

Telecom companies specifically targeted African American leaders to support the COPE Act without network neutrality provisions. Rush, the co-chair of the Energy and Commerce Committee where all telecommunications legislation originates, received $15,500 in campaign contributions from AT&T, making them the second largest contributor to his coffers in 2006. In addition, Comcast and the NCTA gave him $10,000 each, tying for fourth on his list. Other top-twenty contributors included Verizon and the U.S. Telecommunications Association.[51]

Perhaps most controversially, AT&T's SBC Foundation awarded a $1 million grant to the Rebirth of Englewood Community Development Corporation (ROE CDC) community center founded by the Congressman.[52] *Black Commen-*

tator noted in its "CBC Monitor Report," "We at CBC Monitor were puzzled as to what would compel Rep. Rush to even consider supporting such egregious legislation, let alone be pawned as a Democratic co-sponsor of this bill. Now we know why."[53]

Verizon also targeted the CBC as a whole through their lobbying efforts. While Verizon does much of its own lobbying, they also contract with a number of different outside firms, including Dellums and Associates, headed by CBC founder Ron Dellums, a former representative from California. In 2006, Verizon paid the lobbying firm $100,000 for services, constituting over 40 percent of their annual receipts.[54]

In addition to persuading members of Congress directly, the telecom industry curried favor with civil rights and leadership organizations in the African American community in order to influence policymakers. While Jeffrey Chester notes that this has been a long-term strategy to temper criticism within the black community of market-based efforts to bridge gaps in service provision, the network neutrality debates prompted the industry to take things to a new level.[55]

For example, telcos "rented the traditional contingent of black preachers" and created the front group, the Ministerial Alliance Against the Digital Divide (MAADD) in 2006.[56] Invoking the language of informationism, MAADD declares itself "a next generation civil rights organization... promoting personal and economic development in low-income and minority communities across the country."[57] Among the group's supporters was the National Coalition on Black Civic Participation (NCBCP) with union leaders and then Democratic Party chair Howard Dean on its board.[58]

The telecom industry's strategy was quite successful. While 46 percent of Democrats voted against the bill, only 13 out of 40 or one-third of CBC members opposed the COPE Act. Bruce Dixon of *Black Commentator* declared after the vote that the CBC could no longer claim to be the conscience of the Congress, having sold out its constituents to the highest bidder.[59] Although several caucus members, most prominently Rep. Diane Watson (D–CA), were vocal supporters of network neutrality and opposed the COPE Act, they were marginalized. Watson, along with Rep. Hilda Solis (D–CA), offered a motion to recommit the legislation after the vote, on the grounds that it would have restricted broadband access within communities of color and encouraged redlining.[60] Thus, the primary issue of concern remained whether government regulations or market forces would be the best way to bridge the digital divide, with questions of Internet content remaining a secondary issue.

By encouraging black leaders to focus on questions of access, telecom companies helped to paint network neutrality as a "white issue," a concern for those who had the privilege of using high speed broadband. African American advocates for neutrality were accused of "playing into the hands of white media activists" as some black leaders told their community that network neutrality was not "our issue."[61] To some extent, the African American community's skepticism about network neutrality made sense. As blogger Matt Stoller wrote,

> I sympathize with...various African-American leaders who believe that the telecom companies are operating in good faith, and that the Save the Internet and the Google crew represent a new and weird group that doesn't really understand their community . . . Techies haven't been there in terms of broadband or telecom policy for a long time, so at least [Rush is] getting something. And it doesn't hurt that Rush gets $1 million from AT&T pushed to one of his pet community projects. Say what you will about perceptions of corruption, from Bobby Rush's perspective it sure looks like AT&T wants to serve your constituents more than, say, Google, or the blogs.[62]

While Google had successfully branded itself as a company that provides a public service to the tech savvy, the telecom companies did the same for those on the other side of the digital divide. Here again informationism constricted the terms of the debate over network neutrality.

As the debate over network neutrality continued through the decade, the elections of Democratic Congresses in 2006 and 2008 prompted the telecom industry to focus even more on winning the support of black and Latino politicians, activists, and citizens. Soon after the 2006 midterm elections, the League of United Latin American Citizens (LULAC) and the National Caucus of Black State Legislators (NCBSL) took firm stances against neutrality.[63] By 2009, the telcos had assembled a large number of organizations representing the African American community to speak on its behalf in the network neutrality debate. The Joint Caucus of Black Elected Officials wrote to the FCC to "ensure that any new rules proposed can clearly be shown to benefit all consumers and not expand the digital divide facing disadvantaged populations."[64]

Rev. Jesse Jackson echoed these sentiments in a letter to the FCC, on behalf of the Rainbow PUSH Coalition. Once again focusing on access over content, Jackson said, "The quickest and most feasible way for low-income and minority individuals to attain a voice of their own is through broadband access and adoption." Showing trust in tech companies to enable this, he argued "sustained private sector investment holds the promise of greater access to affordable broadband for 95 percent of Americans." In a slight against network neutrality, he stated, "We want to make sure that the Commission's proposed rules will not have the unintended consequences of making broadband unaffordable to the countless disadvantaged Americans we serve. We continue to call on the Commission to conduct a facts-driven analysis of the possible impact that its planned regulations may have on deployment and adoption rates."[65]

The politics of network neutrality continued to divide the black community, and the progressive movement more generally. David Honig of the Minority Media and Telecommunications Council (MMTC) criticized the pro-net neutrality civil rights organization Color of Change for their objections to Rep. Rush being made ranking member of the Telecommunications Congressional Sub-committee. Rush, according to Honig, has "a commitment to underserved communities and low income people who are not online. While these people are not representative of Color of Change's many online members, Rush's commitment to them should hardly disqualify him from congressional leadership."[66]

Similarly, Navarrow Wright at *Black Web 2.0* criticized the pro-neutrality organization Public Knowledge as "digital elites" who do not believe that black leaders "are intelligent enough to think for themselves."[67] One commenter on the same blog called neutrality supporters "self-righteous Poindexters," and noted that organizations such as Free Press are typically "comprised primarily of the upper middle class, well to do, and digitally connected . . . It's easy to criticize underserved communities who accept charitable contributions when you have the digitally connected ready, willing and ABLE to fund your efforts at the click of a mouse. This self-righteous indignation of yours does nothing to eradicate the digital divide."[68] Noting the racial privilege that many media reformers have, much of the African American political community placed their faith in the private sector to solve the digital divide, rather than building a movement for online communications devoted to democracy over profit.

Conclusion

When Google and Verizon announced their pact, network neutrality advocates were outraged. Dubbing the agreement "a backroom deal between industry giants," Free Press called on legislators to reject the new policy framework.

> If codified, this arrangement will lead to toll booths on the information super-highway. It will lead to outright blocking of applications and content on increasingly popular wireless platforms. It would give companies like Verizon, Comcast and AT&T the right to decide which content will move fast and which should be slowed down. And it will destroy the open Internet as a platform for small business innovation and job creation, cementing companies like Google's dominant market power online.[69]

While still painting the ideal image of the Internet as one of capitalist ingenuity, Free Press for the first time publicly acknowledged that Google had joined the ranks of the telecom companies and was part of the corporate communications infrastructure.

Google's betrayal of the principles of network neutrality highlights their preference for corporate hegemony over a truly open Internet, and the extent to which their policy positions are direct reflections of concerns about their bottom line. However, debates over the Stop Online Piracy Act (SOPA) in late 2011 and early 2012, which would have allowed the government to shut down websites merely accused of hosting content that infringed on copyright, once again placed media reformers on the same side as major online content providers. Calling on old media stalwarts—news directors at ABC, CBS and Fox—to end the "SOPA news blackout," the SavetheInternet coalition declared, "Social media sites like Reddit, Tumblr and Twitter, companies like Google, Yahoo! and eBay and some of the biggest websites on the Internet have joined with the nation's largest Internet rights advocates in opposition to this legislation."[70] While the SOPA bill was defeated, media reformers rarely distinguished their political goals from those of their strange bedfellow corporate allies.

This raises an important question: can policy discourses operate outside of informationism? Streeter suggests that it became impossible to speak about broadcasting policy outside the corporate liberal framework during that medium's early years.[71] Perhaps this is true of informationism and the Internet today. Media justice advocates argue that policy reform efforts are severely limited in their efficacy because changes in policy do not necessarily result in a more just distribution of power.[72] Pointing toward media reformer's proclivity towards improved technology, Makani Themba-Nixon writes, "without a vision that seeks to repair the impact of the past and the privilege, we'll have the same old oppression with better, high-speed resolution."[73]

Indeed, McChesney suggests that serious organizing efforts will be necessary in order to complement beltway activity.[74] In order to be most effective, this organizing will have to take place not just among the educated and wired middle class, but among the working class and communities of color. It will have to problematize calls for access, and make demands for power. Such activism may open up space for policy discourse that shirks informationism in favor of a critique of corporate control over our democracy. While the Occupy Wall Street movement has infused mainstream political discourse with the rhetoric of "the 99 percent" as a critique of corporate and financial elites, media coverage has also paid considerable attention to activist use of commercially driven social networking tools, such as Twitter and Facebook, reinscribing the ideology of informationism. Labor unions, civil rights groups, and all those who care about a democratic media system would do well to interrogate the underpinnings of informationism as ideology, and work together toward building a communications system alongside a broader political economy that is not dominated by the needs of capital, but rather by the needs of the people.

Notes

1. "Net Neutrality Lost in Google-Verizon Deal," *San Francisco Chronicle*, August 11, 2010, http://www.sfgate.com/cgi-bin/article.cgi?f=/c/a/2010/08/10/EDRB1ERR Q1.DTL (accessed July 16, 2012).

2. Lauren Kirchner, "FCC Passes Net Neutrality Policy (Sort Of)," *Columbia Journalism Review*, December 21, 2010, http://www.cjr.org/the_news_frontier/fcc_passes_net_neutrality_poli.php?page=all (accessed July 16, 2012).

3. Michelle Rodino-Colocino, "'Feminism' as Ideology: Sarah Palin's Anti-Feminist Feminism and Ideology Critique," *tripleC* 10, no. 2 (2012): 471, citing Marx and Engels 1996, 41.

4. Robert Neubauer, "Neoliberalism in the Information Age, or Vice Versa?: Global Citizenship, Technology and Hegemonic Ideology," in *tripleC* 9 no. 2 (2011): 196.

5. Ibid., 195.

6. Ibid., 200, citing Douglas Kellner, *Media Spectacle* (London: Routledge, 2003), 22–23.

7. Rodino-Colocino, "'Feminism' as Ideology," 462.

8. Dan Schiller, *Digital Capitalism* (Cambridge, MA: MIT Press, 1999).

9. Lizabeth Cohen, *A Consumer's Republic: The Politics of Mass Consumption in Postwar America* (New York: Alfred A. Knopf, 2003); Liz Fones-Wolf, *Selling Free Enterprise: The Business Assault on Labor and Liberalism*, 1945–60 (Urbana: University of Illinois Press, 1995); Paul Buhle, *Taking Care of Business: Samuel Gompers, George Meany, Lane Kirkland and the Tragedy of American Labor* (New York: Monthly Review Press, 1999).

10. Robert W. McChesney, *The Political Economy of Media: Enduring Issues, Emerging Dilemmas* (New York: Monthly Review Press, 2008).

11. Jason Koebler, "Obama Pushes STEM in State of the Union," *U.S. News and World Report*, January 25, 2012, http://www.usnews.com/news/blogs/stem-education/2012/01/25/obama-pushes-stem-in-state-of-the-union (accessed July 16, 2012).

12. Robert Reich, "The Limping Middle Class," *New York Times,* September 3, 2011, http://www.nytimes.com/2011/09/04/opinion/sunday/jobs–will–follow–a–strengthening–of–the–middle–class.html?pagewanted=all (accessed July 16, 2012).

13. McChesney.

14. Bill Marsh, "The Great Prosperity," (graphic), *New York Times.* September 4, 2011, http://www.nytimes.com/imagepages/2011/09/04/opinion/04reich-graphic.html?ref=sunday (accessed July 16, 2012).

15. Kathryn Zickuhr and Aaron Smith, "Digital Differences," *Pew Internet and American Life Project*, April 13, 2012, (http://pewinternet.org/Reports/2012/Digital-differences/Main-Report/Internet-adoption-over-time.aspx (accessed July 16, 2012).

16. Robert Burnett and P. David Marshall, *Web Theory: An Introduction* (New York: Routledge, 2003), 70–78.

17. Lev Grossman, "You—Yes, You—Are *Time*'s Person of the Year," *Time*, December 25, 2006, http://www.time.com/time/magazine/article/0,9171,1570810,00.html (accessed July 16, 2012).

18. Henry Jenkins, *Convergence Culture: Where Old and New Media Collide* (New York: NYU Press, 2006), 247.

19. See, for example, Nicole S. Cohen, "The Valorization of Surveillance: Towards a Political Economy of Facebook," *Democratic Communiqué* 22, no. 1 (2008): 5–22 http://journals.fcla.edu/demcom/article/view/76495 (accessed July 16, 2012).

20. "Steve Jobs Death: Newspaper Front Pages Pay Tribute to Apple Icon," *Huffington Post*, October 6, 2011, http://www.huffingtonpost.com/2011/10/06/steve–jobs–death–newspaper–front–pages_n_997828.html#s392829 (accessed July 16, 2012).

21. Barack Obama, "President Obama's State of the Union Address," Accessed at http://www.nytimes.com/interactive/2012/01/24/us/politics/state-of-the-union-2012-video-transcript.html (accessed July 16, 2012).

22. Eric Alterman, "The Agony and Ecstasy—and 'Disgrace' of Steve Jobs," *The Nation*, November 28, 2011, http://www.thenation.com/article/164499/agony-and-ecstasy-and-disgrace-steve-jobs# (accessed July 16).

23. Rodino-Colocino, 464–465.

24. McChesney, *Communication Revolution: Critical Junctures and the Future of Media* (New York: The New Press, 2007), 184–185.

25. Dan Berger, "Defining Democracy: Coalition Politics and the Struggle for Media Reform," *International Journal of Communication* 3 (2009): 15.

26. Thomas Streeter, *Selling the Air: A Critique of the Policy of Commercial Broadcasting in the United States* (Chicago: University of Chicago Press, 1996), 115–120.

27. McChesney, "Understanding the Media Reform Movement," *International Journal of Communication* 3 (2009): 49.

28. "Free Press Group Leverage Ties to Google and Obama," *Roger Hedgecock Show*, March 2, 2012, http://www.rogerhedgecock.com/story/17064385/free-press-group-leverage-ties-to-google-and-obama (accessed July 16, 2012).

29. Free Press, "Free Press Responds to Supreme Court Rulings in Brand X and Grokster Cases," *Free Press*, June 27, 2005 http://www.freepress.net/release/80 (accessed July 16, 2012).

30. "Brand X: Statement of Consumer Groups on The Supreme Court's Decision," June 27, 2005 www.google.com/url?sa=t&rct=j&q=&esrc=s&source=web&cd=1&ved=0CCIQFjAA&url=http%3A%2F%2Fwww.savetheinternet.com%2Fsites%2Fdefault%2Ffiles%2Freleases%2F06.27.05_CFA_Brand_X_release.doc&ei=1pQFUJ-XKOHy0gGf7O3cCA&usg=AFQjCNFnhuganv5a1hrYD7KW6_BNiq5x6g (accessed July 16, 2012).

31. Free Press, "Strange Bedfellows United to Save the Internet," *Free Press*, April 24, 2006 http://www.freepress.net/release/128 (accessed July 16, 2012).

32. "Building the Internet Toll Road," *Wired*, February 26, 2006, http://www.wired.com/techbiz/media/news/2006/02/70292?currentPage=all (accessed July 16, 2012).

33. Siva Vaidhyanathan, *The Googlization of Everything (And Why We Should Worry)* (Berkeley: University of California Press, 2011), 40.

34. Matthew Hindman, *The Myth of Digital Democracy* (Princeton, N.J.: Princeton University Press, 2009), 60–63; 38–57; 113–118.

35. Brian Dolber, "A Rock and a Hard Place: The CWA's Approach to Media Policy, 1984–2002," *Democratic Communiqué* 22 no. 2 (2008): 66–84.

36. Ibid., 68–70.

37. Ibid., 72–79.

38. Communications Workers of America, "CWA Opposed Move Toward Internet Regulation," May 26, 2006, *CWA–Union.org*, http://www.cwa-union.org/news/entry/cwa_opposes_move_toward_internet_regulation#.UAW_SnCr_-Y (accessed July 16, 2012).

39. Ibid.

40. Brian Cook, "Not Neutrality," *In These Times*, March 26, 2007, http://www.inthesetimes.com/article/3081/not_neutrality/ (accessed July 16, 2012).

41. Ibid.

42. Speed Matters, "Test Your Speed," *Speed Matters*, http://www.speedmatters.org/pages/test-your-speed (accessed July 16, 2012).

43. Linda Foley, "Media Reform From the Inside Out: The Newspaper Guild–CWA," in *Future of Media: Resistance and Reform in the 21st Century*," ed. by Robert W. McChesney, Russell Newman and Ben Scott (New York: New Press, 2005), 41–9.

44. Speed Matters, "Principles for High Speed Internet Policy," *Speed Matters*, http://www.speedmatters.org/pages/principles/ (accessed July 16, 2012).

45. Speed Matters, "Speed Matters Partners," *Speed Matters*, http://www.speedmatters.org/content/partners/ (accessed July 16, 2012).

46. Speed Matters, "Principles."

47. U.S. Congressional Record, 109th Congress,. H3585, http://thomas.loc.gov/cgi–bin/query/F?r109:2:./temp/~r109PUNeQf:e351473: (accessed July 16, 2012).

48. Center for Responsive Politics, "Lobbying: AT&T," *OpenSecrets*, http://www.opensecrets.org/lobby/clientsum.php?year=2006&lname=AT%26T+Inc (accessed July 16, 2012).

49. Center for Responsive Politics, "Lobbying: Verizon Communications," *OpenSecrets*, http://www.opensecrets.org/lobby/clientsum.php?year=2006&lname=Verizon+Communications (accessed July 16, 2012); Center for Responsive Politics, "Lobbying: National Cable and Telecommunications Assn," *OpenSecrets*, http://www.opensecrets.org/lobby/clientsum.php?id=D000022131&year=2006 (accessed July 16, 2012).

50. Center for Responsive Politics, "Communications/Electronics: Long Term Contribution Trends," *OpenSecrets*, http://www.opensecrets.org/industries/contrib.php?ind=B&cycle=2006 (accessed July 16, 2012).

51. Center for Responsive Politics, "Top Contributors: Bobby L. Rush 2005–2006," *OpenSecrets*, http://www.opensecrets.org/politicianscontrib.phpcycle=2006&cid=N00004887&type=I&newmem=N (accessed July 16, 2012).

52. "Rush Takes the Heat on Franchise Bill," *Telecom Policy Report*, May 1, 2006, http://findarticles.com/p/articles/mi_m0PJR/is_18_4/ai_n16135790/ (accessed July 16, 2012).

53. Leutisha Stills, "CBC Monitor Report: Rep. Bobby Rush: AT&T's Million Dollar Man," *Black Commentator*, April 27, 2006, http://www.blackcommentator.com/181/181_cbc_monitor_bobby_rush_pf.html 2006 (accessed July 16, 2012).

54. Center for Responsive Politics, "Lobbyists: Dellums and Associates," *OpenSecrets*, http://www.opensecrets.org/lobby/firmsum.php?id=F23686&year=2006 (accessed July 16, 2012).

55. Jeffrey Chester, *Digital Destiny* (New York: New Press, 2006), 81–82.

56. Bruce Dixon, "The Black Stake in the Internet: Net Neutrality Is an African American Issue," *Black Commentator*, Issue 183, May 11, 2006, http://www.blackcommentator.com/183/183_cover_black_stake_internet.html (accessed July 16, 2012).

57. Ministerial Alliance Against the Digital Divide, "About MAADD," *maadd.org*, http://www.maadd.org/about.php (accessed July 16, 2012).

58. Dixon.

59. Dixon, "Black Caucus Caves to Corporate Power: Two-Thirds Vote against Black Interests," *Black Commentator*, June 15, 2006, http://www.blackcommentator.com /188/188_cover_cbc_www_dixon.html (accessed July 16, 2012).

60. U.S. Congressional Record.

61. Dixon, "The Black Stake."

62. Matt Stoller, "On Building a Progressive Governing Coalition around Network Neutrality," *MyDD*, December 6, 2006, http://mydd.com/2006/12/6/on-building-a-progressive-governing-coalition-around-net-neutrality (accessed July 16, 2012).

63. Ibid.

64. Lesly Simmons, "Black Elected Officials Urge FCC to Keep Digital Divide in Mind," *Black Web 2.0*, November 20, 2009, http://www.blackweb20.com/2009/ 11/20/black-elected-officials-urge-fcc-to-keep-the-digital-divide-in-mind/#.UARM 6nCr-fQ (accessed July 16, 2012).

65. Davey D., "The AT&Tea Party: We're in the Business of Silencing People and Net Neutrality," *Davey D's Hip Hop Corner* (blog), September 23, 2010, http://hiphopandpolitics.wordpress.com/2010/09/23/attea-party-were-in-the-business-of-silencing-people-on-the-net-the-telecoms-new-tactic-to-dead-net-neutrality/ (accessed July 16, 2012).

66. David Honig, "Civility—And Why Bobby Rush Should Be the Ranking Communications Subcommittee Member," *Huffington Post*, November 22, 2010, http://www.huffingtonpost.com/david-honig/civility-and-why-bobby-ru_b_786065.html (accessed July 16, 2012).

67. Navarrow Wright, "Who Should We Trust When it Comes to Net Neutrality?" *Black Web 2.0*, October 26, 2009, http://www.blackweb20.com/2009/10/26/who-should-we-trust-when-it-comes-to-net-neutrality/#.UARpE3Cr8b3 (accessed July 16, 2012).

68. Calvin in Comments on "Lawmakers Urge Incentives to Increase Broadband Adoption," *Black Web 2.0*, December 30, 2009, http://www.blackweb20.com/2009/ 12/30/lawmakers-urge-incentives-to-increase-broadband-adoption/#.UAR1DHCr8b0 (accessed July 16, 2012).

69. Free Press, "Free Press Urges Policymakers to Reject Google–Verizon Pact," *Free Press*, August 9, 2010, http://www.freepress.net/press–release/2010/8/9/free-press-urges-policymakers-reject-google-verizon-pact (accessed July 16, 2012).

70. Free Press, "Why Is the Media Ignoring SOPA?" *Free Press*, http://act2.freepress.net/sign/media_sopa/ (accessed July 16, 2012).

71. Streeter, 59–110.

72. Malkia A. Cyril, "Media and Marginalization," in *The Future of Media: Resistance and Reform in the 21st Century*, ed. Robert McChesney, Russell Newman, and Ben Scott (New York: Seven Stories Press, 2005), 97–104.

73. Makani Themba-Nixon, cited in Cyril, 97.

74. McChesney, "Understanding the Media Reform Movement."

Part IV: Socio-Cultural Implications

Chapter 9

A Critical Theory of Technology Approach to the Study of Network Neutrality

Tina Sikka

Network neutrality is a critical principle that defines the Internet's network design. Broadly, network neutrality refers to the notion that "the network itself should be neutral and not specialized for any specific applications or platforms." As such, it should "treat all kinds of information, content and sites equally."[1] Debates over network neutrality center around whether or not Internet network operators should be able to alter the quality of access to content based on a content provider's ability to pay for faster download speeds or speedier access.

In the course of this chapter, I present an overview of a critical theory of technology approach, as developed by Andrew Feenberg, and demonstrate how this perspective can be used to advocate for network neutrality and the democratization of the Internet's development. Feenberg views technologies and their development as inherently historical, value-laden, flexible, and political. This constructivist perspective is reflected in a number of cross-disciplinary approaches to technology as well the philosophy of technology, the sociology of science and technology (STS) and critical theory of technology among others.

I undertake this complex study in a number of stages beginning with a brief summary of arguments opposed to network neutrality. I then draw on Feenberg's critical theory of technology approach to examine network neutrality on three levels: sociology, technology, and policy. Finally, I close the chapter with a discussion of what this critical approach has to offer in relation to preserving network neutrality through a discussion of the democratization of design as well as perspectives on public participation in technological controversies.

My objective is to make an interdisciplinary case for network neutrality and concerted action in its defense since the objective of this approach is to strengthen democratic participation in the development and design of technological artifacts. Facilitating the ability for the public to get involved in technological design is therefore imperative. This is particularly necessary since, as Feenberg contends,

The legislative authority of technology increases constantly as it becomes more and more pervasive. But if technology is so powerful, why don't we apply the same democratic standards to it we apply to other political institutions? By those standards the design process as it now exists is clearly illegitimate.[2]

It is essential to acknowledge that the so-called fair or neutral treatment of content is not, nor has it ever been, inevitable. For Feenberg, the Internet is a concrete technological artifact; when examined historically and in light of relations of power, the Internet is seen for what it is: a product of technical and social decisions about design and use. Feenberg makes clear that "technology is socially relative and," as such, "the outcome of technical choices is a world that supports the way of life of one or another influential social group."[3] This underlying assumption, and its relevance to network neutrality, forms the foundation of this chapter. I begin by outlining some of the arguments against network neutrality that will have to been considered in any future determinations.

The Case against Network Neutrality

Opponents argue that a policy of network neutrality will limit the ability of telecommunications companies to generate enough capital for investment in costly infrastructure because money that might be made from content providers will be lost. Another claim, made by such groups as the Internet Freedom Coalition and Citizens Against Government Waste, is the much more ideologically charged argument that prohibiting a tiered Internet undermines the free market norms that form the basis of our capitalist economy.

Some have also argued that breaching network neutrality is required in order to protect end users from viral Distributed Denial of Service (DDoS) attacks which "may provide a valid basis for restricting providers' practice of discriminatory traffic handling."[4] Most of these arguments tend to focus on the need to regulate "bad traffic" in a limited way.

Finally, opponents of network neutrality including Ryan Brannen of the Texas Public Policy Foundation and right wing media personality Glenn Beck, have also charged that any kind of government control over the Web will lead to increased censorship and the invasion of users' privacy. This line of reasoning has thus discursively positioned network neutrality in opposition to the basic tenets of freedom and democracy itself.

It must be noted that much of this rhetoric, repeated publically by right-wing politicians and think tanks, is based upon a fundamental misunderstanding of network neutrality as evidenced by Michelle Bachmann's response to a question about this issue in 2010:

So whether they're attacking conservative talk radio, or conservative TV or whether it's Internet sites, I mean, let's face it, what's the Obama administration doing? They're advocating net neutrality, which is essentially censorship of the Internet. This is the Obama administration advocating censorship of the Internet. Why? They want to silence the voices that are opposing them. Despite the fact that they continue to have much of the mainstream media still providing cover for all of these dramatic efforts that the Obama administration is taking. So they're very specifically and pointedly going after voices that they see are effectively telling the truth about what the Obama administration is trying to do."[5]

While such hyperbole may be brushed aside, when a large number of powerful individuals and organizations repeat the same flawed argument, they tend to take on an air of credibility or even truth. Feenberg maintains that such conflicts around issues of censorship, freedom and democracy can have one of two outcomes: the development of the Internet directed by corporate interests, or under public control with some government protection.

Moreover, Feenberg makes clear that the seemingly high costs of public participation in technological development is a burden that must be borne—particularly if we are to ensure that the Internet does not suffer the fate of other communication technologies by operating in corporate interests rather than those of the public. In the following sections, I further develop this argument by articulating what a critical theory of technology approach contributes to the network neutrality debate on the sociological, technical, and policy levels.

Critical Dimensions of Network Neutrality

There are a number of important concepts, categories and theories that comprise Feenberg's critical theory of technology. I present the parts of this sophisticated model most illuminating to the issues of network neutrality, distinguishing between the sociological, technical, and policy levels. It should be noted, however, that this is a purely analytical distinction and that these three levels are in fact co-extensive.

Sociological Dimensions

On the sociological level, primary and secondary instrumentalization can be used to unpack some of the ideas and values that lay at the core of the Internet. To begin with, however, it is useful to define what Feenberg terms a technology's formal bias.

Formal bias refers to the often prejudicial social arrangements that form around technologies and which favor the interests of one group over another.

The formal bias of technologies such as the Internet can be further divided into two types: constitutive bias, which "refers to the values embodied in the nature of design," and the implementation bias, which refers "to the values realized through contextualization."[6]

In his later work, Feenberg reconsiders this division and develops his theory of formal and substantive bias into a more nuanced theory of instrumentalization, encompassing both the technology's social dimensions as well as those "distinctive operations that define a technical relation to the world."[7] Feenberg argues that a critical theory of technology must incorporate functionality with social analysis.

From this, Feenberg makes an analytic distinction between primary and secondary instrumentalizations (which, to a certain degree, corresponds with constitutive and implementation bias). Primary instrumentalization refers the process of opening artifacts such that their functionality is open to manipulation, while secondary instrumentalization refers to the social choices and contexts that determine how a technology is used.

Put another way, primary instrumentalization refers to those aspects of technology that stem from "the functional relation to reality," while secondary instrumentalizations emerge "from social involvements and implementation."[8] In the case of the Internet, which was originally intended to facilitate a narrow form of government and military communication, it was only on the level of secondary instrumentalization that social actors intervened to shape its development as a socially rich tool for communication.

Feenberg explains that the problem with studying technologies abstractly (i.e., only on the level of formal bias or primary rationalization) tends to suppress "the dimensions of contextual relatedness and potentiality" of technologies as well as transforming "its objects into mere means, an operation that prejudices their status as much as any valuative choice."[9] On the subject of network neutrality, this kind of formal bias or rationalization, if left unchecked, can evolve such that the interests of capital, efficiency, and profitability come to predominate (as they have in other communication technologies including radio and television). As such, the discriminatory principles that define our modern capitalist system, as well the unequal socio-political and economic structures can coalesce in technologies—even if that technology contains a technically neutral infrastructure that is somewhat resistant to this kind of transformation.

Take for example reports that Comcast, America's largest Internet provider, has been exempting its own video services from caps on bandwidth that it imposes on other streaming services. According to a March 28, 2012 report in *The Raw Story*, in addition to violating the principles of network neutrality in this way, Comcast has been instituting policies that limit users' movements and access by tying access to gaming with video (you must subscribe to both services). As author Stephen C. Webster argues,

Internet freedom activists have long warned that the "cableization" of the Internet was coming, and if Comcast were to open up its own "private IP network" to other major content providers—for a fee, of course—it would represent the creation of a super–tiered Internet of sorts, where moneyed players essentially run the show, forsaking the public Internet for the private Internet and hauling millions of users along with them into a new environment with entirely different rules.[10]

This violation of non-discrimination principles entrenches a formal bias into the very code of Internet technology based on rationalized principles of control and profit. Further, this action skirts between embedding a bias on the constitutive or primary level, since it begins to tinker with the very codes of the Internet itself, as well as on the level of context or implementation (secondary instrumentalization). As Netflix CEO Reed Hastings asserted in response to the Comcast story, Comcast has used, "The same device, the same IP address, the same Wi-Fi, the same Internet connection, but totally different cap treatment . . . In what way is this neutral?"[11]

A related example is the privatization of the Internet's backbone via new technologies that make preferential treatment of content possible. These Quality of Service Technologies (QoS) allow corporations to "manage network traffic to expedite the delivery of affiliated content while demoting competitive material to second-class service," while also creating "the ability to segregate traffic [which] impacts the backbone industry by favoring large backbone providers over smaller ones." For effective QoS across a network, "it is necessary to maintain control of the network traffic over the entire length of the network."[12] This privatization is directly connected to network neutrality as it feeds this process of rationalization and makes content discrimination possible.

The introduction of this formalized bias using QoS technologies, on both a constitutive and contextual level, threatens the open nature of the Internet system. In opposition to these trends, it is only through concerted democratic rationalization that this kind of institutionalized social rationality can be stopped. The saving grace for the Internet, therefore, is that it remains an open technology that can further develop along a number of different paths with corresponding interests and relations of power.

Overall, the Internet currently favors the values of fairness, neutrality, openness and non-discrimination discussed previously. The interests of the public have thus been intentionally incorporated into the very infrastructure of the Internet, thereby allowing anyone to access and create content in a manner that is relatively fair and equitable. These values, and by extension the way in which Internet has evolved thus far, appear natural to us. However, Feenberg argues that this bias is neither natural nor inevitable and can be fundamentally transformed if more profit and corporate driven interests are prioritized in the Internet's future development.

It is thus imperative that the specifics of the technical code that makes up the Internet be considered. As Storsull asserts, it is the Internet Protocol's end-to-end principle which insures that the "network connects the end users, or the ends of the network and is neutral to what is communicated between these ends."[13] This more technical aspect of a critical theory of technology, and its relation to network neutrality, is the focus of the next section.

Technical Aspects

Andrew, Craig, and Jon Flanagin provide a comprehensive overview of the development of the Internet using Andrew Feenberg's conception of the technical code. They make two significant claims with respect to the relationship between design and values as it relates to the Web. First, they argue that the very structure of the Internet contains and reflects particular social and political values because of its distributed and decentralized nature, privileging "enhanced individual agency and a renegotiated sense of individual and collective authorship."[14] Network neutrality is another such sociopolitical value or affordance reflected in the Internet's structural design.

Flanagin, Flanagin, and Flanagin also make the case that that it is the intentional choices of interested parties that will either support or undermine these features in the future. The fact that the Internet has the capacity to facilitate democratic participation, collaboration, and fair treatment of information does not mean such qualities are inherent. A notable example is how peer-to-peer file sharing has, through provisions of the Digital Millennium Copyright Act (DMCA), resulted in the strengthening of digital copyright law. This clash between openness and regulation highlights the disjuncture between the "innovativeness designed into the internet"[15] and the increasingly corporate-centered values being enacted through the DMCA.

With respect to network neutrality, this perspective makes clear that despite the Internet's decentralized and open characteristics, its malleability as a technological artifact also makes it possible to track down copyright violators and to throttle Internet traffic.

In line with the social construction of technology perspective (SCOT), this view also draws upon the concept of interpretive flexibility—the fact that users often utilize technologies in ways not initially anticipated.[16] Because of the neutrality of its network and its flexibility, the Internet has allowed for its use as a social network, an economic conduit, a political tool, and a creative outlet.

A useful way of parsing out and unpacking the unique technical characteristics of the Internet is by drawing on the sociological notion of "layering." A variety of layering techniques used in the study of technology are applicable to network neutrality and help us to unpack structural arguments favoring network neutrality, as well as initiating debates about the Internet's future role in public participation. On a vertical level (as opposed to a horizontal level which might focus more intently on sociotechnical arrangements), these layers helps to parse out and deal with complex technologies that often combine a large number of functionalities, ideas, norms and regulations in one artifact.

For example, Darryl Cressman draws on Feenberg's approach to divide the study of technology into three interconnected layers: ideas, policies and design.[17] At present, the battle over the future vision of the Internet is being fought on all three levels. On the level of technical design, it is important to note that is the use of nonproprietary protocols (TCP/IP) has allowed all users of the Web to access content in an equitable manner (i.e., content has not been artificially blocked or slowed). The ability to offer choice, encourage the free flow of ideas and content, provide access to and develop new kinds of content and services are all thought to be logical outcomes of an Internet system that retains a neutral or impartial architectural base.

It is at this design level that telecommunications firms are exerting pressure on governments to enact rules and regulations that would dismantle network neutrality. It is also important to keep in mind that even at the technical level of design, social priorities, discourses, ideologies, values, and norms are thoroughly embedded in technologies. Finally, on the constitutive design level, a further level of layering of the Internet has been described by Galloway and Thacker who discuss the complex interconnections that exist between and betwixt four levels: the application layer (e.g., Telnet, the Web), the transport layer (e.g., TCP), the Internet layer (e.g., IP), and the link (or media-access) layer (e.g., Ethernet).[18]

Network neutrality aims to protect the protocols that make up each individual level and the holistic interrelated system. Intervention proposed by firms such as Comcast and Verizon include the link or media-access layer, whereby ISPs will be able to filter content. Due to their interrelation, such filtering will necessarily affect the other three layers. Thus, as Lessig argues, when the Transmission Control Protocol (TCP) and the Internet Protocol (IP) become compromised, the entire structure of the Web as a locus of free access and participation will be undermined. What it comes down to, Lessig asserts, is that

> Just as we are beginning to see the power that free resources produce, changes in the architecture of the Internet—both legal and technical—are sapping the Internet of this power. Fueled by bias in favor of control, pushed by those whose financial interests favor control, our social and political institutions are ratifying changes in the Internet that will reestablish control, in turn, reduce innovation on the Internet and in society generally.[19]

Thus far, the Web has been a self-regulated and neutral technology wherein the transfer of data is negotiated by network protocols. Because these protocols are encased in a distributed network, there is no hierarchization of information, nor a point through which such a hierarchy can be introduced. This means that a blog on election issues can be accessed with the same speed as a major news network. Network neutrality is thus coded into the very protocols that make up the Web. This is in contrast to centralized networks, which direct all information through one central hub, or a decentralized network, which spreads power over several hubs or gateways.

The problem, however, is that in our society where principles of efficiency, profit and economic outcomes are so highly valued and engrained, these values can appear as a kind of hegemonic inevitability under which no other guiding principles can direct technological development. When applied to the Internet, this would present the interests of the major telecommunications firms and ISPs as not only unavoidable but logical.

Against the principle of network neutrality articulated earlier, most ISPs have been lobbying governments for two forms of power. The first is to shape traffic, which gives ISPs the capacity to monitor how customers are using bandwidth and, if they disapprove (as in the case of the use of peer–to–peer software such as BitTorrent), to direct speeds to other applications or reduce the connection speed (a practice known as throttling).

Second, ISPs seek the power to offer tiered service, whereby they can require consumers and content providers to pay for faster download services. In support of this arrangement, ISPs, media corporations, and industry specialists have argued that network neutrality should be treated as a matter of market competition, and as such, favor

> Regulation that enables operators to benefit from their investments, recommending "light touch" regulation that only regulates neutrality in markets where operators have significant market power and sets a minimum standard for broadband above which operators can prioritize third party traffic, and encourages transparency of billing and competitive market entry for a variety of operators.[20]

Yet, as Feenberg repeatedly underlines, the further development of the Internet along these lines is neither necessary nor inevitable. Rather, he makes clear that efficiency is never the sole criterion in explaining the success or failure of a technology "since several viable options usually compete at the inception of a line of development. Technology, therefore, should be considered 'underdetermined' by the criterion of efficiency and responsive to the various particular interests that select among these options."[21] This means that while the further development of the Internet *can* follow the logic of efficiency and profitability, it is not inevitable that it must.

Feenberg goes on to assert that technical standards (which become design codes when black boxed), also tend to take on an air of durable intractability. In constructivist studies of technology, black boxing points to the "stabilization of a technology, together with concomitant ('co-produced') social relations." These technologies are consequently "no longer a site for controversy,"[22] and as such, the way in which they are taken up and deployed by social groups comes to be seen as settled. However, as will be demonstrated further on, due to a variety of social, political, and economic factors, these closures can be pried opened and renegotiated at critical junctures.

This is precisely what has happened with the Internet. For years, the Internet's role as a means for communication has been black-boxed and taken for granted. Time and an increasing awareness of the profit-potential of the Web on a variety of fronts have opened this black-box, renegotiated by several actors with conflicting interests. Feenberg refers to these conflicts as emergent technological controversies, conflicts over the social control of a variety of technological artifacts. Tanja Storsul calls this a technological tussle, "the tensions and disputes between conflicting interests, trying to promote solutions that may be to their advantage."[23]

If the interests of users are ignored within this interpretive flexibility, it is possible that the Internet will develop in ways that, through the layering of new technologies and manipulation of the Internet's infrastructure, will result in a two-tiered Internet structure. As Klein and Kleinman argue, the power of particular elite social groups to do this is reflected in the fact that

> Through the control of administration, this elite may impose its interests on the entire organization by avoiding actions that jeopardize elite privilege. When these elites participate in a design process as representatives of their association, they may impose their own meanings on the artifact. The division of labor internal to a social group and the resulting class structure can allow an elites' system of meaning to dominate the whole group.[24]

With respect to the Internet and network neutrality, these interests are reflected in a variety of hearings and committees on the future policy of the Web formed by governments all over the world. Notably, they tend to be front-loaded with representatives of the private sector for whom network neutrality, and the democratic spaces that it opens for citizens, are not a priority.

Feenberg deals with technological controversies in a unique way by connecting the sociological and technical levels of analysis. He begins by likening design codes to laws in democratic states in that, like legal norms, evolve out of controversies and competing interests that often pit the "specifications formulated by experts on the one hand" against "the expressions of desire and complaints by lay users or victims on the other." This tension is not necessarily antagonistic, but requires a critical and ongoing process of translation between "a technical discourse and social, cultural and political discourses."[25] On the subject of network neutrality, this means that those political and technical "experts" in charge of the future of the Internet must work to preserve the open and progressive parts of the Web's design code. To that extent, law and policy governing Internet communication will directly affect future development of the Internet and its structure.

Law and Policy

Whenever technological controversies arise, a primary locus of conflict is over what kind of technological future will be enshrined in legal norms. Feenberg argues that mapping this kind of technical politics is essential as legal codifications around technology institutionalize particular social interests over others. In doing so, legal norms have the capacity to black-box particular technological usages and applications, or codify more democratic structures of openness. When examining network neutrality through this lens, it is useful to have some idea of the current status of legislation as it exists in the United States and European Union, as such an understanding illuminates the spaces of openness and closure that exist within the network neutrality debate.

In America, legislators and free speech advocates have lobbied the U.S. Congress to introduce legislation aimed at prohibiting "broadband providers from blocking, impairing, degrading or discriminating against the ability of any person to use broadband connections to access the content of service available on broadband networks."[26] Groups advocating for strong legislation have made it clear that the protections against unreasonable interference and discrimination by ISPs have been eroded by the FCC's deliberate choice to remove the obligations of nondiscrimination and common carriage that traditionally come with being a provider of telecommunication services. The result, as Nunziato argues, is that

> By allowing broadband providers to restrict the free flow of information and ideas, the current regime allows these private gatekeepers of speech to obstruct the "dissemination of information from diverse and antagonist sources" and to thwart the "public discussion an informed deliberation that . . . democratic government presupposes and the First Amendment seeks to achieve."[27]

In response, the FCC passed "Open Internet" rules in 2010, aimed at protecting the neutrality of the Internet. The norms established by the FCC include:

> First, transparency: fixed and mobile broadband providers must disclose the network management practices, performance characteristics, and commercial terms of their broadband services. Second, no blocking: fixed broadband providers may not block lawful content, applications, services, or non-harmful devices; mobile broadband providers may not block lawful websites, or block applications that compete with their voice or video telephony services. Third, no unreasonable discrimination: fixed broadband providers may not unreasonably discriminate in transmitting lawful network traffic.[28]

While these rules may appear to uphold the principles of network neutrality at first glance, closer inspection reveals that they are relatively weak, vague, and difficult to enforce.

For example, the use of the term "lawful," as it relates to the proviso about content leaves the door open for providers to block so-called illegal content (the definition of which is unclear). Moreover, a number of telecom operators, including Verizon, have launched legal challenge to these rules. Most importantly, wireless carriers remain free to alter the speeds of connections to websites based on said site's willingness to pay for faster speeds. What this opening portends is the potential that similar rules will migrate to the broadband Internet in the future.

The relatively weak legislation ensuring network neutrality in the United States reveals how thoroughly social, political, and thus underdetermined, the Internet is. Law and policy will continue to play a pivotal role in how the Internet evolves in the coming years. Having the ability to participate in the shaping of the Internet on sociological and technical and legal layers is not only a public right, but is also an obligation. In the final section of this piece I outline and discuss such a way forward.

Public Participation
and the Science/Technology Divide

There has been a significant amount of work done in the philosophy of science on the subject of public participation in the creation, understanding, and evolution of scientific knowledge.[29] Traditionally, the hard sciences have understood technology as the most efficient application of science, and thus consisting of tools needed to solve problems and extend human capacities. Science, on the other hand, tends to be defined as the accumulation of knowledge.

However, recent work in the philosophy and sociology of science and technology has drawn attention to the unclear and artificial nature of this boundary between science and technology. Technology must be understood in light of its material aspects and its non-material elements. Therefore, as Green argues, it becomes clear that

> Once knowledge comes into play, technology is implicated in social processes, and there is nothing neutral about society . . . The knowledge of how to create and enhance technology, and of how to use technology, is socially bound knowledge. Each society operates to determine who will acquire this knowledge, and in which circumstances. Knowledge is no more neutral than technology.[30]

Understood in this way, technology and science can be viewed as interrelated parts of a complex social system where science, like technology, is no longer entirely neutral, universal, or value-free. This being the case, examination of scientific knowledge, particularly with respect to the role of the public plays in its creation, understanding, and application, can illuminate the study of technologies including the Internet.

Thus, network neutrality should be considered in light of the political affordances that it contributes to the Internet's operation. This supports the arguments put forth by Feenberg and others that as a technological artifact whose present form is rooted in decisions made by a variety of actors, the Internet is political, ambivalent, and underdetermined. In addition, a more philosophical approach can contribute to the net neutrality debate by providing a theoretical foundation for the role of public participation in the development of science and design of technology.

In *The Philosophy of Science and Technology Studies*, Steve Fuller argues that conflicting models of the role of public participation in scientific development and deployment can be traced back to three distinct philosophical positions that illuminate competing views of the role of the public in technological controversies. First, the Comtean view would see an elite group of apolitical experts lead a fickle public through scientific and technological change.

In contrast, Mill and Dewey advocate that it is the public who should guide scientific and technological development through communication and understanding. Here, the public has a clear interest and role in scientific evolution and technological change made possible by mass education.[31]

In opposition to these views is what Fuller calls Gnostic scientism, which asserts that there is a kind of personal, quasi-religious salvation in science that is of direct impact and import to the general public. This view, which incorporates spiritual concerns into social ones, demonstrates the role that public scientists play in shaping the worldview of the public—particularly in regards to their relationship to scientific knowledge.

Fuller unpacks the deeply historical roots of these perspectives while arguing that science is an area of knowledge inextricably linked to issues of social concern. Thought of in this way, technological artifacts have a similar relationship with the public as it relates to their evolution. Yet this relationship can only be fruitful with an actively engaged public, which Fuller notes is often lacking in scientific and technological development. Conversely, a participatory attitude toward technology would treat its development as a partisan affair, and provides a means for more democratically organized discourse surrounding science and technological development.

It is from this theoretical foundation that Feenberg's model of a democratization of technology can provide a more concrete way to protect network neutrality and ensure that technology remains subordinate to social goals and needs. This normative approach contains a kind of technical micropolitics whose realization occurs only when "social groups excluded from the original design network articulate their unrepresented interests politically."[32] The formation of collegial organizations and other kinds of citizen groups are therefore needed to combine "democratic rationalization of technical codes with electoral controls on technical institutions."[33]

Finally, Feenberg argues that in light of these complexities, we need to acknowledge that "new technology can also be used to undermine the existing social hierarchy or to force it to meet needs it has ignored."[34] This is particularly applicable to the case of the Internet and network neutrality as evidenced by the examples of citizen initiatives—many of which have used the Web to mobilize in support of network neutrality.

Democratic Movements

Activists embracing this kind of critical approach have developed creative and innovative strategies to mobilize against threats to network neutrality while posing alternative ways to move forward. In one such example, Lawrence Lessig advocates for the dismantling of the FCC in favor of creating what he calls the Innovative Environmental Protection Agency (iEPA). The iEPA's core objective would be to encourage "minimal intervention to maximize innovation," while avoiding both excessive government regulation and monopolization of the Web.[35] Other suggestions might include allowing for municipalities to deliver cheaper and faster Wi-Fi, a complete ban on the throttling of connections and laws prohibiting telecoms from charging websites for speedier access.

Groups working for these kinds of changes include entities such as the Save the Internet Coalition, Free Press, and Latinos for Internet Freedom. These grassroots organizations have used the Internet to lobby for the preservation and protection of those affordances of the Web dedicated to free speech, open connectivity, information, and access provided on a nondiscriminatory basis. What is most significant about this particular umbrella group is that its members range from Google to the American Civil Liberties Union and even the National Rifle Association. However, it must be noted that groups such as Save the Internet Coalition have come under criticism for politicizing the Internet by asserting the seemingly natural quality of Internet principles such as freedom and openness. Doing so fails to acknowledge that this mode of thinking "enshrines openness as equivalent to freedom, leaving aside the necessary complexities of managing networks that depend on protocol. As Web scientists know, balancing openness and control is one of the key requirements for creating systems of collaboration."[36]

In Canada, SaveOurNet.ca (part of the larger OpenMedia.ca group) is another grassroots organization that, in a manner similar to the U.S.-based Save the Internet Coalition, aims to preserve the freedom of access and usage that network neutrality makes possible. On their website, SaveOurNet.ca underlines the very fact that:

> When it comes to surfing the web, the Internet user, not big telecom, should be
> in the driver's seat. But a handful of companies want a discriminatory or "gate-
> keeper" network so they can control Canadians' access to the Internet. They
> have already been caught throttling or slowing Internet traffic to businesses and
> consumers, blocking access to websites that criticized them and crippling con-
> sumer devices and applications.[37]

Through the use of their website's "Stop the Meter" Campaign as well as their
Twitter feed, policy submissions, reports, videos, brochures, and resources for
youth and adults, SaveOurNet.ca has compiled a considerable amount of information in pursuit of network neutrality protections. Moreover, its members'
advocacy encompasses larger issues of media concentration, affordability, surveillance, copyright restrictions, and an important call for more democratic digital policy-making.

  Also of note are groups on the other side of the debate arguing in an equally
forceful way that network neutrality is fundamentally flawed on a number of
fronts. Most visible on this side of the debate have been industry giants such as
Verizon, who have threatened consumers with higher fees if network neutrality
is codified into law, and politicians like Senator John McCain and an Representative Ron Paul, who connect network neutrality to the erosion of liberty.[38]

  In addition to corporations and politicians, conservative think tanks such as
the Cato Institute have used another tactic to argue that the attempt to institutionalize network neutrality through regulation and law is a nonstarter: denial.
For example, in response to statements made by the Coalition of Broadband
Users and Innovators (CBUI) in support of network neutrality, the director of
telecommunication studies at the Cato Institute argued that

> There is no evidence that broadband operators are unfairly blocking access to
> websites or online services today, and there is no reason to expect them to do so
> in the future. No firm or industry has any sort of "bottleneck control" over or
> market power in the broadband marketplace; it is very much a competitive free-
> for-all, and no one has any idea what the future market will look like with so
> many new technologies and operators entering the picture.[39]

While these conflicting views underscore that technological controversies can be
difficult, antagonistic, and involve seemingly incommensurable positions, they
also highlight the need for these heterogeneous interests to play out openly, enacting the kind of technical micropolitics advocated by Feenberg and others.

Conclusion

Network neutrality has developed into a technological controversy requiring
greater scrutiny and public participation in all aspects of its resolution. The key

consideration here is that the Web's capacity to deliver information in a nondiscriminatory way (the very definition of network neutrality), is reflected in the social, technical, and policy layers of the Internet itself. A critical theory of technology approach develops a clear connection between the study of the value-laden affordances, design, and technical capabilities of a given technology and an examination of how these technologies have been taken up by individual users. In the case of network neutrality, we have a case of technical affordances that have allowed for this decentralized technology to provide nondiscriminatory access to information and communication increasingly facing challenge by corporate actors.

Feenberg argues that "technology and society are not alien realms." Rather, "Goals are "coded" [into technology] in the sense of ranking items as ethically permitted or forbidden, aesthetically better or worse, or more or less socially desirable."[40] It is the formation of these codes, and how they express themselves in technological use, that require a strong public interested in creating and preserving those affordances that are socially enriching and that aid in democratic participation. As Doppelt argues, this not only requires that technology and technical complexities are demystified, but also that they become more concretely connected to "a more thoroughgoing critical philosophy of liberal democratic values."[40]

Finally, for Feenberg, these kinds of interventions are necessary in that they are the only means through which to ensure that technological development and deployment fulfill the needs of the users and the public, rather than corporations or political elites. He argues that whenever "the public is involved in technological design, it will likely favor advances that enlarge opportunities to participate in the future over alternatives that enhance the operational autonomy of technical personnel)."[42]

With respect to network neutrality, this means a concerted push to ensure that the Internet remains an open, fair and informationally rich space where money should not be used to throttle its democratic technological affordances; otherwise, we jeopardize the integrity not only of the Internet's existing structure of data exchange, but of the democratic nature of discourse and decision-making in technological development.

Notes

1. Tanja Storsul, "Television in Cyberspace. The Net Neutrality Tussle in Norway," in *The Digital Public Sphere: Challenges for Media Policy*, ed. Jostein Gripsrud and Hallvard Moe (Sweden: Nordicom, 2010), 85.

2. Andrew Feenberg, *Critical Theory of Technology* (New York: Oxford University, 1991), 131.

3. Andrew Feenberg, "Critical Theory of Technology," 2004, http://www.sfu.ca/~andrewf/ctt.htm (accessed February 15, 2012).

4. Jon M. Peha, William M. Lehr, and Simon Wilkie, "The Status of the Debate on Network Neutrality," *International Journal of Communication* 1 (2007): 711.

5. Andy Birkey, "Bachmann: Net Neutrality Is Censorship," *The Minnesota Independent* (April 20, 2010), http://minnesotaindependent.com/57830/Bachmann-net-neutrality-is-censorship, (accessed April 12, 2012).

6. Andrew Feenberg, "From Critical Theory of Technology to Rational Critique of Rationality" *Social Epistemology* 22, no. 1 (2008): 10.

7. Feenberg, "Critical Theory of Technology."

8. Andrew Feenberg, *Between Reason and Experience: Essays in Technology and Modernity* (Cambridge, Mass.: MIT, 2010), 72.

9. Feenberg, *Critical Theory of Technology*, 170.

10. Stephen C. Webster, "Netflix CEO Blasts Comcast for Shredding Net Neutrality," *The Raw Story,* April 6 2012, http://www.rawstory.com/rs/2012/04/16/Netflix-ceo-blasts-comcast-for-shredding-net-neutrality/ (accessed April 19, 2012).

11. Ibid.

12. Rajiv C. Shah and Jay P. Kesan, "The Privatization of the Internet's Backbone Network" *Governing with Code,*" 2012, http://www.governingwithcode.org/journal_articles/pdf/Backbone.pdf (accessed April 17, 2012): 13.

13. Storsul, "Television in Cyberspace: The Net Neutrality Tussle in Norway," in *The Digital Public Sphere. Challenges for Media Policy*, ed. Jostein Gripsrud and Hallvard Moe (Gøteborg: Nordicom), 85.

14. Andrew J. Flanagin, Craig Flanagin, and Jon Flanagin, "Technical Code and the Social Construction of the Internet." *New Media and Society* 12, no. 2 (2010): 184.

15. Ibid., 189.

16. Trevor Pinch, "The Social Construction of Technology: A Review," in *Technological Change: Methods and Themes in the History of Technology*, ed. Robert Fox (Australia: Harwood Academic Publishers, 1996), 23.

17. Darryl Cressman, "The Concert Hall as a Medium of Musical Culture," (Ph.D. dissertation, Simon Fraser University, 2012), 29.

18. Alexander R. Galloway and Eugene Thacker, "Protocol, Control and Networks." *Grey Room* 17, (2004): 14.

19. Lawrence Lessig, *The Future of Ideas: The Fate of the Commons in a Connected World* (New York: Random House, 2001), 7.

20. Alison Powell, "Lessons from the Net Neutrality Lobby: Balancing Openness and Control in a Networked Society," *Proceedings of the WebSci'09 Society,* March 18–20, 2009, http://journal.webscience.org/130/1/websci09_submission_32.pdf (accessed April 12, 2012), 2.

21. Andrew Feenberg, "Critical Theory of Technology."

22. Philip Brey, "Social Constructivism for Philosophers of Technology: A Shopper's Guide," *Society for Philosophy and Technology* 2, no. 3/4 (Spring/Summer 1997), http://scholar.lib.vt.edu/ejournals/SPT/v2_n3n4html/brey.html? (accessed April 3, 2012).

23. Storsul, 83.

24. Hans K. Klein and Daniel Lee Kleinman, "The Social Construction of Technology: Structural Considerations," *Science, Technology and Human Values* 27, no. 1. (Winter 2012): 38.

25. Andrew Feenberg, *Between Reason and Experience: Essays in Technology and Modernity* (Cambridge, Mass.: MIT, 2010), 179.

26. Dawn C. Nunziato, *Virtual Freedom: Net Neutrality and Free Speech in the Internet* Age. (Stanford, Calif.: Stanford University, 2009), 131.

27. Ibid., 141.

28. FCC, "Open Internet," *fcc.gov*, 2012, http://www.fcc.gov/topic/open-internet (accessed March 5, 2012).

29. See Richard Sclove, *Democracy and Technology* (New York: Guilford, 1995); Steven Epstein, *Impure Science: AIDS, Activism, and the Politics of Knowledge* (Berkeley: University of California Press, 1996); Alan Irwin, *Citizen Science: A Study of People, Expertise, and Sustainable Development* (London: Routledge, 1995).

30. Leila Green, *Communication, Technology and Society* (London: Sage Publications, 2001), 5–6.

31. Steven Fuller, *The Philosophy of Science and Technology Studies* (Oxford: Routledge, 2005), 130; John Dewey, *Democracy and Education: an Introduction to the Philosophy of Education* (New York: Free Press, 1916), 223.

32. Andrew Feenberg, *Questioning Technology* (London: Routledge, 1999), 94.

33. Ibid., 147.

34. Ibid., 76.

35. Lawrence Lessig, "Reboot the FCC," *Newsweek,* December 23, 2008, Final Ed: 4.

36. Alison Powell, "Lessons," 1.

37. OpenMedia, "SaveOurNet.ca: Protecting Your Internet's Level Playing Field," *Openmedia.ca* (2012) http://openmedia.ca/saveournet (accessed April 15, 2012).

38. A number of US politicians vocally support network neutrality as well, including Senators Mark Udall and Al Franken.

39. Adam D. Thierer, "Policy Analysis: "Net Neutrality" Digital Discrimination or Regulatory Gamesmanship in Cyberspace?" *Cato Policy Analysis*, 507 (2004).

40. Feenberg, *Between Reason and Experience*, 68.

41. Gerald Doppelt, "Democracy and Technology," in *Democratizing Technology: Andrew Feenberg's Critical Theory of Technology*, ed. Tyler J. Veak (New York: State University of New York, 2006): 98.

42. Feenberg, *Between Reason and Experience,* 135.

Chapter 10

Network Neutrality, Mobile Networks, and User-Generated Activism

Michael Daubs

Although the issue of network neutrality has sparked several vigorous debates, the principles behind it are seemingly and perhaps deceptively simple. Tim Wu, the Columbia Law School professor who coined the phrase "network neutrality," claims that it is "best defined as a network design principle. The idea is that a maximally useful public information network aspires to treat all content, sites, and platforms equally."[1] At its most basic, in other words, net neutrality is simply the belief that a network such as the Internet should have no central control mechanisms and that those who own a network's infrastructure should have no control over the data that runs through it.[2] Proponents of net neutrality argue that there should be no central control over Internet content; opponents argue that net neutrality prevents efficient network traffic management, upgrades, and service.[3]

The popularity of "smartphones"—multi–function mobile phones with broadband mobile data and Internet connectivity—has added an additional level of complexity to net neutrality debates. A December 2010 ruling of the Federal Communications Commission (FCC) on the "Open Internet" recognized the growth of the mobile data market by outlining net neutrality rules for mobile providers, but the limited bandwidth of the mobile spectrum led regulators to treat mobile data differently from more conventional "fixed" connections. Thus, while this ruling did stipulate that fixed broadband Internet providers "may not block lawful content, applications, services, or non-harmful devices," it prevents mobile network providers only from blocking websites and applications that "compete with their voice or video telephony services."[4] That wording allows mobile data providers to throttle or even prevent the use of specific mobile applications. Considering the central role mobile technologies have played in recent social and political movements such as the recent #Occupy movement in the United States, this divided approach not only severely compromises net neutrality in general, but also makes it possible for mobile providers to restrict participation in public debates.

Network Neutrality and Civic Participation

The beliefs at the heart of net neutrality policies are also the foundation of the "end-to-end" principle of network design which, according to Mark A. Lemley and Lawrence Lessig, "counsels that the 'intelligence' in a network be located at the top of a layered system—at its 'ends,' where users put information and applications onto the network—and that the communications protocols themselves (the 'pipes' through which information flows) be as simple and general as possible."[5] Wu argues that the end-to-end principle is a "close cousin, if not the direct ancestor of network neutrality."[6] Both principles suggest that less specialized or "dumb" networks are the most valuable—at least to users—in that they can support any application and carry any information. Lemley and Lessig in fact argue that this general idea has guided the development of the Internet since its inception.[7]

Net neutrality and the end-to-end principle are also related to a much older concept: the "common carrier," a term used to refer to a private institution that performs a public service. For centuries, common carriage laws have applied to shipping and transportation services such as port authorities and, later, railroads. In the nineteenth and twentieth centuries, however, the term common carrier was applied to telecommunications services and mass media such as the telegraph, telephone, radio and television in order to guarantee the interoperability of various networks and the "separation of carriers and content" so that all content—i.e., data—is treated equally.[8] The ultimate goal is to ensure universal access to what are considered to be essential services and to guarantee that customers of various service providers—competing telephone systems, for example—can still communicate with one another. Perhaps due to it similarity to or roots in common carrier laws, debates on network neutrality often center upon a user's ability to access information and engage in interpersonal communication. The potential for Internet providers to block certain websites and file-sharing programs or "throttle" (limit download speeds of) certain online applications, services, or websites is often cited as a reason for the need for regulations that ensure network neutrality.[9]

These concerns are certainly valid and demand attention. Equally important, however, is an examination of how regulatory policies concerning net neutrality also affect the ability for users to contribute to social debates. Kenneth J. Gergen argues that civic participation is important in "generating independent deliberation about political issues, enabling expressions of resistance, inviting independent initiatives, and mobilizing organized expression."[10] The Internet is often heralded for its ability to allow people to engage in this kind of civic participation. Adam Joinson notes that "[w]hen a new technology develops, there inevitably follow forecasts envisaging a variety of positive outcomes."[11] This tendency can be seen after the removal of access restrictions to the Internet and Tim Berners-Lee's development of the World Wide Web in the 1990s. Jeffrey Wimmer suggests that a special democratizing potential has always been attributed to digital media, in part because of the perceived nullification of the separation between producers and audiences or senders and receivers.[12]

Net neutrality is necessary for the realization of this potential. The decentralized and accessible structure of the Internet, coupled with the kinds of personalization, interactivity, and participation possible there, fuel what Jean Burgess and Joshua Green call a "digital utopianism" that "surfaces repeatedly as part of the DIY ideology of participatory culture, the valorization of amateur and community media, and hopeful ideas about the democratization of cultural production."[13] Hans Magnus Enzensberger sees social participation as central to what he calls the "digital gospel" (*das digitale Evangelium*) and compares the beliefs of "digital evangelists" (*digitalen Evangelisten*) to similar hopes Bertolt Brecht had for the democratizing potential of radio.[14]

This evangelism can be seen in the work of Henry Jenkins, who espouses the virtues of the new participatory culture made possible by digital media.[15] Indeed, the ability for "average" people to create and distribute their own media content is one of the most important pillars of this digital utopianism. Barbara van Schewick asserts that the Internet has "improved democratic discourse, and created a decentralized environment for social and cultural interaction in which anyone can participate."[16] Terry Flew and Jason Wilson similarly note that academic and popular discourse has paid a considerable amount of attention to digital media forms that "generate content and comment 'from below' and reinvigorate the public sphere,"[17] while Axel Bruns argues that "produsers"—a combination of "users" and "producers"—can fundamentally alter the production of information and inform public debates.[18]

Inspired by this idea, *Time* magazine named "You" as its 2006 "Person of the Year" for "seizing the reins of the global media, for founding and framing the new digital democracy, for working for nothing and beating the pros at their own game."[19] Since then, popular discourse has cited YouTube and Twitter as integral to the success of modern activist movements from the Green Wave in Iran to the Arab Spring and, most recently, the #Occupy movement that began in 2011.[20] These protests, taking place outside and away from traditional personal computers with wired Internet connections and, in many cases, away from wireless (Wi–Fi) Internet access highlight the importance of the mobile phone, data networks, and mobile applications or "apps" as a way to access online services. Current FCC regulations concerning mobile data networks and net neutrality in the United States, however, have the potential to severely constrain the ability of those within activist movements to participate freely in public debates and present a significant challenge to net neutrality in a mobile age.

Before Smartphones: Mobiles, Counterpublics, and Democratic Participation

The relevance of mobile phones to net neutrality and civic participation might not be obvious at first, but becomes more evident through a brief examination of the role of mobile technologies in past activist movements. Since their inception, mobile communication technologies have made it easier for people to become more active participants in social debates. Mobile phones are the most used and most rapidly expanding communication technology on the planet. Once a mere status symbol for the rich and powerful, the mobile phone rapidly became what Leopoldina Fortunati, citing Francesco Alberoni, refers to as a "citizenship commodity"—a "must-have" device for modern-day citizens.[21] In 2011, an estimated 35 percent of the world's population used the Internet. In comparison, there were approximately 5.9 billion mobile phone subscriptions, with market penetration reaching 87 percent globally, including 79 percent in developing nations.[22]

As with other new technologies, the introduction of the mobile phone coupled with its accessibility and rapid dissemination have generated discussions of its democratizing and even revolutionary potential. Mobile technologies have been credited with significantly narrowing the digital divide by providing Internet access to teens from lower-income families in the United States and to developing areas of the world, particularly Africa.[23] Howard Rheingold argues that the "power to persuade and communicate, joined with the power to organize and coordinate . . . poses a disruptive political potential that could equal or surpass that of the printing press, landline telephone, television, or the Internet."[24] By labelling it a "citizenship commodity," Fortunati suggests that the mobile phone is becoming a standard communication technology with democratizing potential. It is perhaps for this reason that she argues that the mobile phone could match the Internet's ability to generate a "planetary consciousness."[25]

While Fortunati's visions of a planetary consciousness might evoke images of a reinvigorated Habermasian bourgeois *Öffentlichkeit* or public sphere,[26] others see mobile technologies as a potential advantage for people or groups often excluded from public debates. Manuel Castells coined the term the "Fourth World" to refer to those who live a "form of marginalized existence that exists across the globe in both rich and poor nations."[27] He views the emergence of this Fourth World as "inseparable from the rise of informational global capitalism."[28] Although he often focuses on the socioeconomic marginalization of the Fourth World, the voices of its members are also disregarded in public debates. Those who seek to have their voices heard through the organization of social justice movements form what Gergen refers to as a politically "proactive Mittelbau that is a structure of political communication lodged between the national government and the local or civil society, capable of both drawing participation from the local culture and speaking to government."[29] This Mittelbau was first enabled in the 1950s and 1960s by television, in part due to television's ability to make distant events such as the civil rights protests and feminist demonstrations of the era more immediate.

The Fourth World and proactive Mittelbau are similar to the concept of *Gegenöffentlichkeiten* or counterpublic spheres. While the public sphere is supposed to be representative of a society and its culture, counterpublic spheres represent smaller, niche segments of a population that embody a culture or ideology that is significantly different from that of the supposedly inclusive public sphere. Nancy Fraser refers to these groups as "subaltern counterpublics in order to signal that they are parallel discursive arenas where members of subordinated social groups invent and circulate counterdiscourses, which in turn permit them to formulate oppositional interpretations of their identities, interests, and needs."[30]

Michael Warner argues, however, that a counterpublic is more than a subaltern group with ideas for reform; instead, it is a "dominated group [that] aspires to re-create itself as a public and, in doing so, finds itself in conflict not only with the dominant social group, but also with the norms that constitute the dominant culture as a public."[31] A counterpublic's message is therefore often "regarded with hostility or with a sense of indecorousness."[32] Although Jürgen Habermas suggests that counterpublics did not evolve until the late nineteenth century, nearly 200 years after the public sphere first emerged as capitalism and mercantilism expanded at the expense of feudalism, Fraser notes that, "[v]irtually from the beginning, counterpublics contested the exclusionary norms of the bourgeois public, elaborating alternative styles of political behavior and alternative norms of public speech."[33]

Writing in part as a critique of Habermas' originally dismissive attitude toward "proletariat" movements, Oskar Negt and Alexander Kluge argue that counterpublic spheres could be forces of political and social transformation. They suggest that the formation of counterpublic spheres can be a source of solidarity for burgeoning social movements.[34] Jonathan Donner explicitly relates media use to social visibility, asserting that "a community's use of ICTs [information communication technologies] is one of the central determinants of its participation in the informational system, or its relegation to the Fourth World."[35] In other words, he sees an opportunity for marginalized segments of society to seize upon the political potential of mobile technologies and notes several researchers have examined "how users can draw on mobile technology to redistribute political power, giving the previously disenfranchised a voice in the dialogue."[36] Gergen similarly argues that mobile technologies allow formerly private and disconnected streams of thought to easily contribute to public debates, resulting in an exchange that is essential to the democratic process.[37] This information exchange is dependent upon an open or "neutral" network. Once network access providers begin to discriminate against particular content, the democratizing potential of that system is limited.

In the absence of such discrimination, however, participation through the use of ICTs can indeed assist counterpublic spheres with fomenting democratic potential and "representing marginalised positions in an advocatory way."[38]

Habermas himself has refined the position he set forth in *Strukturwandel der Offentlichkeit* to address changes in the relationship between society and the public sphere. As Fraser notes, Habermas originally believed a "single, overarching public sphere is a positive and desirable state of affairs, whereas the proliferation of a multiplicity of publics represents a departure from, rather than an advance toward, democracy."[39] He has since revised his interpretation and now sees the democratic potential in a "pluralistic, internally much differentiated mass public[.]"[40]

Specifically, Habermas points to political mobilizations that seek to generate a counterpublic sphere and asks whether these groups are actually capable of initiating new communicative processes.[41] He observes that "in periods of mobilisation, the structures that actually support the authority of a critically engaged public begin to vibrate."[42] Grassroots or counterpublic access to the general public is only granted in what Habermas refers to as moments of "crisis" or periods in which there is political, economic, or ideological uncertainty. During these moments, a "normative self-understanding" of media as a servant of the people emerges which provides the opportunity for increased representation of counterpublic content and ideas and enables a shift of media (and therefore political) power to civic groups.[43]

The political mobilizations to which Habermas refers take the form of social activist groups. These groups are increasingly empowered by mobile technologies which, in the past, have made an "increasingly powerful contribution to the efficacy of political activism."[44] Indeed, the mobile phone has been a primary tool in social activist movements. Text messaging in particular has been a popular method for the organization of protest actions. Rheingold notes the use of mobile phones and text messaging has been used to organize "smart mobs"—a term he uses to refer to rapidly formed and highly coordinated groups—throughout the world including countries in North America, Europe, Asia, and Africa.[45] The use of mobile devices to communicate between local groups has also generated organized, horizontally structured national movements that lack a centralized leadership structure.[46] As a result, participation within movements is democratized.

The combination of the Internet and mobile communication provides additional flexibility to organizers of social movements, as protests dubbed the "Battle in Seattle" against the World Trade Organization (WTO) during their annual meeting in Seattle in 1999 demonstrate. A number of scholars, journalists, and activists have detailed the use of both mobile and Internet-based communications to organize the mass anti-WTO actions.[47] A similar overlap between Web and mobile communication can be seen in the Web application TXTmob, which allows users to transmit text messages to multiple mobile numbers at once. TXTmob was employed to organize mass protests against the Republican and Democratic National Conventions in 2004, which also attracted a significant amount of traditional and grassroots media attention and led to sympathetic protests in other cities such as Madrid.[48]

Smartphones, Mobile Apps,
and Activist Movements

In recent years, activist groups have taken advantage of a more literal convergence between mobile and Internet technologies. Smartphones have become a primary tool for organizing, mobilizing, and publicizing protest actions, and one of the fastest growing ICTs in general. Broadband mobile data subscriptions grew at a rate of 45 percent from 2007-2011, outpacing even fixed broadband subscriptions.[49]

Accessing email and Web browsing on Internet-capable smartphones are certainly common uses of mobile broadband services, but the popularity of mobile apps—small, specialty applications that can be downloaded to mobile smartphones—is difficult to ignore. In 2011, Apple's App Store—the largest and most popular source for mobile applications which launched in July 2008—boasted 500,000 apps available for download for use its popular iPod, iPhone, and iPad mobile devices while its closest competitor, Google's Android Marketplace, had 294,000 apps.[50] That same year, aggregate mobile downloads surpassed the 30 billion mark and, for the first time since their introduction in 2008, users spent more time in mobile applications on average than in traditional web browsers.[51] Their popularity can be attributed to their convenience and speed. Since people tend to carry their mobile devices with them, they can share information, images, or even video instantly from any location rather than having to upload content later from a personal computer. Apps designed to work for specific devices also tend to operate faster than Web-based applications, which makes them more responsive to user needs.

The March 2012 purchase of Instagram for $1 billion by social networking giant Facebook signalled how "momentum in the tech world is shifting to mobile from computers."[52] Instagram had previously been a mobile social network centred on photo sharing and is just one example of a growing number of start-ups that eschew Web development in favor of mobile-only services left vulnerable to blocking or throttling in the recent FCC net neutrality policy. Many apps are made by established media companies. A growing number, however, are produced by upstart media companies or independent produsers. The focus on a mobile app offers developers several advantages, including a simplified design process and popular pre-existing distribution channels in the form of the Apple App Store and Google's Android Marketplace. With this in mind, coupled with the recent history of the use of mobile devices to organize protest actions, it is perhaps not terribly surprising that mobile apps, designed to make use of mobile broadband connections, have been developed for activist movements.

The #Occupy movement that began in 2011 provides several excellent examples of specialty apps made for activist purposes and demonstrates how a counterpublic sphere can gain access to the public through the media in a moment of "crisis" as Habermas described. The impetus for the movement can be traced to the global economic crisis brought about by the abuses of multinational banks, rising unemployment rates in the face of record corporate profits, and growing awareness of income disparities between the world's richest residents and the rest of the population which inspired the movement's "We are the 99%" slogan. The official start of the #Occupy movement is usually credited to July 13, 2011 blog entry simply titled "#OCCUPYWALLSTREET" on the website of the Canadian anti-consumerist magazine *Adbusters* which claimed it was time to protest against "the greatest corrupter of our democracy: Wall Street, the financial Gomorrah of America."[53]

Inspired by mass uprisings and social movements in Egypt and Spain, the post suggests a new kind of demonstration—not a temporary demonstration, but rather a prolonged protest action: "On September 17, we want to see 20,000 people flood into lower Manhattan, set up tents, kitchens, peaceful barricades and occupy Wall Street for a few months. Once there, we shall incessantly repeat one simple demand in a plurality of voices."[54] Though falling well short of the stated goal of 20,000 demonstrators, roughly a thousand protestors did indeed descend on the Wall Street area, eventually resulting in a weeks–long takeover of Zucotti Park at 1 Liberty Plaza in Lower Manhattan. *AdBusters'* inclusion of the Twitter hashtag—the symbol (#) used to identify keywords which help categorize posts or "tweets" so that they show up more easily in searches on the site—signals the importance of online communication to this activist movement. Hashtags such as #occupywallstreet, and #ows, as well as location-specific hashtags such as #occupyboston, were regularly used to mark tweets related to the protests. Protestors and bystanders also "uploaded video and commentary to a variety of social media sites almost instantly, so that it was almost as if the incident were being streamed."[55]

Once again, mobile phones played a key role, particularly because the primary tactic of the #Occupy movement—namely, "occupation" of a public space—means wired or even Wi-Fi Internet connections were often unavailable to protestors. The occupation of a physical public space, in other words, was coupled with the "occupation" of another (albeit virtual) public resource: the mobile spectrum. In fact, the physical occupation of areas such as Zucotti Park was heavily dependent upon the savvy use of mobile technologies.[56] Activists and protestors have used smartphone apps for existing Web services such as YouTube, Twitter, and Facebook to rapidly disseminate user-generated information, images, and videos of #Occupy protests in order to publicize events or report alleged police aggression.

In addition, several mobile applications were developed for a variety of smartphones for the #Occupy movement in particular. One app created by Pedro Miranda for Apple devices simply called *Occupy* focuses on giving users easy access to information about the movement by compiling "official (and unofficial) news feeds, the latest videos, the press, photos, chat, and a lot more."[57] A company called Quadrant 2, supposedly inspired by a real #Occupy-related event, developed an Android app called *I'm Getting Arrested* which allows people to quickly and easily broadcast a custom text message to the mobile phones of selected friends and loved ones at the push of a button in case they are arrested.[58] The basic function resembles that of the TXTmob Web application from a few years earlier, but is more accessible and immediate as a mobile app.

Other apps are specifically designed to help users share information and coordinate #Occupy-related protests. An app called *WhatsApp*, available for multiple mobile platforms including iPhone, Android, and Blackberry devices, allows users to send unlimited and encrypted text messages so that "sensitive communication between two users cannot not be tied to individuals if it were to be intercepted by snoops."[59] Though the company behind *WhatsApp* claims no affiliation with the #Occupy movement, the advantages for protest organizers—both in terms of cost and security—are obvious. *Go HD*, an app from pro-#Occupy development company Hollr, allows people to share "anonymous location-based messages, photos and videos" about protests and events, while *Protest4*—an app which has apparently been "embraced by free speech movements and political demonstrations in Indonesia, Pakistan Egypt, and even Italy" in addition to those in the #Occupy movement—lets users search for nearby protests in progress.[60] Yet another app, *Shouty*, turns a smartphone into a streaming media server so that people at the back of a crowd or on the other side of the globe can tune into protest speeches.[61]

The examples listed here are just a few of the dozens of mobile apps that have been employed to aid the coordination, effectiveness, and communicative capabilities of activist movements, and the increasing use of mobile apps by groups such as #Occupy—many of which rely on mobile broadband data connections—reveals how the FCC's current network neutrality policies present a significant challenge to this rapidly emerging form of democratic participation in the United States. In addition, the increasing reliance on mobile broadband networks in general demonstrates that current policy is ill-suited to an ever-evolving broadband environment.

Wireless Network Neutrality and Restricting Debate

Their combination of mobile telephony and data services make smartphones more useful to organizers, but it also effectively transforms them from devices providing communication services into devices providing what the FCC, in its 1996 Telecommunications Act, refers to as "information services"—that is, "the offering of a capability for generating, acquiring, storing, transforming, processing, retrieving, utilizing, or making available information via telecommunications."[62] This is no small distinction since the FCC considers telecommunications and information services to be two distinct categories. The former are regulated, "basic" common carrier services while the latter are not.

This distinction might explain why the December 2010 ruling of the FCC prevents mobile network providers only from blocking websites and applications that compete with their voice or video telephony services, which problematizes the neutrality of mobile data networks.[63] That wording allows mobile data providers to throttle or even prevent the use specific mobile applications, which in turn makes it possible for them to restrict participation in activist movements. Consider, for example, if a group used a particular smartphone app to organize a protest against one of the major mobile providers in the United States such as Verizon or AT&T. What would prevent them from blocking access to those apps in order to circumvent a potential public relations problem? Or what if a provider decided to block access to an app designed for a particular social movement in order to avoid the appearance of supporting that movement?

These questions are, of course, speculative and hypothetical but past events suggest such actions are not out of the realm of possibility. During a 2005 strike by members of the Telecommunications Workers Union (TWU) in Canada, for example, Canadian telecommunications company Telus blocked its Internet customers from accessing "Voices for Change," a website that was both run by and openly supported the TWU.[64] The move was widely criticized, particularly because most of the striking workers were also Telus customers. Neil Barratt and Leslie Regan Shade argue the decision to block access to the site "points out the power of telecommunications companies in controlling content and stifling public access to content that the company deems unnecessary."[65]

While the 2010 FCC ruling prevents this type of website blocking in the United States for both mobile and fixed Internet customers, nothing would prevent a telecom company from blocking an app that was perceived as a potential threat. Positioning the "right to reach an audience" as a cornerstone of free speech, Jennifer A. Chandler argues that "[i]f selection intermediaries block or discriminate against a speaker on grounds that listeners would not have selected, that speaker's ability to speak freely has been undermined."[66] Blocking access to mobile apps dedicated to social movements would not only prevent people from accessing information, but also sharing it. Indeed, the FCC's current network neutrality policy allows mobile network providers to act as a new "selection intermediary" and effectively prevents the formation of the "decentralized environment for social and cultural interaction" described by van Schewick earlier.

Beyond #Occupy:
Future Considerations for a Mobile World

Mobile apps designed to help those in activist movements such as #Occupy to organize their activities and publicize their goals are only an entry point for a larger discussion about mobile broadband network neutrality. The current FCC policy on mobile networks has the potential to be detrimental to the dissemination of all user-generated content and severely compromises the visions of unfettered participation in social debates and democratization of cultural production. The rapid increase in the use of mobile technologies suggests that the FCC will need to revise these policies sooner rather than later or risk having a completely ineffectual approach to network neutrality.

It is also important to note that mobile broadband net neutrality is not an issue limited to the United States. Developing areas of the world, for example, are experiencing some of the highest growth rates in mobile penetration.[67] Furthermore, mobile broadband connections are more likely to be the only option for Internet access available to those within developing countries.[68] Ensuring mobile broadband network neutrality in these countries takes on an even greater importance especially considering the United Nations declared Internet access a basic human right in 2011 and specifically questioned the validity of filtering and blocking content.[69] Developed nations that often claim to want to encourage the spread of democracy and aid developing countries can set a positive example by supporting mobile network neutrality both at home and abroad.

That said, it is impossible to ignore that there are significant differences in the underlying infrastructure of wired and mobile broadband systems. Limited spectrum space for mobile communications, especially high-bandwidth data, is a legitimate concern for mobile providers, and spectrum space will become a more urgent issue as more customers in the United States switch to next-generation 4G devices. The FCC's decision to open large blocks of unused spectrum space left vacant after the switch to digital television systems for unlicensed wireless broadband networks demonstrates the Commission's awareness of spectrum issues.[70] However, as Barratt and Shade argue, "cable and telephone companies understand the changing climate of the industry and the potential for profits."[71] The FCC and regulatory bodies in other countries needed to be equally aware of the potentials and pitfalls of this changing climate and ensure their net neutrality policies evolve accordingly, even in the face of fervent resistance from mobile providers. Otherwise, they risk the development of a fractured system that privileges wireless providers, limits the full interoperability of various networks, and institutionalizes limits on the communicative capabilities of users.[72]

Notes

1. Tim Wu, "Network Neutrality FAQ," *timwu.org*, http://timwu.org/network_neutrality.html (accessed August 13, 2012).

2. Neil Barratt and Leslie Regan Shade, "Net Neutrality: Telecom Policy and the Public Interest," *Canadian Journal of Communication* 32, no. 2 (2007): 296.

3. For a summary of debates, see Christine M. Stover, "Network Neutrality: A Thematic Analysis of Policy Perspectives across the Globe," *Global Media Journal—Canadian Edition* 3, no. 1 (2010).

4. Federal Communications Commission, *Report and Order in the Matter of Preserving the Open Internet Broadband Industry Practices*, December 21, 2010, http://www.fcc.gov/Daily_Releases/Daily_Business/ 2010/db1223/FCC-10-201A1.pdf (accessed January 20, 2011). 2.

5. Mark A. Lemley and Lawrence Lessig, "The End of End-to-End: Preserving the Architecture of the Internet in the Broadband Era," *UC Berkeley Law and Econ Research Paper No. 2000–19* (2000): 5.

6. Wu, "Network Neutrality FAQ."

7. Lemley and Lessig.

8. Barratt and Shade, 296.

9. See, for example, Stover, "Network Neutrality: A Thematic Analysis of Policy Perspectives across the Globe"; Barbara van Schewick and David Farber, "Network Neutrality Nuances: A Discussion of Divergent Paths to Unrestricted Access of Content and Applications Via the Internet," *Communications of the ACM* 52, no. 2 (2009).

10. Kenneth J. Gergen, "Mobile Communication and the Transformation of the Democratic Process," in *Handbook of Mobile Communication Studies*, ed. James E. Katz (Cambridge, Mass.: MIT Press, 2008), 298.

11. Adam Joinson, *Understanding the Psychology of Internet Behaviour: Virtual Worlds, Real Lives* (Basingstoke, UK: Palgrave Macmillan, 2002), 116.

12. Jeffrey Wimmer, *(Gegen–)Öffentlichleit in Der Mediengesellschaft: Analyse Eines Medialen Spannungsverhältnisses* (Wiesbaden, Germany: VS Verlag, 2007), 139–140.

13. Jean Burgess and Joshua Green, *YouTube*, Digital Media and Society Series (Malden, Mass.: Polity, 2009), 12.

14. Hans Magnus Enzensberger, "Das Digitale Evangelium," *Der Spiegel* (2000), http://www.spiegel.de/spiegel/print/d-15376078.html (accessed August 8, 2012).

15. Henry Jenkins, *Convergence Culture: Where Old and New Media Collide* (New York: New York University Press, 2006), 246.

16. van Schewick and Farber, 33.

17. Terry Flew and Jason Wilson, "Journalism as Social Networking: The Australian Youdecide Project and the 2007 Federal Election," *Journalism* 11, no. 2 (2010): 132.

18. Axel Bruns, "Some Exploratory Notes on Produsers and Produsage," Snurblog, http://snurb.info/index.php?q=node/329 (accessed August 8, 2012).

19. Lev Grossman, "Time's Person of the Year: You," *Time* 168 (2006), http://www.time.com/time/magazine/article/0,9171,1569514,00.html (August 13, 2012).

20. See, for example, Lev Grossman, "Iran Protests: Twitter, the Medium of the Movement," *TIME* (2009), http://www.time.com/time/world/article/ 0,8599,1905125,00.html (accessed August 8, 2012); Sarah Maslin Nir, "Wall Street Protesters Broadcast Arrests on Social Media," *The New York Times*,

http://cityroom.blogs.nytimes.com/2011/09/24/wall-street-protesters-broadcast-arrests-on-social-media (accessed August 8, 2012).

21. Leopoldina Fortunati, "The Mobile Phone: Towards New Categories and Social Relations," *Information, Communication and Society* 5, no. 4 (2002).

22. International Telecommunication Union, "The World in 2011: ICT Facts and Figures,"(2011), http://www.itu.int/ITU-D/ict/facts/2011/material/ICTFactsFigures2011.pdf (Accessed August 13, 2012).

23. For some examples, see Katie Brown, Scott W. Campbell, and Rich Ling, "Mobile Phones Bridging the Digital Divide for Teens in the Us?," *Future Internet* 3, no. 2 (2011); Jeffrey James, "Sharing Mobile Phones in Developing Countries: Implications for the Digital Divide," *Technological Forecasting and Social Change* 78, no. 4 (2011); Peter A. Kwaku Kyem and Peter Kweku LeMaire, "Transforming Recent Gains in the Digital Divide into Digital Opportunities: Africa and the Boom in Mobile Phone Subscription," *The Electronic Journal on Information Systems in Developing Countries* 28, no. 5 (2006).

24. Howard Rheingold, "Mobile Media and Political Collective Action," in *Handbook of Mobile Communication Studies*, ed. James E. Katz (Cambridge, Mass.: MIT Press, 2008), 225–226.

25. Fortunati, 521.

26. Jürgen Habermas, *Strukturwandel Der Öffentlichkeit* (Frankfurt am Main: Suhrkamp, 1990).

27. Jonathan Donner, "Shrinking Fourth World? Mobiles, Development, and Inclusion," in *Handbook of Mobile Communication Studies*, ed. James E. Katz (Cambridge, Mass.: MIT Press, 2008), 30.

28. Manual Castells, *End of Millennium* (Malden, Mass.: Wiley, 2010), 169–170.

29. Gergen, 300.

30. Nancy Fraser, "Rethinking the Public Sphere: A Contribution to the Critique of Actually Existing Democracy," in *Habermas and the Public Sphere*, ed. Craig Calhoon (Cambridge, Mass.: MIT Press, 1992), 67.

31. Michael Warner, *Publics and Counterpublics* (New York: Zone Books, 2002), 112.

32. Ibid., 119.

33. Fraser, 61.

34. Oskar Negt and Alexander Kluge, *Public Sphere and Experience: Toward an Analysis of the Bourgeois and Proletarian Public Sphere*, trans. Peter Labanyi, Jamie Daniel, and Assenka Oksiloff (Minneapolis: University of Minnesota Press, 1993), 160–186.

35. Donner, 30.

36. Ibid., 32.

37. Gergen, 304.

38. Jeffrey Wimmer, "Counter-Public Spheres and the Revival of the European Public Sphere," *The Public* 12, no. 2 (2005): 101.

39. Fraser, 66.

40. Jürgen Habermas, "Further Reflections on the Public Sphere," in *Habermas and the Public Sphere*, ed. Craig Calhoun (Cambridge, Mass.: MIT Press, 1992), 438.

41. Ibid., 427.

42. Jürgen Habermas, *Between Facts and Norms: Contributions to a Discourse Theory of Law and Democracy*, trans. William Rehg (Cambridge, Mass.: MIT Press, 1996), 379.

43. Ibid., 379–381.

44. Gergen, 305.

45. Rheingold, 226.

46. Gergen, 297–298; Rheingold, 227.

47. See, for example, Matthew Eagleton-Pierce, "The Internet and the Seattle WTO Protests," *Peace Review* 13, no. 3 (2001); Okoth Fred Mudhai, "Exploring the Potential for More Strategic Civil Society Use of Mobile Phones," in *Reformatting Politics: Information Technology and Global Civil Society*, ed. Jodi Dean, Jon W. Anderson, and Geert Lovink (New York: Routledge, 2006); Howard Rheingold, *Smart Mobs: The Next Social Revolution* (Cambridge, Mass.: Perseus, 2002).

48. Tad Hirsch and John Henry, "Txtmob: Text Messaging for Protest Swarms," in *CHI '05 Extended Abstracts on Human Factors in Computing Systems* (Portland, Ore., ACM, 2005); Rheingold.

49. International Telecommunication Union.

50. Philip Elmer-Dewitt, "Apple's Itunes Store: 500,000 Ios Apps and Counting," *CNNMoney*, http://tech.fortune.cnn.com/2011/05/24/apples-itunes-store-500000-ios-apps-and-counting/ (accessed January 20, 2012).

51. Erica Ogg, "By the Numbers: Mobile Apps in 2011," *GigaOM*, http://gigaom.com/2011/12/30/by-the-numbers-mobile-apps-in-2011 (accessed March 15, 2012); Erica Ogg, "The Year in Mobile Apps: Where We've Been, Where We're Going," *GigaOM*, http://gigaom.com/2011/12/25/the-year-in-mobile-apps-where-weve-been-where-were-going/ (accessed March 15, 2012).

52. Jenna Wortham, "A Billion-Dollar Turning Point for Mobile Apps," *New York Times*, http://www.nytimes.com/2012/04/11/technology/instagram-deal-is-billion-dollar-move-toward-cellphone-from-pc.html (accessed April 10, 2012).

53. Adbusters, "#Occupywallstreet," *AdBusters*, http://www.adbusters.org/blogs/adbusters-blog/occupywallstreet.html (accessed October 13, 2011).

54. Ibid.

55. Nir.

56. The government-regulated mobile spectrum is arguably more "public" than the "privately owned public space" Zuccotti Park. See http://www.nyc.gov/html/dcp/html/priv/priv.shtml and http://www.nyc.gov/html/dcp/html/priv/mndist1.shtml for more information.

57. A. T. Faust III, "'Occupy' App Gives You Even More News on Growing Global Phenomenon," *AppAdvice*, http://appadvice.com/appnn/2011/11/occupy-app-gives-you-even-more-news-on-growing-global-phenomenon (accessed January 13, 2012).

58. Jaymar Cabebe, "Help, I'm Getting Arrested!," *CNet*, http://reviews.cnet.com/8301-19736_7-20119537-251/help-im-getting-arrested/ (accessed October 12, 2011).

59. Chikodi Chima, "Apps for Occupiers Make Organizing, Communicating and Sharing Easier," *VentureBeat*, http://venturebeat.com/2011/11/19/apps-for-occupy-wall-street/ (accessed November 30, 2011).

60. Ibid.

61. Tyler Kingkade, "New Protest Apps Crowd-Sourced from Occupy Wall Street Hackers," *Huffington Post*, http://www.huffingtonpost.com/2011/10/26/occupy-wall-street-a-diy-tech-tools-protest_n_1032518.html (accessed November 30, 2011).

62. *Telecommunications Act of 1996* S.652, 104th Cong., 2nd sess. http://frwebgate.access.gpo.gov/cgi-bin/getdoc.cgi?dbname=104_cong_bills&docid=f:s652enr.txt.pdf (accessed August 8, 2012).

63. Interestingly, the policy stipulates that "mobile broadband providers may not block lawful websites" but states that only fixed broadband providers may not "unreasonably discriminate in transmitting lawful network traffic." Mobile providers may still "discriminate" against (or throttle) individual websites.

64. "Telus Cuts Subscriber Access to Pro–Union Website," *CBC News*, http://www.cbc.ca/news/canada/story/2005/07/24/telus-sites050724.html (accessed March 2, 2012); Barratt and Shade.

65. Barratt and Shade, 298. Relatedly, in 2010, the online payment service company PayPal prevented donations to WikiLeaks, an international non–profit organization known for publishing classified information including over 250,000 diplomatic cables from the U.S. State Department. Though not directly a net neutrality issue (PayPal claims they disabled the WikiLeaks account due to a violation of the company's Acceptable Use Policy), their decision does demonstrate that companies are willing to interrupt service to activist organizations in order to avoid the appearance of support. See Kevin Poulson, "Paypal Freezes Wikileaks Account," *Wired* (2010), http://www.wired.com/threatlevel/2010/12/paypal-wikileaks/ (accessed August 8. 2012).

66. Jennifer A. Chandler, "A Right to Reach an Audience: An Approach to Intermediary Bias on the Internet," *Hofstra Law Review* 35, no. 3 (2007): 1098.

67. Donner, 29.

68. International Telecommunication Union.

69. United Nations General Assembly, "Report of the Special Rapporteur on the Promotion and Protection of the Right to Freedom of Opinion and Expression," New York, 2011.

70. Federal Communications Commission, *Order in the Matter of Unlicensed Operation in the TV Broadcast Bands: Additional Spectrum for Unlicensed Devices Below 900 Mhz and in the 3 GHz Band*, 2011, http://hraunfoss.fcc.gov/edocs_public/ attachmatch/DA-11-131A1.pdf (accessed August 13, 2012). The Canadian government's highly anticipated 2013 auction of similar spectrum space referred to as the 700MHz auction demonstrates the desire for more wireless broadband spectrum is not limited to the US.

71. Barratt and Shade, 302.

72. The author wishes to thank Vince Manzerolle and Dr. Zachary Stiegler for their incredibly generous comments and suggestions on this chapter.

Chapter 11

Beyond the Series of Tubes:
Strategies for Advancing Media Reform

John Nathan Anderson

In 2005, I was a graduate student at the Institute of Communications Research at the University of Illinois. Unlike my fellow colleagues-in-training, who taught classes or worked on professors' pet projects, my funding came through Free Press, the nation's largest nonpartisan media reform organization. Utilizing more than a decade's worth of experience in radio journalism, I developed and produced a weekly headline news program on issues of media policy and activism. *Media Minutes* became Free Press' premier broadcast campaign vehicle and was heard on hundreds of stations both on air and online for nearly eight years.[1]

I vividly remember when the Supreme Court handed down its *Brand X* decision that June, thereby turning the entire concept of network neutrality on its head. Every week, Free Press staffers hold a conference call to discuss the pressing policy issues of the moment. Little did I realize that a massive battle at the Federal Communications Commission and Congress over network neutrality was in the works, and would come to dominate media policy news—both on *Media Minutes* and elsewhere—for the next several years. Our initial challenge was to frame network neutrality as an indispensable attribute of the Internet and thus beat back the potential exploitation of the Supreme Court's regulatory rationale in ways that would further weaken the principle. *Media Minutes* helped raise the alarm and launched the Save the Internet campaign, whose first major activity, the circulation of a petition to Congress pleading for the preservation of network neutrality as a point of law, collected more than a million signatures from concerned citizens within the first six weeks.[2]

The term "network neutrality" was originally used in a 2003 letter to FCC Chairman Michael Powell by legal scholars Tim Wu and Lawrence Lessig, and further popularized in an article Wu wrote later that year. It essentially refers to the concept of nondiscrimination: simply put, the ability for data to transit the Internet should not depend primarily on *whose* data it is.[3] However, for the purpose of engaging the public in a battle over what was otherwise considered an

201

esoteric point of media policy, the principle needed popular explication. Thus net neutrality became "the First Amendment of the Internet"—cable and telephone companies wanted to create "toll booths" and "fast lanes" online which would inherently diminish the Internet's potential for democratic communication.[4] Opponents of network neutrality actually helped fuel popular discontent through their own expressions of stunning ignorance and avarice. On the avarice front, then SBC CEO Ed Whitacre's declaration that content providers wouldn't get away with using "my pipes" for "free" put a fine point on the profit maximization designs of Internet access providers in a world where network neutrality was not protected.[5]

The ignorance of regulators first went on full display at a Senate Commerce Committee hearing in June of 2006, when Chairman Ted Stevens (R–AK) ranted about his perceptions of how the Internet worked. It "is not something that you just dump something on. It's not a big truck. It's a series of tubes," he opined. "And if you don't understand, those tubes can be filled and if they are filled, when you put your message in, it gets in line and it's going to be delayed by anyone that puts into that tube enormous amounts of material."

Stevens' outburst initially seemed like manna from heaven for proponents of network neutrality. Here was a lawmaker, in charge of the Senate committee under which the authority for Internet regulation fell, completely unable to comprehend the fundamentals of online communication. The entire episode compellingly called into question the validity of *any* law or rule promulgated under Stevens' watch. That Congress did not ultimately advance any legislation regarding network neutrality could thus be considered a good outcome. However, mocking those in power when they express their ignorance of the Internet doesn't necessarily advance—and may actually sidetrack—advocacy for more democratic media policy.[6] Such stunning displays of ignorance are much more than humorous—they are downright alarming.

The battle over network neutrality, and similar skirmishes that have followed since (SOPA, PIPA, and CISPA) are quite illustrative of the state of what passes for media policy discourse in the United States. The fact that most of them have been successful in halting the implementation of laws that would restrict the Internet's democratic nature is certainly testament to the growing power of the modern U.S. media reform movement, but they also demonstrate how much more there is to do to reach the point where public interest might actually drive media policy. To get there, media reform needs to open up two new fronts: one that illuminates and attacks the dominance of neoliberal ideology on media policy and another to advance principles of media literacy, both as a point of educational policy and in the classroom.

I share the view of James Carey that our culture is dominated by the commercial, and that "what exists of politics is formed as a metaphor of commerce and an imperative of markets."[7] We view much of our world—including education and advances in communications technology—through the neoliberal prism.[8] Such fundamentalism, like all fundamentalisms, creates a dangerous vacuum of common knowledge and wisdom, as faith in the ideology replaces empirical truths as a means for understanding reality. In conditions like these, the very language we use to communicate becomes "increasingly defined as an instrument for manipulating objects, not a device to establish the truth but to get others to believe what we want them to believe."[9] The challenge of resisting neoliberalism in media policy is difficult because its influence is so pervasive that most who engage in such discourse take it for granted—so much so that neoliberal principles have become baked-in to the realpolitik of Washington, D.C. Fortunately, because the evidence of neoliberalism's democratically-destructive tendencies exists all around us, it is not difficult to define and resist; the major barrier is the political will to do so.

Advancing principles of media literacy is a cause all its own. Empowering citizens to speak for themselves on issues of media policy, beyond campaigns of clicktivism or superficially organized protest blitzes, will require the fundamental education of the populace about the media environment in which we live. This is a multidimensional task for which no real organizational foundation currently exists in the United States. The ultimate goal should be the implementation of media literacy curricula in school districts nationwide. It is already a good fit in subjects ranging from science to social studies. However, this is a task of years, if not decades; in the interim, the time is ripe for the rhizomatic spread of media literacy education in schools.

An informed and engaged public is absolutely necessary for the promulgation of democratic media policy, not to mention the perpetuation of democracy itself. Carey once lamented the synonymization of "information" and "knowledge," and its concomitant effect on the agency afforded new media technologies: we can get so caught up in knowing *things* that we lose control of the paradigms for *thinking about what we know.*[10] Reclaiming and asserting the importance of knowledge, especially in the present political-economic context, is essential for advancing the issue of network neutrality—and the cause of democratic media reform more generally—beyond the status quo, where the avoidance of disaster passes for victory.

* * *

The scholastic consensus on the U.S. network neutrality battle seems to point to a draw: the principle still exists as a point of policy, but in a dramatically weakened fashion with loopholes large enough to drive a big truck through. Some attribute this outcome to the "sometimes paradoxical and frequently culturally grounded" flow of the debate itself.[11] Regulatory discourse in particular was surprisingly devoid of language directly relating to the history or operation of Internet technology.[12] It is difficult to make coherent media policy without a fundamental understanding of how the technology at its heart works.[13] This is not to say that advocates and opponents of network neutrality didn't employ nuanced arguments; it's just that nuance mattered little in the end, as both policymakers and the public fixated more on the "egalitarian connotations" of "neutrality" and less on the "network" at issue.[14] In a thought-provoking analysis of the contemporary media policymaking process published in 2006, Des Freedman spoke on background with a number of U.S. media policy lobbyists and public interest advocates. One of them, a "public policy advocate on media issues," summarized the state of play: "Most members of Congress haven't got any idea about communications policy. They get beyond the surface-level discussion of the issues and they are completely lost. So you're really talking about 30 to 40 members of Congress . . . in total who understand the issues well enough to legislate on them."[15]

In an environment of such ignorance, it comes as no surprise that a debate on the substance of network neutrality is challenging, if not impossible, to have. What resulted instead was "a high stakes game" in which all stakeholders worked "to redefine or obscure the issue to favor their own position, while policy-makers struggle[d] to make sense of the apparent contradictions."[16] In such a "confusing" situation, policymakers will default to the comfort of the familiar, which in the U.S. context privileges a neoliberal paradigm.[17] If context is key to promoting progressive Internet policy,[18] neglecting to firmly connect the issue of network neutrality to a critique of the dominant ideological frame under which its debate took place put its proponents at a disadvantage from the outset.

Today, the ethos of corporate rationalization drives the regulation of new media technologies.[19] Its discourse is coded in terms that privilege the status of consumer over that of citizen.[20] To be blunt, corporations have a voice in the communications policymaking process that is nearly impossible for the public to match, unless the public is willing to accept a role that subjugates it. This is unacceptable when constitutive choices about the future development of important media platforms such as the Internet are being made.

Constitutive choices define the design and operation of a media system. According to Paul Starr, oftentimes they are made through the process of "slowly crystallizing cultural practices or gradual economic and political change," but in some cases they arise in "bursts set off by social and political crises, technological innovation, or other triggering events, and at these pivotal moments the choices may be encoded in law, etched into technologies, or otherwise embedded in the structure of institutions."[21] Constitutive choices have three primary effects on the nature of democratic communications: they determine "the general legal and normative rules concerning such issues as free expression, access to information, privacy, and intellectual property; second, the specific design of communications media, structure of networks, and organization of industries; and third, institutions related to the creation of intangible and human capital—that is, education, research, and innovation."[22] Good constitutive choices are made when all three factors are taken into account and balanced in such a manner as to maximize a media system's democratic potentiality.

The history of network neutrality shows that the principle crystallized over time as the Internet's primary architects developed its basic infrastructure and protocols—a constitutive choice etched into early iterations of Internet technology and manifested through an informal policy of consensus. The Telecommunications Act of 1996, which shifted the paradigm of media policy into a firmly neoliberal orientation and promoted the explosive public growth of the Internet itself, was a disruptive event that kicked off "a decade's worth of steps on the slippery slope of broadband access deregulation" which actively challenged the neutrality principle.[23] The Supreme Court's *Brand X* decision in 2005 was essentially a "triggering event" which has forced a new constitutive choice upon us regarding how future network administrators will handle issues of data discrimination. Failure to maintain the principle of network neutrality can only serve to reduce the democratic potentiality of Internet-based communication.[24]

There may be no better representative of the triumph of neoliberalism in modern politics than the FCC, the place where principles like network neutrality become policy (or go to die). The ideology has been instrumental in shaping the agency's contemporary policy history. Thomas Streeter has observed that the function of media policymaking has shifted toward "actions as a matter of neutral, technological necessity in service of the social system."[25] If such systems are increasingly characterized by "technologically enabled commodification and exchange of intangibles," policymaking itself "provides us with an example of one way that such commodification can be accomplished, and of the problems that are likely to be encountered if that path is taken."[26]

The neoliberal foundation of modern media policymaking also creates a stratification of power among the constituents involved in it, where the "core [is] dominated by an alliance of corporate and government elites" and a subaltern "economic periphery of smaller enterprises and a political periphery of electoral politics" exists.[27] As a result, policymakers equate the "public interest" component of regulation "more and more rigidly with the supposedly neutral and desirable state of marketplace competition,"[28] which predisposes regulators away from functionally democratic decision-making.[29] For example, the FCC's historic rationale to promulgate policy in the "public interest, convenience and necessity" was actively redefined by the Telecommunications Act of 1996 to privilege economic metrics over all others, and the makeup of key FCC management and staff has gradually shifted away from people with legal or technical backgrounds to those with expertise in politics and economics.[30]

The language of economics framed the debate about net neutrality.[31] Despite the nuance of arguments raised both for and against the principle, "innovation" was the concept most frequently raised by all sides, and most notably defined from a market perspective.[32] Citizens were "largely characterized" as "consumers," both by proponents and opponents of network neutrality, which depoliticizes the concept of public agency in policymaking.[33] Media coverage similarly favored the phrase "consumer interests" over "the public interest" when defining the public's stake in the policy battle.[34]

Institutionally, the FCC operates under burdensome constraints and pressure from several directions (constituents, Congress, and the courts). These impediments lead regulators to ignore or downplay actual public sentiment regarding the policies they promulgate, especially when the public attempts to assert a larger role in the policymaking process than regulators have already allowed for.

Mark J. Braun has catalogued the "immense workloads and small staffs" that "contribute to a hectic FCC decision-making environment,"[35] which only becomes more turgid when policymaking becomes publicly controversial. In such situations, decisions are made in an ad-hoc, typically conservative fashion, as the FCC attempts to placate all the groups that pressure it, rather than thinking proactively about the issue at hand.[36] This is precisely why, for example, the FCC's Open Internet Order in 2010 pledged to preserve basic network neutrality principles on wired broadband infrastructure, but left "the rapidly growing mobile broadband sector vulnerable to discrimination."[37]

Furthermore, the FCC's increasing reliance on regulated industries for information that directly dictates the trajectory of policy outcomes promotes regulatory capture.[38] If the data underlying a new policy favors a particular outcome, it is quite likely that such an outcome will result.[39] Lobbyists freely admit that their job is to "take the body of fact as it exists and present it in a favorable fashion."[40] "Data" becomes "fetishized" as a "means of marginalizing the public in the policy process and safeguarding it for the economists, lawyers and executives" which the process privileges.[41]

This modus operandi was quite clear in the regulatory and media discourse surrounding network neutrality. Between 2004 and 2009, Congress held nine hearings on the principle (though it came up as a subject of discussion at 43 hearings in all), while the FCC held three, and hundreds of stories were written about the debate. Corporate representatives were well—represented in all fora, accounting for 50 percent of the testimony at Congressional hearings, 35 percent of the testimony at FCC hearings, and "about 40%" of the sources used in mainstream media, while advocacy groups (of all stripes) settled for 12.4 percent of the sources used in newspapers, 10 percent of the appearances at FCC hearings, and 14.7 percent of the testimony at Congressional hearings. Incidentally, academics in the fields of mass communication, journalism, or communication studies were noticeably absent from this discourse. Of the top 18 recurring sources the mainstream media relied upon to frame the issue, two-thirds were corporate representatives, lawmakers, or regulators, while the rest were academics (in law) and spokespeople for advocacy groups.[42]

At the very moment when our "information society" requires both citizens and policymakers to be better-versed in the intricacies of the technologies which define our lives,[43] the FCC appears to be moving toward what Sandra Braman characterizes as "narrative simplicity, even as the data upon which state narratives are placed become more diverse and complex."[44] Although policymakers may *think* they are designing rules and institutions using the language of facts, "their role in policy-making is more likely to belong to the rhetoric of decision-making processes rather than their content."[45] When it comes to the design and justification of media policy, economic metaphors are an inadequate stand-in for directed inquiry and scientific analysis, and they lead to the promulgation of regulation "without a sound empirical basis" that "contribute[s] to. . . inconsistency and ambiguity . . . in communications policy."[46]

Former communications regulators have been surprisingly candid about this state of affairs. Nicholas Johnson, who served as FCC Commissioner from 1966 to 1973, described "a 'subgovernment' of industry lobbyists, specialty lawyers, trade associations, trade press, Congressional subcommittee staff members, and Commission personnel who dominate" the policymaking process.[47] More recently, Jonathan Adelstein, who spent most of the first decade of the twenty-first century as a Commissioner, found the agency's data collection process and decision cycle so devoid of actual facts that he dubbed the FCC's activity "faith—based regulation."[48] This process is fueled by a revolving door between industry and government, as media and telecommunications firms spend billions on lobbying, conducted on their behalf by hundreds of former regulators and civil servants who parlay their connections inside government for large private sector paydays.[49]

Where does the public fit in the media policymaking process? The intimate relationship of industry and government inherently marginalizes the exercise of democratic will.[50] Furthermore, there are many obstacles to obtaining data relevant to regulation, ranging from "opaque pricing structures and restrictive licenses for commercial data, to legal barriers to access, to the basic adversarial nature of contemporary communications policymaking" itself.[51] Public interest groups have repeatedly tried to intervene in communications policy debates at the FCC—as they did by flooding its Open Internet docket with the most public comment on any communications policy in U.S. history— but the agency has no coherent way of dealing with such input. The treatment of public comment is left up to the discretion of FCC staff working on a particular issue and they are free to disregard it as they see fit.[52] Staff also expect commenters to "do their homework," and are much more inclined to disregard comments if they arrive in the form of petitions,[53] thereby setting a bar for "quality input" so high that the average American has difficulty reaching it, even if they have something heartfelt to say.[54] The efforts of media reformers may make "the public" more visible to regulators, but hardly guarantees policy outcomes in the public interest.[55]

* * *

The battle over network neutrality is just one of the latest in an ongoing struggle against neoliberalism's penchant "to turn all information into private property" in direct contradiction to the "development of a system to provide information widely and cheaply to all."[56] A neoliberal regulatory paradigm is designed to discourage public involvement, ignore such involvement if it cannot be avoided, and generally keep any semblance of public agency off the table until *after* constitutive choices have been made.[57] It goes a long way to explain the opaque and seemingly inchoate manner by which regulators wrestle with controversial issues.[58] It is indisputable that massive citizen pushback to the idea of removing the principle of network neutrality from the regulatory lexicon certainly helped to parry the attempts at its legislative evisceration. But it's also important to remember that this "victory" did nothing to make telecommunications policy any more informed or forward thinking; it was a victory in the defensive sense only.

This is an unfortunately common outcome of the major media policy battles of the twenty-first century.[59] Robert McChesney traces the genesis of the modern U.S. media reform movement to the flourishing of unlicensed ("pirate") radio stations in the late twentieth century and the resultant LPFM service that the FCC promulgated in response to this uprising of electronic civil disobedience.[60] McChesney calls this activity a key ingredient that helped to open the contemporary "critical juncture" in our media environment, which has made all subsequent debates over media policy possible.[61] LPFM, however, led to the actual *creation* of media policy that opened new opportunities for public access to the airwaves. It happened because activists around the country first took it upon themselves to learn the necessities of the science of broadcasting and FCC policy: self-empowerment that led to effective direct action. Congress' intervention into LPFM came at the behest of broadcast incumbents, who found themselves uncharacteristically on the uncomfortable side of a major media policy development. Though they succeeded in eviscerating the scope of the service, they could not kill it, and thousands of new community radio stations exist today.

Efforts that lead to the creation of tangibly democratic media policy far outweigh those that only parry the worst anti-democratic tendencies of neoliberalism. The battles over media policy in which the public has engaged since LPFM, however, flip the script back to the more familiar pattern, where the public mobilizes to stop incipient disaster. Despite the impressive popular outrage over the FCC's 2003 plan to do away with most media ownership regulations, the worst of it was ultimately blocked by an act of the Third Circuit of the U.S. Court of Appeals. Network neutrality may still get lip service from regulators, but that's a far cry from being a bedrock of policy. Even the impressive public backlash generated against proposed laws that would have directly meddled with the Internet's technical workings in the name of "anti-piracy" concerns was a net defensive play. The exercise of soft political power by Google, Reddit, Wikipedia, and others that impressed public opinion on policymakers regarding the Stop Online Piracy Act and Protect IP Act was ridiculously easy for them to do, amounting to little more than building a splash-page with a call to action. "Imagine a world without us" is also a powerful hook on which to foment public concern. The SOPA/PIPA debate exemplifies the power of frictionless clicktivism, which certainly stunned Congress in its speed and ferocity, but did little to advance its inherent understanding of how the Internet actually works.[62] For less than three months after the firestorm, lawmakers found themselves in the crosshairs of another organized cyber-protest for proposing to ravage the principle of online privacy in the name of national security.[63] As it stands, those engaged in media reform have got the game plan down for halting really bad things from happening in the policy realm, but this is a long way from the world where tangible victories become the norm.

Playing by the rules of a stringently neoliberal paradigm will unfortunately lead to more of the same. In the context of network neutrality, cable and telecommunications lobbyists still managed to outgun the people, for the lack of enforceable regulation on the issue is almost as good as regulations crafted for the benefit of the incumbent oligopoly.[64] Freedman remains unconvinced that a true sense of pluralism exists now in the world of media policy.[65] According to McChesney, if "the critical question facing us is whether . . . new technologies can rejuvenate . . . political democracy or whether the corporate, commercial domination of . . . the communication industries will be able to subsume the technologies within the profit net and assure that the corporate domination of both U.S. society and the global political economy remain unquestioned and unchallenged,"[66] then it is imperative that attempts to reform our media environment directly confront it. In fact, one of the most effective planks of Free Press' campaign to preserve the principle network neutrality was its dogged illumination of the use of "astroturf" groups funded by telecommunications companies, which vividly illustrated the process by which corporate actors skew regulatory dialogue surrounding issues of media policy toward the neoliberal paradigm.[67] In addition, the economic crash of 2008, and the Occupy movement that has risen from its ashes, has pushed the neoliberal paradigm toward public trial, which can only help to fuel the potentiality of the contemporary critical juncture. Although, McChesney laments the fact that "critical scholarship remains a minority phenomenon" to date and substantive debate "regarding the control and structure of the media" may be difficult under present circumstances, this is no excuse not to try.[68] This sentiment is not new or terribly radical: James Carey once remarked in 1978 that "scholarship, like many of the arts, flourishes when it stands in determined opposition to the established order."[69] Considering that the Internet is a global network with roots in the United States, and the United States was the first country to take up the principle of network neutrality as a point of policy, what happens here still has the potential to define the global perspective.[70] In the short term, this necessitates heightened, focused resistance to the neoliberal paradigm that shapes our world. Shifting the paradigm itself, however, may be the work of generations.

* * *

The triumph of neoliberalism in modern society did not happen overnight. Corporate America spent billions of dollars over more than a hundred years to shape our perceptions of the world in a massive effort to align them with a market orbit. These efforts included advertising, public relations, and public education campaigns, all of which were assisted greatly by the corporate media.[71] This included the promotion and circulation of curricula designed to instill American students at all grade levels with political and economic values that privilege consumption over citizenship. The work has been so successful that the mechanisms by which consumer capitalism functions are now considered the natural order of things or, at the very least, pillars of "principle" that denote "modern" civilization.

Given the increasing amount of time we spend interacting with our media environment, it behooves us to have some basic level of understanding about how it works, both technologically and culturally. An increasing number of educators agree that concepts of media literacy should be part and parcel of our public education. Dr. Ernest Wilson, dean of the Annenberg School of Communication at the University of Southern California, has described media literacy as "the new humanities."[72] Indeed, many countries teach concepts of media literacy as part of their core national curriculum. In the United States, however, the issue has only been considered in a fragmentary fashion by a smattering of federal agencies, foundations, and inspired scholars.[73] Although references to the importance of media literacy can be found in the educational standards documents of all 50 states,[74] it has never found a firm foothold as an identifiable subject of study in K–12 education.[75] In the realm of higher education, concepts of media literacy are not taught in any meaningfully interdisciplinary fashion, relegated to the archipelago of communication-related departments found across many campuses.[76]

When concepts of media literacy are taught, it occurs in a similarly fragmented fashion.[77] Two perspectives shape the field: the "protectionist" and "empowerment" schools of thought. The former focuses on education about media effects, and works to equip students with the skills necessary to understand and resist them, while the latter seeks to teach students the tools to be both critical media consumers and producers. Of the two, the protectionist perspective is much older, giving it a place of primacy in the field.[78] However, the empowerment perspective treats students much more holistically, providing education far beyond media effects to include the structure of the media ecosystem in which we live and how we can proactively interact with it. Unfortunately, principles of empowerment remain a minority phenomenon in the teaching of media literacy. A school's use of digital media in the classroom, for example, is typically designed to make students literate in a strictly technical sense, obviating any discussion about the implications of digital media technologies on modern life more generally—educational elements that are absolutely essential to facilitating a well-rounded understanding of our modern media environment.[79] The empowerment school of media literacy also takes as a starting point the lived experience of students themselves.[80] Any good teacher will tell you that learning is more effective when lessons are made relevant to a student's real life. With the increasingly fluid and multidimensional nature of our modern media environment, it is critically important that any attempt at media literacy education be similarly structured.[81]

The protectionist versus empowerment schism is well reflected in the two largest media literacy education advocacy groups in the United States. The National Association for Media Literacy Education, founded in 1997, represents the protectionist wing of the field. Its "Core Principles of Media Literacy Education" stress the need to "expand the concept of literacy (i.e., reading and writing) to all forms of media"[82] and "affirms that people use their individual skills, beliefs and experiences to construct their own meanings from media messages."[83] NAMLE is much more of a professional organization for educators interested in the subject of media literacy than it is a direct advocate for promoting such education in the nation's schools. It publishes the online *Journal of Media Education* which allows educators to network and share research,[84] but does not develop curricular tools for direct use in the classroom.

On the empowerment side of the coin, the Action Coalition for Media Education (ACME), founded in 2002, asserts a critical political-economic stance on the teaching of media literacy.[85] Endorsed by such radical scholars as Sut Jhally and Robert McChesney, ACME takes no money from "Big Media" and highlights aspects of media literacy such as the corporate control of media systems, the pervasive and persuasive nature of advertising, and the unsettling penchant for media organizations to promote war. It has developed teaching aids for use in the classroom, all of which are published under a Creative Commons license.[86] Furthermore, ACME offers a "seal of approval" to externally produced media literacy curricula (books, films, multimedia tools, websites, etc.) that meet exacting standards, such as being funded "with no direct financial support from transnational media conglomerates." Approved curricula should also include "supporting . . . resources—questions and answers, pre- and post-viewing activities, and/or background or supplemental materials for classroom and community educators."

Perhaps more importantly, ACME encourages the production of a media literacy curriculum that espouses "media-related activism in one's school and/or community, encouraging students to move from 'passive consumer' to 'active citizen,'" and challenges "the current corporately-owned Big Media status quo in a specific, documented, and fearless manner."[87] To date, however, only six media literacy projects have received ACME's seal of approval—just a drop in the bucket of what is necessary to teach a well-rounded liberatory media literacy program.[88] In the past, NAMLE and ACME have been at loggerheads, with NAMLE worried that ACME lacks the professionalism to entice the widespread adoption of media literacy programs by educators, and ACME critical of NAMLE for failing to address the pervasive influence of neoliberalism on our modern media environment.

Under more utopian conditions, media literacy would be tied, in the words of Douglas Kellner and Jeff Share, "to the project of radical democracy and concerned with developing skills that will enhance democratization and participation." Media literacy should go beyond the development of critical thinking skills to empower students "to use media as instruments of social communication and change."[89] Unfortunately, the neoliberal bent of American society also means that the ideology has a strong purchase in the nation's schools, and this opens the concept of media literacy to cooptation. For example, in 2002 the U.S. Department of Education, in conjunction with Microsoft, Apple, and AOL Time Warner (to name a few), founded the Partnership for Twenty-First Century Skills, which purports to advocate for the teaching of media literacy in schools.[90]

However, the Partnership primarily aspires to teach students digital media literacy skills which find their maximum value in the workplace: this "absence of a social justice agenda demonstrate[s] the influence of business interests" in media literacy education itself.[91]

In a policy context, much work remains to be done to organize the foundation necessary to promote the development and uptake of media literacy education in the United States. This work is necessary, however, if a coherent media literacy strategy is ever to find root in American classrooms. At present, the worlds of media policy and educational policy have no substantial ties to each other. Scholars in both arenas must ultimately join forces to underwrite a solid media literacy curriculum, preferably one that promotes principles of empowerment rather than protectionism. Once this is accomplished, a major campaign will be required to lobby public educators in all fifty states—at both the state and local levels—to adopt and implement such curricula, and a period of professional education will be required to bring teachers up to speed on just what media literacy education is and why it is important. Bridging the gaps between media policy and educational policy are also essential to harness the expertise of both fields without wasting time on duplicative efforts. These tasks require long-term commitment.

In the meantime, there are many ways by which teachers can begin to advance principles of media literacy on their own volition within the constraints of the current educational environment. For example, network neutrality could be taught in general or computer science classes under the rubric of instruction about the fundamental workings of the Internet; the principle itself undergirds the efficacy of the packet-switching process that stands at the root of Internet-based communication. It is not the place for a teacher to advocate for or against network neutrality, though I believe that the technical facts speak for themselves, and students are more likely to comprehend the importance of the principle once they understand the nature of the Internet's functionality. It's also not as if schools haven't taught the simple principles of media systems before: the basics of radio and television are taught in science classes, and have been for decades, on the justification that a basic understanding of how such systems work is necessary to fully appreciating and utilizing them. The Internet, at a minimum, should be treated no differently.

The realm of social studies might also provide another entry-point for the integration of media literacy education into classrooms of the present. Lessons that delve into citizens' rights and responsibilities and how public policy is made, for example, can easily accommodate a discussion of network neutrality. In the former, the right to freedom of speech online is an issue of growing importance, taking on contours never before seen in the development of a media system; network neutrality dovetails nicely as a teachable example of how these contours are shaped. In the latter, the battle over network neutrality can be used to illustrate not just the dark side of the policymaking process (in a case that involves all three branches of government to boot), but also to explore and confront the dominant ideologies that drive public policy formulation.

The potential for the integration of principles of media literacy education into the classroom is bounded only by the imaginations of clever teachers, and the general trend toward collaborative or team-teaching already encourages the cross-pollination of topics and objectives across classes. Thanks to the collaborative potential of the Internet itself, the experiences of individual educators can be shared and multiplied. Such individuals will also be crucial for the grassroots advancement of district or statewide policy initiatives to formalize the instruction of media literacy education, by providing an effective advocate with meaningful local experience on which to make the curricular case. The movement-building necessary to take media reform itself to the next level will require the construction of coalitions between interests that may be presently perceived as unrelated or disparate. Considering that many scholars are already active in the arena of media reform, reaching out to a wider circle of educators to promote the importance of media literacy in modern public education makes both tactical and strategic sense in this process. More importantly, the ultimate goal of media literacy is to make for a better-informed and participatory democracy, from which progressive media policies may evolve. In the long run, such an environment stands to be much more fruitful and sustainable than the contemporary practice of fighting piecemeal policy battles under a paradigm which disincentivizes the understanding of the technical foundations of our modern media environment and is downright hostile to progressive public agency.

* * *

The rise of the modern U.S. media reform movement has been historic. From its humble beginnings as a loose collection of radio pirates, the movement has grown in less than a decade to command a seat at the table in the arenas where media policy is made. Battles with corporate giants over issues such as media ownership and network neutrality have demonstrated the power of how an organized public interest constituency can influence the trajectory of policy-making. Had these issues arisen at the end of the last century, there's little doubt that corporate interests would have had their way with Congress, the courts, and the FCC.

Yet much work remains to be done before media reform truly becomes a force that can exert an influence strong enough to proactively foster the formation of fundamentally democratic media policies. The strategies outlined here will not be easy to implement, nor will they pay immediate dividends. The first, confronting and resisting the dominance of neoliberalism on modern politics, will involve the challenge of bucking some of the temptations to play within the boundaries of realpolitik—but if Carey's dictum that "Our models of communication...create what we disingenuously pretend they merely describe" is true, then confronting the dominant regulatory paradigm is of paramount importance.[92] While presenting the initial findings of my dissertation research on the privatization of digital radio at a media policy conference sponsored by the

Social Science Research Council in 2007, I had policy analysts from two prominent media reform organizations tell me that my work was undoubtedly interesting, but "isn't presented in a way that makes it useful in a policy context." I
hope this perspective shifts once the work is published,[93] but in the interim I
would submit that the problem might not be with the language of the research
but rather the language of policy.

Resisting the influence of neoliberalism in the media policy arena will involve shifting the contemporary paradigm to something where metrics and metaphors that promote values other than those firmly grounded in market philoso-
phies are allowable, if not preferred. At first such efforts may be ignored or
ridiculed, but with time and growing participation, such a shift is possible. There
has already been one attempt to organize an "Academic Brain Trust" of scholars
committed to exploring the contemporary critical juncture, with an eye toward
changing the culture of media policymaking "to expose the vending-machine
research and demand a commitment to integrity."[94] Although the formal inaugu-
ration of such a cadre fell through for lack of funding, the need for it remains.
On a larger scale, the funding dilemma itself is something that will unfortunately
continue to beleaguer the media reform movement for the foreseeable future, as
a growing number of organizations chase after a pot of dollars that pales in
comparison to the amount of money media and telecommunications corporations invest in coin—operated "policy institutes" and "think tanks."[95]

A campaign to formalize media literacy education is currently beyond the
capacity of the modern media reform movement. Alliances will be necessary
between those engaged in media and educational policy; the groundwork for
these will require some collaborative self-education about not just what media
literacy is (and might be), but why it is important that it be a requisite component of our nation's system of public education. There is only so much that policy wonks alone can accomplish in this effort: the real impetus for the implementation of media literacy education must come from teachers themselves, who
already have the opportunity and agency to creatively introduce its principles
and concepts into existing curricula. In this regard, the role of scholars invested
in media literacy research desperately needs to move beyond the infighting over
its traditions and toward collaboration that fosters the uptake of media literacy
education which can exploit the potential of the contemporary critical juncture.[96]
The dominant traditions of media literacy education are not mutually exclusive:
protectionism provides a necessary prophylactic that helps to form the conditions from which the empowerment of students—as citizens first and consumers
second—can be realized.

Critical junctures are temporary phenomena, and while the modern media
reform movement has already accomplished an impressive amount under the
most trying of conditions, just imagine the possibilities of a movement fueled by
a public predisposed toward democratic politics more generally. In the interim,
battles like those over network neutrality will continue to provide useful opportunities to hone the tactics of media reform in a direction that allows for the

movement's transformational evolution into an authentically progressive force for change.

Notes

1. See Free Press, "Media Minutes," accessed April 12, 2012, http://www.freepress.net/newsroom/mediaminutes and John Anderson, "Media Minutes: 2004–2012," *DIYmedia.net*, May 7, 2012, accessed May 14, 2012, http://diymedia.net/archive/0512.htm#050712.

2. See Free Press, "Saving the Internet: A History," accessed April 23, 2012, http://www.savetheinternet.com/timeline.

3. See Minjeong Kim, Chung Joo Chung, and Jang Hyun Kim, "Who Shapes Network Neutrality Policy Debate? An Examination of Information Subsidizers in the Mainstream Media and at Congressional and FCC Hearings," *Telecommunications Policy* 35 (2011): 315; Alison Powell and Alyssa Cooper, "Net Neutrality Discourses: Comparing Advocacy and Regulatory Arguments in the United States and the United Kingdom," *The Information Society: An International Journal* 27, no. 5 (2011): 311.

4. Zack Stiegler and Dan Sprumont, "Mediated Voices: Framing the Net Neutrality Debate" (paper presented at the 97th annual convention of the National Communication Association, New Orleans, LA, November 16–19, 2011).

5. See Jonathan Krim, "Executive Wants to Charge for Web Speed," *Washington Post*, December 1, 2005, accessed April 12, 2012, http://www.washingtonpost.com/wp-dyn/content/article/2005/11/30/AR2005113002109.html.

6. This mea culpa is not mine alone. Bill Herman, then an intern at Public Knowledge, initially unleashed the "series of tubes" meme online. He immediately had second thoughts about what he had wrought, and "quickly began to push for greater decorum and on-point discussion of the policy debate at hand." However, the genie was already out of the bottle. See Bill D. Herman, "Opening Bottlenecks: On Behalf of Mandated Network Neutrality," *Federal Communications Law Journal* 59, no. 1 (2006–2007): 108, footnote 18.

7. James W. Carey, "The Press, Public Opinion, and Public Discourse: On the Edge of the Postmodern," in *James Carey: A Critical Reader*, eds. Eve Stryker Munson and Catherine A. Warren (Minneapolis: University of Minnesota Press, 1997), 229.

8. James W. Carey, "A Cultural Approach to Communication," in *Communication as Culture: Essays on Media and Society* (New York: Routledge, 1992), 34.

9. James W. Carey, "Reconceiving 'Mass' and 'Media'," in *Communication as Culture*, 83.

10. James W. Carey and John J. Quirk, "The History of the Future," in *Communication as Culture*, 193–195.

11. Powell and Cooper, 312.

12. Ibid., 321–322.

13. Christian Sandvig, "Network Neutrality Is the New Common Carriage," *Info: The Journal of Policy, Regulation, and Strategy* 9. no. 2/3 (2007): 139.

14. Powell and Cooper, 316.

15. Des Freedman, "Dynamics of Power in Contemporary Media Policy-Making," *Media Culture and Society* 28 (2006): 913.

16. Jon M. Peha, William H. Lehr, and Simon Wilkie, "The State of the Debate on Network Neutrality," *International Journal of Communication* 1 (2007): 710–711.

17. Freedman, 921.

18. Peha et al., 712.

19. See David S. Allen, *Democracy, Inc.: The Press and the Law in the Corporate Rationalization of the Public Sphere* (Urbana: University of Illinois Press, 2005), 2; Nicholas Garnham, *Capitalism and Communication: Global Culture and the Economics of Information,* ed. Fred Inglis (London: Sage, 1990), 111; Robert W. McChesney, *The Political Economy of the Media: Enduring Issues, Emerging Dilemmas* (New York: Monthly Review Press, 2008), 157, 247, 345, 371; Robert W. McChesney, *Rich Media, Poor Democracy: Communication Politics in Dubious Times* (New York: The New Press, 2000), 124-125; Edward S. Herman and Robert W. McChesney, *The Global Media: The New Missionaries of Global Capitalism* (London: Cassell, 1997), 7; Dan Schiller, *How to Think about Information* (Urbana: University of Illinois Press, 2007), 55; Thomas Streeter, *Selling the Air: A Critique of the Policy of Commercial Broadcasting in the United States* (Chicago: University of Chicago Press, 1996), 320; and Frank Webster, *Theories of the Information Society, Third Edition* (London: Routledge, 2006), 270–271.

20. See Francois Fortier, *Virtuality Check: Power Relations and Alternative Strategies in the Information Society* (London: Verso, 2001), 103 and Armand Mattelart, *Networking the World: 1794–2000,* trans. Liz Carey-Libbrecht and James A. Cohen (Minneapolis: University of Minnesota Press, 2000), 104–105.

21. Paul Starr, *The Creation of the Media: Political Origins of Modern Communications* (New York: Basic Books, 2004), 4.

22. Ibid., 5.

23. Lee L. Selwyn, "Revisiting the Regulatory Status of Broadband Internet Access: A Policy Framework for Net Neutrality and an Open Competitive Internet," *Federal Communications Law Journal* 63, no. 1 (2010–2011): 92–93.

24. Herman, 154.

25. Streeter, 79–80.

26. Ibid., xi–xii.

27. Ibid., 39.

28. Schiller, 110.

29. See Robert Britt Horwitz, *The Irony of Regulatory Reform: The Deregulation of American Telecommunications* (New York: Oxford University Press, 1989), 36, 44; Sven B. Lundstedt and Michael W. Spicer, "Latent Policy and the Federal Communications Commission," *Telecommunications, Values, and the Public Interest,* ed. Sven B. Lundstedt (Norwood, NJ: Ablex Publishing Corporation, 1990), 290–292; and Robert W. McChesney, *Telecommunications, Mass Media, and Democracy: The Battle for Control of U.S. Broadcasting, 1928–1935* (New York: Oxford University Press, 1993), 28–29.

30. Philip M. Napoli, *Foundations of Communications Policy: Principles and Process in the Regulation of Electronic Media* (Cresskill, NJ: Hampton Press, 2001), 266.

31. Christine Quail and Christine Larabie, "Net Neutrality: Media Discourses and Public Perception," *Global Media Journal–Canadian Edition* 3, no. 1 (2010): 34.

32. Powell and Cooper, 319.

33. This particular shift in policy lexicon has been underway for more than two decades. See Sandra Braman, "Where Has Media Policy Gone? Defining the Field in the Twenty-First Century," *Communication Law and Policy* 9, no. 2 (2004): 172.

34. Quail and Larabie, 41.

35. Mark J. Braun, *AM Stereo and the FCC: Case Study of a Marketplace Shibboleth* (Norwood, NJ: Ablex, 1994), 167.

36. See Braun, 141; Hernan Galperin, *New Television, Old Politics: The Transition to Digital TV in the United States and Britain* (Cambridge, U.K.: Cambridge University Press, 2004), 7, 70, 244; Horwitz, 38–39, 48, 88, 155; Erwin G. Krasnow and Lawrence D. Longley, *The Politics of Broadcast Regulation* (New York: St. Martin's Press, 1973), 80–81; Vincent Mosco, *Broadcasting in the United States: Innovative Challenge and Organizational Control* (Norwood, NJ: Ablex Publishing Corporation, 1979), 5, 46, 61, 126–127; and Napoli, 75–77, 215–216, 273.

37. Stiegler and Sprumont, 5.

38. Lundstedt and Spicer, 292–293.

39. Napoli, 268–269.

40. Freedman, 916.

41. Ibid., 920–921.

42. Kim et al., 318–322.

43. Daniel Bell, *The Coming of Post-Industrial Society: A Venture in Social Forecasting* (New York: Basic Books, 1973), 364–365.

44. Sandra Braman, *Change of State: Information, Policy, and Power* (Cambridge, MA: MIT Press, 2006), 319.

45. Ibid., 325.

46. Ibid., 254.

47. See Jeff Chester, *Digital Destiny: New Media and the Future of Democracy* (New York: The New Press, 2007), 46–64; John Dunbar, "Who Is Watching the Watchdogs?," in *The Future of Media: Resistance and Reform in the 21st Century,* eds. Robert W. McChesney, Russell Newman, and Ben Scott (New York: Seven Stories Press, 2005), 131; Lundstedt and Spicer, 295.

48. Transcript of remarks delivered by FCC Commissioner Jonathan Adelstein, Media Policy Research Pre-Conference to the National Conference for Media Reform, Memphis, TN, January 11, 2007, accessed April 12, 2012, http://mediaresearchhub.ssrc.org/news/transcript-of-fcc-commissioner-adelsteins-remarks-at-media-policy-research-pre-conference.

49. Freedman, 917.

50. Ibid., 918.

51. Philip M. Napoli and Joe Karaganis, *Toward a Federal Data Agenda for Communications Policymaking* (New York: Social Science Research Council, 2007), 15.

52. See JoAnne Holman and Michael A. McGregor, "'Thank You for Taking the Time to Read This': Public Participation via New Communication Technologies at the FCC," *Journalism and Communication Monographs* 2, no. 4 (Winter 2001), 162, 164, 182; Michael A. McGregor, "When the 'Public Interest' Is Not What Interests the Public," *Communication Law and Policy* 11, no. 2 (Spring 2006), 210.

53. See McGregor, 209, 223–224, and Holman and McGregor, 185, 187.

54. Napoli, 73, 233.

55. Ibid., 230.

56. Garnham, 127

57. Nicholas Garnham, "Information Society Theory as Ideology: A Critique," *Studies in Communication Sciences* 1 (2001): 164.

58. See Oscar H. Gandy, Jr. *Beyond Agenda Setting: Information Subsidies and Public Policy* (Norwood, NJ: Ablex Publishing Company, 1982), 8 and Streeter, xi–xii, xv.

59. Robert W. McChesney, "Media Policy Goes to Main Street: The Uprising of 2003," *The Communication Review* 7 (2004): 250.

60. Ibid., 224–225.

61. Robert W. McChesney, *Communication Revolution: Critical Junctures and the Future of Media* (New York: The New Press, 2007), 147–148.

62. See Joshua Kopstein, "Dear Congress, It's No Longer Okay to Not Know How The Internet Works," *Motherboard*, December 16, 2011, accessed April 16, 2012, http://motherboard.vice.com/2011/12/16/dear-congress-it-s-no-longer-ok-to-not-know-how-the-internet-works.

63. See Trevor Timm, "Cybersecurity Bill FAQ: The Disturbing Privacy Dangers in CISPA and How to Stop It," Electronic Frontier Foundation, April 15, 2012, accessed April 16, 2012, https://www.eff.org/deeplinks/2012/04/cybersecurity-bill-faq-disturbing-privacy-dangers-cispa-and-how-you-stop-it.

64. Kim et al., 316, 322.

65. Freedman, 922.

66. Napoli, 235.

67. See "Corruption Road: How Corporate Money and Astroturf Corrupt Media Policy," accessed April 12, 2012, http://corruptionroad.freepress.net/.

68. McChesney, *The Political Economy of the Media*, 350–353.

69. James W. Carey, "The Ambiguity of Policy Research," in *Communication Researchers and Policy-Making*, ed. Sandra Braman (Cambridge, MA: MIT Press, 2003), 440.

70. Powell and Cooper, 314.

71. See Roland Marchand, *Creating the Corporate Soul: The Rise of Public Relations and Corporate Imagery in American Big Business* (Berkeley: University of California Press, 2001).

72. Renee Hobbs, "The State of Media Literacy: A Response to Potter," *Journal of Broadcasting and Electronic Media* 55, no. 3 (2011): 422.

73. Ibid., 421.

74. Douglas Kellner and Jeff Share, "Toward Critical Media Literacy: Core Concepts, Debates, Organizations, Policy," *Discourse: Studies in the Cultural Politics of Education* 26, no. 3 (September 2005): 379.

75. Ibid., 371.

76. Hobbs, 428.

77. W. James Potter, "The State of Media Literacy," *Journal of Broadcasting and Electronic Media* 54, no. 4 (2010): 683.

78. Hobbs, 422–423.

79. Hobbs, 426.

80. Renee Hobbs, "The State of Media Literacy: A Rejoinder," *Journal of Broadcasting and Electronic Media* 55, no. 4 (2011): 602.

81. Fidelia van der Linde, "The Necessity of a Media Literacy Module within Journalism or Media Studies Curricula," *Global Media Journal: African Edition* 4, no. 2 (2010): 2.

82. National Association for Media Literacy Education, "Core Principles of Media Literacy Education in the United States," 2009, http://namle.net/wp—content/uploads/2009/09/NAMLE-CPMLE-w-questions2.pdf, 4.

83. Ibid., 6.

84. See http://jmle.org/, accessed April 12, 2012. The journal was founded in 2009.

85. See http://www.acmecoalition.org/, accessed April 12, 2012.

86. See ACME Coalition, "Free Teaching Resources," accessed April 12, 2012, http://www.acmecoalition.org/free_acme_teaching_resources.

87. See ACME Coalition, "ACME Curriculum Standards," accessed April 12, 2012, http://www.acmecoalition.org/acme_curriculum_standards.

88. See ACME Coalition, "Curriculum Reviews," accessed April 12, 2012, http://www.acmecoalition.org/curriculum_reviews.

89. Kellner and Share, 372–373.

90. See http://www.21stcenturyskills.org/, accessed April 12, 2012.

91. Kellner and Share, 381.

92. Carey, "A Cultural Approach to Communication," 32.

93. John Nathan Anderson, *Radio's Digital Dilemma: Broadcasting in the 21ˢᵗ Century* (New York: Routledge, forthcoming, 2013).

94. McChesney, *Communication Revolution*, 175–177.

95. The recent closure of Media Access Project demonstrates the tenuousness of the media reform movement's funding base. MAP, with its a *39—year* legacy of advocating for the public interest regarding issues of media policy and law, has been instrumental in many of the media reform movement's largest accomplishments, including the launch of LPFM and stopping the evisceration of the FCC's media ownership rules, among many others. Andrew J. Schwartzmann, MAP's policy director, cited funding difficulties that necessitated the shop's closure: "The problem isn't that there are too many groups; the problem is that there isn't enough money" to go around. See Tony Romm, "Media Access Project to Fold in May," *Politico*, April 3, 2012, accessed April 27, 2012, http://www.politico.com/news/stories/0412/74800.html, and Juliana Gruenwald, "Media Access Project to Shut Down," *NationalJournal Tech Daily Dose*, April 3, 2012, accessed April 27, 2012, http://techdailydose.nationaljournal.com/2012/04/media-access-project-to-shut-d.php.

96. See Douglas Kellner and Jeff Share, "Critical Media Literacy Is Not an Option," *Learning Inquiry* 1, no. 1 (2007): 59–69.

Bibliography

13tongimp. "DJ Ted Stevens Techno Remix: 'A Series of Tubes.'" YouTube. July 14, 2006. http://www.youtube.com/watch?v=EtOoQFa5ug8 (accessed August 13, 2012).

"A 'National Broadband Plan,'" *Wall Street Journal*, January 20, 2010. http://online.wsj.com/article/SB10001424052748703652104574652501608376552. html (accessed March 20, 2011).

Abbate, Janet. *Inventing the Internet*, 2nd ed. Cambridge, Mass.: MIT Press, 2000.

ACME Coalition. "ACME Curriculum Standards." http://www.acmecoalition.org/acme_ curriculum standards (accessed August 8, 2012).

———. "Curriculum Reviews." http://www.acmecoalition.org/curriculum_reviews (accessed August 8, 2012).

———. "Free Teaching Resources." July 23, 2007. http://www.acmecoalition.org/ free_acme_teaching_resources (accessed August 8, 2012).

Adbusters. "#Occupywallstreet." *AdBusters*, http://www.adbusters.org/blogs/adbusters-blog/occupywallstreet.html (accessed October 13, 2011).

Adelstein, Jonathan. Statement of Commissioner Jonathan S. Adelstein at En Banc hearing on Broadband Management Practices, Harvard Law School, Cambridge, Massachusetts, February 25, 2008. http://hraunfoss.fcc.gov/edocs_public/ attachmatch/DOC-280441A1.pdf (accessed August 8, 2012).

———. Statement of Commissioner Jonathan S. Adelstein at En Banc Hearing on Broadband Network Management Practices, Stanford Law School, Palo Alto, CA, April 17, 2008. http://hraunfoss.fcc.gov/edocs_public/attachmatch/ DOC–281626A1.pdf (accessed August 8, 2012).

———. Transcript of remarks at the Media Policy Research Pre–Conference to the National Conference for Media Reform, Memphis, Tennessee, January 11, 2007. http://mediaresearchhub.ssrc.org/news/transcript-of-fcc-commissioner-adelsteins-remarks-at-media-policy-research-pre-conference (accessed August 8, 2012).

Akamai Technologies. "Akamai Releases Fourth Quarter 2011 'State of the Internet' Report." Akamai Press Release, April 30, 2012. Akamai Technologies web site. http://www.akamai.com/html/about/press/releases/2012/press_043012.html (accessed August 13, 2012).

Albanesius, Chloe. "Net Neutrality: The Heavy Hitters React." *PC Magazine*, December 21, 2010.

Allen, David S. *Democracy, Inc.: The Press and the Law in the Corporate Rationalization of the Public Sphere.* Urbana: University of Illinois Press, 2005.

Alterman, Eric. "The Agony and Ecstasy—and 'Disgrace' of Steve Jobs." *The Nation*, November 28, 2011.

American Library Association v. Federal Communications Commission, 406 F.3d 689, 692 (D.C. Cir. 2005).

America Online, Inc. v. GreatDeals.net, 49 F. Supp. 2d 851 (E.D. Va. 1999).

Anderson, John Nathan. "Media Minutes: 2004–2012." *DIYmedia.net*, May 7, 2012. http://diymedia.net/archive/0512.htm#050712 (accessed August 8, 2012).

———. *Radio's Digital Dilemma: Broadcasting in the 21st Century*. New York: Routledge, 2013.

Anderson, Nate. "Blind Refs and Baby Kissers: Senators Brawl Over Neutral Net." *Ars Technica*. April 2010. http://arstechnica.com/tech–policy/news/2010/04/senate-brawls–over–network–neutrality.ars (accessed August 8, 2012).

———. "Why Everyone Hates New Net Neutrality Rules—Even NN Supporters." *Ars Techica*. February 2011. http://arstechnica.com/tech–policy/news/2010/12/why-everyone-hates-new-net-neutrality-ruleseven-nn-supporters.ars (accessed September 1, 2011).

Angelopoulos, Christina. "Dutch University Blocks BitTorrent Pre-Emptively Breaking New Net Neutrality Law." *Institute for Information Law* (March 28, 2012). http://kluwercopyrightblog.com/2012/03/28/dutch-university-blocks-bittorrent-pre-emptively-breaking-new-net-neutrality-law/ (accessed August 8, 2012).

Armstrong, Mario, and Farai Chideya. "Net Neutrality Battle Goes to Washington." *News and Notes*. Radio program. June 26, 2006. NPR. http://www.npr.org/templates/story/story.php?storyId=5511150 (accessed August 13, 2012).

Associated Press, "Investigation Dropped by Wickersham; Telephone Combine Question Referred to Commerce Commission; Deep Probe Is Planned," *Pittsburgh Gazette Times*, January 21, 1913, 1.

"At SBC, It's All About 'Scale and Scope'; CEO Edward Whitacre Talks about the AT&T Wireless Acquisition and How He's Moving to Keep Abreast of Cable Competitors." November 7, 2005. *Bloomburg Businessweek Online Extra*. http://www.businessweek.com/magazine/content/05_45/b3958092.htm (accessed August 8, 2012).

AT&T Inc. *Comments of AT&T Inc.* FCC Docket No. 07–52. January 14, 2010. http://apps.fcc.gov/ecfs/document/view?id=7020377279 (accessed August 13, 2012).

———. *Comments of AT&T on Petitions of Free Press and Vuze*. FCC Docket No. 07–52. February 13, 2008. http://apps.fcc.gov/ecfs/document/view? (accessed August 8, 2012).

———. "In–State Connection Fee." http://www.consumer.att.com/instate-connectionfee/ (accessed August 13, 2012).

Ball, Carolyn. "What Is Transparency?" *Public Integrity* 11, no. 4 (October 2009): 293–307.

Bangeman, Eric. "Amazon Exec: Net Neutrality Necessary Because of 'Little Choice' for Consumers." *Ars Technica*. May 12, 2006. http://arstechnica.com/uncategorized/2 006/05/6817-2/ (accessed August 8, 2012).

Barratt, Neil, and Leslie Regan Shade. "Net Neutrality: Telecom Policy and the Public Interest." *Canadian Journal of Communication* 32, no. 2 (2007): 295–305.

Bell, Daniel. *The Coming of Post-Industrial Society: A Venture in Social Forecasting*. New York: Basic Books, 1973.

"Beck through the Looking Glass: Smears Net Neutrality as a Marxist Plot to Take Over the Internet." *Media Matters for America.* October 21, 2009. http://mediamatters.org/research/200910210026 (August 8, 2012).

Ben-Shahar, Omri, and Carl E. Schneider. "The Failure of Mandated Disclosure." *University of Pennsylvania Law Review* 159 (2012): 647–749.

Benkler, Yochai. "Ending the Internet's Trench Warfare." *New York Times*, March 20, 2010, http://www.nytimes.com/2010/03/21/opinion/21Benkler.html (accessed August 8, 2012).

Berger, Dan. "Defining Democracy: Coalition Politics and the Struggle for Media Reform." *International Journal of Communication* 3 (2009): 3–22.

Berkman Center for Internet and Society at Harvard University. "Next Generation Connectivity: A Review of Broadband Internet Transitions and Policy from around the World." February 16, 2010, http://cyber.law.harvard.edu/pubrelease/ broadband (accessed August 8, 2012).

Berners-Lee, Tim. "The Neutrality of the Net." *Decentralized Information Group, MIT Computer Science and Artificial Intelligence Laboratory.* May 2, 2006. http://dig.csail.mit.edu/breadcrumbs/node/132 (accessed August 8, 2012).

———. "Net Neutrality: This Is Serious." *Decentralized Information Group, MIT Computer Science and Artificial Intelligence Laboratory.* June 21, 2006. http://dig.csail.mit.edu/breadcrumbs/node/144 (accessed August 8, 2012).

Birkey, Andy. "Bachmann: Net Neutrality Is Censorship." *The Minnesota Independent.* April 20, 2010, http://minnesotaindependent.com/57830/bachmann-net-neutrality-is-censorship (accessed April 12, 2012).

Birkinshaw, Patrick. "Transparency as a Human Right." In *Transparency: The Key to Better Governance?*, edited by Christopher Hood and David Heald. Oxford: Oxford University Press, 2006.

Blackstone, William, *Commentaries on the Laws of England.* Oxford: Clarendon Press, 1765–1769.

Boltanski, Luc, and Laurent Thevenot. *On Justification.* Trans. Catherine Porter. Princeton, N.J.: Princeton University Press, 2006.

Bonner, Elizabeth Austin. "Network Neutrality Disclosures: More and Less Information." *I/S: A Journal of Law and Policy for the Information Society* 8, no. 1 (Winter 2012): 179–209.

Bosker, Bianca. "Watch Obama's Net Neutrality Promises, Promises, Promises." *Huffington Post.* August 13, 2010. http://www.huffingtonpost.com/2010/08/13/net-neutrality-obama-see_n_681695.html (accessed March 10, 2011).

Braman, Sandra. *Change of State: Information, Policy, and Power.* Cambridge, MA: MIT Press, 2006.

———. "Where Has Media Policy Gone? Defining the Field in the Twenty-first Century." *Communication Law and Policy* 9, no. 2 (2004): 153–182.

"Brand X: Statement of Consumer Groups on The Supreme Court's Decision." *SavetheInternet.com*, June 27, 2005. http://www.google.com/url?sa= t&rct=j&q= &esrc=s&source=web&cd=1&ved=0CCIQFjAA&url=http%3A%2F%2Fwww. savetheinternet.com%2Fsites%2Fdefault%2Ffiles%2Freleases%2F06.27.05_CFA_ Brand_X_release.doc&ei=1pQFUJXKOHy0gGf7O3cCA&usg=AFQjCNFnhuganv5 a1hrYD7KW6_BNiq5x6g (accessed July 16, 2012).

Braun, Mark J. *AM Stereo and the FCC: Case Study of a Marketplace Shibboleth.* Norwood, NJ: Ablex, 1994.

Brey, Philip. "Social Constructivism for Philosophers of Technology: A Shopper's Guide." *Society for Philosophy and Technology* 2, no. 3/4 (Spring/Summer 1997), http://scholar.lib.vt.edu/ejournals/SPT/v2_n3n4html/brey.html? (accessed April 3, 2012).

Briffault, Richard. "Campaign Finance Disclosure 2.0." *Election Law Journal* 9, no. 4 (December 2010): 273–303.

Brito, Jerry, and Ellig, Jerry. "A Tale of Two Commissions: Net Neutrality and Regulatory Analysis." *CommLaw Conspectus* 16, no. 1 (2007): 1–15.

Brown, Katie, Scott W. Campbell, and Rich Ling. "Mobile Phones Bridging the Digital Divide for Teens in the Us?" *Future Internet* 3, no. 2 (2011): 144–158.

Brown, William R. "Attention and the Rhetoric of Social Intervention." *Quarterly Journal of Speech* 68, no. 1 (1982): 17–27.

———. "The Holgraphic View of Argument." *Argumentation* 1, no. 1 (1987): 89–102.

———. "Power and the Rhetoric of Social Intervention." *Quarterly Journal of Speech* 53, no. 2 (1986): 180–199.

Bruns, Axel. "Some Exploratory Notes on Produsers and Produsage." *Snurblog*, http://snurb.info/index.php?q=node/329 (accessed August 21, 2011).

Buhle, Paul. *Taking Care of Business: Samuel Gompers, George Meany, Lane Kirkland and the Tragedy of American Labor.* New York: Monthly Review Press, 1999.

"Building the Internet Toll Road." *Wired.* February 26, 2006. http://www.wired.com/techbiz/media/news/2006/02/70292?currentPage=all (accessed July 16, 2012).

Burgess, Jean, and Joshua Green. *YouTube*, Digital Media and Society Series. Malden, Mass.: Polity, 2009.

Burnett, Robert, and P. David Marshall. *Web Theory: An Introduction.* New York: Routledge, 2003.

Cabebe, Jaymar. "Help, I'm Getting Arrested!" *CNet*, http://reviews.cnet.com/8301-19736_720119537-251/help-im-getting-arrested/ (accessed October 12, 2011).

Callaghan, Karen, and Frauke Schnell. "Assessing the Democratic Debate: How the News Media Frame Elite Policy Discourse." *Political Communication* 18, no. 2 (2001): 183–212.

Carey, James W. "A Cultural Approach to Communication." In *Communication as Culture: Essays on Media and Society*, 13–36. New York: Routledge, 1992.

———. "The Ambiguity of Policy Research." In *Communication Researchers and Policy-Making*, edited by Sandra Braman, 437–444. Cambridge, MA: MIT Press, 2003.

———. "The Press, Public Opinion, and Public Discourse: On the Edge of the Postmodern." In *James Carey: A Critical Reader*, edited by Eve Stryker Munson and Catherine A. Warren, 228–260. Minneapolis: University of Minnesota Press, 1997.

———. "Reconceiving 'Mass' and 'Media.'" In *Communication as Culture: Essays on Media and Society*, 69–88. New York: Routledge, 1992.

Carey, James W., and John J. Quirk. "The History of the Future." In *Communication as Culture: Essays on Media and Society*, 173–200. New York: Routledge, 1992.

Castells, Manual. *End of Millennium.* Malden, Mass.: Wiley, 2010.

Center for Responsive Politics. "Communications/Electronics: Long Term Contribution Trends." http://www.opensecrets.org/industries/contrib.php?ind= B&cycle=2006 (accessed July 16, 2012).

———. "Lobbying: AT&T." http://www.opensecrets.org/lobby/clientsum.php?year=2006&lname=AT%26T+Inc (accessed July 16, 2012).

———. "Lobbyists: Dellums and Associates." http://www.opensecrets.org/lobby/firmsum.php?id=F23686&year=2006 (accessed July 16, 2012).

————. "Lobbying: National Cable and Telecommunications Assn." http://www.opensecrets.org/lobby/clientsum.php?id=D000022131&year=2006 (accessed July 16, 2012).

————. "Lobbying: Verizon Communications." http://www.opensecrets.org/lobby/clientsum.php?year=2006&lname=Verizon+Communications (accessed July 16, 2012).

————. "Top Contributors: Bobby L. Rush 2005–2006." http://www.opensecrets.org/politicianscontrib.phpcycle=2006&cid=N00004887&type=I&newmem=N (accessed July 16, 2012).

Cerf, Vinton G. "Prepared Statement of Vincent G. Cerf." Speech delivered to US Senate Committee on Commerce, Science, and Transportation Hearing on Net Neutrality. February 7, 2006. http://commerce.senate.gov/pdf/cerf-020706.pdf (accessed August 13, 2012).

Cerf, Vinton G., Stephen D. Crocker, David P. Reed, Lauren Weinstein, and Daniel Lynch. "Open Letter to FCC Chairman Julius Genachowski." *Open Internet Coalition.* http://www.openinternetcoalition.org/files/FCC_NN_Letter_Cerf.pdf (accessed August 13, 2012).

Chandler, Jennifer A. "A Right to Reach an Audience: An Approach to Intermediary Bias on the Internet." *Hofstra Law Review* 35, no. 3 (2007): 1095–138.

Chen, Jim. "The Authority to Regulate Broadband Internet Access Over Cable." *Berkeley Technology Law Journal* 16 (2001): 677–727.

Chen, Stephanie & Chris Brown, "Saving the Open Internet: The Importance of Network Neutrality." Greenlining Institute. March 2012. http://stage.greenlining.org/resources/pdfs/GLIonNetNeutrality.pdf (accessed August 13, 2012).

Chester, Jeffery. *Digital Destiny: New Media and the Future of Democracy.* New York: New Press, 2006.

Chima, Chikodi. "Apps for Occupiers Make Organizing, Communicating and Sharing Easier." *VentureBeat,* http://venturebeat.com/2011/11/19/apps-for-occupy-wall-street/ (accessed November 30, 2011).

Clark, David D. "Network Neutrality: Words of Power and 800-Pound Gorillas." *International Journal of Communication* 1 (2007): 701–708.

Clemmitt, Marcia. "Controlling the Internet." *CQ Researcher* 16 (May 12, 2006): 409–432.

Cloud, Dana L., and Joshua Gunn. "Introduction: W(h)ither Ideology." *Western Journal of Communication* 75, no. 4 (2011): 407–420.

Cloud, Dana, Steve Macek, and James Arnt Aune. "'The Limbo of Ethical Simulacra' a Reply to Ron Greene." *Philosophy and Rhetoric* 39, no. 1 (2006): 72–86.

Clyburn, Mignon L., Statement of Commissioner, *A National Broadband Plan for Our Future,* GN Docket No. 09–51 (March 16, 2010).

Coase, Ronald. "The Problem of Social Cost." *Journal of Law and Economics* 3, no. 1 (1960): 1–44.

Cobb, Kelly William. "Defining and Confining the Internet: Regulation by Another Name Is Still Regulation," *Washington Times,* May 26, 2010. http://www.washingtontimes.com/news/2010/may/25/defining-and-confining-the-internet/ (accessed March 25, 2011).

Coglianese, Cary, and Robert A. Kagan, eds. 2007. *Regulation and Regulatory Processes.* Burlington: Ashgate.

Cohen, Adam. "Why the Democratic Ethic of the Web May Be about to End." *New York Times.* May 28, 2006. http://www.nytimes.com/2006/05/28/opinion/28sun3.html (accessed August 13, 2012).

Cohen, Lizabeth. *A Consumer's Republic: The Politics of Mass Consumption in Postwar America.* New York: Alfred A. Knopf, 2003.

Cohen, Nicole S. "The Valorization of Surveillance: Towards a Political Economy of Facebook." *Democratic Communiqué* 22, no. 1 2008: 5–22. http://journals.fcla.edu/demcom/article/view/76495 (accessed July 16, 2012).

Comcast Corporation. *Comments of Comcast Corporation.* FCC Docket No. 07-52. January 14, 2010. http://apps.fcc.gov/ecfs/document/view?id=7020376090 (accessed August 13, 2012).

Comcast Corp. v. FCC. 600 F.3d 642, 645 (D.C. Cir. 2010).

Consumers Union. "The Telecommunications Act: Consumers Still Waiting for Better Phone and Cable Services on the Sixth Anniversary of National Law." press release, February 6, 2002. Consumers Union website. http://www.consumersunion.org/telecom/sixthdc202.htm (accessed August 13, 2012).

Cook, Brian. "Not Neutrality." *In These Times.* March 26, 2007. http://www.inthesetimes.com/article/3081/not_neutrality/ (accessed July 16, 2012).

Corley, J. Russ. "A Communication Study of Arthur F. Holmes as a Worldview Advocate." Doctoral Dissertation, The Ohio State University, 1983.

Copps, Michael J. "Concurring Statement of Michael J. Copps re: Preserving the Open Internet, GN Docket No. 09-191, *Broadband Industry Practices,* WC Docket No. 07-52." December 21, 2010. http://hraunfoss.fcc.gov/edocs_public/attachmatch/FCC-10-201A3.pdf (accessed August 18, 2012).

Correa, David K. "Assessing Broadband in America: OECD and ITIF Broadband Rankings." *The Information Technology and Innovation Foundation,* April 2007, http://www.itif.org/files/BroadbandRankings.pdf (accessed August 8, 2012).

Council of the European Union. "Council Conclusions on the Open Internet and Net Neutrality in Europe 3134." *EU Transport, Telecommunications and Energy Council Meeting,* 2011, http://www.consilium.europa.eu/uedocs/cms_data/docs/pressdata/en/trans/126890.pdf (April 12, 2012).

Coursey, David. "Comcast May Now Regret Suing the FCC Over Net Neutrality." *PCWorld.* May 6, 2010. http://www.pcworld.com/businesscenter/article/195794/comcast_may_now_regret_suing_the_fcc_over_net_neutrality.html (accessed August 8, 2012).

Crawford, Susan. "An Internet for Everybody." *New York Times.* April 11, 2010. http://www.nytimes.com/2010/04/11/opinion/11crawford.html (accessed August 8, 2012).

———. "The Internet and the Project of Communications Law." *UCLA Law Review* 55, no. 2 (2007): 359.

Cressman, Darryl. "The Concert Hall as a Medium of Musical Culture." Ph.D. dissertation, Simon Fraser University, 2012.

Crovitz, L. Gordon. "Do Monopolies Rule the Internet?" *Wall Street Journal,* November 28, 2010. http://online.wsj.com/article/SB10001424052748704693104575638401052783466.html?mod=WSJ_Opinion_BelowLEFTSecond (accessed March 20, 2011).

"CWA Opposed Move toward Internet Regulation," CWA, May 26, 2006. http://www.cwa-union.org/news/entry/cwa_opposes_move_toward_internet_regulation#.UCML9nCr81h (accessed July 16, 2012).

Cyril, Malkia A. "Media and Marginalization." In *The Future of Media: Resistance and Reform in the 21st Century*, edited by Robert McChesney, Russell Newman, and Ben Scott, 97–104. New York: Seven Stories Press, 2005.

Czwartacki, John. "Preserving the Open Internet." *Verizon PolicyBlog.* September 22, 2009. http://policyblog.verizon.com/BlogPost/668/PreservingtheOpenInternet.aspx (accessed August 8, 2012).

Davidson, Alan. "Vint Cerf Speaks Out on Net Neutrality." *Google Official Blog.* November 8, 2005. http://googleblog.blogspot.com/2005/11/vint-cerf-speaks-out-on-net-neutrality.html (accessed August 8, 2012).

Davidson, Alan, and Thomas J. Tauke. "Google and Verizon Joint Submission on the Open Internet." *In the Matter of Preserving the Open Internet.* FCC GN Docket 09-191. January 14, 2010. http://fjallfoss.fcc.gov/ecfs/document/view?id=7020378826 (accessed August 8, 2012).

Derkacz, Evan. "Markey Introduces Net Neutrality Act: The Fight for the First Amendment of the Internet Is On." *AlterNet.* May 2, 2006. http://www.alternet.org/story/35728// (accessed August 8, 2012).

Dewey, John. *Democracy and Education: An Introduction to the Philosophy of Education.* New York: Free Press, 1916.

Dixon, Bruce. "Black Caucus Caves to Corporate Power: Two-Thirds Vote against Black Interests." *Black Commentator* 188, June 15, 2006. http://www.blackcommentator.com/188/188_cover_cbc_www_dixon.html (accessed July 16, 2012).

———. "The Black Stake in the Internet: Net Neutrality Is an African American Issue." *Black Commentator* 183, May 11, 2006. http://www.blackcommentator.com/183/183_cover_black_stake_internet.html (accessed July 16, 2012).

Doctorow, Cory. "Phone Company Blocks Access to Telecoms Union's Website." *BoingBoing.* July 24, 2005. http://boingboing.net/2005/07/24/phone-company-blocks.html (accessed August 8, 2012).

Dolber, Brian. "A Rock and a Hard Place: The CWA's Approach to Media Policy, 1984–2002." *Democratic Communiqué.* 22, no. 2 (2008): 66–84.

Donner, Jonathan. "Shrinking Fourth World? Mobiles, Development, and Inclusion." In *Handbook of Mobile Communication Studies*, edited by James E. Katz, 29–42. Cambridge, Mass.: MIT Press, 2008.

Doppelt, Gerald. "Democracy and Technology," in *Democratizing Technology: Andrew Feenberg's Critical Theory of Technology*, edited by Tyler J. Veak, New York: State University of New York, 2006, 85–100.

"Down the Tubes: Internet Television Moves From the Computer to the Living Room." *The Economist*, April 24, 2009. http://www.economist.com/node/13562114 (August 13, 2012).

Drawbaugh, Kevin. "House Rejects FCC's 'Open' Internet Rules." *Reuters.* April 8, 2011. http://www.reuters.com/article/2011/04/08/us-congress-internet-idUSTRE7376UR20110408 (accessed August 13, 2012).

Dubro, Alec. "Court Rules to Hear Net Neutrality Challenge." *Speed Matters.* March 9, 2012. http://www.speedmatters.org/blog/archive/court-rules-to-hear-net-neutrality-challenge/#.T6pBbb-9-88 (accessed August 13, 2012).

Dunbar, John. "Who Is Watching the Watchdog?" In *The Future of Media: Resistance and Reform in the 21st Century,* edited by Robert W. McChesney, Russell Newman, and Ben Scott, 127–140. New York: Seven Stories Press, 2005.

Dunn, Scott. "Net Neutrality Is a Ruse." Television broadcast, KSL TV. February 29, 2012. http://www.ksl.com/?nid=1014&sid=19286087 (accessed August 8, 2012).

Eagleton-Pierce, Matthew. "The Internet and the Seattle WTO Protests." *Peace Review* 13, no. 3 (2001): 331–337.

Edwards, Jason A. *Navigating the Post-Cold War World: President Clinton's Foreign Policy Rhetoric.* Lanham: Lexington Books, 2008.

Eggerton, John. "Genachowski, Again, Voices Opposition to Fairness Doctrine." *Broadcasting & Cable,* September 17, 2009. http://www.broadcastingcable.com/article/354411-Genachowski_Again_Voices_Opposition_to_Fairness_Doctrine.php (accessed March 18, 2011).

———. "Obama Does Not Support Return of the Fairness Doctrine." *Broadcasting & Cable,* June 25, 2008. http://www.broadcastingcable.com/article/114322-Obama_Does_Not_Support_Return_of_Fairness_Doctrine.php (accessed March 18, 2011).

———. "Obama Restates Opposition to Return of Fairness Doctrine." *Broadcasting & Cable,* Feb. 18, 2009. http://www.broadcastingcable.com/article/174455-Obama_Restates_Opposition_to_Return_of_Fairness_Doctrine.php?rssid=20065 (accessed March 18, 2011).

———. "President Says He Would Veto Fairness Doctrine Imposition." *Broadcasting & Cable.* March 11, 2008, http://www.broadcastingcable.com/article/112821-President_Says_He_Would_Veto_Fairness_Doctrine_Imposition.php (accessed March 18, 2011).

Eisner, Marc Allen. *Regulatory Politics in Transition.* Baltimore: Johns Hopkins University Press, 2000.

Elmer–Dewitt, Philip. "Apple's Itunes Store: 500,000 Ios Apps and Counting." *CNNMoney,* http://tech.fortune.cnn.com/2011/05/24/apples-itunes-store-500000-ios-apps-and-counting/ (accessed January 20, 2012).

Elrick, Kathy. "Themes from Clinton's 1992 Speeches: Frames, Puritan Influence, and Rhetoric." Presentation at the annual convention of the Midwestern Political Science Association, Chicago, IL, April 2007.

Entman, Robert. "Framing: Toward Clarification of a Fractured Paradigm." *Journal of Communication* 43, no. 4 (1993): 51–58.

Enzensberger, Hans Magnus. "Das Digitale Evangelium." *Der Spiegel,* (2000), http://www.spiegel.de/spiegel/print/d-15376078.html (accessed August 13, 2012).

Epstein, Steven. *Impure Science: AIDS, Activism, and the Politics of Knowledge.* Berkeley: University of California Press, 1996.

"Evolution of Cable Television." *FCC Encyclopedia.* http://www.fcc.gov/encyclopedia/evolution-cable-television#sec46 (accessed August 8, 2012).

Express Company v. Caldwell, 88 U.S. 264 (1874).

Faulhaber, Gerald. R. "The Economics of Network Neutrality: Are "Prophylactic" Remedies to Nonproblems Needed?" *Cato Institute,* 2011–2012, http://www.cato.org/pubs/regulation/regv34n4/v34n4-4.pdf (April 12, 2012).

Faust III, A. T. "'Occupy' App Gives You Even More News on Growing Global Phenomenon." *AppAdvice,* http://appadvice.com/appnn/2011/11/occupy-app-gives-you-even-more-news-on-growing-global–phenomenon (accessed January 13, 2012).

"FCC Classifies DSL as Information Service." *Tech Law Journal,* last modified August 5, 2005. http://www.techlawjournal.com/topstories/2005/20050805a.asp (accessed October 20, 2012).

"FCC Nominees Oppose Fairness Doctrine Reincarnation." *Radio World,* July 16, 2009. http://www.rwonline.com/article/fcc-nominees-oppose-fairness-doctrine-reincarnation/1480 (accessed February 18, 2011).

Federal Communications Commission. "Appropriate Regulatory Treatment for Broadband Access to the Internet Over Wireless Networks." Declaratory Ruling. March 23, 2007. http://hraunfoss.fcc.gov/edocs_public/attachmatch/FCC-07-30A1.pdf (accessed August 13, 2012).

———. "Broadcast Applications and Proceedings; Fairness Doctrine and Digital Broadcast Television Redistribution Control; Fairness Doctrine, Personal Attacks, Political Editorials and Complaints Regarding Cable Programming Service Rates." *Federal Register* 76, no. 175 (September 9, 2011): 55817–55819.

———. "Connecting America: The National Broadband Plan." March 16, 2010. http://download.broadband.gov/plan/national-broadband-plan.pdf (accessed August 13, 2012).

———. *Consent Decree in the Matter of Madison River Communications, LLC and Affiliated Companies.* 2005. http://hraunfoss.fcc.gov/edocs_public/attachmatch/DA-05-543A2.pdf (accessed January 20, 2011).

———. *Declaratory Ruling In the Matter of Appropriate Regulatory Treatment for Broadband Access to the Internet Over Wireless Networks.* March 23, 2007. http://hraunfoss.fcc.gov/edocs_public/attachmatch/FCC-07-30A1.pdf (accessed August 13, 2012). http://www.fcc.gov/Bureaus/Cable/News_Releases/2002/ nrcb0201.html (accessed August 7, 2012).

———. "FCC Classifies Cable Modem Service as 'Information Service': Initiates Proceeding to Promote Broadband Deployment and Examine Regulatory Implications of Classification." 2002. http://transition.fcc.gov/Bureaus/Cable/News_Releases/ 2002/nrcb0201.html (accessed October 25, 2012).

———. "FCC Statement on *Comcast v. FCC Decision*." April 6, 2010. hraunfoss.fcc.gov/edocs_public/attachmatch/DOC-297355A1.pdf (accessed August 18, 2012).

———. "Final Rule: Preserving the Open Internet." *Federal Register* 76, no. 185 (September 23, 2011): 59192–59235. http://www.gpo.gov/fdsys/pkg/FR-2011-09-23/pdf/2011-24259.pdf (accessed August 13, 2012).

———. *Notice of Inquiry in the Matter of Broadband Industry Practice.* Docket No. 07-52, March 22, 2007. http://hraunfoss.fcc.gov/edocs_public/attachmatch/FCC-07-31A1.pdf.

———. *Notice of Proposed Rulemaking in the Matter of Preserving the Open Internet.* 2009. http://hraunfoss.fcc.gov/edocs_public/attachmatch/FCC-09-93A1.pdf (accessed August 13, 2012).

———. Order in the Matter of Unlicensed Operation in the TV Broadcast Bands: Additional Spectrum for Unlicensed Devices Below 900 Mhz and in the 3 GHz Band. 2011. http://hraunfoss.fcc.gov/edocs_public/attachmatch/DA-11-131A1.pdf (accessed August 13, 2012).

———. *Policy Statement in the Matter of Inquiry Concerning High Speed Access to the Internet Over Cable and Other Facilities.* 2005. http://www.publicknowledge.org/ pdf/FCC-05-151A1.pdf (accessed January 20, 2011).

———. *Report and Order in the Matter of Preserving the Open Internet Broadband Industry Practices.* 2010. http://www.fcc.gov/Daily_Releases/Daily_Business/2010/ db1223/FCC-10-201A1.pdf (accessed January 20, 2011).

Federal Communications Commission v. Midwest Video Corp., 440 U.S. 689 (1979).

Feenberg, Andrew. *Questioning Technology*. London: Routledge, 1999.

———. *Between Reason and Experience: Essays in Technology and Modernity.* Cambridge, Mass.: MIT, 2010.

———. *Critical Theory of Technology.* New York: Oxford University, 1991.

———. "Critical Theory of Technology." 2004. http://www.sfu.ca/~andrewf/ctt.htm (accessed April 15, 2012).

———. "From Critical Theory of Technology to Rational Critique of Rationality." *Social Epistemology* 22, no. 1 (2008): 5–28.

———. *Questioning Technology*. Kentucky: Taylor and Francis, 2004.

Felczak, Michael. "(Re)Designing the Internet: A Critical Constructivist Analysis of the Next Generation Internet Protocol." Master's thesis, Simon Fraser University, 2005. http://summit.sfu.ca/item/9695 (accessed August 8, 2012).

Feld, Harold. "Forget the First Amendment, BART Messed With The Phone System. Violated CA and Federal Law." *Wetmachine*. August. 22, 2011. http://tales-of-the-sausage-factory.wetmachine.com/forget-the-first-amendment-bart-messed-with-the-phone-system-violated-ca-and-federal-law/ (accessed August 8, 2012).

———. "Meanwhile, Back at the D.C. Circuit . . . . The Open Internet Litigation Plods Along." *Public Knowledge*. March 27, 2012. http://www.publicknowledge.org/blog/meanwhile–back–dc–circuit–open–internet–litig (accessed August 8, 2012).

Felten, Edward W. "Nuts and Bolts of Network Neutrality." *Center for Information Technology Policy*. Princeton University, 2006. www.cs.princeton.edu/courses/archive/fall09/cos109/neutrality.pdf (accessed August 8, 2012).

Fenster, Mark. "Seeing the State: Transparency as Metaphor." *Administrative Law Review* 62, no. 3 (Summer 2010): 617–672.

Fernandez, Bob. "FCC Chair Blasts Comcast." *Philadelphia Inquirer*. August 2, 2008. http://articles.philly.com/2008-08-02/business/25258241_1_michael-copps-high-speed-internet-service-jonathan-adelstein (accessed August 8, 2012).

Fisher, Elizabeth. "Transparency and Administrative Law: A Critical Evaluation." *Current Legal Problems* 63: 272–314.

Fisher, Ken. "SBC: Ain't No Way VoIP Uses Mah Pipes!" *ArsTechnica*. October 31, 2005. http://arstechnica.com/old/content/2005/10/5498.ars (accessed August 8, 2011).

Flanagin, Andrew J., Craig Flanagin, and Jon Flanagin. "Technical Code and the Social Construction of the Internet." *New Media and Society* 12, 2 (2010): 179–196.

Flew, Terry, and Jason Wilson. "Journalism as Social Networking: The Australian Youdecide Project and the 2007 Federal Election." *Journalism* 11, no. 2 (2010): 131–147.

Foley, Linda. "Media Reform from the Inside Out: The Newspaper Guild–CWA." In *The Future of Media: Resistance and Reform in the 21st Century*, edited by Robert W. McChesney, Russell Newman, and Ben Scott, 41–49. New York: New Press, 2005.

Fones-Wolf, Liz. *Selling Free Enterprise: The Business Assault on Labor and Liberalism, 1945–60*. Urbana: University of Illinois Press, 1995.

Fortier, Francois. *Virtuality Check: Power Relations and Alternative Strategies in the Information Society*. London: Verso, 2001.

Fortunati, Leopoldina. "The Mobile Phone: Towards New Categories and Social Relations." *Information, Communication and Society* 5, no. 4 (2002): 513–528.

Foucault, Michel. *The Archaeology of Knowledge and the Discourse on Language*. Translated by Rupert Swyer. New York: Vintage, 1982.

———. "Governmentality." In *The Foucault Effect: Studies in Governmentality*, edited by Graham Burchell, Colin Gordon, and Peter Miller, 87–104. Chicago: University of Chicago Press, 1991.

———. *The History of Sexuality, Volume II: The Use of Pleasure*. Translated by Robert Hurley. New York: Vintage, 1990.

———. "The Order of Discourse." In *Untying the Text*, edited by Robert Young, translated by Ian McLeod, 48–78. New York: Routledge, 1981.

Fox Special Report with Bret Baier. December 21, 2010. New York City: Fox News Channel, Cable television program.

Fraser, Nancy. "Rethinking the Public Sphere: A Contribution to the Critique of Actually Existing Democracy." In *Habermas and the Public Sphere*, edited by Craig Calhoon, 109–142. Cambridge, Mass: MIT Press, 1992.

Free Press. *Comments of Free Press*. FCC Docket No. 09-51. June 8, 2009. http://www.freepress.net/files/FP_National_broadband_plan.pdf (accessed August 8, 2012).

———. *Comments of Free Press*. FCC Docket No. 07-52. January 14, 2010. http://apps.fcc.gov/ecfs/document/view?id=7020378792 (accessed August 8, 2012).

———. *Comments of Free Press et al*. FCC Docket No. 05-72. February 13, 2008. http://apps.fcc.gov/ecfs/document/view?id=6519841216 (accessed August 8, 2012).

———. "Corruption Road: How Corporate Money and Astroturf Corrupt Media Policy." http://web.archive.org/web/20110715234834/http://corruptionroad.freepress.net (accessed August 8, 2012).

———. "Free Press Responds to Supreme Court Rulings in Brand X and Grokster Cases." *Free Press*, June 27, 2005. http://www.freepress.net/release/80 (accessed July 16, 2012).

———. "Free Press Urges Policymakers to Reject Google-Verizon Pact." *Free Press*, August 9, 2010. http://www.freepress.net/press-release/2010/8/9/free-press-urges-policymakers-reject-google-verizon-pact (accessed July 16, 2012).

———. "Future of the Internet." http://www.freepress.net/media_issues/internet (accessed June 20, 2011).

———. "Join the Fight for Internet Freedom." http://www.freepress.net/savetheinternet (accessed December 15, 2011).

———. "Media Minutes." http://www.freepress.net/media-minutes (accessed August 8, 2012).

———. *Notice of Ex Parte Filing*. Docket No. 07-52. October 24, 2008. http://apps.fcc.gov/ecfs/document/view?id=6520179100 (accessed August 8, 2012).

———. *Reply Comments of Free Press et al*. FCC Docket No. 05-72. February 28, 2008. http://apps.fcc.gov/ecfs/document/view?id=6519856406 (accessed August 8, 2012).

———. *Reply Comments of Free Press*. Docket No. 07-52, April 26, 2010. http://apps.fcc.gov/ecfs/document/view?id=7020437471 (accessed August 13, 2012).

———. "Saving the Internet: A History." http://web.archive.org/web/20110708053546/http://www.savetheinternet.com/timeline (accessed August 8, 2012).

———. "Strange Bedfellows United to Save the Internet." *Free Press*, April 24, 2006. http://www.freepress.net/release/128 (accessed July 16, 2012).

———. "Why Is the Media Ignoring SOPA?" *Free Press*. http://act2.freepress.net/sign/media_sopa/ (accessed July 16, 2012).

Free Press and Public Knowledge. *Formal Complaint of Free Press and Public Knowledge Against Comcast Corporation for Secretly Degrading Peer-to-Peer Applications*. 23 FCC Rcd 13028. November 1, 2007. http://www.publicknowledge.org/pdf/fp_pk_comcast_complaint.pdf (accessed August 13, 2012).

"Free Press Group Leverage Ties to Google and Obama." *Roger Hedgecock Show*, March 2, 2012. http://www.rogerhedgecock.com/story/17064385/free-press-group-leverage-ties-to-google-and-obama (accessed July 16, 2012).

Freedman, Des. "Dynamics of Power in Contemporary Media Policy–making." *Media Culture and Society* 28, no. 6 (2006): 907–923.

Frischmann, Brett. "An Economic Theory of Commons and Infrastructure Management." *Minnesota Law Review* 89 (2005): 917–1030.

Frontier Broadcasting Co. v. Collier, 24 F. C. C. 251 (1958).

Fund, John. "The Net Neutrality Coup," *Wall Street Journal*, December 21, 2010. http://online.wsj.com/article/SB10001424052748703581204576033772053001588. html (accessed March 20, 2011).

Fung, Archong, Mary Graham, and David Weil. *Full Disclosure: The Perils and Promise of Transparency.* New York: Cambridge University Press, 2007.

Fuller, Steven. *The Philosophy of Science and Technology Studies.* Oxford: Routledge, 2005.

Galloway, Alexander R., and Thacker, Eugene. "Protocol, Control and Networks." *Grey Room* 17, (2004): 6–27.

Galperin, Hernan. *New Television, Old Politics: The Transition to Digital TV in the United States and Britain.* Cambridge: Cambridge University Press, 2004.

Gandy, Oscar H., Jr. *Beyond Agenda Setting: Information Subsidies and Public Policy.* Norwood, N.J.: Ablex, 1982,

Garnham, Nicholas. *Capitalism and Communication: Global Culture and the Economics of Information,* edited by Fred Inglis. London: Sage, 1990.

———. "Information Society Theory as Ideology: A Critique." *Studies in Communication Sciences* 1 (2001): 129–166.

Genachowski, Julius. "Preserving a Free and Open Internet: A Platform for Innovation, Opportunity and Prosperity." Address to The Brookings Institution. September 21, 2009. http://hraunfoss.fcc.gov/edocs_public/attachmatch/DOC–293568A1.pdf (accessed March 5, 2011).

———. "The Third Way: A Narrowly Tailored Broadband Framework." *FCC.* May 2010. http://www.broadband.gov/the-third-way-narrowly-tailored-broadband-framework-chairman-julius-genachowski.html (accessed August 13, 2012).

Gergen, Kenneth J. "Mobile Communication and the Transformation of the Democratic Process." In *Handbook of Mobile Communication Studies,* edited by James E. Katz, 297–309. Cambridge, Mass.: MIT Press, 2008.

Glenn Beck. April 5, 2010. New York City: Fox News Channel, Cable television.

Glenn Beck. May 18, 2010. New York City: Fox News Channel, Cable television.

Glenn Beck. September 9, 2010. New York City: Fox News Channel, Cable television.

Glenn Beck. November 22, 2010. New York City: Fox News Channel, Cable television.

Goffman, Erving. *Frame Analysis: An Essay on the Organization of Experience.* Boston: Northeastern University Press, 1986.

Goldfarb, Charles B. *Access to Broadband Networks.* Congressional Research Service. Washington, D.C.: Library of Congress, August 31, 2006. http://opencrs.com/document/RL33496/2006-08-31/download/1005/ (accessed August 13, 2012).

Goldman, David. "AT&T Kills $39 Billion Bid for T–Mobile," *CNNMoney.* December 19, 2011. http://money.cnn.com/2011/12/19/technology/att_tmobile_dead/index.htm (accessed August 13, 2012).

Gonzalez, Alberto. "'Participation' at WMEX–FM: Interventional Rhetoric of Ohio Mexican Americans." *Western Journal of Speech Communication* 53, no. 4 (1989): 398–410.

Goodnight, G. Thomas, and Sandy Green. "Rhetoric, Risk, and Markets: The Dot–Com Bubble." *Quarterly Journal of Speech* 96, no. 2 (2010): 115–140.

"Government Gobbles the Web," *Wall Street Journal*, December 22, 2010. http://online.wsj.com/article/SB10001424052748703581204576033772053001588. html (March 20, 2011).

Graham, Benjamin, and Jason Zewig. *The Intelligent Investor*. Revised Edition. New York: Collins Business, 2003.

Green, Leila. *Communication, Technology and Society*. London: Sage Publications, 2001.

Greene, Ronald. "Another Materialist Rhetoric." *Critical Studies in Media Communication* 15, no. 1 (1998): 21–40.

Grossman, Lev. "Iran Protests: Twitter, the Medium of the Movement." *Time* (2009), http://www.time.com/time/world/article/0,8599,1905125,00.html (accessed August 8, 2012).

———. "Time's Person of the Year: You." *Time* (2006), http://www.time.com/time/magazine/article/0,9171,1569514,00.html (accessed August 13, 2012).

———. "You—Yes, You—Are Time's Person of the Year." *Time*, December 25, 2006. http://www.time.com/time/magazine/article/0,9171,1570810,00.html (accessed July 16, 2012).

Gruenwald, Julia. "Media Access Project to Shut Down." *NationalJournal Tech Daily Dose*, April 3, 2012. http://techdailydose.nationaljournal.com/2012/04/media-access-project-to-shut-d.php (accessed August 8, 2012).

Habermas, Jürgen. *Between Facts and Norms: Contributions to a Discourse Theory of Law and Democracy*. Translated by William Rehg. Cambridge, Mass.: MIT Press, 1996.

———. "Further Reflections on the Public Sphere." In *Habermas and the Public Sphere*, edited by Craig Calhoun, 421–461. Cambridge, Mass: MIT Press, 1992.

———. *Strukturwandel Der Öffentlichkeit*. Frankfurt am Main: Suhrkamp, 1990.

Hachman, Mark. "FCC Proposes 'Third Way' to Regulate Broadband." *PC Magazine*, May 6, 2010. http://www.pcmag.com/article2/0,2817,2363484,00.asp (accessed August 8, 2012).

Hall, Stuart. "Encoding/Decoding." In *Media and Cultural Studies: Key Works*, edited by Gigi Meenkashi Durham and Douglas M. Kellner, 163–173. Malden: Blackwell Publishing, 2006.

Hall, Stuart, and Lawrence Grossberg. "On Postmodernism and Articulation: An Interview with Stuart Hall." *Journal of Communication Inquiry* 10, no. 2 (1986): 45–60.

Hanan, Joshual. "Home Is Where the Capital Is: The Culture of Real Estate in an Era of Control Societies." *Communication and Critical/Cultural Studies* 7, no. 2 (2010): 176–201.

Hannity. December 21, 2010. New York City: Fox News Channel, Cable television.

Hansel, Saul. "F.C.C. Vote Sets Precedent on Unfettered Web Usage." *New York Times*, August 2, 2008, http://www.nytimes.com/2008/08/02/technology/02fcc.html?_r=1 (accessed August 8, 2011).

Hass, Douglas A. "The Never-Was-Neutral Net and Why Informed Users Can End the Net Neutrality Debates." *Berkeley Technology Law Journal* 22: 1565–1635.

Hawkins, Keith. *Law as Last Resort: Prosecution Decision-Making in a Regulatory Agency*. Oxford: Oxford University Press, 2003.

Hayes, Carol M. "Content Discrimination on the Internet: Calls for Regulation of Net Neutrality." *University of Illinois Journal of Law, Technology and Policy* no. 2 (Fall 2009): 493–526.

Hedge, Justin P. "Decline of Title II Common-Carrier Regulations in the Wake of Brand X: Long-Run Success for Consumers, Competition and the Broadband Internet Market." *CommLaw Conspectus* 14 (2006): 427–462.

Hemphill, C. Scott. "Network Neutrality and the False Promise of Zero-Price Regulation." *Yale Journal on Regulation* 25, no. 2 (July 2008): 135–179.

Henriques, Adrian. *Corporate Truth: The Limits to Transparency.* Sterling: Earthscan, 2008.

Herman, Bill D. "Opening Bottlenecks: On Behalf of Mandated Network Neutrality." *Federal Communications Law Journal* 59, no. 1 (2006): 107–159.

Herman, Edward S., and Robert W. McChesney. *Global Media: The New Missionaries of Global Capitalism.* London: Cassell, 1997.

Hilliard, David, and Michael Keith. *The Quieted Voice: The Rise and Demise of Localism in Radio.* Carbondale: Southern Illinois University Press, 2005.

Hindman, Mathew. *The Myth of Digital Democracy.* Princeton, N.J.: Princeton University Press, 2009.

Hingtsman, David, and G. Thomas Goodnight. "From the Great Depression to the Great Recession: The 1932 Hayek-Keynes Debate: A Study in Economic Uncertainty, Contingency, and Criticism." *POROI* 7, no. 1 (2011): 1–22.

Hirsch, Tad, and John Henry. "Txtmob: Text Messaging for Protest Swarms." Paper presented to CHI'05 extended abstracts on Human factors in computing systems, Portland, OR, USA, 2005.

Hobbs, Renee. "The State of Media Literacy: A Rejoinder." *Journal of Broadcasting and Electronic Media* 55, no. 3 (2011): 601–604.

———. "The State of Media Literacy: A Response to Potter." *Journal of Broadcasting and Electronic Media* 55, no. 3 (2011): 419–430.

Holman, JoAnne, and Michael A. McGregor. "'Thank You for Taking the Time to Read This:' Public Participation via New Communication Technologies at the FCC." *Journalism and Communication Monographs* 2, no. 4 (Winter 2001): 158–202.

Holofcener, Adam. "Net Neutrality Besieged by *Comcast Corp. v. FCC*: The Past, Present and Future Plight of an Open Internet." *Journal of Business and Technology Law* 7, no. 2 (2012): 403–424.

Honig, David. "Civility—And Why Bobby Rush Should Be the Ranking Communications Subcommittee Member." *Huffington Post.* November 22, 2010. http://www.huffingtonpost.com/david-honig/civility-and-why-bobby-ru_b_786065.html (accessed July 12, 2012).

Hood, Christopher. "Beyond Exchanging First Principles? Some Closing Comments." In *Transparency: The Key to Better Governance?* edited by Christopher Hood and David Heald. Oxford: Oxford University Press, 2006.

———. "Transparency in Historical Perspective." In *Transparency: The Key to Better Governance? Proceedings of the British Academy.* 135. Ed. Christopher Hood and David A. Heald, 3–23. Oxford: Oxford University Press, 2006.

Horwitz, Robert Britt. *The Irony of Regulatory Reform: The Deregulation of American Telecommunications.* New York: Oxford University Press, 1989.

House Energy and Commerce Committee. "Upton, Walden, and Terry Find FCC's Economic Analysis Lacking." House Energy and Commerce Committee press release, March 8, 2011. House Energy and Commerce Committee website. http://energycommerce.house.gov/news/PRArticle.aspx?NewsID=8315 (accessed September 7, 2011).

Howard, Jen. "FCC Statement on Comcast v. FCC Decision." *FCC.gov.* April 6, 2010. http://hraunfoss.fcc.gov/edocs_public/attachmatch/DOC-297355A1.pdf (accessed August 5, 2011).

Howard v. America Online, 208 F.3d 741, 752 (9th Cir. 2000).

Huffington, Arianna. "'Net Neutrality': Why Are the Bad Guys So Much Better at Naming Things?" *The Huffington Post*, May 3, 2006. http://www.huffingtonpost.com/arianna-huffington/net-neutrality-why-are-th_b_20311.html (accessed August 8, 2012).

Huang, Shaorong. *To Rebel Is Justified: A Rhetorical Study of China's Cultural Movement, 1966–1969.* Lanham, M.D.: University Press of America, 1996.

In re Federal–State Joint Bd. on Universal Serv., 12 F.C.C.R. 87, 123–24 (1996).

International Telecommunication Union. "The World in 2011: ICT Facts and Figures." (2011), http://www.itu.int/ITUD/ict/facts/2011/material/ICTFactsFigures2011.pdf (accessed August 13, 2012).

Irwin, Alan. *Citizen Science: A Study of People, Expertise, and Sustainable Development.* London: Routledge, 1995.

James, Jeffrey. "Sharing Mobile Phones in Developing Countries: Implications for the Digital Divide." *Technological Forecasting and Social Change* 78, no. 4 (2011): 729–735.

Jenkins, Henry. *Convergence Culture: Where Old and New Media Collide.* New York: New York University Press, 2006.

Jenkins, Holman. "End of the Net Neut Fetish?" *Wall Street Journal*, April 7, 2010. http://online.wsj.com/article/SB10001424052702303411604575168053474388236.htm (accessed March 20, 2011).

Jerome, Sara. "Net-neutrality Group Challenged by Ties to MoveOn.org; ACORN." *The Hill.* August 23, 2010. http://thehill.com/blogs/hillicon-valley/technology/115367-as-elections-near-net-neutrality-backers-challenged-by-moveonorg-and-acorn-ties (accessed August 8, 2012).

Jervis, Rick. "Louisiana City Blazes High-speed Web Trail," *USA Today*, February 5, 2012. http://www.usatoday.com/news/nation/story/2012-02-01/broadband–telecom-lafayette/52920278/1 (accessed August 8, 2012).

Joinson, Adam. *Understanding the Psychology of Internet Behaviour: Virtual Worlds, Real Lives.* Basingstoke, UK: Palgrave Macmillan, U2002.

The Journal of Media Literacy Education. http://jmle.org/ (accessed August 8, 2012).

Kang, Cecilia. "Court Dismisses Verizon Lawsuit Against FCC Net Neutrality Rules," *Washington Post*, April 4, 2011. http://www.washingtonpost.com/blogs/post-tech/post/court-dismisses-verizon-lawsuit-against-fcc-net-neutrality-rules/2011/04/04/AFfxDNdC_blog.html (accessed August 8, 2012).

Karr, Rick. "Why Is European Broadband Faster and Cheaper? Blame the Government." *Engadget.* June 28, 2011. http://www.engadget.com/2011/06/28/why-is-european-broadband-faster-and-cheaper-blame-the-governme (accessed August 13, 2012).

Kearney, Joseph D., and Thomas W. Merrill, "The Great Transformation of Regulated Industries Law," 98 *Colum. L. Rev.* 1323 (1998).

Keating, Tom. "Amazon, Google, Yahoo, eBay Fight for Net Neutrality with Letter to Congress." *TMCnet*, July 13, 2006. http://blog.tmcnet.com/blog/tom-keating/news/amazon-google-yahoo-ebay-fight-net-neutrality-with-letter-to-congress.asp (accessed August 13, 2012).

"Keeping a Democratic Web." *New York Times*. May 2, 2006. http://www.nytimes.com/2006/05/02/opinion/02tue3.html (accessed August 13, 2012).

Kellner, Douglas. *Media Spectacle*. London: Routledge, 2003.

Kellner, Douglas, and Jeff Share. "Critical Media Literacy Is Not an Option." In *Learning Inquiry*, edited by J. W. Hunsinger and J. Nolan, 59–69. Springer, 2007.

———. "Toward Critical Media Literacy: Core Concepts, Debates, Organizations, and Policy." *Discourse: Studies in the Cultural Politics of Education* 26, no. 3 (September 2005): 369–386.

Kellner, Mark A. "On Computers: a Call to the Newly Gifted, and a Call to Arms," *Washington Times*, December 22, 2010. http://www.washingtontimes.com/news/2010/dec/21/kellner-a-call-to-the-newly-gifted-and-a-call-to-a/?page=all (accessed March 25, 2011).

Kerpen, Phil. "Silencing Voices of Internet Dissent: FCC's 'Net Neutrality' Puts New Congress to the Test," *Washington Times*, December 15, 2010. http://www.washingtontimes.com/news/2010/dec/14/silencing-voices-of-internet-dissent/ (accessed March 25, 2011).

Kerwin, Cornelius M., and Furlong, Scott. "Rulemaking: How Government Agencies Write Law and Make Policy." 4th ed. Washington, D.C.: CQ Press.

Kim, Minjeong, Chung Joo Chung, and Jang Hyun Kim. "Who Shapes Network Neutrality Policy Debate? An Examination of Information Subsidizers in the Mainstream Media and at Congressional and FCC Hearings." *Telecommunications Policy* 35, no. 4 (2011): 314–324.

Kingkade, Tyler. "New Protest Apps Crowd-Sourced from Occupy Wall Street Hackers." *The Huffington Post*, http://www.huffingtonpost.com/2011/10/26/occupy-wall-street-a-diy-tech-tools-protest_n_1032518.html (accessed November 30, 2011).

Kingser, Taren, and Patrick Schmidt. "Business in the Bulls-Eye? Target Corp and the Limits of Campaign Finance Disclosure." *Election Law Journal* 11: 21–35.

Kirchner, Lauren. "FCC Passes Net Neutrality Policy (Sort Of)." *Columbia Journalism Review*. December 21, 2010. http://www.cjr.org/the_news_frontier/fcc_passes_net_neutrality_poli.php?page=all (accessed July 16, 2012).

Klein, Hans K., and Daniel Lee Kleinman. "The Social Construction of Technology: Structural Considerations." *Science, Technology and Human Values* 27, 1 (Winter 2012): 28–52.

Koebler, Jason. "Obama Pushes STEM in State of the Union." *U.S. News and World Report*. January 25, 2012. http://www.usnews.com/news/blogs/stem-education/2012/01/25/obama-pushes-stem-in-state-of-the-union (accessed July 10, 2012).

Kopstain, Joshua. "Dear Congress, It's No Longer Okay to Not Know How the Internet Works." *Motherboard*, December 16, 2011. http://motherboard.vice.com/2011/12/16/dear-congress-it-s-no-longer-ok-to-not-know-how-the-internet-works (accessed August 8, 2012).

Kopytoff, Verne G., "America: Land of the Slow," *New York Times Bits Blog*, Sept. 20, 2011, 4:09 PM, http://bits.blogs.nytimes.com/2011/09/20/america-land-of-the-slow (accessed August 8, 2012).

Krasnow, Erwin G., and Lawrence D. Longley. *The Politics of Broadcast Regulation*. New York: St. Martin's Press, 1973.

Krim, Jonathan. "Executive Wants to Charge for Web Speed." *Washington Post*, December 1, 2005. http://www.washingtonpost.com/wp-dyn/content/article/2005/11/30/AR2005113002109.html (accessed August 8, 2012).

———. "FCC Probes Blocking of Internet Phone Calls." *Washington Post*, February 16, 2005. http://www.washingtonpost.com/wp-dyn/articles/A31082-2005Feb16.html (accessed August 8, 2012).

Krugman. Paul, "The French Connections," *New York Times*, July 23, 2007, Section A, p. 19.

Kuypers, Jim A. *Doing News Framing Analysis: Empirical and Theoretical Perspectives*. New York: Routledge, 2010.

———. *Press Bias and Politics: How the Media Frame Controversial Issues*. Westport: Praeger, 2002.

———. *Rhetorical Criticism: Perspectives in Action*. Lanham: Rowman & Littlefield, 2009.

Kyem, Peter A. Kwaku, and Peter Kweku LeMaire. "Transforming Recent Gains in the Digital Divide into Digital Opportunities: Africa and the Boom in Mobile Phone Subscription." *The Electronic Journal on Information Systems in Developing Countries* 28, no. 5 (2006): 1–16.

Largent, Steve. "Providers Need Flexibility," *USA Today*, August 18, 2010. http://www.usatoday.com/news/opinion/editorials/2010-08-18-editorial18_ST1_N.htm (accessed March 20, 2011).

Lasar, Matthew. "It's Here: FCC Adopts Net Neutrality (lite)." *Ars Technica*. December 21, 2010. http://arstechnica.com/tech–policy/news/2010/12/its-here-fcc-adopts-net-neutrality-lite.ars (accessed August 8, 2011).

Laws of the State of New York, Chap. 340, p. 739, "An Act to Amend the Act Entitled, 'An Act to Provide for the Incorporation and Regulation of Telegraph Company." Passed April 10, 1850.

Lee, Edward A., and David G. Messerschmitt. *Digital Communication*. Norwell, Mass.: Kluwer Academic Publishers, 1994.

Lee, Robin S., and Tim Wu. "Subsidizing Creativity through Network Design: Zero–Pricing and Net Neutrality." *Journal of Economic Perspectives* 23, no. 3 (Summer 2009): 61–76.

Leghart, Kendra. "The FCC's New Network Semi-Neutrality Order Maintains Inconsistency in the Broadband World." *North Carolina Journal of Law and Technology* 12. no. (2011): 199–232.

Lemley, Mark A., and Lawrence Lessig. "The End of End-to-End: Preserving the Architecture of the Internet in the Broadband Era." *UC Berkeley Law and Econ Research Paper No. 2000–19* (2000).

Leroux, Neil. "Frederick Douglas and the Attention Shift." *Rhetoric Society Quarterly* 21, no. 2 (Spring 1991): 36–46.

Lessig, Lawrence. *The Future of Ideas: The Fate of the Commons in a Connected World*. New York: Random House, 2001.

———. "Reboot the FCC." *Newsweek*. December 23, 2008, Final Ed: 4.

"Letter to the Attorney General from the American Telephone and Telegraph Company: Outlining a Course of Action Which It Has Determined Upon," published by the U.S. Government Printing Office, 1914.

Liptak, Adam. "Verizon Blocks Messages of Abortion Rights Group," *New York Times*, September 27, 2007. http://www.nytimes.com/2007/09/27/us/27verizon.html (accessed August 8, 2012).

Lopez, Sarah G. "Evaluation of the AOL Time Warner Consent Decree's Ability to Prevent Antitrust Harm in the Cable Broadband ISP Market." *John's Journal of Legal Commentary* 17, no. 1 (Winter 2003): 127–175.

Lundstedt, Sven B., and Michael W. Spicer. "Latent Policy and the Federal Communications Commission." In *Telecommunications, Values, and the Public Interest,* edited by Sven B. Lundstedt, 289–312. Norwood, NJ: Ablex Publishing Corporation, 1990.

Lutz, Sandy. "Transparency—'Deal or No Deal'?" *Frontiers of Health Services Management* 23, no. 3 (Spring 2007): 13–23.

Manne, Geoffrey. "Net Neutrality and Trinko." *Truth on the Market.* April 4, 2011, http://truthonthemarket.com/2011/04/04/net-neutrality-and-trinko/ (accessed August 8, 2012).

Marchand, Roland. *Creating the Corporate Soul: The Rise of Public Relations and Corporate Imagery in American Big Business.* Berkeley: University of California Press, 2001.

Martinez, Jennifer. "Six GLADD Members Resign Amid AT&T Flap." *Politico.* June 22, 2011. http://www.politico.com/news/stories/0611/57515.html (accessed August 8, 2012).

Marsh, Bill. "The Great Prosperity." Graphic, *New York Times.* September 4, 2011. http://www.nytimes.com/imagepages/2011/09/04/opinion/04reich-graphic.html?ref=sunday (accessed July 16, 2012).

Marx, Karl, and Frederick Engels. *The German Ideology,* edited by C. J. Arthur. New York: International Publishers, 1996.

Mattelart, Armand. *Networking the World: 1794–2000.* Translated Liz Carey-Libbrecht and James A. Cohen. Minneapolis: University of Minnesota Press, 2000.

Mayntz, Renate, and Volker Schneider. "The Dynamics of System Development in a Comparative Perspective: Interactive Videotex in Germany, France, and Britain." In *The Development of Large Technical Systems,* edited by Renate Mayntz and Thomas P. Hughes, 263–298. Frankfurt: Campus Verlag, 1988.

McAdam, Lowell. "Finding Common Ground on an Open Internet." *Verizon PolicyBlog.* October 21, 2009. http://policyblog.verizon.com/BlogPost/675/FindingCommonGroundonanOpenInternet.aspx (accessed August 13, 2012).

McBarnet, Doreen. "Whiter than White Collar Crime: Tax, Fraud Insurance and the Management of Stigma." *British Journal of Sociology* 42, no. 3 (September 1991): 323–344.

McChesney, Robert. *Communication Revolution: Critical Junctures and the Future of Media.* New York: The New Press, 2007.

———. "Media Policy Goes to Main Street: The Uprising of 2003." *The Communication Review* 7 (2004): 223–258.

———. *The Political Economy of Media: Enduring Issues, Emerging Dilemmas.* New York: Monthly Review Press, 2008.

———. *The Problem of the Media: U.S. Communication Politics in the 21st Century.* New York: Monthly Review Press, 2004.

———. *Rich Media, Poor Democracy: Communication Politics in Dubious Times.* New York: The New Press, 2000.

———. *Telecommunications, Mass Media, and Democracy: The Battle for Control of U.S. Broadcasting, 1928–1935.* New York: Oxford University Press, 1993.

———. "Understanding the Media Reform Movement." *International Journal of Communication* 3(2009): 47–53.

McChesney, Robert, and John Nichols. *The Death and Life of American Journalism: The Media Revolution that Will Begin the World Again.* Philadelphia: Nation Books, 2010.

McCloskey, Diedre. *The Bourgeois Virtues.* Chicago: University of Chicago Press, 2006.

———. *The Rhetoric of Economics.* Chicago: University of Chicago Press, 1994.

McCullagh. Declan. "FCC Formally Rules Comcast's Throttling of BitTorrent was Illegal." *CNET.* August 1, 2008. http://news.cnet.com/8301-13578_3-10004508-38.html (accessed August 8, 2012).

———. "eBay Tries E–mail in Net Neutrality Fight." CNET News. June 1, 2006. http://news.cnet.com/eBay-tries-e-mail-in-Net-neutrality-fight/2100-1028_3-6079291.html (accessed August 8, 2012).

———. "Microsoft's New Push in Washington." CNET News. June 30, 2003. http://news.cnet.com/2010-1071_3-1021938.html (accessed August 8, 2012).

———. "Telco Agrees to Stop Blocking VoIP calls." March 3, 2008, http://news.cnet.com/Telco-agrees-to-stop-blocking-VoIP-calls/2100-7352_3-5598633.html (accessed August 30, 2011).

McDowell, Robert M. "The FCC's Threat to Internet Freedom," *Wall Street Journal*, May 24, 2010, http://online.wsj.com/article/SB1000142405274870339520457602 23452250748540.html (March 20, 2011).

———. Opening Statement of Commissioner Robert M. McDowell at Second Public En Banc hearing on Broadband Management Practices, Stanford Law School, Palo Alto, California, April 17, 2008. http://hraunfoss.fcc.gov/edocs_public/attachmatch/DOC–281646A1.pdf (accessed August 8, 2012).

McGee, Michal Calvin. "The 'Ideograph:' A Link Between Rhetoric and Ideology." *Quarterly Journal of Speech* 66, no. 1 (1980): 1–16.

McGregor, Michael A. "When the 'Public Interest' Is Not What Interests the Public." *Communication Law and Policy* 11 (Spring 2006): 207–224.

Meinrath, Sascha, and Victor Pickard. "The New Net Neutrality: Criteria for Internet Freedom." *International Journal of Communication Law and Policy* 12 (2008): 225–243.

Miller, Stephen. "FCC's Third Way: The FCC's Broadband Regulation Proposal and its Impact on Journalism." *The News Media & The Law* (Fall 2010): 36. http://www.rcfp.org/browse-media-law-resources/news-media-law/news-media-and-law-fall-2010/fccs-third-way (accessed August 8, 2012).

Ministerial Alliance Against the Digital Divide. "About MAaDD," *maadd.org*, http://www.maadd.org/about.php (accessed July 16, 2012).

Mischel, Lawrence. "Regulatory Uncertainty: A Phony Explanation for Our Jobs Problem." *Economic Policy Institute Report.* September 27, 2011. http://www.epi.org/publication/regulatory-uncertainty-phony-explanation/ (accessed August 8, 2012).

Mosco, Vincent. *Broadcasting in the United States: Innovative Challenge and Organizational Control.* Norwood, N.J.: Ablex Publishing Corporation, 1979.

Moyers on America: The Net at Risk. PBS television broadcast Oct. 18, 2006. http://www.pbs.org/moyers/moyersonamerica/print/netatrisk_transcript_print.html (accessed August 8, 2012).

Moylan, Andrew. "Spare Us the Broadband Plan; Everything Is Working Just Fine without Obama's Meddling," *Washington Times*, April 1, 2010. http://www.washingtontimes.com/news/2010/mar/31/spare-us-the-broadband-plan/ (accessed March 25, 2011).

Mudhai, Okoth Fred. "Exploring the Potential for More Strategic Civil Society Use of Mobile Phones." In *Reformatting Politics: Information Technology and Global Civil Society*, edited by Jodi Dean, Jon W. Anderson, and Geert Lovink, 107–120. New York: Routledge, 2006.

Mueller, Milton, et al. "Net Neutrality as Global Principle for Internet Governance." *Internet Governance Project.* Syracuse University, 2007.

http://www.internetgovernance.org/pdf/NetNeutralityGlobalPrinciple.pdf (accessed August 8, 2012).

Muhammed, Arshad. "Verizon Executive Calls for End to Google's 'Free Lunch.'" *Washington Post*. February 6, 2006. http://www.washingtonpost.com/wp-dyn/content/article/2006/02/06/AR2006020601624.html (accessed August 8, 2012).

Murphy, Kate. "How to Muddy Your Tracks on the Internet," *New York Times*, May 2, 2012. http://www.nytimes.com/2012/05/03/technology/personaltech/how-to-muddy-your-tracks-on-the-internet.html (accessed August 8, 2012).

Napoli, Philip M. *Foundations of Communications Policy: Principles and Process in the Regulation of Electronic Media*. Cresskill, N.J.: Hampton Press, 2001.

Napoli, Philip M., and Joe Karaganis. *Toward a Federal Data Agenda for Communications Policymaking*. New York: Social Science Research Council, 2007.

National Association for Media Literacy Education. "Core Principles of Media Literacy Education in the United States." 2009, http://namle.net/wp-content/uploads/2009/09/NAMLE-CPMLE-w-questions2.pdf (accessed August 8, 2012).

National Cable & Telecommunications Assn. v. Brand X Internet Services, 545 U.S. 967, 980 (2005).

Negt, Oskar, and Alexander Kluge. *Public Sphere and Experience: Toward an Analysis of the Bourgeois and Proletarian Public Sphere*. Translated by Peter Labanyi, Jamie Daniel and Assenka Oksiloff. Minneapolis: University of Minnesota Press, 1993.

"Net Neutrality." eBay Main Street. http://www.ebaymainstreet.com/issues/net–neutrality (accessed August 8, 2012).

"Net Neutrality." *Google Policy Blog*. August 12, 2010. http://googlepublicpolicy.blogspot.com/search/label/Net%20Neutrality (accessed August 8, 2012).

"Net Neutrality End Run," *Wall Street Journal*, December 4, 2010. http://online.wsj.com/article_email/SB10001424052748704369304575632522873994634-lMyQjAxMTAxMDIwMzEyNDMyWj.html (accessed March 20, 2011).

"Net Neutrality Lost in Google-Verizon Deal." *San Francisco Chronicle*, August 11, 2010. http://www.sfgate.com/cgi-bin/article.cgi?f=/c/a/2010/08/10/EDRB1ERRQ1.DTL (accessed July 16, 2012).

Neubauer, Robert. "Neoliberalism in the Information Age, or Vice Versa?: Global Citizenship, Technology and Hegemonic Ideology." *tripleC* 9, no. 12 (2011): 195–230.

New Jersey Steam Navigation Co. v. Merchants' Bank, 47 U.S. 344, at 382 (1848).

Nir, Sarah Maslin. "Wall Street Protesters Broadcast Arrests on Social Media." *New York Times*, http://cityroom.blogs.nytimes.com/2011/09/24/wall-street-protesters-broadcast-arrests-on-social-media (accessed September 25, 2011).

Nunziato, Dawn. *Virtual Freedom: Net Neutrality and Free Speech in the Internet Age*. Stanford, Calif.: Stanford University Press, 2009.

The O'Reilly Factor. November 22, 2010. New York City: Fox News Channel, Cable television.

Obama, Barack. "President Obama's State of the Union Address." *New York Times*, January 24, 2012. http://www.nytimes.com/interactive/2012/01/24/us/politics/ state-of-the-union-2012-video-transcript.html (accessed July 16, 2012).

Oestreich, Marc. "Research and Commentary: FCC's Data-Roaming Mandate." Heartland Institute. April 3, 2011. http://heartland.org/policy-documents/research-commentary-fccs-data-roaming-mandate (accessed August 8, 2012).

Ogg, Erica. "By the Numbers: Mobile Apps in 2011." *GigaOM*, http://gigaom.com/2011/12/30/by-the-numbers-mobile-apps-in-2011/ (accessed March 15, 2012).

———. "The Year in Mobile Apps: Where We've Been, Where We're Going." *GigaOM*, http://gigaom.com/2011/12/25/the-year-in-mobile-apps-where-weve-been-where-were-going/ (accessed March 15, 2012).

Omnibus Budget Reconciliation Act of 1993, Pub. L. No. 103–66, § 6002(b), 107 Stat. 312, 392 (codified in scattered sections of 47 U.S.C. (1994)).

Open Internet Coalition. "Why an Open Internet." *Open Internet Coalition.* http://openinternetcoalition.org/index.cfm?objectid=8C7857B0–5C6A–11DF–9E27000C296BA163 (accessed August 8, 2012).

OpenMedia. "SaveOurNet.ca: Protecting Your Internet's Level Playing Field." Openmedia.ca. 2012. http://openmedia.ca/saveournet (accessed April 15, 2012).

Opt, Susan K., and Mark A. Gring. *The Rhetoric of Social Intervention: An Introduction.* Los Angeles: Sage, 2009.

Ott, Brian L., and Eric Aoki. "The Politics of Negotiating Public Tragedy: Media Framing of the Matthew Shepard Murder." *Rhetoric and Public Affairs* 5, no. 3 (2002): 483–505.

Owen, Bruce. "Antecedents to Net Neutrality." *Cato Regulation* (Fall 2007): 14–17.

———. "The Net Neutrality Debate: Twenty-Five Years after *United States v. AT&T* and 120 Years after the Act to Regulate Commerce." Stanford Law & Economics Olin Working Paper No. 336 (2007). http://ssrn.com/abstract=963623 (accessed August 8, 2012).

Pandects, ninth title of the fourth book, in Samuel P. Scott, trans., *The Civil Law* (Cincinnati: Central Trust Co., 1932).

Peha, Jon. "The Benefits and Risks of Mandating Network Neutrality and the Quest for a Balanced Policy." *International Journal of Communication* 1 (2007): 644–668.

Peha, Jon M., William M. Lehr, and Simon Wilkie. "The Status of the Debate on Network Neutrality." *International Journal of Communication* 1(2007): 709–716.

Pinch, Trevor. "The Social Construction of Technology: A Review." *Technological Change: Methods and Themes in the History of Technology*, edited by Robert Fox, 17–35. Australia: Harwood Academic Publishers, 1996.

Pociask, Stephen. "Don't 'Fix' the Internet: Interweb's Tubes and Wires Not Broke," *Washington Times*, February 16, 2010. http://www.washingtontimes.com/news/2010/feb/16/dont-fix-the-internet/ (accessed March 25, 2011).

Polaski, Adam. "Examining Other Minority Group's Opposition to Net Neutrality, Support of AT&T Merger." *The Bilerco Project.* June 12, 2011, http://www.bilerico.com/2011/06/examining_other_minority_groups_opposition_to_net.php (accessed August 8, 2012).

Potter, W. James. "The State of Media Literacy." *Journal of Broadcasting and Electronic Media.* 54, no. 4 (2010): 675–696.

Poulson, Kevin. "Paypal Freezes Wikileaks Account." *Wired* (2010), http://www.wired.com/threatlevel/2010/12/paypal-wikileaks/ (accesed August 8, 2012).

Powell, Alison. "Lessons from the Net Neutrality Lobby: Balancing Openness and Control in a Networked Society." *Proceedings of the WebSci '09 Society*, 18–20 March 2009, http://journal.webscience.org/130/1/websci09_submission_32.pdf (April 12, 2012).

Powell, Alison, and Alyssa Cooper. "Net Neutrality Discourses: Comparing Advocacy and Regulatory Arguments in the United States and the United Kingdom." *The Information Society: An International Journal* 27, no. 5 (2011): 311–325.

Powell, Michael. "Preserving Internet Freedom: Guiding Principles for the Industry." *The Digital Broadband Migration: Toward a Regulatory Regime for the Internet Age.* University of Colorado School of Law. 2004. http://www.educause.edu/library/ resources/preserving-internet-freedom-guiding-principles-industry (accessed August 13, 2012).

Press Release, "Akamai Releases Fourth Quarter 2011 'State of the Internet' Report," April 30, 2012, http://www.akamai.com/html/about/press/releases/2012/ press_043012.html (accessed August 8, 2012).

Primrose v. Western Union Telegraph Co., 154 U.S. 1 (1894).

Pruden, Wesley. "Pruden on Politics: Nothing Neutral About this Unholy Scheme," *Washington Times,* December 21, 2010. http://www.washingtontimes.com/ news/2010/dec/20/nothing-neutral-about-this-unholy-scheme/ (accessed March 25, 2011).

Quail, Christine, and Christine Larabie. "Net Neutrality: Media Discourses and Public Perception." *Global Media Journal—Canadian Edition* 3, no. 1 (2010): 31–50.

Radio Television Digital News Association. "Code of Ethics and Professional Conduct." *RTNDA.org.* September 14, 2000. http://www.rtdna.org/pages/media_items/code-of-ethics-and-professional-conduct48.php (accessed April 2, 2011).

Ramsay, Maisie. "Verizon, MetroPCS Net Neutrality Suit to Proceed." *Wireless Week,* March 2, 2012. http://www.wirelessweek.com/News/2012/03/Policy-and-Industry-Verizon-MetroPCS-Net-Neutrality-Suit-to-Proceed-Legal/ (accessed March 10, 2011).

Reardon, Marguerite. "Debunking the Internet Apocalypse." *CNN.com.* Aug. 17 2010. http://edition.cnn.com/2010/TECH/web/08/17/cnet.internet.apocalypse/index.html?h pt=Sbin (accessed March 5, 2011).

Reg. and Policy Problems Presented by the Interdependence of Computer and Communications Services, Final Decision, 28 FCC2d 267, 21 Rad. Reg.2d (P & F) 1561 (1971).

Reich, Robert. "The Limping Middle Class." *New York Times,* September 3, 2011. http://www.nytimes.com/2011/09/04/opinion/sunday/jobs-will-follow-a-strengthening-of-the-middle-class.html?pagewanted=all (accessed July 16, 2012).

Reicher, Alexander. "Redefining Net Neutrality After Comcast v. FCC." *Berkeley Technology Law Journal* 26, no. 1 (2011): 733–763.

Religious Technology Center v. Netcom On–Line Communication Services, Inc., 907 F. Supp. 1361 (N.D. Cal. 1995).

Rheingold, Howard. "Mobile Media and Political Collective Action." In *Handbook of Mobile Communication Studies,* edited by James E. Katz, 225–239. Cambridge, Mass.: MIT Press, 2008.

———. *Smart Mobs: The Next Social Revolution.* Cambridge, Mass: Perseus, 2002.

Roberts, Lawrence G. "The Evolution of Packet Switching." Dr. Lawrence G. Roberts: Homepage. 1978. Last modified January 28, 2001. http://www.packet.cc/files/ev-packet-sw.html (accessed August 8, 2012).

Rodino–Colocino, Michelle. "'Feminism' as Ideology: Sarah Palin's Anti-Feminist Feminism and Ideology Critique." *tripleC* 10, no. 2 (2012): 457–473.

Romm, Tony. "Media Access Project to Fold in May." *Politico.* April 3, 2012, http://www.politico.com/news/stories/0412/74800.html (accessed August 8, 2012).

Ruane, Kathleen Ann. "The FCC's Authority to Regulate Net Neutrality after Comcast v. FCC." Report, Congressional Research Service, December 2, 2010. http://www.hsdl.org/?view&did=12737 (accessed August 8, 2012).

"Rush Takes the Heat on Franchise Bill." *Telecom Policy Report.* May 1, 2006.http://findarticles.com/p/articles/mi_m0PJR/is_18_4/ai_n16135790/ (accessed July 16, 2012).

Saltzer, Jerome H., David P. Reed, and David D. Clark. "End-to-End Arguments in System Design." *ACM Transactions in Computer Systems* 2, no. 4 (1984): 277–288.

Salus, Peter H. *Casting the Net: From ARPANET to Internet and Beyond.* Reading, Mass.: Addison-Wesley, 1995.

Sandvig, Christian, "Network Neutrality Is the New Common Carriage." *Info: The Journal of Policy, Regulation, and Strategy.* 9, no. 2/3 (2007): 136–147.

Sashkin, Davina. "Failure of Imagination: Why Inaction on Net Neutrality Regulation Will Result in a de Facto Regime Promoting Discrimination and Consumer Harm." *CommLaw Conspectus* 15, no. 1 (2006): 261–309.

Save the Internet Coalition. "Join Us." *Save the Internet.* http://www.savetheinternet.com/members (accessed August 10, 2010).

———. "Statement of Principles." http://www.savetheinternet.com/statement-principles (accessed June 8, 2011).

Schatz, Amy. "Net Neutrality Case Heads to D.C. Circuit Court." *Wall Street Journal.* October 6, 2011. http://blogs.wsj.com/digits/2011/10/06/net-neutrality-case-heads-to-d-c-circuit-court (accessed August 8, 2012).

Schiller, Dan. *Digital Capitalism.* Cambridge, Mass.: MIT Press, 1999.

———. *How to Think About Information.* Urbana: University of Illinois Press, 2007.

Schmidt, Eric. "A Note to Google Users on Net Neutrality." *Google Policy Blog,* 2006. http://www.google.com/help/netneutrality_letter.html (accessed August 8, 2012).

Schmidt, Patrick. *Lawyers and Regulation: The Politics of the Administrative Process.* New York: Cambridge University Press, 2005.

———. "Securities Lawyers and the Ethical Quagmires of Disclosure." In *Lawyers in Practice: Ethical Decision Making in Context,* edited by Leslie Levin and Lynn Mather. Chicago: University of Chicago Press, 2012.

Sclove, Richard. *Democracy and Technology.* New York: Guilford, 1995.

Scott, Ben, Mark Cooper, and Jeannine Kenney for Free Press et al. "Why Consumers Demand Internet Freedom." *Free Press.* May 2006. http://www.freepress.net/files/nn_fact_v_fiction_final.pdf

Scott, Samuel P., trans., *The Civil Law.* Cincinnati: Central Trust Co., 1932.

Selwyn, Lee L., and Helen Golding. "Revisiting the Regulatory Status of Broadband Internet Access: A Policy Framework for Net Neutrality and an Open Competitive Internet." *Federal Communications Law Journal* 63, no. 6 (2010–2011): 91–139.

Shah, Rajiv C., and Jay P. Kesan. The Privatization of the Internet's Backbone Network. *Governing With Code.* http://www.governingwithcode.org/journal_articles/pdf/Backbone.pdf (accessed August 8, 2012).

Simmons, Lesley. "Black Elected Officials Urge FCC to Keep Digital Divide in Mind" *Black Web 2.0,* November 20, 2009. http://www.blackweb20.com/2009/11/20/black-elected-officials-urge-fcc-to-keep-the-digital-divide-in-mind/#.UARM6nCr–fQ (accessed July 16, 2012).

Síthigh, Daithí Mac. "Regulating the Medium: Reactions to Network Neutrality in the European Union and Canada." *Journal of Internet Law* 14, no. 8 (February 2011): 3–14.

Society of Professional Journalists. "Code of Ethics." n.d. http://www.spj.org/ethicscode.asp (accessed April 2, 2011).

SOCAN v. Canadian Association of Internet Providers et al., (2002) FCA 166.

Speed Matters. "Principles for High Speed Internet Policy." *Speed Matters*. http://www.speedmatters.org/pages/principles/ (accessed July 16, 2012).

———. "Speed Matters Partners." *Speed Matters*. http://www.speedmatters.org/content/partners/ (accessed July 16, 2012).

———. "Test Your Speed." *Speed Matters*. http://www.speedmatters.org/ pages/test-your-speed (accessed July 16, 2012).

Starr, Paul. *The Creation of the Media: Political Origins of Modern Communications*. New York: Basic Books, 2004.

"Steve Jobs Death: Newspaper Front Pages Pay Tribute to Apple Icon." *Huffington Post*, October 6, 2011. http://www.huffingtonpost.com/2011/10/06/steve-jobs-death-newspaper-front-pages_n_997828.html#s392829 (accessed July 16, 2012).

Stevens, Neil. "Danger at the FCC: An Omnibus Warning." *RedState*. March 27, 2010. http://www.redstate.com/neil_stevens/2010/03/27/danger-at-the-fcc-an-omnibus-warning/ (accessed August 8, 2012).

Stiegler, Zack, and Dan Sprumont. "Mediated Voices: Framing the Net Neutrality Debate." Presented at the 97th Annual Convention of the National Communication Association, New Orleans, Louisiana, November 16–19, 2011.

Stills, Leutisha. "CBC Monitor Report: Rep. Booby Rush: AT&T's Million Dollar Man." *Black Commentator*, April 27, 2006, http://www.blackcommentator.com/181/181_cbc_monitor_bobby_rush_pf.html (accessed July 16, 2012).

Stoller, Matt. "On Building a Progressive Governing Coalition Around Network Neutrality." *MyDD*, December 6, 2006, http://mydd.com/2006/12/6/on-building-a-progressive-governing-coalition-around-net-neutrality (accessed July 16, 2012).

Stoner, Mark R. "Understanding Social Movement as Social Intervention." *The Speech Communication Annual* 3 (1989): 27–43.

Storsul, Tanja. "Television in Cyberspace. The Net Neutrality Tussle in Norway." *The Digital Public Sphere: Challenges for Media Policy,* edited by Jostein Gripsrud and Hallvard Moe, 83–96. Sweden: Nordicom, 2010.

Stover, Christine M. "Network Neutrality: A Thematic Analysis of Policy Perspectives across the Globe." *Global Media Journal—Canadian Edition* 3, no. 1 (2010): 75–86.

Streeter, Thomas. "The Cable Fable Revisited: Policy, Discourse, and the Making of Cable Television." *Critical Studies in Media Communication* 4, no. 2 (1987): 174–200.

———. "Blue Skies and Strange Bedfellows: The Discourse of Cable Television." In *The Revolution Wasn't Televised: Sixties Television and Social Conflict*, edited by Lynn Spigel and Michael Curtin, 221–242. New York: Routledge, 1997.

———. *Selling the Air: A Critique of the Policy of Commercial Broadcasting in the United States*. Chicago: University of Chicago Press, 1996.

Sunstein, Cass R. "Open Government is Analytic Government and Vice–Versa." Speech, 30th Anniversary of the Regulatory Flexibility Act, Washington, D.C., September 21, 2010.

Sutter, John D. "FCC Chairman Proposes 'Net Neutrality' Regulations." *CNN Tech*. December 1, 2010. http://articles.cnn.com/2010-12-01/tech/fcc.net.neutrality_1_google-and-verizon-mobile-internet-net-neutrality?_s=PM:TECH (accessed March 5, 2011).

Tanenbaum, Andrew S. *Computer Networks*, 4th ed. Upper Saddle River, N.J.: Prentice Hall, 2002.

Tate, Deborah Taylor. Statement of Commissioner Deborah Taylor Tate at En Banc hearing on Broadband Management Practices, Stanford Law School, Palo Alto, CA,

April 17, 2008. http://hraunfoss.fcc.gov/edocs_public/attachmatch/DOC-281629A1.pdf (accessed August 8, 2012).

Taylor, Chris. "All Your Base Are Belong to Us." *Time*, February 25, 2001. http://www.time.com/time/magazine/article/0,9171,100525,00.html (accessed August 8, 2012).

Tech Law Journal. "FCC Classifies DSL as Information Service." Last modified August 5, 2005. http://www.techlawjournal.com/topstories/2005/20050805a.asp (accessed August 8 2012).

Telegraph Company v. Texas, 105 U.S. 460 (1881).

"Telus Cuts Subscriber Access to Pro–Union Website." *CBC New.s* http://www.cbc.ca/news/canada/story/2005/07/24/telus–sites050724.html (accessed March 2, 2012).

"The Google-Verizon Deal." *Wall Street Journal.* August 14, 2011. http://online.wsj.com/article/SB10001424052748704164904575421472481509784.html (accessed March 20, 2011).

Thierer, Adam. "Net Neutrality and the First Amendment." *The Technology Liberation Front.* August 8, 2010, http://techliberation.com/2010/08/08/net–neutrality–the–first–amendment/ (accessed August 8, 2012).

Thierer, Adam D. "Policy Analysis: "Net Neutrality" Digital Discrimination or Regulatory Gamesmanship in Cyberspace?" *Cato Policy Analysis*, 507, 2004.

Thierer, Adam, and Mike Wendy. "Big Government the Real Threat to the Internet." *CNN.com.* August 6, 2010. http://articles.cnn.com/2010–08–06/opinion/thierer.net.neutrality_1_net–neutrality–first–amendment–al–franken?_s=PM:OPINION (accessed March 5, 2011).

Time Warner Telecom Inc., et. al, v. FCC, 507 F.3d 205, 221 (3d Cir. 2007).

Timm, Trevor. "Cybersecurity Bill FAQ: The Disturbing Privacy Dangers in CISPA and How to Stop It." *Electronic Frontier Foundation.* April 15, 2012, https://www.eff.org/ deeplinks/2012/04/cybersecurity-bill-faq-disturbing-privacy-dangers-cispa-and-how-you-stop-it (accessed April 16, 2012).

Travis, Hannibal. "The FCC's New Theory of the First Amendment." *Santa Clara Law Review* 51, no. 2 (2010): 101–197.

United Nations General Assembly. "Report of the Special Rapporteur on the Promotion and Protection of the Right to Freedom of Opinion and Expression." New York, 2011.

U.S. Congress. 1860. *An Act to Facilitate Communication between the Atlantic and Pacific States by Telegraph*. 36th Cong., 1st sess., 1860.

U.S. Congress. 1910. *Mann–Elkins Act*. 61st Cong., 2nd sess, 1910.

U.S. Congress. 1996. *Telecommunications Act of 1996*. 104th Cong., 2nd sess. 1996. S.652. http://frwebgate.access.gpo.gov/cgi-bin/getdoc.cgi?dbname=104_cong_bills&docid=f:s652enr.txt.pdf (accessed August 8, 2012).

U.S. Congress. House. *Disapproving the Rule Submitted by the Federal Communications Commission with Respect to Regulating the Internet and Broadband Industry Practices*. 112th Cong., 1st sess. 2011.

———. H.J. Res. 37 *Internet Freedom Preservation Act of 2008*. 110th Cong., 2nd sess., 2008.

U.S. Congress. House. *Report 112–51*. 112th Cong., 1st sess. (April 1, 2011). http://www.gpo.gov/fdsys/pkg/CRPT-112hrpt51/pdf/CRPT-112hrpt51.pdf (accessed August 8, 2012).

U.S. Congress. Senate. *Disapproving the Rule Submitted by the Federal Communications Commission with Respect to Regulating the Internet and Broadband Industry Practices.* 112th Cong., 1st sess. 2011. S.J. Res. 6.

U.S. Congressional Record, 109th Congress. p. H3585. http://thomas.loc.gov/cgi-bin/query/F?r109:2:./temp/~r109PUNeQf:e351473: (accessed July 16, 2012).

U.S. Department of Transportation. "Essential Air Service Program." http://ostpxweb.dot.gov/aviation/X-50%20Role_files/essentialairservice.htm (accessed August 8, 2012).

U.S. v. Southwestern Cable Co., 392 U.S. 157 (1968).

Valenzano, Joseph M. "Framing the War on Terror in Canadian Newspapers: Cascading Activation, Canadian Leaders and Newspapers." *Southern Communication Journal* 74, no. 2 (2009): 174–190.

Van der Linde, Fidelia. "The Necessity of a Media Literacy Module within Journalism or Media Studies Curricula." *Global Media Journal: African Edition* 4, no. 2 (2010): 212–227.

van Schewick, Barbara. *Internet Architecture and Innovation.* Cambridge, Mass.: MIT Press, 2010.

———. "Towards an Economic Framework for Network Neutrality." *Journal on Telecommunications and High Technology Law* 5 (2007): 329–391.

van Schewick, Barbara, and David Farber. "Network Neutrality Nuances: A Discussion of Divergent Paths to Unrestricted Access of Content and Applications Via the Internet." *Communications of the ACM* 52, no. 2 (2009): 32–37.

———. "Point/Counterpoint: Network Neutrality Nuances." *Communications of the ACM* 52, no. 31 (2009): 34.

Verizon and Verizon Wireless. *Comments of Verizon and Verizon Wireless.* FCC Docket No. 07-52. February 13, 2008. http://apps.fcc.gov/ecfs/document/view?id=6519841190 (accessed August 8, 2012).

Verizon and Verizon Wireless. *Comments of Verizon and Verizon Wireless.* FCC Docket No. 07-52. January 14, 2010, http://apps.fcc.gov/ecfs/document/view?id=7020378541 (accessed August 8, 2012).

"Verizon-Google Legislative Framework Proposal." *Google Public Policy Blog.* August 9, 2010. http://www.google.com/googleblogs/pdfs/verizon_google_legislative_framework_proposal_081010.pdf (accessed August 8, 2012).

Wabash v. Illinois, 118 U.S. 557 (1886).

Warner, Michael. *Publics and Counterpublics.* New York: Zone Books, 2002.

Webster, Frank. *Theories of the Information Society*, 3rd Edition. London: Routledge, 2006.

Webster Stephen C. "Comcast Exempts Its New Streaming Video Service from Bandwidth Caps." *The Raw Story,* 28 March 2012, http://www.rawstory.com/rs/2012/03/28/comcast-exempts-its-new-streaming-video-service-from-bandwidth-caps/ (accessed April 6, 2012).

———. "Netflix CEO Blasts Comcast for Shredding Net Neutrality." *The Raw Story,* April 16, 2012, http://www.rawstory.com/rs/2012/04/16/netflix-ceo-blasts-comcast-for-shredding-net-neutrality/ (accessed April 19, 2012).

Western Union Telegraph Co. v. Call Publishing Co., 181 U.S. 92 (1901).

Wimmer, Jeffrey. "Counter-Public Spheres and the Revival of the European Public Sphere." *The Public* 12, no. 2 (2005): 93–110.

———. *(Gegen–)Öffentlichleit in Der Mediengesellschaft: Analyse Eines Medialen Spannungsverhältnisses.* Wiesbaden, Germany: VS Verlag, 2007.

Worden, Nat. "Time Warner Cable CEO Wary of Net Rules Limiting Options," *Wall Street Journal,* August 16, 2010. http://online.wsj.com/article/ SB10001424052748704023404575430252734689506.html (accessed March 20, 2011).

Wortham, Jenna. "A Billion–Dollar Turning Point for Mobile Apps." *New York Times,* http://www.nytimes.com/2012/04/11/technology/instagram-deal-is-billion-dollar-move-toward-cellphone-from-pc.html (accessed April 10, 2012).

Wright, Navarrow. "Who Should We Trust When It Comes to Net Neutrality?" *Black Web 2.0,* October 26, 2009, http://www.blackweb20.com/2009/10/26/who-should-we-trust-when-it-comes-to-net-neutrality/#.UARpE3Cr8b3 (accessed July 16, 2012).

"www.internet.gov." *Wall Street Journal.* December 30, 2010. http://online.wsj.com/ article/SB10001424052970203525404576049951815563410.html (accessed March 20, 2011).

Wu, Tim. 2003. "Network Neutrality, Broadband Discrimination." *Journal of Telecommunications and High Technology Law* 2: 141–179.

———." Network Neutrality FAQ." *timwu.org,* http://timwu.org/network_neutrality.html (accessed August 8, 2012).

———. "Is Net Neutrality Dead?" *Slate.* April 13, 2010. http://www.slate.com/articles/news_and_politics/jurisprudence/2010/04/is_net_neutr ality_dead.html (accessed August 8, 2012).

———. *The Master Switch: The Rise and Fall of Information Empires.* New York: Alfred A. Knopf, 2010.

Wyatt, Edward. "U.S. Court Curbs F.C.C. Authority on Web Traffic." *New York Times.* April 6, 2010, A1. http://www.nytimes.com/2010/04/07/technology/07net.html (accessed August 8, 2012).

Yoo, Christopher S. 2004. "Would Mandating Broadband Network Neutrality Help or Hurt Competition? A Comment on the End-to-End Debate." *Journal of Telecommunications and High Technology Law* 3: 23–68.

Zickuhr, Kathryn, and Aaron Smith. "Digital Differences." *Pew Internet and American Life Project.* April 13, 2012, http://pewinternet.org/Reports/2012/Digital-differences/Main-Report/Internet-adoption-over-time.aspx (accessed July 16, 2012).

Zinman, Jack, et. al. Statement of AT&T Associate General Counsel. *Framework for Broadband Internet Service.* GN Docket No. 10-127 (December 7, 2010).

Zittrain, Jonathan. *The Future of the Internet and How to Stop It.* New Haven, Conn.: Yale University Press, 2008.

Index

About the Contributors

John Nathan Anderson has been researching and writing on media policy and activism for the last two decades. A pirate radio and remix culture practitioner, former broadcast journalist, and refugee from the Telecommunications Act of 1996, he is now an Assistant Professor and Director of Broadcast Journalism in the Department of Television and Radio, Brooklyn College, City University of New York.

Jeremy Carp recently graduated with a B.A. in Sociology from Macalester College in St. Paul, Minnesota. His prior publications focus on the creation of state-level regulatory systems and the evolution of Sino–United States relations. In 2013 he will be pursuing a J.D. degree with an emphasis in regulatory law.

Benjamin Cline received his Ph.D. in 2005 from Bowling Green State University in Bowling Green, Ohio. His past research has dealt primarily with rhetorics of social intervention, especially in the areas of religious communication and new media. He has taught in several different institutions throughout the United States and now serves as Assistant Professor of Speech and Communication at Western New Mexico University in Silver City, New Mexico. He lives in Silver City with his wife, Jamie, two dogs, and a cat.

Michael Daubs researches the influence of user-generated media on the production, consumption, distribution, and understanding of media. In the past, he has investigated aesthetic remediation, participatory journalism and animation and his recent work examines activist movements, social networking, and inter–media agenda setting. He is currently an Assistant Professor in the Faculty of Information and Media Studies at the University of Western Ontario.

Brian Dolber is Assistant Professor of Mass Communication at SUNY College at Oneonta. His research interests are at the intersection of media history, media activism and labor. Dolber served as the Entertainment Industries Caucus Congressional fellow in the office of Rep. Diane Watson (D–CA), where he worked on net neutrality legislation and other media policy issues. His dissertation is the winner of the 2012 American Journalism Historians Association Margaret A. Blanchard Doctoral Dissertation Prize.

Dan Faltesek has worked in the legacy media, new media, and is Assistant Professor of Social Media at Oregon State University.

Michael Felczak is a PhD candidate in the School of Communication at Simon Fraser University (Vancouver, Canada) whose research interests span culture, communication, and technology. He has recently published and presented work on the politics of network neutrality, social diversity and technology, pedagogy and wikis, communication rights and policy, scholarly communication, and the practices of free/open source software.

Mark Grabowski is Assistant Professor at Adelphi University in Long Island, where he teaches media law and Web journalism. Previously, he was a columnist for AOL News and a reporter for the *Providence Journal* and *Arizona Republic*. He holds a J.D. from Georgetown Law. His most recent scholarly work, "Are Technical Difficulties at the Supreme Court Causing a 'Disregard of Duty'?" was published in 2012 in the *Journal of Law, Technology and Internet* and republished in *The Romanian Judges' Forum Review*.

Pallavi Gunigani is currently a Legal Fellow at the American Civil Liberties Union of Delaware. She holds a B.A. in English and economics from the University of Virginia, a J.D. from the Columbia University School of Law and a PG.D. in European Union competition law from King's College London. She was an early adopter of blogging and a laggard for Facebook and Twitter.

Danny Kimball is a PhD candidate in the Media and Cultural Studies program in the Communication Arts department at the University of Wisconsin–Madison. He is writing a dissertation on the role of network neutrality policies and open Internet infrastructures in shaping the potential for a more inclusive and participatory public sphere. He has presented his work at international communications and media studies conferences and has served as coordinating editor for *The Velvet Light Trap*.

Isabella Kulkarni is a B.A. student at Macalester College in St. Paul, Minnesota.

Patrick Schmidt is an Associate Professor of Political Science and Co-Director of Legal Studies at Macalester College, St. Paul, Minnesota. He holds a B.A. from the University of Minnesota and a Ph.D. in Political Science from the Johns Hopkins University. He has published articles in a variety of journals, including *Election Law Journal, Judicature, Justice System Journal, Law and History Review*, and *Political Research Quarterly*, and his the author of *Lawyers and Regulation: The Politics of the Administrative Process* (2005), *Human Rights Brought Home: Socio-Legal Perspectives on Human Rights in the National Context* (2004), and *Conducting Law and Society Research: Reflections* *on Methods and Practices* (2009), the latter two in collaboration with Simon Halliday.

Tina Sikka is a Lecturer in Communication Studies at Fraser International College, housed within Simon Fraser University in Burnaby, British Columbia. Since completing a SSHRC Postdoctoral Fellowship, Dr. Sikka has been working on a number of projects involving the application of a critical theory of technology approach to the study of new media and the environment. She is currently writing a book for Springer Press on geoengineering and climate change.

Dan Sprumont is a Project Manager at BarkleyREI, a full-service interactive web marketing agency specializing in higher education and tourism. Sprumont graduated from Indiana University of Pennsylvania in 2010 with a bachelor's in Communications Media and in 2011 with a master's in Adult Education and Communication Technology. Sprumont currently lives and works in Pittsburgh, Pennsylvania.

Zack Stiegler is Assistant Professor of Communications Media at Indiana University of Pennsylvania. His research and teaching focus on communication law and policy, media history and theory, and critical approaches to popular culture. His research has appeared in the *Journal of Communications Media Studies*, *Sociology Study*, the *Journal of Popular Music Studies*, *Javnost: The Public*, and the *Journal of Radio and Audio Media*.

DATE DUE